Real Options
in Theory and Practice

Financial Management Association
Survey and Synthesis Series

Real Options
in Theory and Practice

Graeme Guthrie

UNIVERSITY PRESS

2009

OXFORD
UNIVERSITY PRESS

Oxford University Press, Inc., publishes works that further
Oxford University's objective of excellence
in research, scholarship, and education.

Oxford   New York
Auckland   Cape Town   Dar es Salaam   Hong Kong   Karachi
Kuala Lumpur   Madrid   Melbourne   Mexico City   Nairobi
New Delhi   Shanghai   Taipei   Toronto

With offices in
Argentina   Austria   Brazil   Chile   Czech Republic   France   Greece
Guatemala   Hungary   Italy   Japan   Poland   Portugal   Singapore
South Korea   Switzerland   Thailand   Turkey   Ukraine   Vietnam

Published by Oxford University Press, Inc.
198 Madison Avenue, New York, New York 10016
www.oup.com

Oxford is a registered trademark of Oxford University Press

Library of Congress Cataloging-in-Publication Data
Guthrie, Graeme A. (Graeme Alexander), 1967-
Real options in theory and practice / Graeme Guthrie.
p. cm. – (Financial Management Association survey and
synthesis series)
Includes bibliographical references and index.
ISBN 978-0-19-538063-7
1. Real options (Finance) I. Title.
HG6042.G88 2009
332.63–dc22   2008043028

9 8 7 6 5 4 3 2 1

Printed in the United States of America
on acid-free paper

For MG (1930–1980),
who would have rather enjoyed this

Preface

Decision makers face a staggering array of problems in business and economics. For example, managers of growing firms have to decide when to exercise growth options and expand their business. Governments have to decide whether to undertake large infrastructure investments. Managers of oil firms must decide how rapidly to deplete their reserves. While these problems seem quite diverse, they share many important features. In each case, the decision maker must choose when to take a particular action that will be difficult, if not impossible, to reverse. In each case, the consequences of taking (or not taking) that action are uncertain. And, in all cases, the timing and nature of the actions taken by the decision makers directly affect the cash flows generated by the entities they manage.

The traditional discounted cash flow (DCF) analytical techniques taught to students, and still being used by many practitioners, do a very poor job of analyzing such situations. The simplest approach, static DCF analysis, assumes that decision makers commit to all future actions now and do not change these plans in the light of new information that might arrive in the meantime. This ignores the fact that expansion of a successful business can be delayed until conditions are such that the manager is confident that making an irreversible investment in new facilities is justified. Similarly, the traditional valuations of oil reserves assume that the future extraction of oil will follow a pre-determined schedule, even if future oil prices fall so far that the oil is better off kept in the ground until prices rebound. In short, static DCF analysis assumes that decision makers do not fully and rationally exploit the flexibility available to them.

An alternative piece of the traditional toolkit, decision tree analysis, does allow decision makers to respond to the arrival of new information. However, like static DCF analysis, it typically uses a constant discount rate to value all cash flows.

This approach to valuation is at odds with modern financial theory, which recognizes that when decision makers are able to respond to new information as it arrives, different cash flows received at different dates can have quite different risk profiles and therefore require quite different discount rates.

What is needed is an approach that recognizes that decision makers are rational—in particular, each time they act they base their decisions on all of the information that is currently available to them—and correctly incorporates the implications of the resulting behavior into discount rates. Fortunately, there is a well-established branch of finance that does exactly this: the theory and practice of pricing the derivative securities that are traded in financial markets. Participants in these markets are confronted with problems similar to those described above. For example, the owner of an American call option on IBM stock must decide whether to exercise the option to buy an IBM share for the price specified in the option contract and, if she decides to do so, must decide exactly when to buy the share. Like the manager of the firm with the growth option described above, she must decide when to commit to a lump sum payment (the option's "strike price") that will lead to a series of uncertain future cash flows (the dividends generated by the IBM share); she knows that exercising the option cannot be reversed (she cannot sell the share back at the strike price if IBM shares subsequently fall in value); and she can decide when (not just whether) to exercise the option. The other decisions described above can also be compared to financial derivatives or, more commonly, portfolios of financial derivatives.

The observation that real-world business and economic decisions and financial derivative exercise decisions share many common features has led to the technique known as "real options analysis", which takes the methods that have been developed to value financial derivatives and uses them to analyze the "real options" that are embedded in real-world projects. As a result, real options analysis is based on underlying assumptions that decision makers act in order to maximize market value or some other well-defined objective function, and that they use all available information when making decisions. In other words, it has all the properties required to analyze real-world business and economic decisions. Analysts with expertise in real options analysis will give much better advice than their counterparts who use only traditional DCF techniques.

Many journal articles (and quite a few books) offer an intuitive introduction to real options analysis. However, this literature does not give practitioners an effective means of actually implementing real options analysis. Thus, we have a situation where other authors have created an environment in which decision makers are aware of—and eager to use—real options analysis, but they have not shown them how to use it. This book aims to meet the resulting demand for a text that shows practitioners how to actually carry out real options analysis.

All introductions to real options analysis highlight the relationship between the real options embedded in many capital budgeting problems and the derivative securities that make up such a large part of the modern financial system. They correctly point out that the valuation techniques being applied to real options have their origins in the models used to price financial derivatives. Some authors and practitioners have gone the next step and tried to analyze real options in exactly the same way that they would analyze financial derivatives—with a small set of models that can supposedly be applied to a wide variety of real options problems. However, there is a fundamental difference between financial derivatives and real options, which severely limits this approach.

- Financial derivatives are highly standardized, so that a single model can be used to price a large number of different contracts on different underlying assets traded on different exchanges at different dates.
- In contrast, the real options that arise in the real world will often vary radically from one problem to another. These differences may arise due to the particular real options embedded in the projects and the order in which they can be exercised. They may arise due to different underlying sources of uncertainty (with possibilities ranging from easily observable commodity prices to almost unquantifiable factors such as the technological viability of a project). The possibilities are almost endless.

Therefore, in this book we develop a relatively small set of essential tools that can be applied to any real options problem, rather than a "black box" to solve a small set of standardized problems. By the time we have worked through to the end of the book, we will be able to take an unstructured problem and implement real options analysis in a structured manner. The technique that we use to analyze any particular problem will not necessarily be the most efficient one available, but this is the price we pay for the generality that our approach offers. And, of course, reading this book should be regarded as exercising the first of a series of growth options: understanding a very general technique is the perfect springboard for developing the refinements that can enhance its efficiency for specific problems of interest.

Acknowledgments

I would like to thank Glenn Boyle, Eli Grace-Webb, Dinesh Kumareswaran, and Steen Videbeck for reading drafts of several chapters at various stages, and—especially—Lew Evans, who read almost everything in this book at least once and set me right on more occasions than I care to remember. Ten years of students at Victoria University of Wellington have seen some of the material in this book in various guises and, perhaps without realizing it, have contributed to its current form. Finally, I would like to thank my colleagues at the School of Economics and Finance for tolerating my frequent absences during the final few months of this book's preparation.

Contents

Real Options
in Theory and Practice

1

Introduction

1.1 THE AIM OF REAL OPTIONS ANALYSIS

We begin this book the way we will end it—by discussing three case studies that demonstrate the range of problems to which real options analysis can be applied. In the first one, a land owner needs to decide when to harvest a forest. The owner has considerable flexibility regarding the harvest date. Timber prices are highly volatile, so if the owner can get the harvest timing right there is potential to add considerable value to the forest. The second case considers the problem of whether, and how, to develop a natural gas field. Completing the process will be expensive and time consuming, and most of the development expenditure cannot be recovered if the project is abandoned prior to completion. The developer's problem is complicated by the volatility of natural gas prices and the uncertainty surrounding the actual development time required. The developer needs to decide when to begin developing the field and, once development is underway, whether to continue. In the third case, the owner of an ethanol plant confronted by falling ethanol prices and rising corn prices is considering temporarily suspending production, mothballing the plant, or shutting it down permanently. While suspending production can reduce losses in the short run, mothballing the plant will reduce them further—but at the cost of making it more difficult to resume production when market conditions improve. The owner needs to decide how long to wait before mothballing the plant, and then how long to wait before reactivating it in the future.

Each of these situations features a decision maker who observes exogenous factors that combine with the decisions he or she makes to determine a firm's cash flows. For example, the owner of the forest receives cash flows that depend on timber prices and the harvest policy adopted. The net cash flow received by the developer of the gas field depends on the price of natural gas and on the development policy. The ethanol plant produces a cash flow that depends on the prices of ethanol and corn, as well as on how the plant is operated.

The decision maker in each of these examples faces a series of choices that are complicated by the uncertainty surrounding the future paths of the exogenous factors and the difficulty in reversing decisions in the future. For example, if the owner of the forest harvests the trees immediately then it could be another 50 years before the next trees planted on the land are old enough to be harvested. This makes it important that the trees currently on the land are harvested at a time when timber prices are high. The forest owner will not want to harvest the trees two years from now only to see timber prices climb to historically high levels shortly afterwards. But while the owner delays the harvest, waiting for high timber prices to arrive, the eventual cash flow is also being delayed and (all else equal) its present value is being reduced. The forest owner needs to balance the costs and benefits of waiting for higher timber prices.

Real options analysis is a technique for identifying the actions that managers should take and the consequences for the market values of the firms that they manage. It uses analytical techniques originally developed for pricing financial derivatives to ensure that decision makers take account of all relevant information and correctly incorporate market attitudes to risk when making decisions.

1.2 PLACING REAL OPTIONS ANALYSIS IN CONTEXT

Real options analysis is not the only technique that aims to inform managerial decision making. Students of corporate finance are taught several techniques, which can be collected under the heading "discounted cash flow" (DCF) analysis. Before embarking on a study of real options analysis, it is useful to place the various approaches in context.

1.2.1 Static DCF Analysis

The first capital budgeting problems that students meet are usually relatively simple. For example, a manager might have to decide whether or not to undertake a new project, with the investment having to be undertaken immediately or not at all. The completed project may generate a stream of many future cash flows, but each one will be assumed to have the same risk-adjusted discount rate (RADR). For these problems, students are taught that the project should go ahead if and only if the market value of its incremental cash flows—that is, the cash flows received by the firm's owners if the project goes ahead, minus the cash flows they receive if it does not go ahead—is greater than the initial financial outlay. They are also taught that this market value equals the present value of the incremental cash flows, which is calculated by discounting the expected value of the cash flows by a common RADR. This approach (which we call static DCF analysis) maximizes the market value of a firm's existing equity when it is applied to such simple problems.

Provided it is applied carefully, static DCF analysis can also correctly analyze many variations of these problems. In some variations, the expected cash flows will be calculated by specifying expected paths for sales, output prices, input costs, and other factors. In some cases the RADR will be specified as part of the problem, while in others it will be estimated using the costs of capital of firms in a similar industry. In more complicated problems, in which cash flows are made up of components with different risks, students will have to use a different RADR for each component and calculate the present value of each component separately.

Unfortunately, we do not have to go far beyond the first problems we meet as students to find situations where static DCF analysis will *not* give the correct answer. Indeed, static DCF analysis should be avoided in any situation where the decision maker is going to have to make decisions in the future that will affect the incremental cash flows. With such dynamic decision making, future cash flows will be determined by future actions, which can be chosen only in the context of information available at the (future) time. Since we do not know what that information will be, the only way to apply static DCF analysis to such situations is to force the decision maker to choose all future actions today. While this allows us to use the techniques of static DCF analysis, it is inherently irrational in a dynamic setting: it effectively assumes that the decision maker will ignore some important information when making future decisions.

Consider, for example, the forest harvest decision introduced at the beginning of this chapter. Static DCF analysis of this problem requires that we force the forest owner to decide now when to harvest the forest. Once the forest owner has chosen a harvest date, we can identify the relevant expected incremental cash flows, apply a sensible RADR, and estimate the market value of the forest. We can repeat this procedure for a selection of different possible harvest dates and then choose the one that leads to the highest market value for the forest. However, this market value will be correct only if the forest owner does not deviate from the specified policy—regardless of what might happen between now and that harvest date. For example, the timber price might spike upwards prior to the scheduled harvest, but the owner cannot be tempted into harvesting early. The price might fall to historically low levels at the time of the scheduled harvest, but the owner will harvest anyway. A rational forest owner will not behave in this way, yet static DCF analysis relies on such behavior whenever it is applied to situations outside that class of simple capital budgeting problems for which it is suited.

1.2.2 Decision Tree Analysis

Static DCF analysis should not be applied to situations involving dynamic decision making. However, corporate finance students will often meet another relatively simple technique that appears more suitable. This approach, known as decision tree analysis, digs a little deeper than static DCF analysis when calculating cash flows. It recognizes that future cash flows depend on future actions, and that they potentially depend on future information. Decision tree analysis of a problem begins by mapping out the sequence of actions that the decision maker can potentially carry out over time, representing them in a decision tree, and then works backwards through the tree, identifying the best action to take at each point where the tree branches out. Because we work backwards through time, at each branch point in the decision tree the decision maker's future actions have already been determined and already been incorporated into the future cash flows. The market value of these future cash flows is usually estimated by discounting their expected value using a constant discount rate.

It is this use of a constant discount rate that is the main shortcoming of decision tree analysis. Dynamic decision making has a subtle effect on the risk of cash flow streams. Future cash flows depend on the manager's future actions, which depend on future information. This potentially makes risk, as well as the cash flows, sensitive to the arrival of future information. Thus, the RADR need not be constant over time. If decision tree analysis gets the RADR wrong then, while the decision maker is maximizing something, it will not be the market value of the firm's equity.

1.2.3 Real Options Analysis

Like static DCF analysis, real options analysis follows the fundamental principle of maximizing market value. It uses much the same inputs and can use the same financial models to adjust for risk. The only difference is that real options analysis recognizes that decision makers use all available information when making decisions, whereas static DCF analysis requires decision makers to make choices years in advance and follow them through regardless of what may happen in the meantime. It should therefore be used in place of static DCF analysis whenever the decision-making process will be carried out over time.

Real options analysis uses the same "backward induction" approach as decision tree analysis, but it combines this with a consistent valuation model. That is, rather than using a constant discount rate to calculate the present value of the cash flow stream resulting from each possible action, real options analysis uses a valuation model that recognizes the impact of dynamic decision making on the risk of the cash flow stream. Conceptually, at least, it leaves valuation to the market: it estimates the market value of each cash flow stream by finding a portfolio of traded securities that generates the same cash flow stream and then uses the observed market value of this portfolio as the estimate of the market value of the cash flow stream. The precise procedure for carrying out this portfolio replication was originally developed to value stock options and other financial derivatives, which is the source of the "real options" label for this technique.

1.3 OUTLINE OF THE BOOK

The book is divided into four distinct parts, with the first one describing the foundations of real options analysis. This is essential preparation for the later chapters. Chapter 2 introduces the basic modeling framework and explains why it is appropriate to make maximizing the market value of a firm's equity the decision-making criterion. Chapter 3 develops the basic valuation approach that is used throughout the book, introducing it in the context of a model with a single time period. We derive a variety of formulations of the binomial option pricing model that is used to value financial derivatives, including one that yields valuations consistent with the CAPM. Chapter 4 applies this theory to situations involving multiple time periods. By the end of that chapter we will have acquired all of the techniques we need in order to value any cash flows appearing in this book. Chapter 5 introduces the general algorithm that is the basis of the remainder of the book. It combines the valuation model of Chapters 3 and 4 with the decision maker's response to the arrival of new information as discussed in Chapter 2. In Chapter 5 we motivate the backward induction technique that lies at the heart of the approach, and sketch the overall algorithm to be followed.

The second part of the book features a series of examples that show how the general approach described in Chapter 5 is implemented. The material in Part II is organized to help us gradually deepen our understanding of the general algorithm and apply it to increasingly complex situations. Each chapter is based on a particular underlying option structure. Within each chapter, the examples are chosen so that we can gradually develop the ability to apply real options analysis to that particular option structure.

Chapter 6 considers the simplest real options, cases where decisions taken today do not affect the choices available in the future. Chapter 7 introduces the next simplest situation, in which a decision maker has to decide when to carry out a particular action (such as investing in a new project or abandoning an existing one) that has long-term consequences. Chapters 8 and 9 extend this discussion to cases where the decision maker has to decide when to carry out each of a series of actions (such as when to invest in each stage of a complex capital expansion program). Chapter 10 introduces another dimension to the range of real options by allowing the decision maker to reverse earlier decisions. For example, we consider the problem of when to shut down a production facility and when to reopen it. Chapter 11 explains how real options analysis can be implemented when the decision maker can take actions that reveal information that would otherwise be unknown. These so-called "learning options" are crucial components of many real-world business decisions.

Chapters 6–11 provide the key to understanding and implementing real options analysis. Within each of these chapters, there is a sequence of examples that build towards a general technique for analyzing a specific type of real option. This sequence of chapters has been organized so that each chapter builds on the previous one, allowing readers to gradually develop the skills needed to analyze the problems confronted in the real world, which can contain quite complex combinations of the "component" options considered in the individual chapters.

By the time we have worked through Part II, we will have a thorough understanding of real options and how to analyze them. However, if real options analysis is to be useful in a practical setting then we must be able to calibrate the models that we build. Because real options analysis delegates much of the determination of market value to financial markets (in principle, anyway), practitioners make extensive use of market data in calibrating the underlying models. Even if they are not always efficient, financial markets are likely to do a more reliable job of estimating market value than the decision maker. Part III, comprising Chapters 12–14, shows how to go about implementing this part of real options analysis.

Chapter 12 considers a common situation where the key source of risk is described by the level of the price of an item. We see how the price process can be modeled and how our valuation model can be calibrated so that it produces market value estimates that are consistent with observed price behavior. Chapter 13 presents some techniques that allow us to build models consistent with the prices of financial options and other derivative securities traded in financial markets. Although these techniques will not be suitable for every problem we encounter, when they are available they provide a very effective means of calibrating our models. Finally, Chapter 14 considers problems for which the source of risk may be a non-price variable. Sometimes we are able to apply modified versions of the techniques from Chapter 12 to these situations. On other occasions we might be able to use historical share price data for firms exposed to similar risks. Both approaches are described in Chapter 14.

At this point of the book, all of the building blocks have been introduced. We finish, in Part IV, with three case studies that are designed to show how these building blocks fit together. Each one begins with a description of a real-world problem and works through the process of identifying the key sources of risk, identifying the most appropriate real option structure, calibrating the model, implementing the real options algorithm, and analyzing and interpreting the results. Chapter 15 shows how real options analysis can be used to value a forest and decide on the optimal harvest policy. Chapter 16 considers the optimal development of a gas reserve. Chapter 17 uses real options analysis to determine how soon to mothball an ethanol plant when the ethanol price falls relative to input prices. These case studies demonstrate the potential of real options analysis, but they also suggest some areas where we might wish to develop or extend the tools we have available. Chapter 18 briefly discusses some ways in which our real options toolkit might be expanded.

1.4 SPREADSHEETS

Spreadsheets provide a very effective tool for developing a thorough understanding of the theory of real options analysis and the modeling techniques used to implement this theory. The enclosed CD contains spreadsheets for each of the numerical examples contained in this book. One purpose of these spreadsheets is to demonstrate how the examples can be implemented. Another, equally important, purpose is to allow readers to develop their real options intuition in a setting where conjectures can readily be tested. One of the most effective approaches to learning how real options work is to play around with simple models. How does the optimal exercise policy change if the state variable becomes more volatile? Is market value affected by restricting some of the decision maker's flexibility? Which aspects of the situation lead the real options valuation to differ from one using static DCF analysis? Such questions can be answered by making some quite small changes to the examples covered in the book. The exercises at the end of each chapter give some guidance as to the modifications that can be interesting, but readers should treat them as a starting point, not an exhaustive list.

However, spreadsheets will often not be the best tool to use when solving real-world problems due to the large size (and number) of tables that are often needed. Fortunately, the step from simple spreadsheet models to full implementations requires only fairly basic programming skills. The notation in the book has been chosen to make the transition from spreadsheet to full implementation as painless as possible.

Finally, the numerical calculations reported in the text are only rounded for presentational purposes—the calculations themselves are carried out using greater precision than might at first appear to be the case. As a result, it will not always be possible to exactly reproduce the outputs using the intermediate inputs reported. Nevertheless, the outputs are all consistent with the original inputs for each problem. Where there is any confusion, inspection of the relevant spreadsheet should clear it up.

Part I

FOUNDATIONS

2

The Modeling Framework

If we are to analyze projects properly, we need to know how managers will exploit the flexibility embedded in those projects. To do this we need to understand managers' objective functions. Section 2.1 explains why the manager of any firm should seek to maximize the market value of existing shareholders' stake in the firm. The manager's job is made more difficult by the uncertainty about the future consequences of any action. Modeling this uncertainty is a crucial part of real options analysis. Section 2.2 introduces the structure (called a binomial tree) that we use to model the risk associated with future cash flows. We use this structure in Section 2.3 to highlight the importance of dynamic decision making—that is, of using all available information to make future decisions.

This chapter establishes the foundations on which the rest of the book is built. It is the glue that binds Part I together. For example, once we have determined that a manager should maximize the market value of the existing equity in a firm, it is clear that we need a means of estimating that market value. This is why we spend Chapters 3 and 4 developing an approach for estimating the market value of cash flow streams. Similarly, once we understand how dynamic decision making links managers' decisions with the arrival of new information, we need to develop a method for identifying optimal decisions when information arrives over time. This is exactly what we do in Chapter 5. By the time we reach the end of that chapter we will have acquired all the tools we need to undertake real options analysis.

2.1 CHOOSING AN OBJECTIVE FUNCTION

As we discussed in Chapter 1, many real investment projects contain substantial opportunities for managers to influence future cash flows. If we are to fully understand a project, we must understand how its manager exercises this flexibility. In some applications we use real options analysis when managing a project ourselves, so that we need to decide how we will exercise the project's various embedded real options. Exactly what we do will depend on what we are trying to achieve, which is formalized in the so-called objective function that we are trying to maximize. Are we, for example, trying to maximize current profits? Should we aim to maximize the accounting rate of return? Or should we maximize the market value of equity instead? In other applications we use real options analysis to estimate the market value of a firm or project that is being managed by another individual. We need to predict how this individual will exercise the embedded real options, and this once again depends on the manager's objective function. An essential task, therefore, is to determine just what objective function managers should choose.

2.1.1 Shareholder Unanimity

Firms are ultimately owned by their shareholders, and each individual shareholder of a firm would like the manager to act in that shareholder's best interest. However, different shareholders have different attitudes to risk and different time profiles of desired consumption, to mention just two sources of variation. As a result, we might think that there is the potential for substantial disagreement amongst shareholders regarding the actions of a firm's manager. For example, some shareholders may want the firm to invest in projects that generate low-risk, short-term cash flows, while others may prefer the firm to invest in higher risk projects that do not begin to generate cash flows until much further in the future. However, it turns out that provided the manager's actions affect shareholders' consumption and investment opportunities only through the impact on their personal wealth, and not on the prices they face, all shareholders will agree that the firm's manager should maximize the market value of the existing equity—that is, all shareholders will agree on the objective function that they would like the firm's manager to adopt.

To put this in context, consider the example of the manager of a firm that is contemplating undertaking a new project that will increase the market value of the firm's equity. We assume that the incremental cash flows generated by the project are spanned by securities that are already traded in financial markets—that is, the project's incremental cash flows can be exactly replicated using some portfolio of existing traded securities. We say that partial spanning holds, or that financial markets are sufficiently complete. In addition, we assume that the project is sufficiently small that prices are unaffected by the manager's decision; that is, the decision maker is a price-taker.

Note that these assumptions are not unique to real options analysis: they are implicit in static DCF analysis as well.[1] Indeed, finance theory does not

---

1. Arnold and Shockley (2002) discuss the assumptions underlying market-value maximization at a similar technical level to that of this chapter, but in more detail.

provide practical solutions to capital budgeting problems when these assumptions do not hold, since then all prices in the economy potentially change following investment in the new project. Different shareholders might well be affected by such a change in different ways, introducing the possibility of conflicts of interest amongst a firm's shareholders and making it impossible to determine an objective function for a manager who wishes to work in the best interests of shareholders. The precise objective function adopted would depend on factors such as the relative size of individual shareholders' stakes in the firm and the coalitions of shareholders that might form. Consideration of such possibilities would take us far beyond what is feasible in practical capital budgeting problems. Therefore, we make the partial-spanning and price-taking assumptions throughout this book.

Consider the problem facing an individual shareholder of this firm. She allocates her resources in order to fund her consumption both now and in the future. These resources comprise her current income and portfolio of financial securities. At each date she must use these resources to pay for her immediate consumption and the portfolio that she will use to transfer wealth over time. The utility that she is able to achieve ultimately depends on her budget set, which depends on the market value of her asset portfolio.

Our two assumptions (partial spanning and price taking) mean that the prices at which the shareholder can shift wealth over time and across states of nature will be unaffected by the manager's action. However, because her equity in the firm has increased in value, the shareholder's budget constraint will be relaxed, thereby enlarging the set of affordable consumption–portfolio combinations and (potentially) raising the utility that she can achieve: the enlargement of her budget set cannot make the shareholder worse off, and it might make her better off. As a result, the shareholder will support any action of the manager that raises the market value of her stake in the firm. So will all other shareholders.

Therefore, throughout this book we assume that the decision maker maximizes the market value of existing shareholders' stake in the firm. This is sensible when we are using real options analysis for decision-making purposes, since then theory shows that our objective function should be the market value of the firm's existing equity. We adopt the same objective function when we are using real options analysis to value a firm being managed by another party. Although theory dictates that this manager should also be maximizing the market value of the firm's existing equity, we need to recognize that managers are likely to work in their own best interests. They may, for example, seek to build an empire by having the firm invest in projects even when these projects do not increase the market value of the firm's existing equity; they might seek to entrench their position as manager by having the firm invest in projects that are closely related to their own special skills, even if this lowers the market value of equity. Shareholders will design executive compensation schemes that attempt to give managers the incentive to maximize market value, but these incentive schemes are unlikely to work perfectly. Thus, when valuing a firm managed by another party, our calculated market value should be regarded as an estimate of what the firm *could* be worth if it were managed optimally, not what it necessarily *is* worth.[2]

2.1.2 A Special Case: The Net Present Value Rule

In this section we discuss a special situation and the familiar capital budgeting rule that then applies. A firm is confronted with a "now-or-never" investment opportunity: either the firm can invest in a particular project immediately or the opportunity is lost forever. Investment requires immediate expenditure of I and changes the market value of the firm's future cash flows from V to V'. The investment rule—that the net present value (NPV) of the investment must be greater than or equal to zero—arises from requiring that a firm's manager maximizes the market value of the firm's existing equity.

If the manager rejects the investment opportunity the firm will have market value V, comprising debt (worth D) and equity (worth E); that is,

$$V = D + E.$$

Suppose, instead, that the manager exercises the investment opportunity. Undertaking the investment requires an initial cash outlay of I, which has to come from somewhere. We consider the case that the firm issues new securities worth N that raise exactly I from investors. (This could be new debt, new equity, or some other security; its precise nature is unimportant.) Immediately afterwards, the firm will have market value V', comprising the original debt (now worth D'), the original equity (now worth E'), and the new securities (worth N); that is,

$$V' = D' + E' + N.$$

Thus, the original shareholders' equity is worth

$$E = V - D$$

if the investment opportunity is rejected and

$$E' = V' - D' - N$$

if investment occurs. The manager maximizes the market value of the firm's existing equity by undertaking the investment if and only if $E' \geq E$, which occurs if and only if

$$V' - D' - N \geq V - D.$$

Equivalently, the manager should invest if and only if

$$(V' - V) - N \geq D' - D. \tag{2.1}$$

At this point, we need to make two further assumptions. First, we suppose that the new securities are issued at a "fair" price, which means that their true market

---

2. See Chapter 18 of Grinblatt and Titman (2002) for a discussion of manager–shareholder conflict.

value equals the amount that investors pay for them; that is, $N = I$. This assumption is far from innocuous. One of the difficulties firms face is that it can be costly to raise funds from external capital markets, meaning that N often exceeds I. For example, new investors will typically demand a discount in order to compensate them for the fact that insiders know more about the firm's future prospects than they do, and the discount will be larger for those firms with the greatest information asymmetries. Nevertheless, it is standard in capital budgeting applications to assume that there are no such frictions in external capital markets. Second, we assume that investing in the new project does not affect the market value of the firm's existing debt, so that $D' = D$. Again, this assumption is not innocuous. For firms with high debt levels, new investment can benefit existing bondholders by reducing default risk. This phenomenon, known as the debt overhang problem, is also typically assumed away in capital budgeting applications.[3]

With these two assumptions in place, condition (2.1) reduces to

$$(V' - V) - I \geq 0.$$

The term inside the brackets on the left-hand side is the increase in market value of the firm's future cash flows that occurs as a result of the investment. In other words, $V' - V$ is the market value of the future incremental cash flows that can be attributed to the new project. It follows that $(V' - V) - I$ equals the NPV of the investment opportunity. Thus, a now-or-never investment opportunity should be exercised if and only if the associated NPV is greater than or equal to zero.[4]

The standard NPV investment rule is therefore consistent with maximizing the market value of existing equity in the special case of a now-or-never investment opportunity (in a world without capital market frictions, at least). However, throughout Part II we will see many examples of situations where the appropriate investment rule changes when the assumption of now-or-never investment is relaxed. In some cases, the market value of existing shareholders' stake in a firm will be maximized by undertaking a project with a negative NPV. In other cases, it will be maximized by not undertaking a project with a positive NPV. Real options analysis leads to optimal (that is, market-value maximizing) decisions in all cases, unlike the standard NPV approach still favored by many practitioners, which is appropriate in only a relatively small set of special cases.

2.1.3 Calculating the Objective Function

There is one complication that we should mention before we continue. We have said that our objective function is the market value of existing shareholders' stake in the firm. Suppose we are considering taking action A or action B. With this

---

3. Most corporate finance textbooks discuss the effect of asymmetric information on the cost of raising external capital and the debt overhang problem. For example, see pp. 674–678 and pp. 563–567 of Grinblatt and Titman (2002) on these two topics.

4. This assumes that there are no costs associated with accessing external capital markets and that debt overhang does not arise.

approach, in principle we would compare the market value of the existing equity if we take action A (call it V_A) with the market value if we take action B (call it V_B). We would take action A only if $V_A \geq V_B$. However, the existing equity's market value will be revealed only *after* the decision is taken, so we cannot actually make this comparison. Instead, we need to estimate the after-effects of an action *before* that action is taken. In effect, our objective function is the *predicted* market value of existing equity. Therefore, we need a means of predicting market values; that is, we need a valuation model.

Our partial-spanning and price-taking assumptions mean that the prices at which investors can shift wealth over time and across states of nature are unaffected by the manager's decision. Since these prices do not change, we can use the current prices of financial securities to predict the market value of the firm's existing equity for each possible action taken by the manager. In Chapters 3 and 4 we present a valuation model, which we use throughout this book, that estimates market values using the current market prices of financial securities. However, before we get into the details of estimating market values we need to discuss the general structure upon which our valuation model is built. This is the subject of the next section.

2.2 MODELING RISK AND TIME

A key feature of actual business behavior is that managers manage. They observe the current state of the world and the states of the projects they manage and decide on courses of action that will affect the future cash flows associated with these projects. The manager of a copper mine may increase production when she observes high levels of the copper price. The owner of vacant land may develop the land when he observes high demand for office space. The manager of a gas-fueled power plant may shut it down during periods when the wholesale price of electricity is relatively low. In each case, the manager observes some indicator of the state of the world (the price of copper; the demand for office space; the wholesale electricity price) and takes an action (increase production; develop land; suspend production) that affects the project's cash flows.

If a valuation model is to be suitable for real options analysis then it must admit this type of behavior. In particular, it must recognize that a project's future cash flow does not generally evolve completely outside of the manager's control. Rather, it is determined by some combination of the manager's past and current actions and the evolution of variables that the manager cannot influence.

Therefore, the starting point of a real options model is the choice of a state variable (possibly more than one, although we restrict attention to a single state variable). The state variable is unaffected by the manager's actions and describes the main sources of risk that affect the project under consideration. The manager observes the state variable and takes actions that, together with the current state of nature, determine the cash flow. As discussed in Section 2.1, the manager chooses actions that maximize the market value of the existing shareholders' stake in the project.

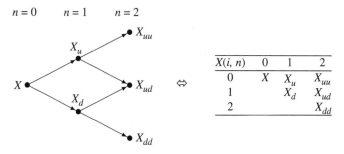

Figure 2.1. Different representations of a binomial tree

Once we have chosen the state variable, we need to specify how its magnitude changes over time. We assume that its behavior can be represented by a binomial tree. Figure 2.1 shows two ways to represent such a process. The left-hand representation shows the state variable taking the value X at date 0 and evolving to take one of the values X_u and X_d at date 1. We call the change from X to X_u an "up" move and one from X to X_d a "down" move. A sequence of two up moves results in the state variable taking the value X_{uu} at date 2, while a sequence of two down moves leads to a value of X_{dd}. We generally assume that the order in which moves occur has no effect on the underlying state variable: as shown in the left-hand representation, the state variable takes the value X_{ud} after one up and one down move, no matter which move occurred first.

The right-hand representation, which is much more useful in spreadsheet implementations, shows the same information in table form. $X(i, n)$ denotes the value of the state variable at date n if exactly i down moves have occurred since date 0. Just as in a spreadsheet or a matrix, i refers to the row of the table (which corresponds to the number of down moves) and n refers to the column (which corresponds to the date). For example, at date 1, if there has been one down move, the state variable takes the value $X(1, 1) = X_d$, while if there have been no down moves (and hence one up move), it takes the value $X(0, 1) = X_u$.

There is no reason to stop evolution of the state variable at date 2. We can add as many future dates as we like, but each additional period means that we must add one extra set of branches to the tree on the left-hand side of Figure 2.1. If we extend the tree out to date 3 there will be four "terminal nodes", labeled $X_{uuu}, X_{uud}, X_{udd}$, and X_{ddd}.[5] Similarly, each additional period means that we must add one extra column and one extra row to the table on the right-hand side of Figure 2.1.

The process shown in Figure 2.1 probably appears hopelessly unrealistic. After all, in practice there will usually be many different paths that the state variable

---

5. We continue to assume that the order in which moves occur is unimportant. Thus, for example, the state variable takes the value X_{udd} if any combination of a single up move and two down moves occurs.

can take, not the small number shown in the figure. However, when we actually apply the modeling framework described here, we make each period represent just a small length of time. As we squeeze more and more periods into each year, the number of possible paths that the state variable can take over the course of a year will increase.[6] Moreover, as we will see in Chapters 12–14, our approach is sufficiently flexible that we are able to model a wide range of behavior for the state variable.

We are typically faced with the task of valuing a stream of cash flows whose magnitude at any date depends on the level of the state variable at that date. For example, we might need to value an asset that generates a cash flow of $Y(i, n)$ at each node (i, n) of the binomial tree in Figure 2.1. In this case, the owner of the asset receives:

- cash flow of $Y(0, 0)$ at date 0;
- cash flow of either $Y(0, 1)$ or $Y(1, 1)$ at date 1, depending on whether the state variable equals X_u or X_d at date 1; and
- cash flow of $Y(0, 2)$ or $Y(1, 2)$ or $Y(2, 2)$ at date 2, depending on whether the state variable equals X_{uu} or X_{ud} or X_{dd} at date 2.

The first cash flow (received at date 0) is therefore risk free. However, the remaining two cash flows are risky. We do not know the magnitude of the date 1 cash flow because we do not know what value the state variable will take at date 1.[7] Similarly, we do not know the magnitude of the date 2 cash flow because we do not know what value the state variable will take at date 2.

2.3 STATIC VERSUS DYNAMIC DECISION MAKING

The distinction between static and dynamic decision making revolves around the future actions that managers will take. The market value of a project at date 0 potentially depends on the actions that the manager of that project takes at all future dates. In principle, the action chosen by the manager at date n can depend on all information available to the manager at that date—this comprises all information available at date 0 as well as all new information revealed between dates 0 and n. Under static decision making, the manager's actions at every future date n depend *only* on information available to the manager at date 0. In contrast, under dynamic decision making the manager's actions depend on all information available at date 0 *as well as* all new information revealed between dates 0 and n. This is much more realistic than assuming that managers wilfully ignore information that has the potential to dramatically alter the profitability of a project, which is the assumption underlying static decision making.

---

6. As the number of periods per year grows infinitely large, our binomial tree approaches the so-called Itô process that is widely used in the academic real options literature (Dixit and Pindyck, 1994, Chapter 3).

7. In the special case that $Y(0, 1) = Y(1, 1)$, the date 1 cash flow is risk free.

The following example illustrates the differences between the two types of decision making.

Example 2.1. Consider the problem faced by the owner of a piece of land in the central business district of a large city. The land is currently used as a car park, generating a net cash flow of $C = 0.1$ million dollars per period. At any time up to and including date 1 the owner can spend $I = 9$ million dollars to build an office block. If development occurs at node (i, n) then the owner can sell the developed land for $X(i, n)$ million dollars, where $X(i, n)$ evolves according to the binomial tree described in Table 2.1. In order to make this example as simple as possible, we assume that construction is instantaneous and that the car-parking operation does not generate any cash flow after date 1, even if the land is left undeveloped.

The cash flows generated by the land depend on the development policy chosen by the owner. For example, if he decides to develop the land at date 0 there is a one-off cash inflow of $X(0, 0) - I = 10 - 9 = 1$ million dollars; since the developed land is sold at date 0, there is no further cash flow. This information is summarized in the first row of Table 2.2. (Notice that there is no need to specify actions at nodes $(0, 1)$ and $(1, 1)$ for this particular policy because the land will already have been developed by this date.) Suppose, instead, that the owner decides he will develop the land at date 1. Then there is an initial cash flow of $C = 0.1$ million dollars from the car park operation. At date 1 there will be further cash flow of $X(0, 1) - I = 12.5 - 9 = 3.5$ million dollars in the up state and $X(1, 1) - I = 8 - 9 = -1$ million dollars in the down state. This information is summarized in the second row of Table 2.2. If, instead, the owner decides not to develop the land at all the cash flow will equal $C = 0.1$ million dollars at each node, as shown in the third row of the table.

These three policies are examples of static decision making since in each case the action to be taken at date 1 depends only on information available at date 0—most importantly, the action taken at date 1 does not depend on whether an up or down move occurs (which is not known at date 0). For example, if the owner adopts the second policy then he commits to develop the land at date 1 even if, at the time development is to occur, he realizes that the payoff from doing so is negative.

Consider, by way of contrast, the policy that develops the land only at date 1 and then only in the up state. This policy is not consistent with static

Table 2.1. The Market
Value of Developed Land

$X(i, n)$	0	1
0	10.0	12.5
1		8.0

Table 2.2. Possible Development Policies for a Piece of Land
with One Period until the Development Option Expires

Policy	Action at each node			Cash flow at each node		
	(0,0)	(0,1)	(1,1)	$Y(0,0)$	$Y(0,1)$	$Y(1,1)$
Policies consistent with static decision making						
1	Develop	n/a	n/a	1.0	0.0	0.0
2	Wait	Develop	Develop	0.1	3.5	−1.0
3	Wait	Wait	Wait	0.1	0.1	0.1
Policies not consistent with static decision making						
4	Wait	Develop	Wait	0.1	3.5	0.1
5	Wait	Wait	Develop	0.1	0.1	−1.0

decision making because the action taken at date 1 depends on information
that will only be revealed after date 0. The resulting cash flows will be $C = 0.1$ million dollars at nodes $(0, 0)$ and $(1, 1)$ from the car-park operation and
$X(0, 1) − I = 12.5 − 9 = 3.5$ million dollars at node $(0, 1)$ from developing
the land, as shown in the fourth row of Table 2.2. The remaining policy
is to develop the land only at date 1 and then only in the down state. The
resulting cash flows will be $C = 0.1$ million dollars at nodes $(0, 0)$ and $(0, 1)$
and $X(1, 1) − I = 8 − 9 = −1$ million dollars at node $(1, 1)$ from developing
the land, as shown in the bottom row of Table 2.2.   ∎

In Example 2.1 the decision maker must choose one of the five policies
described in Table 2.2. From our discussion in Section 2.1, the chosen policy
should maximize the estimated market value of the land. Anything that restricts
the set of actions that the owner can take will potentially reduce this market
value. Restricting the choice set will either reduce the market value of the land or
will have no effect, but it can never raise the market value. Static decision making
reduces the set of policies the owner can adopt, because it prevents the owner from
reacting to information when it arrives, and so potentially reduces the market value
of the land. The valuation when dynamic decision making is allowed will be at
least as high as the valuation when only static decision making is allowed, and it
will possibly be higher, since allowing more flexibility in decision making raises
(or, at least, does not lower) the value of the land.[8] For example, if the cash flow in
row 1 of Table 2.2 is the most valuable of the five policies considered there, then

---

8. However, this does *not* imply that allowing more flexibility makes investment more
attractive—sometimes incorporating all of the real options in a project makes investment
less attractive. For example, suppose that the policy in row 1 of Table 2.2 is the best of the
three static policies, but that the policy in row 4 is better still. Then dynamic decision making
increases the market value of the firm (from the market value of the cash flow in row 1 to the

restricting the choice set to policies consistent with static decision making will have no effect on the market value of the land because all it is doing is removing suboptimal policies from consideration. However, if the cash flow in row 4 is the most valuable then static decision making restricts consideration to a set of suboptimal policies and therefore leads to a strictly lower land value.

Once we have developed a method for estimating the market value of any given cash flow stream, the procedure for valuing the undeveloped land is—in principle—straightforward: for each policy in Table 2.2 calculate the estimated market value of the corresponding cash flows and take the largest of the five estimates. The associated policy shows us when (and if) the land should be developed. While this procedure seems straightforward, in practice it is not quite so simple. This is because the number of possible policies can be extremely large in models with a realistic number of periods. The following extension of Example 2.1 shows how quickly the number of possible policies can grow.

Example 2.2. Suppose that the situation introduced in Example 2.1 is extended so that development of the land can be delayed until date 2. There are now four policies consistent with static decision making, corresponding to developing the land at date 0, date 1, or date 2, or not developing it at all. These policies are described in the first four rows of Table 2.3. However, the main growth in the number of policies comes from those that are examples of dynamic decision making. For example, suppose the owner decides not to develop the land at date 0 and to develop it at date 1 only in the up state. The owner needs to decide what to do at date 2 if the first move is down; that is, he needs to specify actions at nodes $(1, 2)$ and $(2, 2)$. Since there are two possible actions at each node, there are $2 \times 2 = 4$ possible combinations. Thus, the single policy in the fourth row of Table 2.2 turns into four different policies in Table 2.3; they are shown in rows 5–8 of the latter table. The other ten policies, shown in rows 9–18, can be constructed from the policies in the third and fifth rows of Table 2.2 in much the same way. ■

When all policies are considered, we are left with 18 different policies for the decision maker in Example 2.2 to choose from.[9] And this is from an example that extends out only to date 2. In practical applications we will want to build models that extend much further into the future than this. Not only will the number of possible policies become huge, but it will become increasingly difficult to actually list the different policies. As a result, it is not feasible to solve real options problems

---

market value of the cash flow in row 4), but the optimal policy changes from one of investing at date 0 to one of waiting.

9. Of course, some of these policies have no chance of being optimal. For example, developing the land when the market value of developed land is low and not developing the land when the market value is high is unlikely to be optimal. Nevertheless, there may well exist a policy amongst the large set shown in Table 2.3 that dominates static decision making. The challenge is to find it.

Table 2.3. Possible Development Policies for a Piece of Land with Two Periods until the Development Option Expires

Policy	Action at each node					
	(0, 0)	(0, 1)	(1, 1)	(0, 2)	(1, 2)	(2, 2)
Policies consistent with static decision making						
1	Develop	n/a	n/a	n/a	n/a	n/a
2	Wait	Develop	Develop	n/a	n/a	n/a
3	Wait	Wait	Wait	Develop	Develop	Develop
4	Wait	Wait	Wait	Wait	Wait	Wait
Policies not consistent with static decision making						
5	Wait	Develop	Wait	n/a	Wait	Wait
6	Wait	Develop	Wait	n/a	Wait	Develop
7	Wait	Develop	Wait	n/a	Develop	Wait
8	Wait	Develop	Wait	n/a	Develop	Develop
9	Wait	Wait	Develop	Wait	Wait	n/a
10	Wait	Wait	Develop	Wait	Develop	n/a
11	Wait	Wait	Develop	Develop	Wait	n/a
12	Wait	Wait	Develop	Develop	Develop	n/a
13	Wait	Wait	Wait	Develop	Wait	Wait
14	Wait	Wait	Wait	Wait	Develop	Wait
15	Wait	Wait	Wait	Wait	Wait	Develop
16	Wait	Wait	Wait	Develop	Develop	Wait
17	Wait	Wait	Wait	Wait	Develop	Develop
18	Wait	Wait	Wait	Develop	Wait	Develop

by simply listing all of the possible policies, constructing their associated cash flow streams, estimating the market value of each stream, and taking the largest estimated market value. This is exactly what we do *in principle*, but it is not what we do *in practice*. The approach we actually use, called dynamic programming, is described in Chapter 5. As we see there, dynamic programming provides a very efficient means of finding optimal policies.

We conclude this section with a brief discussion of the rationality underlying real options analysis or, more precisely, the irrationality embedded in static decision making. The irrationality arises because static decision making rests on an assumption that managers behave in a way that is inherently irrational: they choose not to use all available information when making decisions. In particular, static decision making implicitly assumes that a manager will decide now when to invest in the future and will not change that plan regardless of what happens between now and the scheduled investment date. For example, the market for the intended output of a new factory may collapse (perhaps because a competitor has developed a new product that completely dominates the intended output), yet static decision making assumes that the manager will continue with the investment plan. This situation is worth remembering when people criticize the apparent complexity of real options analysis—the cost of restricting attention to static decision making is that we would have to assume that managers do not manage, they mis-manage.

Of course, project evaluation can be costly, so that the hyper-rationality assumed in real options analysis may be prohibitively costly. In practice, firms do not formally evaluate large investment opportunities every day. A firm may, for example, only evaluate projects once a year. However, no matter how infrequently these evaluations occur, information that has arrived since the preceding evaluation will be an input into the decision-making process. As the following continuation of Example 2.2 illustrates, this reduces the set of possible policies, but it does not reduce it all the way to static decision making.

> **Example 2.3.** Suppose that the owner of the land described in Example 2.2 only evaluates his development option at dates 0 and 2. At date 0 he can choose between developing the land at date 0 or developing the land at date 1 or waiting and reevaluating the development decision at date 2. What he cannot do is allow the date 1 development decision to depend on information unavailable at date 0. Thus, policies 5–12 in Table 2.3 are no longer feasible. However, this still leaves ten policies that are feasible when evaluations are not held at date 1: the four examples of static decision making, numbered 1–4, as well as policies 13–18 in Table 2.3. ∎

At this point we put the issue of static versus dynamic decision making to one side and go on to consider how to estimate the market value of an arbitrary cash flow stream. We return to our discussion of decision making in Chapter 5, when we describe the dynamic programming technique.

2.4 PROBLEMS

2.1. **(Discussion)** A firm has a now-or-never investment opportunity that will require capital expenditure of $10 million. If the firm decides not to invest, its equity will be worth $30 million and its debt $25 million. If the firm does invest, its net cash flows will be worth $67 million.

   (a) If there are no frictions in external capital markets and undertaking the project does not affect the market value of the firm's existing debt, is investment good for the firm's existing shareholders? How much will their equity be worth if the firm invests?

   (b) Suppose that capital market frictions mean the firm must issue securities worth $13 million in order to raise $10 million. The market value of the firm's existing debt is still unaffected by investment. Is investment good for the firm's existing shareholders? How much will their equity be worth if the firm invests?

   (c) Suppose that there are no capital market frictions but that investment raises the market value of the firm's existing debt by 4%. Is investment good for the firm's existing shareholders? How much will their equity be worth if the firm invests?

2.2. **(Discussion)** Suppose that the investment in Section 2.1.2 is financed by issuing new equity. Specifically, after the new shares are issued, the new shareholders own a proportion λ of the firm, with the remainder owned by the original shareholders.

    (a) Explain why the existing shareholders end up owning equity worth $(1 - \lambda)(V' - D')$ if the investment goes ahead.

    (b) Show that the manager should invest if and only if

$$V' - V \geq (D' - D) + \lambda(V' - D').$$

    (c) Explain why this reduces to the standard NPV rule if there are no frictions in external capital markets and the new project does not affect the market value of the firm's existing debt.

2.3. **(Practice)** Recalculate the cash flows in Table 2.2 assuming that the market value of developed land is currently $15 million, that it is equally likely to either rise by 25% or fall by 20%, that the land will cost $12 million to develop, and that it generates a net cash flow of $1 million per period prior to being developed.

2.4. **(Practice)** An all-equity firm has the right to build a new factory on or before date 1. Construction is instantaneous and the factory will be worth $30 million as soon as it is completed. If the firm invests at date 0 the factory costs $28 million to build. However, if the firm invests at date 1 instead then construction will cost either $32 million or $25 million, corresponding to up and down moves respectively. Assume that the firm sells the factory as soon as it is built. Construct the equivalent of Table 2.2 for this situation.

3

Valuing Single-period Cash Flows

This chapter introduces the valuation approach that is used throughout the remainder of the book. By the time we have finished working through its contents we will be able to estimate the market value of a risky cash flow that will be received after one period of time elapses. In the next chapter we see how to use this approach to value a stream of cash flows that will be received in many future periods. Then, in Chapter 5, we modify the approach so that we can simultaneously calculate the market value and identify policies that maximize the market value. For now, though, we focus on the simplest case of valuing a cash flow to be received one period in the future.

We start by using the binomial tree introduced in Section 2.2, together with the so-called law of one price, to reduce the problem of valuing an arbitrary cash flow to the problem of valuing a particular asset known as the spanning asset. Thus, no matter what cash flow we need to value, we must start by valuing the spanning asset. In Section 3.2 we see how to calculate its market value when the state variable is the price of a traded asset, while Section 3.3 shows an alternative approach that is available when forward or futures contracts on the state variable are traded. Section 3.4 shows a different approach, which can be used even when the state variable is not the price of a traded asset. The valuation approach is summarized in Section 3.5.

3.1 ARBITRAGE-FREE ASSET PRICES

Our valuation problem is expressed using the modeling framework introduced in Chapter 2. That is, a state variable currently takes the value X and, after one period has elapsed, will equal either X_u or X_d. We may be interested in estimating the market value of several different cash flows to be received after one period, with each different cash flow corresponding to a particular action that the manager can take. Each cash flow is completely specified by its level in the up state, Y_u, and its level in the down state, Y_d. We therefore need to be able to value an arbitrary cash flow of this type.

The most reliable way to estimate the market value of a future cash flow is to use as much information contained in market prices as possible. Most of the methods derived from finance theory amount to finding a portfolio of traded assets that generates a cash flow stream that is "close" to the one being valued and using the cost of this portfolio as the market value estimate. The rationale for this approach is that financial markets are efficient; in short, market prices can be trusted.[1] The various methods differ according to what they require for two cash flow streams to be close to one another.

The valuation model described in this section, and used throughout the book, rests on one assumption: assets are priced in such a way that arbitrage opportunities do not exist. The most useful implication of this assumption for our purposes is the law of one price—the prices of any two portfolios that generate identical future cash flows must always be equal. If the law of one price ever failed to hold, investors could buy the relatively cheap portfolio and short-sell the relatively expensive one, generating an immediate cash inflow with no requirement for a subsequent cash outflow (that is, they could exploit an arbitrage opportunity). Thus, in our valuation approach two cash flow streams must generate identical cash flows at each future node if they are to be regarded as close.

We are trying to estimate the market value of a cash flow that will be received after one period. This cash flow equals Y_u in the up state and Y_d in the down state. In order to do this, we suppose that there exist two assets: a one-period risk-free bond with a current price of 1 and a certain payoff of R_f after one period;[2] and a so-called spanning asset—which is a risky asset generating a payoff after one period equal to X_u in the up state and X_d in the down state—with a current price of Z. We use the information contained in Z and R_f to value the cash flow described by (Y_u, Y_d).

Our approach is to build a portfolio made up of just enough units of the risk-free bond and the spanning asset that the portfolio generates a cash flow of Y_u in the up state and Y_d in the down state. This is known as the cash flow's replicating portfolio. In Appendix 3.A.1 we show that the replicating portfolio costs

$$V = \frac{\pi_u Y_u + \pi_d Y_d}{R_f}, \tag{3.1}$$

---

1. This is not to say that we necessarily believe that asset markets are always efficient. However, progress in developing rules for capital budgeting in inefficient markets has been limited. For some work in such an environment, see Stein (1996).

2. That is, $R_f = 1 + r_f$, where r_f denotes the one-period risk-free interest rate.

where

$$\pi_u = \frac{ZR_f - X_d}{X_u - X_d} \quad \text{and} \quad \pi_d = \frac{X_u - ZR_f}{X_u - X_d}. \tag{3.2}$$

If there are to be no arbitrage opportunities then the market value of the asset we are valuing must equal the cost of its replicating portfolio—that is, the law of one price must hold. Therefore our estimate of the market value of the cash flow (Y_u, Y_d) is given by equation (3.1). This is our fundamental asset-pricing formula. We use it whenever we need to estimate the market value of a cash flow stream.

Equation (3.1) has an elegant interpretation that can make it easy to remember, but can also lead to confusion about the assumptions underlying our valuation approach. The key to this interpretation can be found in a different world from the one we are considering. All investors in this new world are risk neutral, and up and down moves occur with respective probabilities π_u and π_d.[3] Because risk-neutral investors are indifferent between receiving a risk-free cash flow and a risky one with the same expected value, all investors in this new world attach the same value to the risky cash flow (Y_u, Y_d) as they would to a risk-free cash flow of $\pi_u Y_u + \pi_d Y_d$. Since the latter cash flow is risk free, its market value can be found by discounting the cash flow using the one-period risk-free interest rate, resulting in the expression in equation (3.1). It follows that the market value of the risky cash flow (Y_u, Y_d) satisfies equation (3.1) in this risk-neutral world, just like it does in the world we are really interested in.

Because of this result, equation (3.1) is often known as the risk-neutral pricing formula, and π_u and π_d in (3.2) as the risk-neutral probabilities of up and down moves. We can interpret equation (3.1) as saying that the current market value of a cash flow to be received one period from now equals the expected value of the cash flow (calculated using the risk-neutral probabilities), discounted back at the one-period risk-free interest rate.

It is important to realize that we do *not* have to assume that all investors are risk neutral to get equation (3.1); all we assume is that there are no arbitrage opportunities. Indeed, the asset pricing formula in (3.1) still adjusts for risk, even though the risk-free interest rate (rather than a risk-adjusted discount rate) is used to discount the expected cash flow. Suppose, for example, that investors require a large premium in compensation for exposure to state-variable risk; that is, Z is relatively low. Then (3.2) shows that π_u is relatively low and π_d is relatively high. If the risk premium increases then Z falls, further lowering π_u and raising π_d. The risk adjustment thus appears in the numerator of (3.1), via the risk-neutral probabilities, rather than in the denominator, via the discount rate. As a result, our valuation approach does not rely on all investors being risk neutral.

---

3. As we show in Appendix 3.A.2, π_u and π_d are each greater than zero and less than one. Moreover, it is easily shown that they add up to one. These are exactly the properties that probabilities have.

Before continuing, it is worthwhile pausing and asking just what information we need in order to be able to value the cash flow using equations (3.1) and (3.2). The future levels of the state variable (X_u and X_d) are specified as part of the valuation problem, as are the corresponding levels of the cash flow (Y_u and Y_d), while the return on a one-period risk-free bond (R_f) can be inferred from observed bond prices. This leaves Z, the current price of the spanning asset.

Therefore, we have reduced the problem of valuing an asset that pays Y_u or Y_d after one period to the problem of valuing an asset that pays X_u or X_d after one period. At a first glance, it may not seem as if we have made much progress: we have just replaced one valuation problem with another. However, recall that we often have to estimate the market values of many different cash flows with different combinations of Y_u and Y_d. Indeed, there will be one such combination for each possible action that the decision maker can take. But now all we have to do is value one asset—the one that pays X_u or X_d after one period—and then we can use equations (3.1) and (3.2) to easily estimate the market values of all of the others. This will ensure that each of these cash flows is valued on a consistent basis. We now consider three different approaches for estimating Z.

3.2 VALUATION WHEN THE STATE VARIABLE IS THE PRICE OF A TRADED ASSET

Consider the special case where the state variable is the price of a traded asset, which may pay a dividend or generate a convenience yield that accrues to the asset's owner.[4] For example, we may be attempting to value an oil reserve, in which case a natural choice for the state variable is the spot price of crude oil. Throughout this book we adopt the convention that prices are expressed cum dividend. In the context of our modeling framework, this means that the price at any given date is measured immediately before any cash flows are distributed on that date. Therefore, we suppose that the current price of the traded asset equals X, that it pays a dividend (or an equivalent convenience yield) of C immediately, and that one period from now its (cum dividend) price will equal X_u in the up state and X_d in the down state.

Although it costs X to buy one unit of the asset, because the dividend is received immediately the true cost is really $X - C$. Substituting $Z = X - C$ into equation (3.2) shows that when the state variable is the price of a traded asset the risk-neutral probability of an up move equals

$$\pi_u = \frac{ZR_f - X_d}{X_u - X_d} = \frac{(X - C)R_f - X_d}{X_u - X_d}.$$

---

4. The convenience yield represents the flow of benefits that accrue to the owner of a commodity being held in storage. These benefits derive from the flexibility that is provided by having immediate access to the stored commodity. This flow of benefits is treated in just the same way as a flow of cash dividends.

Dividing both numerator and denominator by X gives an alternative expression for this probability,

$$\pi_u = \frac{\left(1 - \frac{C}{X}\right) R_f - D}{U - D},$$ (3.3)

where $U = X_u/X$ and $D = X_d/X$ are the sizes of up and down moves, respectively, expressed relative to the initial level of the state variable. The corresponding expression for the risk-neutral probability of a down move is[5]

$$\pi_d = \frac{U - \left(1 - \frac{C}{X}\right) R_f}{U - D}.$$ (3.4)

The term C/X captures the market's attitude towards state-variable risk. If investors require relatively high compensation for exposure to this risk, the current price X will be low (so that their average return from holding the asset is high), so that $1 - C/X$ will be low, and the risk-neutral probability of an up move will also be relatively low.

Example 3.1. In this example we estimate the market value of the cash flow generated by an oil field that produces one unit of oil at a cost of $I = 20$. The spot price of crude oil is an obvious choice of state variable for this problem. We suppose that it is currently $X = 120$ and will equal either $X_u = 150$ or $X_d = 96$ after one period. The convenience yield from holding crude oil is assumed to equal 10% of the spot price per period, so that $C = 0.10X = 12$. We assume that the one-period risk-free interest rate is 4%, so that the return on a one-period risk-free bond equals $R_f = 1.04$.

The risk-neutral probability of an up move is equal to

$$\pi_u = \frac{(X - C)R_f - X_d}{X_u - X_d} = \frac{(120 - 12)1.04 - 96}{150 - 96} = 0.3022,$$

while that of a down move is equal to

$$\pi_d = \frac{X_u - (X - C)R_f}{X_u - X_d} = \frac{150 - (120 - 12)1.04}{150 - 96} = 0.6978.$$

---

5. With these risk-neutral probabilities, our valuation model corresponds to the binomial option pricing model originally developed by Cox et al. (1979). There are slight differences in the expressions for π_u and π_d compared to approaches that measure all prices ex dividend and assume that the dividend (or convenience yield) is proportional to the state variable. We use cum dividend prices because this assumption results in tidier expressions in subsequent chapters.

Therefore the risk-neutral pricing formula is

$$V = \frac{\pi_u Y_u + \pi_d Y_d}{R_f}$$

$$= \frac{0.3022 Y_u + 0.6978 Y_d}{1.04}$$

$$V = 0.2906 Y_u + 0.6709 Y_d.$$

Since the oil field produces one unit of oil at a cost of $I = 20$ and oil sells for $X_u = 150$ in the up state, the cash flow there is

$$Y_u = X_u - I = 150 - 20 = 130.$$

Since the spot price is $X_d = 96$ in the down state, the cash flow there is

$$Y_d = X_d - I = 96 - 20 = 76.$$

Therefore

$$V = 0.2906 Y_u + 0.6709 Y_d = 0.2906 \times 130 + 0.6709 \times 76 = 88.77$$

is the estimated market value of the cash flow. ∎

When analyzing real options problems for which the state variable is the price of a traded asset we can use the risk-neutral probabilities in (3.3) and (3.4). The required inputs are either directly observable (R_f) or can be estimated (U, D, and C/X). This approach does not require us to make any assumptions about how the market rewards investors for bearing risk.

3.3 VALUATION USING FORWARD AND FUTURES CONTRACTS

Another approach to calculating risk-neutral probabilities that does not require any additional assumptions about risk premia is possible when there are forward or futures contracts traded on the state variable.[6] A typical forward contract is an agreement between two parties to exchange an item for a specified price (the forward price) at a specified date (the delivery date). Each party's payoff depends on the difference between the forward price and the spot price that applies on the delivery date. The forward price is set at a level such that no cash needs to change hands immediately in order for the two parties to reach agreement on the terms of the contract. Futures contracts are similar to forward contracts, but they are traded on organized exchanges and are marked to market at the end of each trading day, when funds are transferred between the parties according to the

6. Useful background material on forward and futures contracts can be found in Chapter 2 of Hull (2008).

amount by which the futures price has changed from the previous day.[7] Forward and futures contracts do not need to be written on the prices of traded assets—they can also be written on a wide variety of non-price indices. For example, the Chicago Mercantile Exchange trades weather futures contracts, for which the underlying state variables are indices of the temperature in various locations.

Suppose that there exists a forward contract on the state variable and that the forward price equals F. If we enter into a long forward position, we pay nothing immediately and receive a cash flow one period from now equal to $X_u - F$ in the up state and $X_d - F$ in the down state.[8] If we combine the forward position with an investment of F/R_f in a one-period risk-free bond, we need to pay F/R_f immediately and receive, in total,

$$(X_u - F) + F = X_u$$

one period from now in the up state and

$$(X_d - F) + F = X_d$$

in the down state. This is the same payoff as for the spanning asset. Thus, the law of one price implies that $Z = F/R_f$.

Substituting $Z = F/R_f$ into equation (3.2) shows that when there are forward or futures contracts on the state variable the risk-neutral probabilities are

$$\pi_u = \frac{ZR_f - X_d}{X_u - X_d} = \frac{F - X_d}{X_u - X_d} \quad \text{and} \quad \pi_d = \frac{X_u - ZR_f}{X_u - X_d} = \frac{X_u - F}{X_u - X_d}. \tag{3.5}$$

Thus, all we need to know in order to calculate the risk-neutral probabilities are the forward price and the two values that the state variable can take after one period.

3.4 VALUATION WHEN THE STATE VARIABLE IS NOT NECESSARILY THE PRICE OF A TRADED ASSET

In many real options problems we are unable to directly observe a traded asset or portfolio that pays X_u or X_d after one period, either because the state variable is not the price of a traded asset or because suitable forward or futures contracts are not traded. However, recall from Section 2.1 that all capital budgeting derives from an assumption that such an asset (or portfolio) exists, even if we cannot observe it directly. Our approach is to calculate the price that we think such an asset would have. In this section we show how the Capital Asset Pricing Model (CAPM) can be used for this purpose.

---

7. Throughout this book we assume that, although the interest rate can change over time, it does so in an entirely predictable way. One consequence of this assumption is that forward and futures prices are identical (Hull, 2008, Appendix to Chapter 5).

8. If the state variable is the price of a traded asset then we are actually buying that asset on the contract's delivery date for a price of F. More generally, however, the holder of a long position is entitled to the difference between the underlying state variable and the agreed forward price.

3.4.1 Capital Asset Pricing Model

Our approach, which corresponds to use of the CAPM to adjust for risk, is to find a portfolio of traded assets that minimizes what is known as the mean squared tracking error and then to use the cost of this portfolio as our estimate of the price of the spanning asset. This portfolio, known as the spanning asset's tracking portfolio, comprises a holding of one-period risk-free bonds and a stake in the market portfolio of risky assets, which is the hypothetical portfolio comprising all risky assets available to investors in amounts proportional to their individual market values.[9] The tracking error is the difference between the payoffs of the tracking portfolio and the spanning asset, while the mean squared tracking error is the expected value of the square of the tracking error. Thus, positive and negative tracking errors are treated symmetrically, but large tracking errors are penalized disproportionately more harshly than small ones.

Appendix 3.A.3 shows that the cost of the tracking portfolio (and therefore our estimate of the market value of the spanning asset) equals

$$
Z = \frac{E[\tilde{X}] - (E[\tilde{R}_m] - R_f)\left(\frac{\mathrm{Cov}[\tilde{X},\tilde{R}_m]}{\mathrm{Var}[\tilde{R}_m]}\right)}{R_f}, \tag{3.6}
$$

where $\tilde{X}$ denotes the level of the state variable after one period and $\tilde{R}_m$ denotes the total return on the market portfolio over the same period.[10] This is known as the certainty-equivalent form of the CAPM. In the usual rate-of-return formulation of the CAPM, we calculate the market value of the cash flow $\tilde{X}$ by discounting the expected cash flow, using a suitable risk-adjusted discount rate (RADR).[11] In the certainty-equivalent form of the CAPM, the risk adjustment is applied to the numerator (by modifying the expected cash flow) rather than the denominator (by modifying the discount rate). Thus, in (3.6) we estimate the market value of the cash flow $\tilde{X}$ by subtracting a risk premium from the expected value of the cash flow and discounting the resulting quantity back to the present using the risk-free interest rate. The risk premium is the product of the so-called market risk premium, $E[\tilde{R}_m] - R_f$, and

$$
\frac{\mathrm{Cov}[\tilde{X}, \tilde{R}_m]}{\mathrm{Var}[\tilde{R}_m]},
$$

---

9. Luenberger (2002) describes a more general approach in which the tracking portfolio can comprise any combination of the risky assets, rather than just the combination making up the market portfolio. The objective is still to minimize the mean squared tracking error, however.

10. That is, $\tilde{X}$ takes the value X_u in the up state and X_d in the down state. The "~" on $\tilde{X}$ and $\tilde{R}_m$ indicates that they are both treated as random variables.

11. Appendix 3.A.4 shows how equation (3.6) leads to the rate-of-return formulation of the CAPM. Specifically, it shows that buying an asset for Z now and selling it for $\tilde{X}$ after one period has an expected rate of return that satisfies the usual CAPM formula.

which measures the quantity of (systematic) risk and looks just like the usual CAPM beta, but is applied to the state variable rather than a rate of return. The numerator in (3.6) can therefore be interpreted as the certainty equivalent of the risky cash flow $\tilde{X}$.[12]

Example 3.2. A telecommunications network carries $X = 100$ calls at date 0, but this will change to $X_u = 125$ or $X_d = 80$ calls at date 1, with the two outcomes being equally likely. We assume that the market risk premium is $E[\tilde{R}_m] - R_f = 0.10$,

$$\frac{\text{Cov}[\tilde{X}, \tilde{R}_m]}{\text{Var}[\tilde{R}_m]} = 50,$$

and the one-period risk-free interest rate is 5% per period.

The expected value at date 0 of the state variable at date 1 is

$$E[\tilde{X}] = 0.5X_u + 0.5X_d = 0.5 \times 125 + 0.5 \times 80 = 102.5,$$

so that the spanning asset is currently worth

$$Z = \frac{E[\tilde{X}] - (E[\tilde{R}_m] - R_f)\left(\frac{\text{Cov}[\tilde{X},\tilde{R}_m]}{\text{Var}[\tilde{R}_m]}\right)}{R_f}$$

$$= \frac{102.5 - 0.10 \times 50}{1.05}$$

$$Z = 92.86.$$

That is, investors are willing to pay 92.86 at date 0 in return for a payoff of either 125 or 80 at date 1, in the up and down states respectively. ∎

3.4.2 Risk-neutral Probabilities Implied by the CAPM

Recall that the purpose of estimating a price (Z) for a cash flow of $\tilde{X}$ is to evaluate the formulae for the two risk-neutral probabilities,

$$\pi_u = \frac{ZR_f - X_d}{X_u - X_d} \quad \text{and} \quad \pi_d = \frac{X_u - ZR_f}{X_u - X_d}.$$

---

12. The certainty equivalent of a risky payoff is the risk-free payoff that provides an individual with the same level of utility as the risky payoff.

We can use (3.6) to rewrite the risk-neutral probability of an up move as

$$\pi_u = \frac{ZR_f - X_d}{X_u - X_d}$$

$$= \frac{E[\tilde{X}] - (E[\tilde{R}_m] - R_f)\left(\frac{\text{Cov}[\tilde{X},\tilde{R}_m]}{\text{Var}[\tilde{R}_m]}\right) - X_d}{X_u - X_d}$$

$$= \frac{\theta_u X_u + (1 - \theta_u)X_d - (E[\tilde{R}_m] - R_f)\left(\frac{\text{Cov}[\tilde{X},\tilde{R}_m]}{\text{Var}[\tilde{R}_m]}\right) - X_d}{X_u - X_d}$$

$$\pi_u = \theta_u - \left(\frac{E[\tilde{R}_m] - R_f}{X_u - X_d}\right)\left(\frac{\text{Cov}[\tilde{X}, \tilde{R}_m]}{\text{Var}[\tilde{R}_m]}\right), \tag{3.7}$$

where θ_u and θ_d are the actual probabilities of up and down moves, respectively. That is, we calculate the risk-neutral probability of an up move by subtracting an amount from the actual probability of an up move that reflects the covariance between the future value of the state variable and the return on the market portfolio.[13] If the covariance is relatively large then this adjustment will also be relatively large. That is, when the state variable's systematic risk is high we shift more of the weight from an up move to a down move.[14]

In many cases we go one step further and write

$$\pi_u = \frac{\frac{ZR_f}{X} - \frac{X_d}{X}}{\frac{X_u}{X} - \frac{X_d}{X}} \quad \text{and} \quad \pi_d = \frac{\frac{X_u}{X} - \frac{ZR_f}{X}}{\frac{X_u}{X} - \frac{X_d}{X}},$$

so that the risk-neutral probabilities equal

$$\pi_u = \frac{K - D}{U - D} \quad \text{and} \quad \pi_d = \frac{U - K}{U - D}, \tag{3.8}$$

where $U = X_u/X$ and $D = X_d/X$ are the sizes of up and down moves, and

$$K = \frac{ZR_f}{X}$$

$$= \frac{E[\tilde{X}] - (E[\tilde{R}_m] - R_f)\left(\frac{\text{Cov}[\tilde{X},\tilde{R}_m]}{\text{Var}[\tilde{R}_m]}\right)}{X}$$

$$= E\left[\frac{\tilde{X}}{X}\right] - (E[\tilde{R}_m] - R_f)\left(\frac{\text{Cov}[\frac{\tilde{X}}{X}, \tilde{R}_m]}{\text{Var}[\tilde{R}_m]}\right).$$

---

13. When subtracting this amount would make π_u negative, we set the risk-neutral probability of an up move equal to zero; when it would make π_u greater than one, we set the risk-neutral probability of an up move equal to one.

14. Rendleman (1999) also derives the relationship between the risk-neutral and actual probabilities that is implied by the CAPM.

Notice how similar the expressions in (3.8) are to those for the risk-neutral probabilities in the binomial option pricing model. The term $(1 - C/X)R_f$ in (3.3) and (3.4) is replaced by

$$K = E[\tilde{R}_x] - (E[\tilde{R}_m] - R_f)\beta_x, \tag{3.9}$$

where $\tilde{R}_x = \tilde{X}/X$ and

$$\beta_x = \frac{\text{Cov}[\tilde{R}_x, \tilde{R}_m]}{\text{Var}[\tilde{R}_m]}$$

is the usual CAPM beta applied to the proportional change in the state variable.[15] We can thus interpret K as a risk-adjusted growth factor, calculated by subtracting the CAPM risk premium, $(E[\tilde{R}_m] - R_f)\beta_x$, from the expected growth factor, $E[\tilde{R}_x]$, of the state variable. Equation (3.7) for the risk-neutral probability of an up move then reduces to

$$\pi_u = \theta_u - \frac{(E[\tilde{R}_m] - R_f)\beta_x}{U - D}. \tag{3.10}$$

Equation (3.9) offers an effective means of estimating K (and hence the risk-neutral probabilities) using historical state variable data. All that we need is historical data on the state variable, the return on the market portfolio, and the return on risk-free bonds. We regress each period's proportional change in the state variable $(\tilde{R}_x)$ onto the total return on the market portfolio $(\tilde{R}_m)$, use the slope coefficient as our estimate of β_x, and substitute it into (3.9) to evaluate K. (We consider the estimation procedure in detail in Section 12.2.1.)

> **Example 3.3.** In this example we estimate the market value of the cash flow generated by the telecommunications network in Example 3.2. The owner of the network receives revenue of 0.10 for each phone call carried over the network and operating costs are zero. Recall that at date 0 the network carries $X = 100$ calls and that this will change to $X_u = 125$ or $X_d = 80$ calls at date 1, with the two outcomes being equally likely. Consistent with Example 3.2, the "usage beta" is
>
> $$\beta_x = \frac{\text{Cov}[\frac{\tilde{X}}{X}, \tilde{R}_m]}{\text{Var}[\tilde{R}_m]} = \frac{1}{X}\frac{\text{Cov}[\tilde{X}, \tilde{R}_m]}{\text{Var}[\tilde{R}_m]} = \frac{50}{100} = 0.5.$$
>
> As in Example 3.2, we assume that the market risk premium is $E[\tilde{R}_m] - R_f = 0.10$ and the one-period risk-free interest rate is 5% per period.

---

15. The only difference—that total returns R rather than rates of return r appear everywhere—is unimportant. Because the two return measures are related by $R = 1 + r$, the covariance and variance terms are the same whether we use total returns or rates of return. For example,

$$\text{Var}[\tilde{R}] = \text{Var}[1 + \tilde{r}] = \text{Var}[\tilde{r}].$$

The expected proportional change in the state variable is

$$E[\tilde{R}_x] = \frac{0.5X_u + 0.5X_d}{X} = \frac{0.5 \times 125 + 0.5 \times 80}{100} = 1.0250,$$

so that

$$K = E[\tilde{R}_x] - (E[\tilde{R}_m] - R_f)\beta_x = 1.0250 - 0.1 \times 0.5 = 0.9750.$$

The risk-neutral probability of an up move is therefore equal to

$$\pi_u = \frac{K - D}{U - D} = \frac{0.9750 - 0.8000}{1.2500 - 0.8000} = 0.3889,$$

while the risk-neutral probability of a down move equals $\pi_d = 1 - \pi_u = 0.6111$.

The return on a one-period risk-free bond equals $R_f = 1.05$, so that the risk-neutral pricing formula is

$$V = \frac{\pi_u Y_u + \pi_d Y_d}{R_f}$$

$$= \frac{0.3889Y_u + 0.6111Y_d}{1.05}$$

$$V = 0.3704Y_u + 0.5820Y_d.$$

Since the cash flow at date 1 equals $Y_u = 12.5$ if an up move occurs (when usage increases to 125 calls) and $Y_d = 8$ if a down move occurs (when it falls to 80 calls), the estimated market value of this cash flow at date 0 is

$$V = 0.3704Y_u + 0.5820Y_d = 0.3704 \times 12.5 + 0.5820 \times 8 = 9.286.$$

Before we finish with this example, consider how the market value changes if the usage beta is $\beta_x = 0$ instead. Now

$$K = E[\tilde{R}_x] - (E[\tilde{R}_m] - R_f)\beta_x = 1.025 - 0.1 \times 0 = 1.0250,$$

so that the risk-neutral probability of an up move equals

$$\pi_u = \frac{K - D}{U - D} = \frac{1.0250 - 0.8000}{1.2500 - 0.8000} = 0.5,$$

while $\pi_d = 1 - \pi_u = 0.5$. It follows that the estimated market value of the cash flow at date 0 is

$$V = \frac{\pi_u Y_u + \pi_d Y_d}{R_f} = \frac{0.5 \times 12.5 + 0.5 \times 8}{1.05} = 9.762.$$

Thus, the estimated market value rises when the usage beta falls, which is consistent with our intuition that the cash flow becomes more valuable as its systematic risk is reduced.   ∎

3.5 SUMMARIZING THE VALUATION APPROACH

We need to carry out the following steps when estimating the market value of a cash flow to be received next period.

1. Specify a suitable state variable and estimate X, X_u, and X_d. (We describe how to estimate these (and other) parameters in Chapters 12–14.)
2. Use data on observed bond prices to estimate R_f.
3. Calculate the risk-neutral probabilities.

   - If the state variable is the price of a traded asset then we can estimate the dividend or convenience yield in order to calculate C/X and then use (3.3) and (3.4) to calculate π_u and π_d.
   - If forward or futures contracts on the state variable are traded then we can use the period-ahead forward price F in (3.5) to calculate π_u and π_d.
   - Otherwise, estimate K using (3.9) and then use (3.8) to calculate π_u and π_d.

4. Calculate the cash flows, Y_u and Y_d, that we receive after one period.
5. Calculate the estimated market value using (3.1).

3.6 PROBLEMS

3.1. (**Demonstration**) The state variable will take the value $X_u = 100$ if an up move occurs and $X_d = 60$ if a down move occurs. The spanning asset is worth $Z = 68$, while the one-period risk-free interest rate equals 6%. We consider two ways of estimating the market value of a future cash flow.
    (a) First, we use the risk-neutral pricing formula.
        i. Calculate the risk-neutral probabilities of up and down moves.
        ii. Use the risk-neutral pricing formula to estimate the market value of an asset that pays $Y_u = 14$ in the up state and $Y_d = 8$ in the down state.
    (b) Second, we use a replicating portfolio comprising A one-period risk-free bonds and B units of the spanning asset.
        i. Write down expressions for the portfolio's payoff in the up and down states.
        ii. Find values of A and B such that the portfolio pays $Y_u = 14$ in the up state and $Y_d = 8$ in the down state.
        iii. How much does this portfolio cost? Compare the answer to the market value of the same cash flow calculated using the risk-neutral pricing formula.

3.2. (**Practice**) Reevaluate Example 3.1 for the following values of C: -20, -10, 0, 10, 20. Keep all other parameters at their original values. How does the market value of the oil field change as the convenience yield increases? Give an intuitive explanation for this behavior.

3.3. **(Practice)** The spot price of oil is currently $80 and will equal either $100 or $64 after one period. The convenience yield from holding crude oil is 7.5% of the spot price per period and the one-period risk-free interest rate is 4%. Estimate the market value of an asset that generates a cash flow next period that equals zero if the spot price of oil is less than $70 and otherwise equals the amount by which the spot price exceeds $70.

3.4. **(Practice)** Suppose that the state variable currently takes the value 120, but that this is equally likely to change to 144 or 100 after one period. The CAPM beta for the proportional change in this variable is 1.25, while the market risk premium equals 8% and the one-period risk-free interest rate equals 4%.

(a) Calculate the risk-adjusted growth factor and use the answer to calculate the market value of the spanning asset and the risk-neutral probability of an up move.

(b) Calculate the market value of an asset that pays $30 in the up state and $10 in the down state.

(c) How do the answers to these questions change if the CAPM beta is actually 0.75? Is this consistent with the intuition of the CAPM? Explain.

3.5. **(Practice)** The level of the state variable is currently $X = 42$; after one period it is equally likely to be either $X_u = 49$ or $X_d = 36$. The return on one-period risk-free bonds is $R_f = 1.05$ and the market risk premium is $E[\tilde{R}_m] - R_f = 0.06$. Assume that the CAPM holds. In this problem we analyze the effect of β_x on the market value of an asset paying $Y_u = 20$ or $Y_d = 15$. We consider the following values of β_x: $0, 0.5, 1.0, 1.5, 2.0, 2.5$. For each one, calculate the risk-adjusted growth factor, the risk-neutral probability of an up move, the market value of the asset, and the expected rate of return from buying the asset immediately and selling it after one period. Discuss the relationship between β_x and the expected rate of return from holding the asset.

3.A APPENDIX

3.A.1 The Fundamental Asset Pricing Formula

Consider a portfolio comprising A one-period risk-free bonds and B units of the spanning asset. This portfolio generates a cash flow of $AR_f + BX_u$ in the up state and $AR_f + BX_d$ in the down state. We choose A and B in order to replicate the cash flow stream we are interested in valuing. That is, we choose A and B such that

$$AR_f + BX_u = Y_u \quad \text{and} \quad AR_f + BX_d = Y_d.$$

The first equation implies that

$$AR_f = Y_u - BX_u, \tag{3.11}$$

which we can use to eliminate A from the second equation, giving

$$Y_u - BX_u + BX_d = Y_d.$$

Solving this equation for B shows that the replicating portfolio must contain

$$B = \frac{Y_u - Y_d}{X_u - X_d}$$

units of the spanning asset. We can substitute this into equation (3.11), to show that the replicating portfolio must contain

$$A = \frac{X_u Y_d - X_d Y_u}{R_f(X_u - X_d)}$$

units of the risk-free bond. The cost of this portfolio equals

$$A + BZ = \frac{X_u Y_d - X_d Y_u}{R_f(X_u - X_d)} + \frac{(Y_u - Y_d)Z}{X_u - X_d}.$$

Collecting terms involving the cash flows Y_u and Y_d shows that

$$A + BZ = \frac{1}{R_f} \left(\left(\frac{ZR_f - X_d}{X_u - X_d} \right) Y_u + \left(\frac{X_u - ZR_f}{X_u - X_d} \right) Y_d \right),$$

which equals the expression on the right-hand side of equation (3.1).

3.A.2 Properties of the Risk-neutral Probabilities

Recall that we have a risk-free bond with a price of 1 and a payoff of R_f, for a guaranteed total return of R_f. We also have a spanning asset, with a price of Z and a risky payoff of either X_u or X_d; the respective returns are X_u/Z and X_d/Z. Without loss of generality, we can suppose that $X_d < X_u$. Now, if $R_f \leq X_d/Z$ then the lowest possible return from investing in the spanning asset is at least as large as the risk-free return from investing in the bond. This would imply the existence of an arbitrage opportunity involving short-selling bonds and buying the spanning asset. Since we assume that arbitrage opportunities do not exist, it must be the case that $R_f > X_d/Z$. Similarly, if $R_f \geq X_u/Z$ then the risk-free return from investing in the bond is at least as large as the highest possible return from investing in the spanning asset. This would imply the existence of an arbitrage opportunity involving buying bonds and short-selling the spanning asset. Our assumption that arbitrage opportunities do not exist means that we must have $R_f < X_u/Z$. Putting these two results together shows that Z, R_f, X_u, and X_d must satisfy

$$\frac{X_d}{Z} < R_f < \frac{X_u}{Z}.$$

Multiplying through by Z shows that

$$X_d < ZR_f < X_u.$$

It follows that π_u and π_d given by (3.2) are each greater than zero and less than one. To see why, note that the denominators of both π_u and π_d are positive, since $X_d < X_u$. The numerators are also positive, since $ZR_f > X_d$ and $X_u > ZR_f$, so that both π_u and π_d are positive. Moreover, the numerators are less than the denominators, so that both π_u and π_d must be less than one.

3.A.3 The Certainty-equivalent Form of the CAPM

We look for a tracking portfolio comprising A dollars invested in one-period risk-free bonds and B dollars invested in the market portfolio. As in Section 3.1, each dollar invested in risk-free bonds pays R_f dollars after one period. Each dollar invested in the market portfolio pays $\tilde{R}_m$ dollars after one period, where $\tilde{R}_m$ is a random variable. The tracking portfolio therefore delivers a payoff equal to

$$AR_f + B\tilde{R}_m$$

after one period.

If we are trying to track an asset that pays $\tilde{X}$ after one period, then the tracking error (the difference between the two cash flows) is

$$\tilde{X} - \left(AR_f + B\tilde{R}_m\right),$$

so that the mean squared tracking error equals

$$\mathrm{MSE} = E\left[\left(\tilde{X} - \left(AR_f + B\tilde{R}_m\right)\right)^2\right].$$

We choose the tracking portfolio (that is, the portfolio components A and B) in order to minimize this quantity. The respective first-order conditions are

$$0 = \frac{\partial \mathrm{MSE}}{\partial A} = -2E\left[\left(\tilde{X} - \left(AR_f + B\tilde{R}_m\right)\right)R_f\right]$$

and

$$0 = \frac{\partial \mathrm{MSE}}{\partial B} = -2E\left[\left(\tilde{X} - \left(AR_f + B\tilde{R}_m\right)\right)\tilde{R}_m\right].$$

The first equation simplifies to[16]

$$0 = E[\tilde{X}] - AR_f - BE[\tilde{R}_m],$$

so that

$$A = \frac{E[\tilde{X}] - BE[\tilde{R}_m]}{R_f}. \tag{3.12}$$

---

16. Note that this condition implies that the asset and the tracking portfolio have the same expected payoff.

Using this to eliminate A from the second equation shows that

$$0 = E\left[\left(\tilde{X} - \left(AR_f + B\tilde{R}_m\right)\right)\tilde{R}_m\right]$$

$$= E\left[\left(\tilde{X} - E[\tilde{X}] + BE[\tilde{R}_m] - B\tilde{R}_m\right)\tilde{R}_m\right]$$

$$= E\left[\tilde{X}\tilde{R}_m\right] - E\left[E[\tilde{X}]\tilde{R}_m\right] + E\left[BE[\tilde{R}_m]\tilde{R}_m\right] - E\left[B\tilde{R}_m\tilde{R}_m\right]$$

$$= E[\tilde{X}\tilde{R}_m] - E[\tilde{X}]E[\tilde{R}_m] - B\left(E[\tilde{R}_m^2] - (E[\tilde{R}_m])^2\right)$$

$$0 = \text{Cov}[\tilde{X}, \tilde{R}_m] - B\text{Var}[\tilde{R}_m],$$

so that

$$B = \frac{\text{Cov}[\tilde{X}, \tilde{R}_m]}{\text{Var}[\tilde{R}_m]}.$$

We can now substitute the solution for B into (3.12), to obtain

$$A = \frac{E[\tilde{X}] - E[\tilde{R}_m]\frac{\text{Cov}[\tilde{X},\tilde{R}_m]}{\text{Var}[\tilde{R}_m]}}{R_f}.$$

The cost of the tracking portfolio equals

$$Z = A + B$$

$$= \frac{E[\tilde{X}] - E[\tilde{R}_m]\frac{\text{Cov}[\tilde{X},\tilde{R}_m]}{\text{Var}[\tilde{R}_m]}}{R_f} + \frac{\text{Cov}[\tilde{X}, \tilde{R}_m]}{\text{Var}[\tilde{R}_m]}$$

$$Z = \frac{E[\tilde{X}] - (E[\tilde{R}_m] - R_f)\left(\frac{\text{Cov}[\tilde{X},\tilde{R}_m]}{\text{Var}[\tilde{R}_m]}\right)}{R_f},$$

which is equation (3.6).

3.A.4 The RADR Form of the CAPM

In this section we show how the certainty-equivalent form of the CAPM, equation (3.6), can be transformed into the traditional form involving rates of return. Dividing both sides of equation (3.6) by Z, the predicted price of the spanning asset, shows that

$$1 = \frac{E[\tilde{R}_x'] - (E[\tilde{R}_m] - R_f)\left(\frac{\text{Cov}[\tilde{R}_x',\tilde{R}_m]}{\text{Var}[\tilde{R}_m]}\right)}{R_f},$$

where $\tilde{R}_x' = \tilde{X}/Z$ is the total return from buying the spanning asset and holding it for one period. When we solve this equation for $E[\tilde{R}_x']$, the expected return from buying and holding the spanning asset, we obtain

$$E[\tilde{R}_x'] = R_f + (E[\tilde{R}_m] - R_f)\left(\frac{\text{Cov}[\tilde{R}_x', \tilde{R}_m]}{\text{Var}[\tilde{R}_m]}\right) = R_f + (E[\tilde{R}_m] - R_f)\beta_x',$$

where

$$\beta'_x = \frac{\mathrm{Cov}[\tilde{R}'_x, \tilde{R}_m]}{\mathrm{Var}[\tilde{R}_m]}$$

is the standard CAPM beta. Thus, if the price of the spanning asset satisfies equation (3.6) then the expected return from buying and holding the spanning asset satisfies the traditional form of the CAPM.

4

Valuing Multi-period Cash Flows

In Chapter 3 we learned how to value a cash flow that would be received one period in the future. In practice we often need to value cash flows to be received many periods in the future. We also need to value assets that generate an entire sequence of cash flows spread over many future dates. Fortunately, the valuation method introduced in Chapter 3 is easily adapted for use in both of these situations, as we demonstrate in this chapter.

In Section 4.1 we see how the one-period technique can be applied repeatedly to value a single cash flow that will be received many periods in the future, thus breaking a multi-period valuation problem down into a sequence of single-period ones. While this method is quite efficient computationally, its efficiency can be enhanced in two special situations, which we consider in Section 4.2. These situations will not always arise in practical applications, but when they do these more efficient methods should be used.

Once we can value a single cash flow to be received many periods in the future, it is straightforward to value an asset that generates an entire sequence of cash flows spread over many different future dates. One approach, described in Section 4.3, is to treat the cash flow to be received on each different date as a different asset and then apply the valuation methods in Sections 4.1 and 4.2 to each of these assets. Our estimate of the market value of the entire sequence of cash flows will just be the estimated market value of the portfolio of the individual assets. It is possible to estimate the market value of this portfolio without valuing the individual assets separately. We see how this can be done in Section 4.4. As well as being much more efficient than the portfolio approach described in Section 4.3, this method forms the basis of the dynamic programming approach to solving real options problems that we introduce in Chapter 5.

In contrast to Chapter 3, which introduced some fundamentally new material, this chapter does not introduce any new concepts. Rather, it takes the techniques introduced in Chapter 3 and shows how they can be applied to a new class of problems. Thus, this chapter will not be anywhere near as abstract as the previous one. Indeed, most of the discussion revolves around a recurring example of the type of valuation problem that we confront in practice. As well as being of interest in its own right, this example allows us to demonstrate our approach to valuing multi-period cash flow streams. We return to this example throughout this chapter.

Example 4.1. Public–private partnerships are often used to develop or upgrade infrastructure, such as road networks. A private investor, the concessionaire, finances the investment and in return is allowed to collect toll revenue from road users. In practice, mechanisms have been designed that allow the concessionaire and the government to share both upside and downside risk. Often the government will agree to compensate the concessionaire if actual revenue falls below a specified threshold, allowing the two parties to share downside risk. The concessionaire may agree to share revenue above a specified threshold with the government, so that upside risk is shared.

In this example we consider two different roading concessions that each allow the concessionaire to collect revenue of $0.10 from every vehicle that uses a particular road each period between dates 1 and 5. In the first case, the concessionaire bears all the risk of future road usage, while in the second case the government guarantees minimum revenue of $6.80 per period. Our task is to calculate the cost to the government of offering this guarantee.

For the problem considered here a sensible choice of state variable is the number of vehicles using the road each period.[1] We suppose that the number of vehicles currently using the road equals $X(0, 0) = 72$, and that this number grows by a factor of $U = 1.1250$ or $D = 1/U = 0.8889$ each period, with the two outcomes being equally likely.[2] This leads to the process for the state variable that is shown in the top panel of Table 4.1.

The simplest way to construct the top panel is to start by setting the entry in the top left-hand corner equal to the current value of the state variable, $X(0, 0) = 72$. We can then fill in the top row one entry at a time, working from left to right, and inserting the product of the size of an up move and the previous entry in that row. That is, we set $X(0, 1) = 1.1250X(0, 0)$, and then set $X(0, 2) = 1.1250X(0, 1)$, and so on, until the first row is complete. We then move down to the second row. One way to fill in this row is just to set each entry (starting along the diagonal) equal to the product of the

---

1. Because road users pay the same fee, $0.10, in each case, road usage should not depend on whether or not the government guarantees a minimum level of revenue.

2. The calibration technique described in Chapter 12 generates up and down moves having the property that $D = 1/U$, so we adopt this convention in our numerical examples.

Table 4.1. A Roading Concession with Guaranteed Minimum Revenue

$X(i, n)$	0	1	2	3	4	5
0	72.00	81.00	91.13	102.52	115.33	129.75
1		64.00	72.00	81.00	91.13	102.52
2			56.89	64.00	72.00	81.00
3				50.57	56.89	64.00
4					44.95	50.57
5						39.95

$Y(i, n)$	0	1	2	3	4	5
0	0.00	8.10	9.11	10.25	11.53	12.97
1		6.40	7.20	8.10	9.11	10.25
2			5.69	6.40	7.20	8.10
3				5.06	5.69	6.40
4					4.49	5.06
5						4.00

$Y'(i, n)$	0	1	2	3	4	5
0	0.00	8.10	9.11	10.25	11.53	12.97
1		6.80	7.20	8.10	9.11	10.25
2			6.80	6.80	7.20	8.10
3				6.80	6.80	6.80
4					6.80	6.80
5						6.80

size of a down move and the entry in the row above and the column to the left. For example, we set $X(1, 1) = 0.8889X(0, 0)$, and then set $X(1, 2) = 0.8889X(0, 1)$, and so on, until the second row is complete. We then move down to the third, fourth, fifth, and sixth rows, repeating this procedure to fill in the required entries in each row.

The other panels of Table 4.1 show the concessionaire's cash flow for the two cases we consider. The middle panel shows the revenue in the absence of any government guarantee. At each node (excluding date 0), the revenue equals 0.1 times the level of the state variable at that node. That is,

$$Y(i, n) = 0.1 X(i, n).$$

Once the minimum-revenue guarantee is introduced, we are left with the cash flow process shown in the bottom panel of Table 4.1. Revenue is unchanged from the middle panel at those nodes where total traffic is 68 vehicles or greater. At all other nodes, revenue increases from the value in the middle panel to \$6.80. That is,

$$Y'(i, n) = \max\{0.1\, X(i, n), 6.80\},$$

where $\max\{A, B\}$ equals the larger of A and B.

From Table 4.1, the state variable is currently $X = 72$ and will take the value $X_u = 81$ or $X_d = 64$ at date 1. It follows that the expected proportional change in the state variable is

$$E[\tilde{R}_x] = \frac{0.5X_u + 0.5X_d}{X} = \frac{0.5 \times 81 + 0.5 \times 64}{72} = 1.0069.$$

Because of the way in which we constructed the table—the sizes of U and D are constant throughout—the expected proportional change equals 1.0069 at every node. We assume that the market risk premium is $E[\tilde{R}_m] - R_f = 0.10$ and the "usage beta" is $\beta_x = 0.569$ at all dates, so that, from equation (3.9),

$$K = E[\tilde{R}_x] - (E[\tilde{R}_m] - R_f)\beta_x = 1.0069 - 0.1 \times 0.569 = 0.9500.$$

Like U and D, K is constant throughout the table, so that at each node the risk-neutral probability of an up move equals

$$\pi_u = \frac{K - D}{U - D} = \frac{0.9500 - 0.8889}{1.1250 - 0.8889} = 0.2590$$

and the risk-neutral probability of a down move equals

$$\pi_d = 1 - \pi_u = 1 - 0.2590 = 0.7410.$$

We assume that the one-period risk-free interest rate is 5% per period, so that the return on a one-period risk-free bond equals $R_f = 1.05$. The risk-neutral pricing formula in equation (3.1) is therefore

$$V = \frac{\pi_u Y_u + \pi_d Y_d}{R_f}$$

$$= \frac{0.2590Y_u + 0.7410Y_d}{1.05}$$

$$V = 0.2467Y_u + 0.7057Y_d. \tag{4.1}$$

This gives the estimated market value of a cash flow that will be received one period in the future.   ∎

We demonstrate the various valuation techniques in this chapter using this example. By the end of the chapter we will be able to estimate the market value of the roading concession, with and without the minimum-revenue guarantee, with just a few relatively simple calculations.

4.1 VALUING DISTANT CASH FLOWS USING BACKWARD INDUCTION

Our discussion in Chapter 3 focused on valuing a cash flow to be received one period in the future. However, it is important to consider cash flows received many periods in the future because (i) projects typically have such cash flows, and (ii) in practice we often make the amount of time represented by each period as small as possible in order to obtain a more precise valuation, so that even simple one-off cash flows will often be received many periods in the future. Therefore, in this section we explain how a single cash flow is valued when it is to be received an arbitrary number of periods in the future.

The valuation technique involves repeated application of the method for valuing a cash flow to be received one period in the future, so we begin by demonstrating the one-period technique in the context of the roading concession example.

Example 4.2. In both of the roading concessions that we consider, the concessionaire receives $0.10 for each car that uses the road at date 1. In the first case, there is no minimum-revenue guarantee, while in the second the government guarantees minimum revenue of $6.80 per period. When there is no minimum-revenue guarantee, the middle panel of Table 4.1 shows that the cash flow at date 1 equals $Y_u = 8.10$ if an up move occurs (when usage increases to 81 cars) and $Y_d = 6.40$ if a down move occurs (when usage falls to 64 cars). The estimated market value of this cash flow at date 0 is

$$V = 0.2467Y_u + 0.7057Y_d = 0.2467 \times 8.10 + 0.7057 \times 6.40 = 6.51.$$

The bottom panel of Table 4.1 shows that when the minimum-revenue guarantee is in place, the cash flow after an up move is unchanged at $Y'_u = 8.10$, while the cash flow after a down move now equals $Y'_d = 6.80$. The estimated market value of the cash flow at date 0 therefore rises to

$$V' = 0.2467Y'_u + 0.7057Y'_d = 0.2467 \times 8.10 + 0.7057 \times 6.80 = 6.80,$$

showing that the guarantee at date 1 costs the government $6.80 - 6.51 = 0.29$ dollars at date 0. ∎

The simplest way to value a cash flow to be received more than one period from now is to break the multi-period valuation problem into a sequence of one-period valuation problems, starting at the date when the cash flow is received and then working backwards, one period at a time. This procedure is known as backward induction.

Consider a one-off cash flow to be received at date 2. We often write such a cash flow as $Y(\cdot, 2)$, where the "$\cdot$" indicates that the number of down moves is arbitrary. That is, the cash flow equals $Y(0, 2)$ if no down moves occur, $Y(1, 2)$ if one down move occurs, and $Y(2, 2)$ if two down moves occur. The market value of the cash flow immediately before it is to be received is clearly equal to the size of the cash flow itself.[3] For example, if there have been i down moves between date 0 and date 2, so that the cash flow will equal $Y(i, 2)$, the market value of the

---

3. Recall our assumption that all market values are measured cum dividend.

right to the cash flow must equal

$$V(i, 2) = Y(i, 2). \tag{4.2}$$

This must be the case for $i = 0, 1, 2$.

Now consider the situation one period earlier, at date 1. If we are at node $(i, 1)$ then, after one period, the right to the cash flow will be worth $V(i, 2)$ if an up move occurs and $V(i + 1, 2)$ if a down move occurs. This is just our familiar one-period valuation problem, so that the discussion in Section 3.1 shows that the right to the cash flow must be worth

$$V(i, 1) = \frac{\pi_u(i, 1)V(i, 2) + \pi_d(i, 1)V(i + 1, 2)}{R_f} \tag{4.3}$$

at node $(i, 1)$, where $\pi_u(i, 1)$ and $\pi_d(i, 1)$ denote the risk-neutral probabilities at that node.

Finally, we take one more step backwards in time, to date 0. After one period the right to the cash flow will be worth $V(0, 1)$ if an up move occurs and $V(1, 1)$ if a down move occurs. If we did not want to wait until date 2 to receive the cash flow, we could sell the right to the cash flow one period earlier, thus receiving a cash flow of $V(0, 1)$ at date 1 if an up move occurs and one of $V(1, 1)$ if a down move occurs. But this is just like our standard one-period valuation problem. The discussion in Section 3.1 implies that the right to the date 1 sale price, and therefore to the underlying date 2 cash flow, must be worth

$$V(0, 0) = \frac{\pi_u(0, 0)V(0, 1) + \pi_d(0, 0)V(1, 1)}{R_f} \tag{4.4}$$

at node $(0, 0)$, where $\pi_u(0, 0)$ and $\pi_d(0, 0)$ denote the risk-neutral probabilities at that node. This is the current market value of the claim to a one-off cash flow of $Y(\cdot, 2)$ at date 2.

This procedure is shown schematically in Table 4.2. We begin with the last column of the table, filling in the entries one-by-one using equation (4.2), as indicated by the shaded cells. Once this column is completely filled in, we move one column to the left, filling in the entries there using equation (4.3). Finally, we move back to the column representing date 0, and fill in the single entry there using equation (4.4). We demonstrate this procedure using the following example.

Example 4.3. In this example we value the revenue generated at date 2 by the roading concession introduced in Example 4.1. Recall that the state variable (the number of cars using the road) is currently equal to $X(0, 0) = 72$ and grows by a factor of $U = 1.1250$ or $D = 0.8889$ each period, with the two outcomes being equally likely. Road usage will therefore equal $X(0, 2) = 91.13$ if no down moves occur over the next two periods, $X(1, 2) = 72.00$ if exactly one down move occurs during this interval, and $X(2, 2) = 56.89$ if two down moves occur. Our assumptions in Example 4.1 imply that the risk-neutral probability of an up move is $\pi_u = 0.2590$, that the return on a one-period risk-free bond equals $R_f = 1.05$, and that the risk-neutral pricing formula is given by equation (4.1).

Table 4.2. The Procedure for Valuing a Cash Flow that Will be Received Two Periods from Now

Step 1a: Use equation (4.2) with $i = 0$ to evaluate $V(0, 2)$	$V(i, n)$	0	1	2
	0			$V(0, 2)$
	1			
	2			

Step 1b: Use equation (4.2) with $i = 1$ to evaluate $V(1, 2)$	$V(i, n)$	0	1	2
	0			$V(0, 2)$
	1			$V(1, 2)$
	2			

Step 1c: Use equation (4.2) with $i = 2$ to evaluate $V(2, 2)$	$V(i, n)$	0	1	2
	0			$V(0, 2)$
	1			$V(1, 2)$
	2			$V(2, 2)$

Step 2a: Use equation (4.3) with $i = 0$ to evaluate $V(0, 1)$	$V(i, n)$	0	1	2
	0		$V(0, 1)$	$V(0, 2)$
	1			$V(1, 2)$
	2			$V(2, 2)$

Step 2b: Use equation (4.3) with $i = 1$ to evaluate $V(1, 1)$	$V(i, n)$	0	1	2
	0		$V(0, 1)$	$V(0, 2)$
	1		$V(1, 1)$	$V(1, 2)$
	2			$V(2, 2)$

Step 3: Use equation (4.4) to evaluate $V(0, 0)$	$V(i, n)$	0	1	2
	0	$V(0, 0)$	$V(0, 1)$	$V(0, 2)$
	1		$V(1, 1)$	$V(1, 2)$
	2			$V(2, 2)$

We begin with the case of a roading concession with no minimum-revenue guarantee, which is shown in the top panel of Table 4.3. The cash flow will equal \$9.11 if no down moves occur over the next two periods, \$7.20 if exactly one down move occurs during this interval, and \$5.69 if two down moves occur.

Equation (4.2) is used to value the cash flow at date 2, so that $V(i, 2) = Y(i, 2)$. This completes the right-hand column of the top panel in Table 4.3. Now we move back one period, using equation (4.3) to estimate the market value of the cash flow at date 1. When viewed from node (0, 1), the right to the date 2 cash flow will be worth \$9.11 if an up move occurs and \$7.20 if a down move occurs. Applying equation (4.3) shows that the market value at node (0, 1) is

$$V(0,1) = 0.2467V(0,2) + 0.7057V(1,2) = 0.2467 \times 9.11 + 0.7057 \times 7.20 = 7.33.$$

We complete filling in this column of the top panel by considering node (1, 1), from where the right to the date 2 cash flow will equal \$7.20 if an up move occurs and \$5.69 if a down move occurs. Applying equation (4.3) shows that the market value at node (1, 1) is

$$V(1,1) = 0.2467V(1,2) + 0.7057V(2,2) = 0.2467 \times 7.20 + 0.7057 \times 5.69 = 5.79.$$

Finally, we can use equation (4.4) to estimate the current market value of the right to the date 2 cash flow. At node (0, 0) the right to the cash flow will be worth \$7.33 at date 1 if an up move occurs and \$5.79 if a down move occurs. Applying equation (4.4) shows that the market value at node (0, 0) is

$$V(0,0) = 0.2467V(0,1) + 0.7057V(1,1) = 0.2467 \times 7.33 + 0.7057 \times 5.79 = 5.89.$$

The date 2 cash flow is therefore currently worth \$5.89.

The calculation is similar when there is a minimum-revenue guarantee. The higher market values, evident in the bottom panel of Table 4.3, are attributable to the greater cash flow at node (2, 2). This increases $V'(2,2)$, which in turn raises $V'(1, 1)$ and $V'(0, 0)$. Comparison of $V(0, 0)$ and $V'(0, 0)$

Table 4.3. Valuing a Distant Cash Flow Using Backward Induction

$V(i, n)$	0	1	2
0	5.89	7.33	9.11
1		5.79	7.20
2			5.69

$V'(i, n)$	0	1	2
0	6.45	7.33	9.11
1		6.57	7.20
2			6.80

Step 1: Use equation (4.2) to evaluate $V(i, 2)$ for $i = 0, 1, 2$

Step 2: Use equation (4.3) to evaluate $V(i, 1)$ for $i = 0, 1$

Step 3: Use equation (4.4) to evaluate $V(0, 0)$

shows that the minimum-revenue guarantee at date 2 costs the government $0.56 at date 0. ∎

The more general case of a cash flow to be received at date $N \geq 2$ is handled in the same way. That is, if $V(i, n)$ equals the market value at node (i, n) of the right to receive a cash flow of $Y(\cdot, N)$ at some fixed future date N, then V satisfies the terminal condition

$$V(i, N) = Y(i, N), \tag{4.5}$$

together with the recursive equation

$$V(i, n) = \frac{\pi_u(i, n)V(i, n+1) + \pi_d(i, n)V(i+1, n+1)}{R_f}, \tag{4.6}$$

for each $n = N - 1, \ldots, 0$ and each $i = 0, \ldots, n$.

These equations are used as part of the obvious extension of the procedure shown in Table 4.2. We begin with the last column of the table, filling in the entries one-by-one using the terminal condition, (4.5). Once this column is completely filled in, we move one column to the left, filling in the entries there using the recursive equation (4.6). Then we move one further column to the left, filling in the entries there using (4.6) again. We keep repeating this procedure until, finally, we reach the column representing date 0, where we fill in the single entry using (4.6) one last time.

4.2 TWO SITUATIONS WHERE VALUATION CAN BE STREAMLINED

The recursive method for valuing a distant cash flow described in Section 4.1 breaks the valuation problem into a sequence of steps, each one applying the one-period valuation model of Section 3.1. In some circumstances these steps can be recombined in such a way that we can value the cash flow in a single step. We describe two such circumstances—and the simplified valuation approaches that they lead to—in this section. We include them here for two reasons. First, it is very useful to have such techniques available; they can simplify many real options calculations. Second, these two special cases help explain the differences and similarities between the valuation approach used in this book and static DCF valuation.

4.2.1 A "One-shot" Valuation Approach

We consider the case of a single cash flow, $Y(\cdot, N)$, to be received at date N. The approach to valuation described in this section can only be used when the cash flow at each node is known. The cash flow can be risky—meaning that $Y(i, N)$ takes different values for different values of i—but we must know the precise value *at each node* when we carry out the valuation. Often this will not be the case in real options analysis, since $Y(i, N)$ may depend on the actions taken by the decision maker between dates 0 and N. When this happens, the valuation and the determination of the optimal actions to take have to be solved period by period, using a modification of the approach in Section 4.1. (We describe this approach in Chapter 5.) However, when the cash flow at each node is known at date 0, the valuation approach described here is extremely useful. The approach comes into its own when the risk-neutral probabilities are constant throughout the tree, so we make that assumption here. That is, we assume that the risk-neutral probabilities of up and down moves equal the constants π_u and π_d throughout the tree.[4]

Consider the example of a one-off cash flow of $Y(\cdot, 2)$ to be received at date 2, which we first met in Section 4.1. Repeated substitution of the recursive equation (4.6) shows that the cash flow is currently worth

$$V(0, 0) = \frac{1}{R_f} \left(\pi_u V(0, 1) + \pi_d V(1, 1) \right)$$

$$= \frac{1}{R_f} \left(\pi_u \left(\frac{\pi_u Y(0, 2) + \pi_d Y(1, 2)}{R_f} \right) + \pi_d \left(\frac{\pi_u Y(1, 2) + \pi_d Y(2, 2)}{R_f} \right) \right)$$

$$V(0, 0) = \frac{1}{(R_f)^2} \left(\pi_u^2 Y(0, 2) + 2\pi_u \pi_d Y(1, 2) + \pi_d^2 Y(2, 2) \right), \tag{4.7}$$

where we have used the fact that

$$V(0, 1) = \frac{\pi_u Y(0, 2) + \pi_d Y(1, 2)}{R_f}$$

and

$$V(1, 1) = \frac{\pi_u Y(1, 2) + \pi_d Y(2, 2)}{R_f}$$

to derive the second line. This gives us an expression for the market value at date 0 that depends only on the distribution of the cash flow to be received at date 2—there is no need to calculate the subsequent market values (those at dates 1 and 2) using backward induction.

Equation (4.7) has a natural interpretation. To see what it is, note that we arrive at node $(0, 2)$ at date 2 if and only if the first two moves are both up; the (risk-neutral) probability of this occurring is π_u^2. Similarly, we arrive at node $(2, 2)$ if and only if the first two moves are both down, which occurs with (risk-neutral) probability π_d^2. Node $(1, 2)$ can be reached by any path containing one up move and one down move. There are two such paths: an up move followed by a down move, and a down move followed by an up one. Since each path occurs with (risk-neutral) probability $\pi_u \pi_d$, the (risk-neutral) probability of arriving at node $(1, 2)$ equals $2\pi_u \pi_d$. Therefore, we can interpret

$$\pi_u^2 Y(0, 2) + 2\pi_u \pi_d Y(1, 2) + \pi_d^2 Y(2, 2)$$

---

4. As we see in Chapter 12, in many situations we want the risk-neutral probabilities to take different values at different nodes, so the approach in this section is not always available.

as the expected value of the cash flow, provided that it is calculated using the risk-neutral probabilities of up and down moves. It follows that the current market value of the right to receive a cash flow of $Y(\cdot, 2)$ at date 2 equals the expected value of the cash flow—calculated using the risk-neutral probabilities—discounted back two periods using the risk-free interest rate.

As in the one-period case discussed in Section 3.1, the adjustment for risk occurs in the calculation of the expected cash flow rather than in the discount rate. Thus, we use the risk-free rate to allow for the time-value of money and the risk-neutral probabilities to allow for the market reward for bearing risk.

Example 4.4. The first step when applying this valuation approach to the first cash flow considered in Example 4.3 is to calculate the risk-neutral probabilities of ending up at the various terminal nodes. Since $\pi_u = 0.2590$ and $\pi_d = 0.7410$ at each node, the risk-neutral probabilities are

$$\Pr^*[i = 0] = \pi_u^2 = 0.0671, \quad \Pr^*[i = 1] = 2\pi_u\pi_d = 0.3838,$$

$$\Pr^*[i = 2] = \pi_d^2 = 0.5491,$$

where $\Pr^*$ denotes the probability of the indicated event occurring. It follows that the expected value of the cash flow—calculated using the risk-neutral probabilities—equals

$$E^*[Y(\cdot, 2)] = \Pr^*[i = 0]\, Y(0, 2) + \Pr^*[i = 1]\, Y(1, 2) + \Pr^*[i = 2]\, Y(2, 2)$$

$$= 0.0671 \times 9.11 + 0.3838 \times 7.20 + 0.5491 \times 5.69$$

$$= 6.50.$$

When we discount this back two periods using the risk-free interest rate of 5% per period we get a current market value of $5.89, which is the same market value that we calculated using backward induction in Example 4.3. ∎

The calculations in Example 4.4 demonstrate, once again, how the adjustment for risk is performed in the numerator (via the risk-neutral probabilities) rather than the denominator (via the discount rate). Since the actual probability of an up move is 0.5, we actually reach node $(0, 2)$ with probability 0.25, node $(1, 2)$ with probability 0.5, and node $(2, 2)$ with probability 0.25, so that the true expected value of the cash flow to be received at date 2 equals

$$0.25 \times 9.11 + 0.5 \times 7.20 + 0.25 \times 5.69 = 7.30.$$

This compares with the expected value of $6.50 when the risk-neutral probabilities are used instead. We are effectively deducting a risk premium of $0.80 from the expected cash flow rather than adding a risk premium onto the discount rate.

As we might expect, the valuation formula is slightly more complicated than (4.7) in the general case of a one-off cash flow of $Y(\cdot, N)$ to be received at date N. However, the underlying result is the same. That is, the current market value of this cash flow equals the expected value of the cash flow—calculated using the risk-neutral probabilities—discounted back N periods using the risk-free interest rate. The complications arise in calculating the expected value of the cash flow.

In order to calculate the expected cash flow, we need to know the (risk-neutral) probability distribution from which the cash flow is drawn, which means that we need to know the risk-neutral probability of ending up at each one of the possible nodes at date N. We arrive at node (i, N) if and only if the first N moves contain exactly i down moves, in any order. There are $_NC_i = N!/i!(N - i)!$ different ways in which this can occur, where $_NC_i$ is known as the binomial coefficient and $n!$ denotes the factorial of n; that is,

$$n! = 1 \times 2 \times 3 \times \cdots \times (n - 1) \times n.$$

Since each one of these paths occurs with (risk-neutral) probability $\pi_u^{N-i}\pi_d^i$, the total probability of arriving at node (i, N) equals

$$\Pr^*[\text{arrive at node } (i, N)] = \frac{N!}{i!(N - i)!}\pi_u^{N-i}\pi_d^i. \tag{4.8}$$

It follows that the expected cash flow, calculated using the risk-neutral probabilities, is

$$E^*[Y(\cdot, N)] = \sum_{i=0}^{N} \frac{N!}{i!(N - i)!}\pi_u^{N-i}\pi_d^i Y(i, N).$$

To estimate the market value of the cash flow we simply discount this expected value back to date 0 using the risk-free interest rate. Therefore our estimate of the current market value of the claim to a cash flow of $Y(\cdot, N)$ at date N equals

$$\frac{1}{(R_f)^N} \sum_{i=0}^{N} \frac{N!}{i!(N - i)!}\pi_u^{N-i}\pi_d^i Y(i, N). \tag{4.9}$$

4.2.2 Valuing Cash Flows that are Proportional to the State Variable

Another situation often arises in which the backward induction approach in Section 4.1 reduces to a much simpler calculation. In this case, the cash flow is equal to the underlying state variable (or to a constant multiple of the state variable). The roading concession without a minimum-revenue guarantee, introduced in Example 4.1, is one such situation. The simplification occurs provided that the risk-adjusted growth factor, K, that we introduced in Section 3.4.2, is constant throughout the tree.[5]

---

5. In fact, K need not be a constant for the point made here to be relevant, but it makes the expressions simpler. We could allow K to depend on n, just so long as it does not depend on i. Thus, we could have $Z(i, n) = K_n X(i, n)/R_f$ for some constants $K_0, K_1, \ldots$, where $Z(i, n)$ is the price of the spanning asset at node (i, n). This case is considered in Problem 4.3.

Suppose that we are currently at node (i, n) and will receive a cash flow at date $n + 1$ that will equal $X(i, n + 1)$ if an up move occurs and $X(i + 1, n + 1)$ if a down move occurs instead. Applying the discussion in Section 3.4.2 to this situation shows that the right to receive this cash flow (that is, the spanning asset) is currently worth

$$Z(i, n) = \frac{KX(i, n)}{R_f} = \left(\frac{K}{R_f}\right) X(i, n).$$

That is, the market value of the cash flow one period before it is to be received is just equal to the product of the current level of the state variable and the *constant* K/R_f.

We can use this result to simplify the valuation when the cash flow will be received more than one period in the future. For example, consider the case of a one-off cash flow of $X(\cdot, 2)$ to be received at date 2. Before we estimate its market value at date 0, consider its market value at date 1. If the first move is an up move, so that we move to node $(0, 1)$, then the discussion above shows that the cash flow will be worth

$$\left(\frac{K}{R_f}\right) X(0, 1)$$

at date 1. If the first move is down, so that we move to node $(1, 1)$, then the cash flow will be worth

$$\left(\frac{K}{R_f}\right) X(1, 1)$$

at date 1. But, when viewed from date 0, this is equivalent to K/R_f units of an asset that pays $X(0, 1)$ at date 1 if an up move occurs and $X(1, 1)$ if a down move occurs instead. From above, one unit of such an asset is worth

$$\left(\frac{K}{R_f}\right) X(0, 0)$$

at date 0. Therefore, K/R_f units must be worth

$$\left(\frac{K}{R_f}\right)^2 X(0, 0)$$

at the same date. This is our estimate of the market value at date 0 of an asset that pays $X(\cdot, 2)$ at date 2.

Therefore, provided K is constant throughout the tree, we do not need to carry out the recursive valuation procedure of Section 4.1 to value a cash flow of $X(\cdot, 2)$. We do not even need to calculate the expected cash flow (using the risk-neutral probabilities) as in Section 4.2.1. Instead, all we have to do is multiply the current level of the state variable by the factor $(K/R_f)^2$.

Example 4.5. This method can be applied to the cash flow considered in Example 4.4. Since the risk-adjusted growth factor is $K = 0.9500$ and the

return on a one-period risk-free bond is $R_f = 1.05$, the current market value
of a cash flow of $0.1X(\cdot, 2)$ to be received at date 2 is

$$0.1 \left(\frac{K}{R_f} \right)^2 X(0, 0) = 0.1 \left(\frac{0.9500}{1.05} \right)^2 72 = 5.89,$$

as in the earlier example.   ■

The valuation formula for the general case is a straightforward modification of
the one above. That is, the current market value of the right to receive a cash flow
of $X(\cdot, N)$ at date N is

$$\left(\frac{K}{R_f} \right)^N X(0, 0). \tag{4.10}$$

This makes valuation of some cash flow streams extremely straightforward.
However, it also provides some useful insights into how our valuation procedure
relates to the static DCF analysis that many readers will be familiar with.

If X is expected to grow at rate g each period and the RADR is ρ per period,
the static DCF valuation of the cash flow considered above is

$$\frac{E[X(\cdot, N)]}{(1 + \rho)^N} = \frac{(1 + g)^N X(0, 0)}{(1 + \rho)^N} = \left(\frac{1 + g}{1 + \rho} \right)^N X(0, 0).$$

This has the same form as our valuation formula in (4.10), except that the expected
growth factor, $1 + g$, has replaced K, and the RADR factor, $1 + \rho$, has replaced the
return on a one-period risk-free bond. Recall from our discussion in Section 3.4.2
that K can be interpreted as a risk-adjusted growth factor, so all we are really
doing is moving the risk adjustment from the discount rate to the growth factor.
This is consistent with our earlier observation that our valuation approach adjusts
for risk in the numerator (that is, by adjusting the expected cash flow) rather than
the denominator (that is, by adjusting the discount rate).

Our valuation will equal the static DCF valuation provided that

$$\frac{K}{R_f} = \frac{1 + g}{1 + \rho}, \tag{4.11}$$

which will be the case if and only if

$$K = \frac{(1 + g)(1 + r_f)}{1 + \rho} \approx 1 + g - (\rho - r_f),$$

where r_f is the one-period risk-free interest rate. That is, if we set K equal to one
plus the expected growth rate in the state variable minus the risk premium for
X-risk, our market value estimates will be consistent with static DCF valuation.[6]
Achieving such consistency is a desirable goal as it makes it easier for managers
to compare the results of real options analysis with those of static DCF analysis.

---

6. This is essentially what we proposed to do in equation (3.9).

4.3 VALUING MULTI-PERIOD CASH FLOWS AS PORTFOLIOS

In this section we see how the valuation method introduced in Section 4.1 can be used to value streams of cash flows lasting several periods. We continue to use the example of the roading concession introduced in Example 4.1. This situation offers some useful insights because the minimum-revenue guarantee naturally makes the cash flow a nonlinear function of the state variable. As we see in Section 4.3.2, nonlinearities in cash flows effectively render the static DCF valuation method unable to estimate market values that are consistent with standard financial theories of risk adjustment. However, as Section 4.3.3 illustrates, the valuation approach we are developing is consistent with static DCF analysis in those special cases where static DCF analysis is an appropriate valuation technique to use.

4.3.1 The Portfolio Approach

The simplest approach to valuing a cash flow stream is to treat it as a portfolio of separate cash flows and then estimate the market value of each individual cash flow separately. That is, we value the cash flow to be received after one period, then we value the cash flow to be received one period after that, and so on. Finally, we add up the market values to obtain the market value of the portfolio. We will see that there is a much more efficient way to carry out the valuation exercise, but we start by using this approach as it helps illustrate some important concepts.

Example 4.6. Returning to the roading concession introduced in Example 4.1, consider the situation when there is no minimum-revenue guarantee. We value this sequence of cash flows by breaking it into a portfolio of one-off cash flows, one for each date, and applying the method described in Section 4.2.1 to each one. The results are shown in Table 4.4. For example, the date 2 cash flow equals $9.11 with (risk-neutral) probability 0.0671, $7.20 with probability 0.3838, and $5.69 with probability 0.5491. When the expected cash flow of $6.50 is discounted back two periods using the risk-free interest rate of 5% per period, the present value (and hence our estimate of the market value) is $5.89.

We can repeat this procedure for the cash flows occurring at dates 1, 3, 4, and 5, to show that they are currently worth $6.51, $5.33, $4.83, and $4.37, respectively. The entire cash flow stream is therefore worth

$$V(0, 0) = V_1(0, 0) + V_2(0, 0) + V_3(0, 0) + V_4(0, 0) + V_5(0, 0)$$

$$= 6.51 + 5.89 + 5.33 + 4.83 + 4.37$$

$$= 26.93.$$

Table 4.5 shows the results of repeating the whole procedure when there is a minimum-revenue guarantee. The entire cash flow stream is worth

Table 4.4. Valuing Each Cash Flow when Minimum Revenue is Not Guaranteed

	n = 1		n = 2		n = 3		n = 4		n = 5	
i	Prob	$Y(i, n)$	Prob	$Y(i, n)$	Prob	$Y(i, n)$	Prob	$Y(i, n)$	Prob	$Y(i, n)$
0	0.2590	8.10	0.0671	9.11	0.0174	10.25	0.0045	11.53	0.0012	12.97
1	0.7410	6.40	0.3838	7.20	0.1491	8.10	0.0515	9.11	0.0167	10.25
2			0.5491	5.69	0.4266	6.40	0.2210	7.20	0.0954	8.10
3					0.4068	5.06	0.4215	5.69	0.2729	6.40
4							0.3015	4.49	0.3904	5.06
5									0.2234	4.00
$E^*[Y(\cdot, n)]$	6.84		6.50		6.17		5.87		5.57	
$V_n(0, 0)$	6.51		5.89		5.33		4.83		4.37	

Table 4.5. Valuing Each Cash Flow when Minimum Revenue is Guaranteed

	n = 1		n = 2		n = 3		n = 4		n = 5	
i	Prob	$Y'(i, n)$	Prob	$Y'(i, n)$	Prob	$Y'(i, n)$	Prob	$Y'(i, n)$	Prob	$Y'(i, n)$
0	0.2590	8.10	0.0671	9.11	0.0174	10.25	0.0045	11.53	0.0012	12.97
1	0.7410	6.80	0.3838	7.20	0.1491	8.10	0.0515	9.11	0.0167	10.25
2			0.5491	6.80	0.4266	6.80	0.2210	7.20	0.0954	8.10
3					0.4068	6.80	0.4215	6.80	0.2729	6.80
4							0.3015	6.80	0.3904	6.80
5									0.2234	6.80
$E^*[Y'(\cdot, n)]$	7.14		7.11		7.05		7.03		6.99	
$V_n'(0, 0)$	6.80		6.45		6.09		5.78		5.48	

$$V'(0, 0) = V_1'(0, 0) + V_2'(0, 0) + V_3'(0, 0) + V_4'(0, 0) + V_5'(0, 0)$$
$$= 6.80 + 6.45 + 6.09 + 5.78 + 5.48$$
$$= 30.60.$$

The guarantee therefore costs $30.60 - 26.93 = 3.67$ dollars at date 0. ∎

4.3.2 Relationship with Static DCF Analysis

In principle, each of the cash flows featured in Example 4.6 could be valued using static DCF analysis. For the cash flow occurring at date n we would need to calculate the expected value of the cash flow based on all information available at date 0 (using the *actual* probabilities of up and down moves) and then discount it using an appropriate RADR, resulting in a market value of

$$V_n(0, 0) = \frac{E[Y(\cdot, n)]}{(1 + \text{RADR}_n)^n}. \tag{4.12}$$

In order to value a cash flow in this way, we must be able to calculate the correct RADR. However, the standard RADR form of the CAPM cannot be applied when the cash flow is a nonlinear function of the state variable, making it impracticable to calculate the RADR directly. In the case of the roading concession, the minimum-revenue guarantee introduces just such a nonlinearity.

We leave a formal discussion of the difficulties to Appendix 4.A, but consideration of the roading concession gives an indication of the difficulties faced by static DCF valuation. For each individual cash flow featured in Example 4.6, we calculate the RADR that would have to be used if equation (4.12) is to value the cash flow correctly. We do this by rearranging equation (4.12) to get

$$\text{RADR}_n = \left(\frac{E[Y(\cdot, n)]}{V_n(0, 0)}\right)^{1/n} - 1.$$

This is the RADR that we would have to adopt if we were using static DCF analysis to value the cash flow to be received at date n. As the following example suggests, when there is a minimum-revenue guarantee this RADR is a complicated function of the date at which the cash flow will be received. In practical applications it is not feasible to calculate this function, and static DCF valuation is impossible without it.

Example 4.7. The first row in the top panel of Table 4.6 reports the date 0 market values of the five cash flows when there is no minimum-revenue guarantee, as featured in Example 4.6, while the second and third rows in this panel report the expected value of each cash flow and the implied RADR. The expected values, denoted $E[Y(\cdot, n)]$, are calculated using the actual probabilities of up and down moves. Recall from Example 4.1 that up and down moves are equally likely so that, for example, the expected cash flow at date 1 is

$$E[Y(\cdot, 1)] = \frac{1}{2}Y(0, 1) + \frac{1}{2}Y(1, 1) = 0.5 \times 8.10 + 0.5 \times 6.40 = 7.25.$$

Table 4.6. RADRs Implied by the Market Values of Individual Cash Flows

n	1	2	3	4	5
Minimum revenue is not guaranteed					
$V_n(0, 0)$	6.51	5.89	5.33	4.83	4.37
$E[Y(\cdot, n)]$	7.25	7.30	7.35	7.40	7.45
RADR_n	0.1129	0.1129	0.1129	0.1129	0.1129
Minimum revenue is guaranteed					
$V'_n(0, 0)$	6.80	6.45	6.09	5.78	5.48
$E[Y'(\cdot, n)]$	7.45	7.58	7.72	7.82	7.94
RADR_n	0.0961	0.0841	0.0820	0.0785	0.0771

The RADR implied by the market value of \$6.51 is therefore

$$\text{RADR}_1 = \left(\frac{E[Y(\cdot, 1)]}{V_1(0, 0)} \right)^{1/1} - 1 = \left(\frac{7.25}{6.51} \right)^{1/1} - 1 = 0.1129.$$

Derivation of the RADR for the date 2 cash flow is similar, although calculation of the expected cash flow is slightly more complicated. Nodes $(0, 2)$, $(1, 2)$ and $(2, 2)$ occur with probability 0.25, 0.5, and 0.25, respectively, so the expected cash flow is

$$E[Y(\cdot, 2)] = 0.25Y(0, 2) + 0.5Y(1, 2) + 0.25Y(2, 2)$$
$$= 0.25 \times 9.11 + 0.5 \times 7.20 + 0.25 \times 5.69$$
$$= 7.30.$$

The RADR implied by the market value of \$5.89 is therefore

$$\text{RADR}_2 = \left(\frac{E[Y_2(\cdot, 2)]}{V_2(0, 0)} \right)^{1/2} - 1 = \left(\frac{7.30}{5.89} \right)^{1/2} - 1 = 0.1129.$$

Calculation of the remaining RADRs is similar. Note that the RADR equals 11.29% per period for each of the five cash flows.

The calculation is similar when there is a minimum-revenue guarantee, although the results are subtly different—as can be seen in the bottom panel of Table 4.6. The expected value of each of the five cash flows is higher, and the RADR is lower, when the minimum-revenue guarantee is in place. Both of these changes affect the market value of the cash flows in the same direction, consistent with the substantial differences between the market values in the first row of each panel. Moreover, more distant cash flows are more affected by the guarantee: they have higher expected values and lower RADRs than their short-term counterparts.   ∎

Note that the RADR is constant at 11.29% per period across maturities when there is no minimum-revenue guarantee.[7] In contrast, when the government guarantees a minimum level of revenue the RADR is not constant across horizons. In fact, distant cash flows attract a lower RADR. This is consistent with the fact that the minimum-revenue guarantee reduces the risk of the distant cash flows: as can be seen from the bottom panel of Table 4.1, the guarantee is quite likely to be binding for distant cash flows.

The RADR generally depends on the relationship between the cash flow and the state variable. Even if the state variable has a constant RADR, a nonlinear

---

7. Recall that $K/R_f = (1 + g)/(1 + \rho)$, where g is the expected growth rate in the state variable and ρ is the RADR. Thus $\rho = (1 + g)R_f/K - 1$, which, for the parameters used here, equals 0.1129.

function of the state variable will not generally have a constant RADR.[8] And, as we shall see many times, the managerial flexibility that underlies real options analysis introduces just such nonlinearity. This makes it infeasible to calculate RADRs directly, so that we cannot typically use equation (4.12) to estimate the market value of a risky cash flow stream.[9] Instead, we use the risk-neutral pricing formula described by equations (3.1) and (3.2).

4.3.3 Valuing Annuities

We close this section by considering two particular multi-period cash flow streams that often arise in applications: the first is a risk-free annuity and the second is an annuity comprising a cash flow equal to the level of the state variable each period. As well as being useful in their own right, these results will further illustrate the fact that the valuation approach we are developing is consistent with static DCF analysis in those special cases where static DCF analysis is an appropriate valuation technique to use.

In the first case, we consider an asset that generates a cash flow of $G^n C$ at date n for all $n = 1, 2, \ldots, N$, for some constants C and $G > 0$. If $G > 1$ then the cash flow is growing at a constant rate, while if $G < 1$ then it is declining at a constant rate. Since all cash flows are risk free, the market value of this asset at node $(0, 0)$ equals

$$\frac{GC}{R_f} + \frac{G^2 C}{(R_f)^2} + \cdots + \frac{G^N C}{(R_f)^N} = \left(\frac{G}{R_f}\right) \left(1 + \left(\frac{G}{R_f}\right) + \cdots + \left(\frac{G}{R_f}\right)^{N-1}\right) C,$$

which can be simplified to

$$\left(\frac{G}{R_f}\right) \frac{\left(1 - \left(\frac{G}{R_f}\right)^N\right)}{1 - \left(\frac{G}{R_f}\right)} C = \left(1 - \left(\frac{G}{R_f}\right)^N\right) \frac{GC}{R_f - G}. \tag{4.13}$$

As long as $G < R_f$ (so that $(G/R_f)^N$ vanishes as N grows very large), the current market value of a perpetual cash flow of $G^n C$ equals

$$\frac{GC}{R_f - G}, \tag{4.14}$$

which is obtained by letting N grow to infinity in (4.13).

---

8. Hodder et al. (2001) demonstrate the difficulties in using RADRs to value assets with cash flows that are nonlinear functions of the state variable. They use a simple numerical example to show that the appropriate RADR will take different values at different nodes in such cases.

9. The non-constancy of the RADR reinforces the importance of remembering that the RADR relates only to the risk of the cash flow being valued. We should not generally use a firm-wide RADR. Indeed, with different projects having different embedded real options, there is unlikely to be a firm-wide RADR. As we have seen, there may not even be a single RADR for a given cash flow stream.

Similarly, in the second case we calculate the market value of an asset that generates a cash flow of $X(\cdot, n)$ at date n for all $n = 1, 2, \ldots, N$. Provided that the risk-adjusted growth factor, K, is constant throughout the tree, (4.10) implies that the current market value of the cash flow to be received at date n equals

$$\left(\frac{K}{R_f}\right)^n X(0, 0).$$

Therefore, the current market value of the portfolio comprising all N individual cash flows equals

$$\left(\frac{K}{R_f}\right)^1 X(0, 0) + \left(\frac{K}{R_f}\right)^2 X(0, 0) + \cdots + \left(\frac{K}{R_f}\right)^N X(0, 0)$$

$$= \left(\frac{K}{R_f}\right)\left(1 + \left(\frac{K}{R_f}\right) + \cdots + \left(\frac{K}{R_f}\right)^{N-1}\right) X(0, 0),$$

which can be simplified to

$$\left(\frac{K}{R_f}\right)\frac{\left(1 - \left(\frac{K}{R_f}\right)^N\right)}{1 - \left(\frac{K}{R_f}\right)} X(0, 0) = \left(1 - \left(\frac{K}{R_f}\right)^N\right)\frac{KX(0, 0)}{R_f - K}. \qquad (4.15)$$

As above, we can find the market value of the corresponding perpetuity by allowing N to grow to infinity in (4.15). As long as $K < R_f$ (so that $(K/R_f)^N$ vanishes as N grows very large), the current market value of this perpetuity equals

$$\frac{KX(0, 0)}{R_f - K}. \qquad (4.16)$$

The market value of a perpetuity is often expressed in terms of the expected growth rate and the RADR. We can derive such a formula by recalling from equation (4.11) that

$$\frac{K}{R_f} = \frac{1 + g}{1 + \rho},$$

where g is the expected growth rate and ρ is the RADR. Using this to replace K everywhere it appears in (4.16) allows us to rewrite the expression for the current market value of the perpetuity as

$$\frac{KX(0, 0)}{R_f - K} = \frac{\left(\frac{1+g}{1+\rho}\right) X(0, 0)}{1 - \left(\frac{1+g}{1+\rho}\right)} = \frac{(1 + g)X(0, 0)}{\rho - g},$$

which is just the Gordon growth model.[10] The only differences between (4.16) and the Gordon growth model are that the former uses the risk-adjusted growth

10. See, for example, p. 388 of Grinblatt and Titman (2002).

factor (K) instead of the actual growth factor $(1 + g)$ and the risk-free return (R_f) in place of the risk-adjusted one $(1 + \rho)$. That is, we are continuing to adjust for risk via the expected cash flows rather than the discount rate. However, the two formulae will lead to identical estimates of the perpetuity's market value.

4.4 VALUING MULTI-PERIOD CASH FLOWS USING BACKWARD INDUCTION

When analyzing a multi-period cash flow, it is often possible to perform the valuation using a single tree, which can greatly simplify the calculations in large practical applications of real options analysis. The technique, described in this section, is the basis of the dynamic programming approach to valuing real options that we meet in Chapter 5.

The key is to estimate the market value, period-by-period, of the claim to the entire (remaining) sequence of cash flows. Consider, for example, an asset that generates a cash flow of $Y(i, n)$ at each node (i, n), with the last cash flow generated at date N. Suppose that this asset is worth $V(i, n)$ at node (i, n), immediately before the cash flow at that node has been paid out. Its market value at node (i, N), immediately before the final cash flow is to be received, therefore equals the size of the cash flow itself, $Y(i, N)$. That is,

$$V(i, N) = Y(i, N) \qquad (4.17)$$

at any node (i, N), for $i = 0, 1, \ldots, N$.

Now consider what happens at all earlier dates. At node (i, n), the owner of this asset receives a cash flow of $Y(i, n)$ immediately and, after one period elapses, will be left holding an asset that will be worth $V(i, n + 1)$ if an up move occurs and $V(i+1, n+1)$ if a down move occurs. Since the cash flow is received immediately, that part of the owner's return is clearly worth $Y(i, n)$. The valuation approach described in Section 3.1 implies that ownership of the asset immediately after the cash flow is paid out is worth

$$\frac{\pi_u(i, n)V(i, n + 1) + \pi_d(i, n)V(i + 1, n + 1)}{R_f}.$$

The market value of the asset immediately before the cash flow is paid out equals the sum of the market values of these two components to the asset's payoff. Thus

$$V(i,n) = \underbrace{Y(i,n)}_{\text{cash flow at date } n} + \underbrace{\frac{\pi_u(i,n)V(i,n+1)+\pi_d(i,n)V(i+1,n+1)}{R_f}}_{\text{market value of cash flows from date } n+1 \text{ onwards}}. \qquad (4.18)$$

The first term is the (cum dividend) market value at node (i, n) of the cash flow to be received at date n, while the second term is the market value at node (i, n) of all cash flows to be received from date $n + 1$ onwards.[11]

---

11. This equation assumes that investors pay no personal tax. Allowing for personal taxes is straightforward and is covered in Appendix 4.B.

When combined with the terminal condition in (4.17), this recursive equation can be used to value a multi-period cash flow on a single tree. We start by using equation (4.17) to fill in the market value at every terminal node of the tree. We then work backwards in time, using equation (4.18) to fill in the entries in each remaining column of the tree, completing one column before moving on to the next one.

Example 4.8. The results of applying this technique to the stream of cash flows received by the owner of the roading concession with a minimum-revenue guarantee are shown in Table 4.7. We start at the final date by setting the market value of the cash flow stream equal to the final cash flow:

$$V'(i, 5) = Y'(i, 5)$$

for all $i = 0, 1, \ldots, 5$. This allows us to fill in the final column of Table 4.7. We then step back one period, to date 4, and set the market value equal to the sum of the cash flow at date 4 and the market value of the subsequent cash flow; that is,

$$V'(i, 4) = Y'(i, 4) + 0.2467V'(i, 5) + 0.7057V'(i + 1, 5)$$

Table 4.7. Backward Induction when Minimum Revenue is Guaranteed

$V'(i, n)$	0	1	2	3	4	5
0	30.60	34.65	31.71	27.92	21.97	12.97
1		31.24	26.54	22.26	17.36	10.25
2			25.36	19.62	14.00	8.10
3				19.44	13.28	6.80
4					13.28	6.80
5						6.80

Step 1: Use equation (4.17) with $N = 5$ to evaluate $V'(i, 5)$

Step 2: Use equation (4.18) with $n = 4$ to evaluate $V'(i, 4)$

Step 3: Use equation (4.18) with $n = 3$ to evaluate $V'(i, 3)$

Step 4: Use equation (4.18) with $n = 2$ to evaluate $V'(i, 2)$

Step 5: Use equation (4.18) with $n = 1$ to evaluate $V'(i, 1)$

Step 6: Use equation (4.18) with $n = 0$ to evaluate $V'(0, 0)$

for all $i = 0, 1, \ldots, 4$. This allows us to fill in the second-to-last column of Table 4.7. We continue like this, working backwards through the tree, until we come to date 0. Since there is no cash flow at the initial date, we have

$$V'(0, 0) = 0.2467V'(0, 1) + 0.7057V'(1, 1) = 30.60,$$

which equals the market value calculated in Example 4.6. ∎

4.5 SUMMARIZING THE VALUATION APPROACH

We need to carry out the following steps when estimating the market value of a multi-period cash flow.

1. Specify a suitable state variable and estimate $X(i, n)$ at each node in the tree as far out as the date on which the final cash flow is to be received. (We describe how to estimate these (and other) parameters in Chapters 12–14.)
2. Use data on observed bond prices to estimate R_f.
3. Calculate the risk-neutral probabilities at each node.

   - If the state variable is the price of a traded asset then we can estimate the dividend or convenience yield in order to calculate $C(i, n)/X(i, n)$ and then use (3.3) and (3.4) to calculate $\pi_u(i, n)$ and $\pi_d(i, n)$.
   - If forward or futures contracts on the state variable are traded then we can use the period-ahead forward price $F(i, n)$ in (3.5) to calculate $\pi_u(i, n)$ and $\pi_d(i, n)$.
   - Otherwise, estimate $K(i, n)$ using (3.9) and then use (3.8) to calculate $\pi_u(i, n)$ and $\pi_d(i, n)$.

4. Build a tree for the cash flows, $Y(i, n)$, using the relationship between the cash flow and the state variable that is appropriate for the situation being analyzed.
5. Build a tree for the market value of the cash flow.

   (a) Use equation (4.17) to fill in the market value at every terminal node of the tree.
   (b) Use equation (4.18) to fill in the entries in each remaining column of the tree, completing one column before moving on to the next one.

4.6 PROBLEMS

4.1. (Practice) Repeat the calculations in Example 4.3 for the cash flows received at dates 3, 4, and 5.
4.2. (Practice) An asset generates a cash flow at date 4 equal to ten times the state variable on that date. The state variable is currently equal to $X_0 = 8$ and is equally likely to change by a factor of $U = 1.12$ or $D = 1/U$ each period.

The risk-adjusted growth factor is $K = 0.95$ and the return on one-period risk-free bonds is $R_f = 1.02$.

    (a) Use the approach in Section 4.2.1 to value the asset at date 0.

    (b) Use the approach in Section 4.2.2 to value the asset at date 0.

4.3. **(Extension)** Suppose that the price of the spanning asset at node (i, n) is $Z(i, n) = K_n X(i, n)/R_f$ for some constants $K_0, K_1, \ldots$.

    (a) Explain why the claim to a cash flow of $X(\cdot, 1)$ at date 1 is worth $K_0 X(0, 0)/R_f$ at date 0.

    (b) Repeat the analysis in Section 4.2.2 to show that the claim to a cash flow of $X(\cdot, 2)$ at date 2 is worth $K_0 K_1 X(0, 0)/(R_f)^2$ at date 0.

    (c) Show that the claim to a cash flow of $X(\cdot, 3)$ at date 3 is worth $K_0 K_1 K_2 X(0, 0)/(R_f)^3$ at date 0.

4.4. **(Practice)** A firm is considering building a new factory. It will require expenditure of \$10 million at dates 0, 1, 2, and 3, and will result in a factory that can be sold for $X(\cdot, 4)$ at date 4. The state variable is currently $X_0 = 90$ and is equally likely to change by a factor of $U = 1.25$ or $D = 1/U$ each period. The risk-adjusted growth factor is $K = 1.01$ and the return on one-period risk-free bonds is $R_f = 1.05$. Calculate the market value of the cash flow stream that results if the firm invests.

4.5. **(Demonstration)** Suppose the one-period risk-free interest rate (r_f) is 4%, the expected growth rate for the state variable (g) is 2% per period, and the RADR (ρ) is 8% per period. Calculate K and show that it is approximately equal to $1 + g - (\rho - r_f)$.

4.6. **(Practice)** An asset generates a cash flow equal to $X(\cdot, n) - 7$ for $n = 1, 2, 3$. The state variable is currently equal to $X_0 = 12$ and is equally likely to change by a factor of $U = 1.2$ or $D = 1/U$ each period. The risk-adjusted growth factor is $K = 0.95$ and the return on one-period risk-free bonds is $R_f = 1.05$.

    (a) Calculate the RADR implied by U, D, K, and R_f.

    (b) Use the approach in Section 4.3.1 to value the asset at date 0.

    (c) Calculate the expected values at date 0 of the cash flows to be received at dates $n = 1, 2, 3$ and use these to calculate the RADR implied by the market value of each cash flow at date 0. Discuss the results.

4.7. **(Practice)** Use the results of Section 4.3.3 to calculate the market value of the roading concession when minimum revenue is not guaranteed. Explain why we cannot use this approach when the minimum-revenue guarantee is in place.

4.8. **(Practice)** The state variable is currently equal to $X_0 = 15$, the risk-adjusted growth factor is $K = 0.97$, and the return on one-period risk-free bonds is $R_f = 1.03$. An asset generates a cash flow stream equal to the level of the state variable from dates 1 to N, inclusive. Use the results of Section 4.3.3 to calculate the market value of this asset for the following values of N: 1, 2, 5, 10, 20, 50, 100, 1000, 2000. Discuss the results.

4.9. **(Demonstration)** Use (4.16) to derive an expression for the market value of a perpetual cash flow of $X(\cdot, \cdot)$ starting at date 0.

4.10. **(Practice)** This exercise describes an alternative method for estimating the cost to the government of providing the minimum-revenue guarantee for the roading concession introduced in Example 4.1. Construct a table showing the cash flow that the government incurs at each node if it offers the minimum-revenue guarantee. Use the approach in Section 4.4 to estimate the market value of the cash flow stream described by this table. Discuss the results.

4.11. **(Practice)** An asset generates a cash flow of 100 at date 5 if and only if $X(\cdot, 5) \geq 12$. The state variable is currently equal to $X_0 = 10$ and is equally likely to change by a factor of $U = 1.1$ or $D = 1/U$ each period. The risk-adjusted growth factor is $K = 0.98$ and the return on one-period risk-free bonds is $R_f = 1.04$.

    (a) Calculate the RADR implied by U, D, K, and R_f.

    (b) Use the approach in Section 4.1 to value the asset at date 0.

    (c) Use the approach in Section 4.2.1 to value the asset at date 0.

    (d) Calculate the expected payoff of the asset and use this to calculate the RADR implied by its market value. Discuss the result.

4.12. **(Practice)** A firm will extract one unit of copper from a mine at date 3 provided that the spot price of copper exceeds the extraction cost of $0.90. The copper price is currently $1.20; it is equally likely to change by a factor of $U = 1.25$ or $D = 1/U$ each period. The convenience yield at any node equals 5% of the spot price at that node, while the return on one-period risk-free bonds is $R_f = 1.05$.

    (a) Calculate the risk-neutral probability of an up move at any node.

    (b) Use the approach in Section 4.1 to calculate the market value at date 0 of the firm's net cash flow at date 3.

    (c) Use the approach in Section 4.2.1 to calculate the market value of this cash flow.

    (d) Calculate the RADR implied by the market value of this cash flow.

4.13. **(Practice)** A factory produces one unit of output every two periods at a cost of $C = 4$ per unit, starting at date 2. The factory produces five units of output in total. The output price equals $X(i, n)$ at node (i, n), the risk-adjusted growth factor is $K = 0.96$, and the return on one-period risk-free bonds is $R_f = 1.06$. The output price, which is currently $X_0 = 7$, is equally likely to change by a factor of $U = 1.2$ or $D = 1/U$ each period. The factory must operate at full capacity, even if the output price is less than the cost of production.

    (a) Calculate the RADR implied by U, D, K, and R_f.

    (b) Use the approach in Section 4.1 to calculate the market value at date 0 of each of the factory's net cash flows separately. Use the results to calculate the factory's market value.

    (c) Use the approach in Section 4.4 to calculate the factory's market value at date 0.

4.14. (**Practice**) Suppose that the government bears the upside risk in the roading concession introduced in Example 4.1. Specifically, each period the concessionaire keeps all revenue below \$7.60 but pays all revenue above \$7.60 to the government. All other aspects of the situation are unchanged.
  (a) Repeat the calculations in Table 4.5 for this situation.
  (b) Repeat the calculations in Example 4.8 for this situation.

4.15. (**Demonstration**) Sometimes, especially when communicating the results of real options analysis, it is useful to report the expected value of a risky cash flow. This problem demonstrates an efficient way of calculating the expected value of a cash flow to be received at a fixed future date N. If the cash flow equals $Y(\cdot, N)$ and its expected value at node (i, n) is denoted $G(i, n)$, then we can calculate $G(0, 0)$ using the terminal condition

$$G(i, N) = Y(i, N)$$

and the recursive equation

$$G(i, n) = \theta_u(i, n)G(i, n + 1) + \theta_d(i, n)G(i + 1, n + 1),$$

where $\theta_u(i, n)$ and $\theta_d(i, n)$ are the actual probabilities of up and down moves at node (i, n), respectively. This is just like our approach to valuation, except that we do not discount at each step and we replace the risk-neutral probabilities with the actual ones.

Use this approach to calculate the expected values at date 0 of the five cash flows featured in the bottom panel of Table 4.6.

4.A APPENDIX: THE RADR FORM OF THE CAPM

Recall from Appendix 3.A.4 that the expected return from buying and holding the spanning asset for one period equals

$$E[\tilde{R}'_x] = R_f + (E[\tilde{R}_m] - R_f)\beta'_x,$$

where $\tilde{R}'_x = \tilde{X}/Z$ and

$$\beta'_x = \frac{\mathrm{Cov}[\tilde{R}'_x, \tilde{R}_m]}{\mathrm{Var}[\tilde{R}_m]}.$$

This is the traditional RADR form of the CAPM. The main problem with this form is that the price of the spanning asset, Z, appears on both sides of the equation via $\tilde{R}'_x$. Thus, we cannot simply calculate $E[\tilde{R}'_x]$ and then discount $E[\tilde{X}]$ to calculate Z—we need to know Z in order to calculate $\tilde{R}'_x$ and hence β'_x. In other words, $E[\tilde{R}'_x]$ is endogenous to the valuation problem—it is not an exogenous parameter. This endogeneity is especially important when the cash flows are nonlinear functions of the state variable since then, as we saw in Example 4.7, the RADR can vary with the date of the cash flow.

It is possible (although not especially practicable) to calculate the RADR directly from the properties of $\tilde{X}$. We know that

$$E[\tilde{R}'_x] = R_f + \left(\frac{E[\tilde{R}_m] - R_f}{\text{Var}[\tilde{R}_m]}\right) \text{Cov}[\tilde{R}'_x, \tilde{R}_m].$$

If we use $\tilde{R}'_x = \tilde{X}/Z$ to eliminate $\tilde{R}'_x$ from the right-hand side, we find that

$$E[\tilde{R}'_x] = R_f + \left(\frac{E[\tilde{R}_m] - R_f}{\text{Var}[\tilde{R}_m]}\right) \text{Cov}\left[\frac{\tilde{X}}{Z}, \tilde{R}_m\right]$$

$$= R_f + \left(\frac{E[\tilde{R}_m] - R_f}{\text{Var}[\tilde{R}_m]}\right) \frac{\text{Cov}[\tilde{X}, \tilde{R}_m]}{Z}.$$

We can use equation (3.6) to eliminate Z, so that

$$E[\tilde{R}'_x] = R_f + \frac{\left(\frac{E[\tilde{R}_m]-R_f}{\text{Var}[\tilde{R}_m]}\right) \text{Cov}[\tilde{X}, \tilde{R}_m]}{\frac{E[\tilde{X}] - \left(\frac{E[\tilde{R}_m]-R_f}{\text{Var}[\tilde{R}_m]}\right)\text{Cov}[\tilde{X},\tilde{R}_m]}{R_f}}$$

$$= R_f \left(1 + \frac{\left(\frac{E[\tilde{R}_m]-R_f}{\text{Var}[\tilde{R}_m]}\right) \text{Cov}[\tilde{X}, \tilde{R}_m]}{E[\tilde{X}] - \left(\frac{E[\tilde{R}_m]-R_f}{\text{Var}[\tilde{R}_m]}\right) \text{Cov}[\tilde{X}, \tilde{R}_m]}\right)$$

$$E[\tilde{R}'_x] = \frac{R_f E[\tilde{X}]}{E[\tilde{X}] - \left(\frac{E[\tilde{R}_m]-R_f}{\text{Var}[\tilde{R}_m]}\right) \text{Cov}[\tilde{X}, \tilde{R}_m]}.$$

This is an alternative expression for the CAPM. It gives the expected return as a function of the asset's payoff distribution (as well as market-wide parameters). This is not a formula that we use in this book. However, it is useful in explaining why, once we require a usable form of the CAPM (meaning that the expected rate of return must depend only on parameters that we would regard as exogenous to the valuation problem), we end up with a quite different form from what is regarded as the "standard" CAPM.

4.B APPENDIX: VALUATION WITH PERSONAL TAXES

In this appendix we repeat our derivation of the risk-neutral pricing formula, this time from the perspective of an investor who must pay personal taxes. In subsequent chapters we carry out real options analysis from the perspective of tax-exempt investors. However, this material is included here so that we can consider alternative tax scenarios when the situation merits it. We cover personal taxes in this chapter because the relevance of both dividends and capital gains for personal tax calculations means that we need the valuation model for multi-period cash flows. However, we can easily skip this material without altering our understanding of subsequent topics.

4.B.1 Risk-neutral Pricing Formula

We suppose that dividends and capital gains are taxed at the same rate for any particular asset, but allow this common tax rate to vary across assets. Specifically, the representative investor's returns on risk-free bonds are taxed at rate τ_b, returns on the spanning asset are taxed at rate τ_s, and returns on the asset being valued are taxed at rate τ_e.

Consider an asset that generates a pre-personal-tax cash flow of Y immediately after the asset goes ex dividend and that will have a pre-personal-tax payoff of V_u or V_d after one period, depending on whether the next move is up or down. It is convenient to analyze these two sources of value separately. The immediate cash flow is easy to value: since the representative investor will have to pay a proportion τ_e of the cash flow in tax, its value to her equals $(1 - \tau_e)Y$. We estimate the market value of the second component, which we denote $\hat{V}$, using the law of one price. We can then appeal to the law of one price again, to argue that the value of the entire asset must equal the sum of the values of the two components; that is, $V = (1 - \tau_e)Y + \hat{V}$.

Suppose that each unit of the spanning asset is currently worth Z and will be worth either X_u or X_d after one period, depending on whether an up or a down move occurs. Without loss of generality, we assume that the spanning asset does not pay a dividend. We are interested in estimating the market value of an asset that generates no cash now, but generates a payoff of V_u or V_d after one period, depending on whether an up or a down move occurs. We wish to estimate $\hat{V}$, the current market value of the asset. The one-period risk-free interest rate equals r_f.

If an up move occurs, the representative investor receives the payoff of V_u, but must pay tax of $\tau_e(V_u - \hat{V})$;[12] her post-tax payoff is therefore $(1 - \tau_e)V_u + \tau_e\hat{V}$. Similarly, if a down move occurs her post-tax payoff equals $(1 - \tau_e)V_d + \tau_e\hat{V}$. We proceed by building a portfolio of risk-free bonds and the spanning asset with the same post-tax payoff.

Suppose the representative investor buys A one-period risk-free bonds and B units of the spanning asset. This portfolio generates a post-tax cash flow of

$$A\left(1 + (1 - \tau_b)r_f\right) + B\left((1 - \tau_s)X_u + \tau_s Z\right)$$

in the up state and

$$A\left(1 + (1 - \tau_b)r_f\right) + B\left((1 - \tau_s)X_d + \tau_s Z\right)$$

---

12. If $V_u < \hat{V}$, she receives a tax credit of $\tau_e(\hat{V} - V_u)$.

in the down state. We choose A and B to replicate the post-tax payoffs from investing in the asset we are trying to value, so that

$$A\left(1 + (1 - \tau_b)r_f\right) + B\left((1 - \tau_s)X_u + \tau_s Z\right) = (1 - \tau_e)V_u + \tau_e \hat{V}$$

and

$$A\left(1 + (1 - \tau_b)r_f\right) + B\left((1 - \tau_s)X_d + \tau_s Z\right) = (1 - \tau_e)V_d + \tau_e \hat{V}.$$

Solving these equations for A and B shows that the replicating portfolio must contain

$$B = \frac{(1 - \tau_e)(V_u - V_d)}{(1 - \tau_s)(X_u - X_d)}$$

units of the spanning asset and

$$A = \frac{\tau_e \hat{V}}{1 + (1 - \tau_b)r_f} + \left(\frac{1 - \tau_e}{1 - \tau_s}\right)\frac{(\tau_s Z + (1 - \tau_s)X_u)V_d - (\tau_s Z + (1 - \tau_s)X_d)V_u}{(1 + (1 - \tau_b)r_f)(X_u - X_d)}$$

units of the risk-free bond. Notice that since the cash flow we are trying to value depends on $\hat{V}$, the composition of the replicating portfolio will also depend on $\hat{V}$. (It does, via A.) Therefore the cost of this portfolio, which equals $A + BZ$, will also depend on $\hat{V}$. However, the law of one price implies that the cost of the portfolio as a whole must also equal $\hat{V}$. Therefore, $\hat{V}$ must satisfy

$$\hat{V} = A + BZ.$$

Solving this equation for $\hat{V}$ shows that

$$\hat{V} = \frac{\pi_u V_u + \pi_d V_d}{R_f},$$

where

$$\pi_u = \frac{Z\left(1 + \left(\frac{1 - \tau_b}{1 - \tau_s}\right)r_f\right) - X_d}{X_u - X_d}, \quad \pi_d = \frac{X_u - Z\left(1 + \left(\frac{1 - \tau_b}{1 - \tau_s}\right)r_f\right)}{X_u - X_d}, \quad (4.19)$$

and

$$R_f = 1 + \left(\frac{1 - \tau_b}{1 - \tau_e}\right)r_f.$$

The market value of the asset we are trying to value must equal the sum of the market values of the first and second components, $(1 - \tau_e)Y + \hat{V}$. Thus,

$$V = (1 - \tau_e)Y + \frac{\pi_u V_u + \pi_d V_d}{R_f}. \quad (4.20)$$

Three special cases are worth considering. First, when all tax rates are zero, (4.20) reduces to our standard valuation formula, (4.18). Second, when returns on all assets are taxed at the same rate τ, we get our standard valuation formula except that the current date's cash flow is adjusted for personal tax; in particular, we use the pre-personal-tax return on bonds. Third, when returns on the asset being valued and the spanning asset are taxed at the same rate τ (for example, they are both taxed as equity), but returns on bonds are taxed at a different rate, we get our standard valuation formula except that the current date's cash flow is adjusted for personal tax and the return on risk-free bonds is adjusted to reflect the different tax rates.

4.B.2 Valuation when the State Variable is the Price of a Traded Asset

In this section we consider the risk-neutral pricing formula when the state variable is the (cum dividend) price of a traded asset. The current price of the traded asset equals X, it pays a dividend of C immediately, and one period from now its (cum dividend) price will equal X_u in the up state and X_d in the down state.

Although it costs X to buy one unit of the asset, because the dividend is received immediately (and the tax on the investor's dividend income is paid immediately) the true cost is really $X - (1 - \tau_s)C$. Substituting $Z = X - (1 - \tau_s)C$ into equation (4.19) shows that when the state variable is the price of a traded asset the risk-neutral probability of an up move equals

$$\pi_u = \frac{(X - (1 - \tau_s)C)\left(1 + \left(\frac{1-\tau_b}{1-\tau_s}\right)r_f\right) - X_d}{X_u - X_d}.$$

Dividing both numerator and denominator by X gives an alternative expression for this probability,

$$\pi_u = \frac{\left(1 - (1 - \tau_s)\frac{C}{X}\right)\left(1 + \left(\frac{1-\tau_b}{1-\tau_s}\right)r_f\right) - D}{U - D},$$

where $U = X_u/X$ and $D = X_d/X$ are the sizes of up and down moves, respectively. The risk-neutral probability of a down move is

$$\pi_d = \frac{U - \left(1 - (1 - \tau_s)\frac{C}{X}\right)\left(1 + \left(\frac{1-\tau_b}{1-\tau_s}\right)r_f\right)}{U - D}.$$

4.B.3 Valuation Using the CAPM

We can also use the CAPM to calculate the market value of the spanning asset. As in Section 3.4, we find a portfolio of traded assets that minimizes the mean squared tracking error and then use the cost of this portfolio as our estimate of the price of the spanning asset.

The tracking portfolio comprises A dollars invested in one-period risk-free bonds and B dollars invested in the market portfolio. After personal taxes are deducted, each dollar invested in risk-free bonds pays $R_f = 1 + (1 - \tau_b)r_f$ dollars after one period, where τ_b is the tax rate on risk-free bonds and r_f is the one-period risk-free interest rate. Similarly, each dollar invested in the market portfolio pays $\tilde{R}_m = 1 + (1 - \tau_m)\tilde{r}_m$ dollars after one period, where τ_m is the tax rate, and $\tilde{r}_m$ is the rate of return, on the market portfolio. The tracking portfolio therefore delivers a payoff equal to $AR_f + B\tilde{R}_m$ after one period.

We are trying to track an asset that pays

$$\tilde{X} - \tau_s(\tilde{X} - Z) = (1 - \tau_s)\tilde{X} + \tau_s Z$$

after personal tax is deducted. The tracking error (the difference between the two cash flows) is therefore

$$(1 - \tau_s)\tilde{X} + \tau_s Z - \left(AR_f + B\tilde{R}_m\right),$$

so that the mean squared tracking error equals

$$\text{MSE} = E\left[\left((1 - \tau_s)\tilde{X} + \tau_s Z - \left(AR_f + B\tilde{R}_m\right)\right)^2\right].$$

We choose the portfolio components A and B in order to minimize this quantity. The respective first-order conditions are

$$0 = \frac{\partial \text{MSE}}{\partial A} = -2E\left[\left((1 - \tau_s)\tilde{X} + \tau_s Z - \left(AR_f + B\tilde{R}_m\right)\right)R_f\right]$$

and

$$0 = \frac{\partial \text{MSE}}{\partial B} = -2E\left[\left((1 - \tau_s)\tilde{X} + \tau_s Z - \left(AR_f + B\tilde{R}_m\right)\right)\tilde{R}_m\right].$$

The first equation simplifies to

$$0 = (1 - \tau_s)E[\tilde{X}] + \tau_s Z - AR_f - BE[\tilde{R}_m],$$

so that

$$A = \frac{(1 - \tau_s)E[\tilde{X}] + \tau_s Z - BE[\tilde{R}_m]}{R_f}. \tag{4.21}$$

Using this to eliminate A from the second equation shows that

$$0 = E\left[\left((1 - \tau_s)\tilde{X} + \tau_s Z - \left(AR_f + B\tilde{R}_m\right)\right)\tilde{R}_m\right]$$

$$= E\left[\left((1 - \tau_s)(\tilde{X} - E[\tilde{X}]) + BE[\tilde{R}_m] - B\tilde{R}_m\right)\tilde{R}_m\right]$$

$$= (1 - \tau_s)E[\tilde{X}\tilde{R}_m] - (1 - \tau_s)E[\tilde{X}]E[\tilde{R}_m] - B\left(E[\tilde{R}_m^2] - (E[\tilde{R}_m])^2\right)$$

$$0 = (1 - \tau_s)\text{Cov}[\tilde{X}, \tilde{R}_m] - B\text{Var}[\tilde{R}_m],$$

which implies that

$$B = \frac{(1 - \tau_s)\text{Cov}[\tilde{X}, \tilde{R}_m]}{\text{Var}[\tilde{R}_m]}.$$

We can now substitute the solution for B into (4.21), to obtain

$$A = \frac{(1 - \tau_s)E[\tilde{X}] + \tau_s Z - E[\tilde{R}_m]\frac{(1-\tau_s)\text{Cov}[\tilde{X}, \tilde{R}_m]}{\text{Var}[\tilde{R}_m]}}{R_f}.$$

The cost of the tracking portfolio equals

$$Z = A + B$$

$$= \frac{(1 - \tau_s)E[\tilde{X}] + \tau_s Z - E[\tilde{R}_m]\frac{(1-\tau_s)\text{Cov}[\tilde{X},\tilde{R}_m]}{\text{Var}[\tilde{R}_m]}}{R_f} + \frac{(1 - \tau_s)\text{Cov}[\tilde{X}, \tilde{R}_m]}{\text{Var}[\tilde{R}_m]}$$

$$Z = (1 - \tau_s)\left(\frac{E[\tilde{X}] - (E[\tilde{R}_m] - R_f)\frac{\text{Cov}[\tilde{X},\tilde{R}_m]}{\text{Var}[\tilde{R}_m]}}{R_f}\right) + \frac{\tau_s Z}{R_f}.$$

Solving this equation for Z and rearranging gives

$$Z = \frac{E[\tilde{X}] - (E[\tilde{R}_m] - R_f)\frac{\text{Cov}[\tilde{X},\tilde{R}_m]}{\text{Var}[\tilde{R}_m]}}{1 + \left(\frac{1-\tau_b}{1-\tau_s}\right)r_f}.$$

Finally, substituting in the expressions for R_f and $\tilde{R}_m$ gives the following version of the certainty-equivalent form of the CAPM:

$$Z = \frac{E[\tilde{X}] - \left(E[\tilde{r}_m] - \left(\frac{1-\tau_b}{1-\tau_m}\right)r_f\right)\frac{\text{Cov}[\tilde{X},\tilde{r}_m]}{\text{Var}[\tilde{r}_m]}}{1 + \left(\frac{1-\tau_b}{1-\tau_s}\right)r_f}.$$

If, as is reasonable, the tax rates on the spanning asset and the market portfolio are equal, then this is identical to the form of the CAPM in equation (3.6), with the exception that a simple tax adjustment is applied to the risk-free interest rate.

5

Combining Valuation and Decision Making

As we saw in Chapter 2, managers have the potential to influence the cash flow streams generated by the firms that they manage. We argued there that they should exercise this influence in ways that maximize the market value of their existing shareholders' equity. In order to choose the best *current* actions, managers therefore need to know how their actions will affect their firms' future cash flows. However, those future cash flows may themselves be affected by the managers' *future* actions. Thus, in order to decide what to do now, managers need to know what they will do in the future. In order to know what they will do then, they need to know what they will do even further in the future. They do not need to commit unconditionally to a particular course of action immediately. Instead, it will usually be optimal to adopt a policy where future actions are conditional on certain events happening between now and then. For example, it might be optimal to abandon a project at some future date only if it has performed particulary poorly between now and then: if it has performed well, then it will not be abandoned. Our goal in this chapter is to extend the valuation approach in Chapter 4 so that it can be used to identify the complex dynamic policies that maximize the market value of a cash flow stream.

We begin by analyzing the problem facing the manager of a firm with the option to expand its production capacity. Although this example is relatively simple, it introduces most of the techniques that we use throughout the book. However, it is just one example. We need to develop the ability to analyze a much wider variety of problems, and the rest of the chapter introduces the general approach that we use. The first step towards analyzing a problem involving real options is to represent the choices available to the decision maker using a decision tree, which we discuss in Section 5.2. The next step is to use the information contained in the decision tree to build binomial trees for the decision maker's objective function (which, in the context of capital budgeting, will be the market value of a firm's existing shareholders' equity). We develop the key valuation equation in Section 5.3 and show how it can be used to build the required binomial trees in Section 5.4. Finally, Section 5.5 summarizes our overall approach to analyzing problems involving real options.

5.1 A SIMPLE EXAMPLE OF A REAL OPTION

We motivate the ideas introduced in this chapter using a simple example of a firm with a real option. The firm's manager has the option to invest $I = 35$ and expand production. Prior to expansion the firm produces one unit of output per period at a total operating cost of $C = 10$; after expansion it produces two units of output per period at a total operating cost of $C' = 15$. That is, the cost per unit of output falls when the factory is expanded. We let $X(i, n)$ denote the output price at node (i, n). The output price is currently $X_0 = 15$ and each period it changes by a factor of $U = 1.2000$ or $D = 1/U = 0.8333$, each with probability 0.5. The risk-adjusted growth factor is $K = 0.9600$ and the return on a one-period risk-free bond is $R_f = 1.05$, so that the risk-neutral probability of an up move is

$$\pi_u = \frac{K - D}{U - D} = \frac{0.9600 - 0.8333}{1.2000 - 0.8333} = 0.3455$$

at all nodes. The risk-neutral probability of a down move is $\pi_d = 1 - \pi_u = 0.6545$. Production begins at date 1 and lasts until date 5. If the firm expands, then the higher production begins one period after expansion. We assume that the firm is all-equity financed and that all investment expenditure is financed by the existing shareholders. (This is a relatively unimportant assumption: the firm could raise capital in other ways without changing the results.)

5.1.1 Invest Now or Not at All

We start by considering the situation when the firm's manager can expand production only at date 0. This is the classic now-or-never investment problem that we considered in Section 2.1.2. At node $(0, 0)$ the manager must either expand production or let the expansion option lapse. She should only invest if doing so increases the market value of the existing shareholders' equity in the firm.

Suppose first that she allows the option to lapse. Since production begins at date 1, the firm generates zero cash flow at node $(0, 0)$ and a cash flow of

$$Y(\cdot, n) = X(\cdot, n) - C$$

at dates $n = 1, 2, \ldots, 5$. The easiest way to value this cash flow stream is to value the revenue and operating costs separately. From equation (4.13), the market value of the operating cost stream equals

$$\left(1 - \left(\frac{1}{R_f}\right)^5\right) \frac{C}{R_f - 1} = \left(1 - \left(\frac{1}{1.05}\right)^5\right) \frac{10}{1.05 - 1} = 43.29.$$

From equation (4.15), the market value of the revenue stream equals

$$\left(1 - \left(\frac{K}{R_f}\right)^5\right) \frac{K X(0,0)}{R_f - K} = \left(1 - \left(\frac{0.9600}{1.05}\right)^5\right) \frac{0.9600 \times 15}{1.05 - 0.9600} = 57.78.$$

Thus, if the manager allows the expansion option to lapse, existing shareholders' equity in the firm will be worth $57.78 - 43.29 = 14.49$.

Next, suppose that the manager decides to expand the firm's production capacity at date 0. This requires a cash outflow of I at date 0, but the expanded firm generates a cash flow of

$$Y'(\cdot, n) = 2X(\cdot, n) - C'$$

at dates $n = 1, 2, \ldots, 5$. The market value of this cash flow stream equals

$$-I + \left(1 - \left(\frac{K}{R_f}\right)^5\right) \frac{2K X(0,0)}{R_f - K} - \left(1 - \left(\frac{1}{R_f}\right)^5\right) \frac{C'}{R_f - 1}$$

$$= -35 + \left(1 - \left(\frac{0.9600}{1.05}\right)^5\right) \frac{2 \times 0.9600 \times 15}{1.05 - 0.9600} - \left(1 - \left(\frac{1}{1.05}\right)^5\right) \frac{15}{1.05 - 1}$$

$$= 15.62.$$

Thus, the existing shareholders' equity in the firm will be worth 15.62.

If the manager expands production the existing shareholders' equity is worth 15.62, while if she does not expand production it is worth 14.49. Assuming the manager is working in the best interests of the firm's existing shareholders, she should expand production. Anticipating this, financial markets will value the firm's equity at 15.62.

Although it is very simple, this example illustrates the relationship between valuation and managerial decision making. We cannot calculate the market value of the firm until we know the particular action that the manager is going to take, and we do not know which one that will be until we have calculated the market value for *each possible* action. Thus, even in this very simple example, valuation and decision making are linked.

5.1.2 Invest Now or Wait and See

Now we consider the situation when the manager can delay her expansion decision until date 1. That is, if she does not expand production at date 0 then at date 1 the manager gets one last chance to expand production. If she takes this opportunity, then the firm funds expansion at date 1 and output increases between dates 2 and 5.

The manager now faces a more complicated problem at date 0. She can still invest immediately. As above, the firm's existing shareholders will hold equity worth 15.62 if she takes this action. However, it would be a mistake to compare this with the market value of the firm if it does not expand at date 0 that we calculated above, which equals 14.49. In that calculation we assumed that if the firm did not expand at date 0 then it would not expand *at all*. That is clearly not the situation here—just because the firm does not expand at date 0 does not mean that it will not expand at date 1.

So what is the firm worth if the manager does not expand production at date 0? The answer clearly depends on what she will do at date 1. Therefore, the first step in calculating the market value of the firm if she delays expansion at date 0 is to determine what the manager will do at date 1 *if she does not expand production at date 0*. It is quite possible—indeed, we will see that for this example it is optimal—that the manager's action at date 1 will depend on whether the first move is up or down. We therefore consider the two cases separately.

We start by considering the case where the manager did not expand production at date 0 and the first move in the output price is up. The output price is now $X(0, 1) = UX(0, 0) = 18$ and the manager must decide whether to expand production or allow the expansion option to lapse. (Because of the way we set up the problem, she cannot delay the expansion past date 1.) If she expands production, the firm's date 1 cash flow will equal

$$X(0, 1) - C - I = 18 - 10 - 35 = -27$$

and the market value of the cash flows received at dates 2–5 will equal

$$\left(1 - \left(\frac{K}{R_f}\right)^4\right) \frac{2K\, X(0, 1)}{R_f - K} - \left(1 - \left(\frac{1}{R_f}\right)^4\right) \frac{C'}{R_f - 1}$$

$$= \left(1 - \left(\frac{0.9600}{1.05}\right)^4\right) \frac{2 \times 0.9600 \times 18}{1.05 - 0.9600} - \left(1 - \left(\frac{1}{1.05}\right)^4\right) \frac{15}{1.05 - 1}$$

$$= 62.49.$$

The existing shareholders' equity in the firm will therefore be worth

$$-27 + 62.49 = 35.49$$

if the firm expands. In contrast, if the manager allows the expansion option to lapse then the firm's date 1 cash flow will equal

$$X(0, 1) - C = 18 - 10 = 8$$

and the market value of all of its future cash flows will equal

$$\left(1 - \left(\frac{K}{R_f}\right)^4\right) \frac{K\,X(0,1)}{R_f - K} - \left(1 - \left(\frac{1}{R_f}\right)^4\right) \frac{C}{R_f - 1}$$

$$= \left(1 - \left(\frac{0.9600}{1.05}\right)^4\right) \frac{0.9600 \times 18}{1.05 - 0.9600} - \left(1 - \left(\frac{1}{1.05}\right)^4\right) \frac{10}{1.05 - 1}$$

$$= 22.38.$$

The existing shareholders' equity in the firm will therefore be worth

$$8 + 22.38 = 30.38$$

if the firm's expansion option is allowed to lapse. The firm's existing shareholders are better off if the firm expands. This is the action that the manager will adopt; financial markets will anticipate this action and value the existing equity in the firm at $V(0, 1) = 35.49$.

Now we consider the case where the manager did not expand production at date 0 and the output price falls to $X(1, 1) = DX(0, 0) = 12.50$. The manager must decide whether to expand production or allow the expansion option to lapse. If she expands production, the firm's date 1 cash flow will equal

$$X(1, 1) - C - I = 12.50 - 10 - 35 = -32.50$$

and the market value of the cash flows received at dates 2–5 will equal

$$\left(1 - \left(\frac{K}{R_f}\right)^4\right) \frac{2K\,X(1,1)}{R_f - K} - \left(1 - \left(\frac{1}{R_f}\right)^4\right) \frac{C'}{R_f - 1}$$

$$= \left(1 - \left(\frac{0.9600}{1.05}\right)^4\right) \frac{2 \times 0.9600 \times 12.5}{1.05 - 0.9600} - \left(1 - \left(\frac{1}{1.05}\right)^4\right) \frac{15}{1.05 - 1}$$

$$= 27.14.$$

The existing shareholders' equity in the firm will therefore be worth

$$-32.50 + 27.14 = -5.36$$

if the firm expands. In contrast, if the manager allows the expansion option to lapse then the firm's date 1 cash flow will equal

$$X(1, 1) - C = 12.50 - 10 = 2.50$$

and the market value of all of its future cash flows will equal

$$
\left(1 - \left(\frac{K}{R_f}\right)^4\right) \frac{K\,X(1,1)}{R_f - K} - \left(1 - \left(\frac{1}{R_f}\right)^4\right) \frac{C}{R_f - 1}
$$

$$
= \left(1 - \left(\frac{0.9600}{1.05}\right)^4\right) \frac{0.9600 \times 12.50}{1.05 - 0.9600} - \left(1 - \left(\frac{1}{1.05}\right)^4\right) \frac{10}{1.05 - 1}
$$

$$
= 4.71.
$$

The existing shareholders' equity in the firm will therefore be worth

$$
2.50 + 4.71 = 7.21
$$

if the firm's expansion option is allowed to lapse. This time the firm's existing shareholders are better off if the firm does not expand. This is the action that the manager will adopt; financial markets will anticipate this action and value the existing equity in the firm at $V(1, 1) = 7.21$.

To summarize, if the manager does not expand the firm at date 0, then at date 1 she will expand production if an up move occurs (when the firm's existing equity will be worth $V(0, 1) = 35.49$) but she will not expand production if a down move occurs (when the firm's existing equity will be worth $V(1, 1) = 7.21$). It is now a straightforward task to calculate the market value of the firm's existing equity at date 0 assuming expansion does not occur at date 0. Since the cash flow at date 0 is zero in this case, the market value of the firm's existing equity is

$$
V(0, 0) = \frac{\pi_u V(0, 1) + \pi_d V(1, 1)}{R_f} = \frac{0.3455 \times 35.49 + 0.6545 \times 7.21}{1.05} = 16.17.
$$

Thus, if the manager does not expand production at date 0, the firm's existing equity will be worth 16.17. We have already seen that it will be worth 15.62 if she expands the firm's production immediately. The manager should therefore choose not to expand production at date 0, but to wait until date 1 and then expand only if an up move occurs. Anticipating this, financial markets will value the firm's equity at 16.17.

Our example of now-or-never investment showed that we cannot calculate the market value of a firm until we know the particular action that its manager is going to take, and we do not know which action that will be until we have calculated the market value for *each possible* action. When delay is possible, the link between decision making and valuation is even stronger: as this example illustrates, we need to know what the manager will do in the future—at each node, so future actions can still be uncertain—before we can decide what the manager will do today.

This completes the analysis of our first problem involving real options. However, there are many different problems we can expect to confront in practice. Because we cannot cover every possible permutation in this book we need to develop a strategy for dealing with a quite general problem. Developing and describing such a strategy is the subject of the remainder of this chapter.

5.2 DECISION TREES

Our first task when confronted with a problem involving real options is to understand the various actions that the decision maker can take. We use a decision tree to help us develop that understanding. A decision tree summarizes the choices available to the decision maker at each point in time and how the choices are affected by the decision maker's actions. For instance, the decision maker may have one set of choices at date 1 if one particular action is taken at date 0 and an entirely different set if a different action is taken.

Figure 5.1 shows the decision tree for the situation analyzed in Section 5.1. The filled circles indicate terminal nodes of the decision tree, which are nodes after which no further actions are taken. In contrast, the empty circles indicate nodes where the decision maker is still to take some actions in the future. The decision tree has three branches, corresponding to the three different sequences of actions available to the manager. First, she can expand the firm's production at date 0 and then operate the expanded facility from dates 1 to 5 inclusive. This is represented by the top branch of the tree, with E indicating the expansion action and OE showing when the manager operates the expanded facility. Second, the manager can choose not to expand the facility at any date, as indicated by the middle branch of the tree with its sequence of NE actions. Finally, she can choose to not expand production at date 0, to expand at date 1, and then to operate the expanded facility until date 5. This corresponds to the bottom branch of the tree.

It is not necessarily optimal for the manager to decide at date 0 which of these branches to follow. That choice potentially depends on how the output price evolves. For example, she might decide not to expand production at date 0 and then to expand at date 1 only if the output price goes up. Thus, she will end up moving along either the middle or the bottom branch of the decision tree in Figure 5.1, but exactly which of these two possibilities occurs will not be known until date 1 when the output price is revealed.

The best way to construct the decision tree for a problem is to start at date 0 and systematically work forwards in time, tracing out all the various actions that the decision maker can take. We start by listing all the actions that the decision maker can take at date 0. If there are k such actions then the decision maker will find

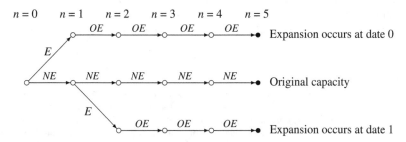

Figure 5.1. Decision tree for the expansion timing problem

herself in exactly one of k different situations at date 1—one for each action she could have taken at date 0. The next step is to consider each one of these situations in turn and repeat the procedure we applied at date 0. That is, for each possible situation at date 1 we list all of the actions that the decision maker can take at that date. Once we have completed this step, we list all of the situations the decision maker might find herself in at date 2—one for each combination of actions she can take at dates 0 and 1—and then repeat the procedure. We continue like this until we reach a date where the decision maker has no more actions to take.[1]

The next example demonstrates this technique by applying it to the situation analyzed in Section 5.1.

Example 5.1. The manager has two actions to choose from at date 0, one corresponding to each arrow leaving the node in Figure 5.1 that represents date 0: she can expand production (labeled E) or she can "not expand" production (labeled NE). She will therefore find herself in exactly one of two possible situations at date 1: the facility has been expanded or it still has its original capacity. If she finds herself in the first situation, then all the manager can do at date 1 is to continue to operate the expanded facility (labeled OE). In contrast, if the firm still has its original capacity at date 1 then she has two actions to choose from: she can expand production (labeled E) or she can not expand production (labeled NE).

It follows that the manager will find herself in exactly one of three possible situations at date 2, depending on the actions she took at dates 0 and 1: (i) expansion occurred at date 0; (ii) expansion occurred at date 1; and (iii) the firm still has its original capacity. Since the manager is not allowed to expand the plant after date 1, and there is no other flexibility described in the problem, there is only a single action possible from now on: to operate the expanded facility if expansion occurred at date 0 or date 1, and operate the original facility if expansion did not occur.

The situation repeats itself from dates 3 to 5 inclusive. The three branches thus extend out as far as date 5 when the firm produces output for the last time and, as no further actions are available to the manager, the decision tree terminates.   ∎

These decision trees can become very complicated very quickly, especially when the decision maker has the option to decide *when* to carry out particular actions. However, sometimes what appear to be separate branches of a decision tree can recombine: two different sequences of actions may end up with an

---

1. Sometimes there will be natural terminal dates, as in the situation analyzed in Section 5.1. However, in other cases we may need to impose an artificial terminal date. For example, if an investment option is perpetual—meaning that its exercise can be delayed until *any* date in the future—we may set the terminal date at some arbitrary point far enough into the future that our analysis is insensitive to the particular date chosen. For instance, the optimal policy at date 0 may be the same whether the option expires at date 100 or date 1000.

indistinguishable outcome. For example, whether a firm shuts down at date 7 or date 8 does not affect its value at date 9.[2] As we see in the next example, the decision tree in Figure 5.1 can be simplified in this way.

Example 5.2. For the situation analyzed in Section 5.1, the problem facing the firm's manager from date 2 onwards depends only on whether expansion has occurred or not—the timing of expansion is irrelevant. For example, the firm's cash flow at node $(i, 3)$ equals $2X(i, 3) - C'$ if capacity expansion occurred at date 0 or if it occurred at date 1. The actions available to the manager are also the same in both cases: continue to produce two units of output per period until date 5 and then cease production. This means that the top and bottom branches of the decision tree in Figure 5.1 can be recombined from date 2 onwards, resulting in the simpler decision tree shown in Figure 5.2. This decision tree makes it clear that from date 1 onwards the firm will really be in one of just two states: its original production capacity or the expanded capacity. In our discussion below we refer to these states as S (for "small") and L (for "large") respectively. ∎

The state of the *world* is described by the state variable that we have been denoting $X(i, n)$. However, this only reflects market-wide information. The state of the *project* may also depend on project-specific information: for example, whether an investment program has begun, how long construction has been underway, and so on. We have to build a separate binomial tree for each such project-state, so that analysis of a single project can often involve the construction of many different binomial trees of market values. The number and the nature of the trees that are needed can be easily extracted from the problem's decision tree. This is one of the most important uses for decision trees—helping us to figure out just how many different market value trees to build.

Example 5.3. The decision tree in Figure 5.2 tells us that we need to build two trees of market values, one for when the firm is in its original state and one for when its capacity has been extended. In our discussion in the next

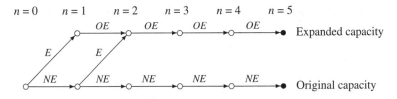

Figure 5.2. A tidier decision tree for the expansion timing problem

---

2. However, it will not always be the case that timing is irrelevant. For example, if machinery lasts exactly four periods, it clearly matters at date 6 whether the machinery was built at date 2 or date 3.

section we denote the market value at node (i, n) by $V_S(i, n)$ in the first case and by $V_L(i, n)$ in the second case. ∎

We have now built the decision tree and used it to identify the various binomial trees that we need to construct. In the next section we see how to use the information contained in the decision tree to calculate the market value of the project at an arbitrary node in one of these binomial trees. Then, in Section 5.4, we see how to fill in each tree.

5.3 FUNDAMENTAL VALUATION EQUATION

Suppose that we are currently at node (i, n) in the binomial tree for the market value of a project when it is in an arbitrary "project state" a. For the time being, suppose that the manager can take only one action at this node when the project is in this state, and suppose that this action transforms the project into state b. This could be the same state (that is, $b = a$), which is what happens when the manager is merely waiting, or it could be one of the other possible project states (that is, $b \neq a$). We suppose that the firm generates a cash flow of $Y_b(i, n)$ immediately and that after one period it will be worth $V_b(i, n + 1)$ if an up move occurs and $V_b(i + 1, n + 1)$ if a down move occurs instead. (For the time being we do not worry about where the market values $V_b(i, n + 1)$ and $V_b(i + 1, n + 1)$ come from. We see how to calculate them later.) The valuation approach developed in Chapters 3 and 4 tells us that the market value of this cash flow stream equals

$$\underbrace{Y_b(i, n)}_{\text{date } n} + \underbrace{\frac{\pi_u(i, n)V_b(i, n + 1) + \pi_d(i, n)V_b(i + 1, n + 1)}{R_f}}_{\text{date } n + 1 \text{ onwards}} \tag{5.1}$$

at node (i, n). It splits naturally into the current cash flow and the current market value of all subsequent cash flows.

Example 5.4. Suppose the manager of the firm described in Section 5.1 exercised the expansion option at date 1. At node $(2, 3)$ all she can do is continue to operate the firm at its increased level of output. That is, the firm is currently in state L and it will remain there after one period. The firm's current cash flow is $Y_L(2, 3) = 2X(2, 3) - C'$ and at date 4 the firm will be worth $V_L(2, 4)$ if an up move occurs and $V_L(3, 4)$ if a down move occurs instead. The market value of the firm is therefore

$$2X(2, 3) - C' + \frac{\pi_u V_L(2, 4) + \pi_d V_L(3, 4)}{R_f}$$

at node $(2, 3)$.[3] ∎

---

3. In this example the risk-neutral probabilities are constant throughout the tree, so we write π_u instead of $\pi_u(i, n)$, and similarly for the risk-neutral probability of a down move.

Now we consider the more complicated situation in which the manager must take one of two actions, which we call b and c. The first action is exactly the same as the one analyzed above: the project is transformed into state b and its market value is still given by (5.1). In contrast, if the manager takes action c, the firm generates a cash flow of $Y_c(i, n)$ immediately and the market value of the project after one period will be $V_c(i, n + 1)$ if an up move occurs and $V_c(i + 1, n + 1)$ if a down move occurs instead. The market value of this cash flow stream at node (i, n) is

$$Y_c(i, n) + \frac{\pi_u(i, n)V_c(i, n + 1) + \pi_d(i, n)V_c(i + 1, n + 1)}{R_f}. \tag{5.2}$$

We assume that whenever managers are called upon to act, they choose actions that maximize the market value of their firms to their existing owners. Thus, if the expression in (5.1) is larger than the one in (5.2), then action b will be chosen and the firm will be worth the amount in (5.1). Similarly, if action c has the more valuable payoff, then it will be chosen instead and the firm will be worth the amount in (5.2). It follows that the market value of the firm equals

$$V_a(i, n) = \max \left\{ Y_b(i, n) + \frac{\pi_u(i, n)V_b(i, n + 1) + \pi_d(i, n)V_b(i + 1, n + 1)}{R_f}, \right.$$
$$\left. Y_c(i, n) + \frac{\pi_u(i, n)V_c(i, n + 1) + \pi_d(i, n)V_c(i + 1, n + 1)}{R_f} \right\}. \tag{5.3}$$

This is our basic valuation equation.[4] We use it throughout this book.

Example 5.5. Suppose the manager of the firm described in Section 5.1 did not exercise the expansion option at date 0. At node $(1, 1)$ she must either exercise it and expand production from date 2 onwards or instead allow the option to lapse. That is, the firm is currently in state S and the manager must either change it to state L or leave it permanently in state S.

If the manager decides not to expand production then the firm's current cash flow is $Y_S(1, 1) = X(1, 1) - C$ and at date 2 the firm will be worth $V_S(1, 2)$ if an up move occurs and $V_S(2, 2)$ if a down move occurs instead. The market value of the firm is therefore

$$X(1, 1) - C + \frac{\pi_u V_S(1, 2) + \pi_d V_S(2, 2)}{R_f}$$

---

4. The generalization to situations where there are more than two possible actions is obvious. We simply calculate the market value of the firm to its existing shareholders for each action and set the market value of the firm equal to the largest of these numbers.

at node $(1, 1)$ if she allows the option to lapse. If she chooses to expand production then the firm's current cash flow is $Y_L(1, 1) = X(1, 1) - C - I$ and at date 2 the firm will be worth $V_L(1, 2)$ if an up move occurs and $V_L(2, 2)$ if a down move occurs instead. The market value of the firm is therefore

$$X(1, 1) - C - I + \frac{\pi_u V_L(1, 2) + \pi_d V_L(2, 2)}{R_f}$$

at node $(1, 1)$ if she chooses to expand production. Putting the pieces together, the market value of the firm will equal

$$V_S(1, 1) = \max \left\{ X(1, 1) - C + \frac{\pi_u V_S(1, 2) + \pi_d V_S(2, 2)}{R_f}, \right.$$
$$\left. X(1, 1) - C - I + \frac{\pi_u V_L(1, 2) + \pi_d V_L(2, 2)}{R_f} \right\}$$

at node $(1, 1)$.   ■

5.4 FILLING IN THE TREES USING DYNAMIC PROGRAMMING

We now have all the information we need to calculate the decision maker's objective function and to find an optimal policy for exercising the project's embedded real options. A separate binomial tree of market values must be constructed for each of the project-states identified in the decision tree. The order in which these binomial trees are constructed will depend on the structure of the problem (as summarized by the decision tree). However, for each tree we start by calculating the project's market value at the terminal nodes and use the fundamental valuation equation, (5.3), to fill in the remainder of the tree, working from right to left.[5]

We demonstrate this technique by applying it to the situation analyzed in Section 5.1.

Example 5.6. We begin by building the binomial tree for the output price, starting with $X(0, 0) = 15$ and filling the tree in from left to right by multiplying the price by $U = 1.2000$ for an up move and $D = 0.8333$ for a down move. The complete tree is shown in the top panel of Table 5.1.

---

5. We will see several shortcuts in Chapters 6–11 that can reduce the amount of calculations required to find a value-maximizing policy for the manager. For example, we will see that it is not always necessary to work all the way to the end of each branch of the decision tree. For this example, at least, once we get to the point where the tree stops branching out we can just use the annuity formula to speed up the valuation process. However, we do not implement such shortcuts in this chapter so as to focus our attention on more important matters.

Table 5.1. Analysis of the Option to Expand Capacity

$X(i, n)$	0	1	2	3	4	5	6	
0	15.00	18.00	21.60	25.92	31.10	37.32	44.79	
1		12.50	15.00	18.00	21.60	25.92	31.10	
2			10.42	12.50	15.00	18.00	21.60	Step 1: Construct binomial
3				8.68	10.42	12.50	15.00←	tree for the state variable
4					7.23	8.68	10.42	
5						6.03	7.23	
6							5.02	

$V_L(i, n)$	0	1	2	3	4	5	6	
0		83.49	95.98	99.68	89.80	59.65	0.00	Step 2a: Fill in final column
1		37.14	49.59	56.12	53.41	36.84	0.00←	using equation (5.4)
2			17.37	25.86	28.14	21.00	0.00	
3				4.86	10.60	10.00	0.00	Step 2b: Fill in remaining
4					−1.59	2.36	0.00←	columns using equation (5.5)
5						−2.94	0.00	
6							0.00	

$V_S(i, n)$	0	1	2	3	4	5	6	
0	16.17	35.49	38.68	42.69	40.02	27.32	0.00	Step 3a: Fill in final column
1		7.21	15.48	20.91	21.82	15.92	0.00←	using equation (5.6)
2			−0.62	5.78	9.19	8.00	0.00	
3				−4.72	0.42	2.50	0.00	Step 3b: Fill in remaining
4					−5.68	−1.32	0.00←	columns using equations
5						−3.97	0.00	(5.7), (5.8), and (5.9)
6							0.00	

The second step is to build the binomial tree for the market value of the firm when its capacity has already been expanded. We denote the market value of the firm in this state by $V_L(i, n)$ at node (i, n). No production is possible from date 6 onwards, so that the firm will be worthless at date 6. Thus

$$V_L(i, 6) = 0. \tag{5.4}$$

From dates 1 to 5 inclusive the firm produces two units of output per period at a cost of C' per period.[6] Since the cash flow at node (i, n) equals $2X(i, n) - C'$

---

6. Since it takes one period to expand production, the earliest that the larger firm can be operating is date 1. Therefore we do not need to calculate $V_L(0, 0)$.

and the firm will still be in state L after one period, the market value of the firm in this state at node (i, n) equals

$$V_L(i, n) = 2X(i, n) - C' + \frac{\pi_u V_L(i, n+1) + \pi_d V_L(i+1, n+1)}{R_f}. \quad (5.5)$$

We use (5.4) to fill in the final column of the binomial tree (shown in the middle panel of Table 5.1), and then we use (5.5) to fill in the rest of the tree, working from right to left.

The third and final step is to build the binomial tree for the market value of the firm when its capacity has not been expanded. We denote the value of the firm in this state by $V_S(i, n)$ at node (i, n). No production is possible from date 6 onwards, so that the firm will be worthless at date 6. Thus

$$V_S(i, 6) = 0. \quad (5.6)$$

From dates 2 to 5 inclusive the firm produces one unit of output per period at a cost of C per period. The cash flow at node (i, n) therefore equals $X(i, n) - C$ and, since the firm will still be in state S after one period, the market value of the firm at node (i, n) equals

$$V_S(i, n) = X(i, n) - C + \frac{\pi_u V_S(i, n+1) + \pi_d V_S(i+1, n+1)}{R_f}. \quad (5.7)$$

At date 1 the manager has the option to expand capacity. If she exercises this option the firm still produces one unit of output at a cost of C, but now the cash flow at node $(i, 1)$ equals $X(i, 1) - C - I$. Since the firm will be in state L after one period, the market value of the firm at node $(i, 1)$ equals

$$V_S(i, 1) = \max \left\{ X(i, 1) - C + \frac{\pi_u V_S(i, 2) + \pi_d V_S(i+1, 2)}{R_f}, \right.$$
$$\left. X(i, 1) - C - I + \frac{\pi_u V_L(i, 2) + \pi_d V_L(i+1, 2)}{R_f} \right\}. \quad (5.8)$$

No production occurs at date 0, but the manager still has the option to expand production. Thus, the market value of the firm at date 0 is

$$V_S(0, 0) = \max \left\{ \frac{\pi_u V_S(0, 1) + \pi_d V_S(1, 1)}{R_f}, -I + \frac{\pi_u V_L(0, 1) + \pi_d V_L(1, 1)}{R_f} \right\}. \quad (5.9)$$

We use (5.6) to fill in the final column of the binomial tree (shown in the bottom panel of Table 5.1), then we use (5.7) to fill in the tree back as far as date 2, (5.8) to fill in the column corresponding to date 1, and finally we use (5.9) to calculate the market value of the firm at date 0. The shaded cell in the table indicates the node of the binomial tree where the manager elects to expand production.

Consistent with our analysis in Section 5.1, the firm is initially worth 16.17 and expansion only occurs at date 1 and then only if the first move is up. ∎

The approach we are using here is known as dynamic programming. It breaks a complicated multi-period optimization problem down into a sequence of simpler problems, where at each date the manager only has to decide what action to take at that date. All relevant information about the past is summarized by the state that the project is currently in; all relevant information about the future is summarized by the market values of the firm after up and down moves.

Past actions stay in the past. Once the manager knows what state the project is in, nothing else about the past matters. All the manager can do at that stage is maximize the market value of the firm's current and future cash flows. It is for this reason that we need to build a tree for every possible project-state: at the time we solve for the manager's actions at date n we do not know what actions will be taken at previous dates, so we need to allow for *all* possibilities.

Future actions can be decided in the future. The manager chooses an action at date n based on what the market value of the firm will be at date $n + 1$ in the up and the down states. These market values have already been calculated as part of the backward induction procedure, and are therefore based on value-maximizing behavior by the manager from date $n + 1$ onwards. Thus, the manager makes decisions at date n anticipating that all future behavior will be optimal, and all of the relevant information about that future behavior is captured by the market value of the firm at date $n + 1$ after up and down moves.[7]

In principle, the procedure is quite straightforward. As we will see in some of the examples in Chapters 6–11, however, when there are multiple interacting real options (and therefore many different binomial trees required) it may not be obvious exactly where to begin. One approach is simply to start anywhere we like, but to be very careful to implement the valuation equation *exactly* as it has been described in Section 5.3. By a process of elimination, we will soon figure out where to begin. For example, we might try to start at node $(0, 0)$, but we will soon realize that we do not have enough information to calculate the market value—we need to know market values at nodes $(0, 1)$ and $(1, 1)$. So we go to node $(0, 1)$ and try to work out the market value there. That does not work, because there we need to know the market values at nodes $(0, 2)$ and $(1, 2)$. We keep on working forwards through the tree until we find a market value that we *can* evaluate—and this is where we start. In practice, this search will lead us to the so-called terminal nodes of one of the trees of

---

7. This is why we can only use the one-shot valuation process described in Section 4.2.1 when we know the actual cash flow at each future node. As long as the decision maker is able to influence that cash flow in the future, we need to apply the backward induction procedure described here. The one-shot approach is very useful in those situations where it can be applied, but we need to be careful not to apply it in situations where its use would be inappropriate.

market values, so the terminal nodes are usually a good place to start this search procedure.

5.5 SUMMARIZING OUR APPROACH TO ANALYZING REAL OPTIONS

We need to carry out the following steps when analyzing a problem involving real options.

1. Build the decision tree for the problem being analyzed, making sure that branches of the tree recombine wherever that is appropriate.
2. Use this decision tree to identify the different project-states at each date. We need to build a separate binomial tree for the market value of the project in each of these states (although, as we see in Chapters 6–11, sometimes this number can be reduced).
3. Build a binomial tree for the state variable.
4. Fill in the binomial trees for the market value of the project in the various states. The order in which these binomial trees are constructed will depend on the structure of the problem (as summarized by the decision tree). However, for each tree we start by calculating the project's market value at the terminal nodes and use the fundamental valuation equation to fill in the remainder of the tree, working from right to left.

This procedure yields the market value of the firm and an optimal policy for exercising the project's real options.

5.6 PROBLEMS

5.1. (**Practice**) Reevaluate the numerical example in Section 5.1 for the following parameter values: $X_0 = 25$, $U = 1.22$, $D = 1/U$, $K = 1.01$, $R_f = 1.04$, $I = 55$, $C = 20$, $C' = 35$. Production begins at date 1 and lasts until date 8, but all other aspects of the situation are unchanged.

5.2. (**Practice**) Redo Table 5.1 for the situation described in Problem 5.1.

5.3. (**Practice**) Redo Table 5.1 for the situation described in Problem 5.1, modified so that expansion can occur at date 0 or 1 or 2 (or not at all). All other aspects of the situation are unchanged.

5.4. (**Practice**) Redo Table 5.1 for the situation described in Problem 5.1, modified so that expansion *must* occur at either date 0 or date 1. All other aspects of the situation are unchanged.

5.5. (**Application: Roading concession with a resale option**) Suppose there is no minimum-revenue guarantee in the roading concession in Example 4.1. Instead, the concessionaire has the right to sell the concession back to the government at any time. Specifically, the government agrees to buy it back for $30 at date 1, or for $25 at date 2, or for $20 at date 3, or for $15 at date 4, or for \$10 at date 5. The transaction would occur immediately before any revenue is collected at that date.

(a) Draw the decision tree for the problem facing the concessionaire.

(b) Use the decision tree to identify the binomial trees needed to analyze the concessionaire's problem.

(c) Derive the terminal conditions and the recursive equations needed to calculate the market value of the concession.

(d) Calculate the market value of the concession and determine an optimal policy for exercising the resale option.

(e) How much is the resale option worth to the concessionaire?

(f) Discuss the form of the optimal policy.

Part II

COMPONENT REAL OPTIONS

6

Options that do not Affect the State of a Project

At the end of 2003, GE Power Systems launched the LMS100 simple-cycle gas turbine (SCGT), designed for use in the power generation industry. The turbine is claimed to require approximately 7.5 million British thermal units (MMBtu) of natural gas to generate each megawatt hour (MWh) of electricity, a considerable improvement in fuel efficiency relative to other SCGTs (which typically require 10–11 MMBtu/MWh).

A useful profitability measure for gas-fired power plants is their "spark spread", which is the amount by which the price of their output exceeds the cost of their fuel input.[1] The left-hand graph in Figure 6.1 shows the evolution of the spark spread during all weekdays in June 2005 for a simple-cycle plant in the PJM market (spanning Pennsylvania, New Jersey, Maryland and nearby states).[2] The spark spread is calculated using the day-ahead electricity price at the PJM-West trading hub (in dollars per MWh) and the day-ahead natural gas price at Transco Zone 6 Non-NY (in dollars per MMBtu) for a plant with a "heat rate"

---

1. For a detailed discussion of the operations of a very successful deregulated electricity market, see PJM (2006). Hsu (1997) discusses the spark spread, explaining how spark-spread options can be used to hedge price risk and to assist in valuing gas-fired power plants.

2. There is a separate electricity price for each hour of the day. We assume that the gas price, for which we have only one observation per day, is the same each hour.

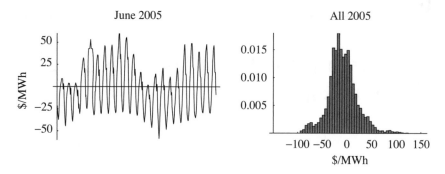

Figure 6.1. Spark spread for a simple-cycle gas-fired power plant

Note: The spark spread is constructed using the day-ahead electricity price at the PJM-West trading hub (in dollars per MWh) and the day-ahead natural gas price at Transco Zone 6 Non-NY (in dollars per MMBtu) for a plant with a heat rate of 7.5 MMBtu/MWh. The left-hand graph shows the spread during all weekdays in June 2005, while the right-hand graph shows the density function for all weekdays in the entire year.

of 7.5 MMBtu/MWh.[3] The right-hand graph plots the density function for all weekdays during the entire year.

The graphs show that, while the spark spread is often negative, it regularly takes positive values for short periods of time (which correspond to the peak load periods each weekday). The average spark spread for this plant is −8.59 dollars per MWh. If the plant had to operate at all times then it could not possibly make money. For example, a representative 100 MW plant that operated continuously during 2005 would have incurred fuel costs that exceeded its electricity revenue by more than $5 million. Allowing for non-fuel costs would make the plant's profitability even worse.

However, because it ignores the real options available to the plant's owner, the average spark spread does not reflect a plant's true profitability. In particular, SCGT plants can start up and reach full load in 10–20 minutes, allowing them to generate only when the spark spread is high. For this reason they are commonly referred to as "peaker plants". When we restrict the sample to observations when the spark spread is positive, the average spark spread for an SCGT plant becomes $21.36/MWh. If a 100 MW plant operated only during periods when the spark spread is positive then its electricity revenue would exceed its fuel costs by more than $4 million, rather than the $5 million shortfall calculated above. Of course, even simple-cycle plants face some restrictions with regard to their operating flexibility, so these figures exaggerate the benefits of production flexibility. Nevertheless, they give

---

3. This combination of prices is used by the Federal Energy Regulatory Commission (FERC) in its regular analysis of the PJM market.

an indication of the value that can be added to a powerplant by a flexible operating policy.[4]

An idealized SCGT plant can be turned on or off instantaneously. Such a facility should be used to generate electricity only when its owners receive more for the electricity output than they pay for fuel and other inputs. Situations such as this are especially easy to analyze because the actions taken at one date have no effect on the actions—neither the available choices nor the outcomes—at any future date. We introduce some examples in Section 6.1 and analyze one in particular—the effect of being able to costlessly suspend and resume production at any time—in Section 6.2. Because the structure of the various problems is so simple, this one example is sufficient for us acquire all the tools we need to analyze a quite general problem of this type. We outline the general technique for analyzing such problems in Section 6.3.

6.1 EXAMPLES OF OPTIONS THAT DO NOT AFFECT THE STATE OF A PROJECT

The defining characteristic of the situations analyzed in this chapter is that the actions taken by a decision maker at one date have no impact on the choices available at any future date. A straightforward example involves a firm operating a factory that can produce a given number of units of output each period at a given operating cost. The firm has the option to suspend production at any time; it can operate at any future date on the same terms, whether or not production occurs now. In practice there will be some frictions that make future choices dependent on current actions. For example, it may take a factory some time to return to full production following a period being idle, so that we cannot simply shut down production at one date and start it up again immediately afterwards. Nevertheless, the frictionless case is useful as a learning tool. Moreover, in some applications it may provide an adequate approximation to the more general (and more realistic) situation.[5]

We often confront situations in which a manager's actions affect short-term cash flows but do not have long-term effects.

Suspension of Production The manager of a factory is able to vary production in response to changes in demand conditions and the cost of inputs. This reduces the owners' downside risk because production can simply be shut down whenever the net revenue from producing is less than the net revenue from suspending production. The latter will not necessarily be zero. For example, it might be

---

4. We have used day-ahead gas and electricity prices here. If, instead, we used real-time prices (which are much more volatile than day-ahead prices), the benefits of operating flexibility would be even greater.

5. More realistic situations will be considered in subsequent chapters, especially Chapters 10 and 17, where we consider the production-suspension problem in detail.

necessary to pay staff to maintain physical equipment ready for production to resume.

Switching between Outputs A food processing plant is able to change from one product line to another. Switching products may occur in response to seasonal fluctuations in prices of the plant's inputs or outputs.

Access Agreements A firm is seeking the right to access the facilities of a separate firm at a fixed price, period-by-period. It will exercise this option whenever the net cash flow from doing so is positive and will otherwise not seek access. (See Problem 6.6 for an example.)

These situations share the same common structure: at each date the decision maker chooses from a menu of actions with the property that whatever action is taken at this date has no effect on the actions available (or on their payoffs) at all future dates; the only effect will be on the current cash flow.

6.2 SOLVING THE PRODUCTION-SUSPENSION PROBLEM

6.2.1 Setting Up the Production-suspension Problem

A firm is currently producing one unit of output per period at a constant cost of C per unit. Production must cease permanently after date 5. However, prior to that date the firm can open and close its factory as many times as it chooses. There is no production when the factory is closed. At any date, immediately before producing output the firm can close the factory if it is currently open—output and operating costs both fall to zero immediately. At any date, the firm can reopen the factory if it is currently closed—output and operating costs both return to their usual values immediately. Opening and closing the factory requires no additional expenditure.

We let $X(i, n)$ denote the output price at node (i, n) and suppose that the risk-adjusted growth factor for the output price equals the constant K. That is, the market value at node (i, n) of the right to a cash flow at date $n + 1$ that will equal $X(i, n + 1)$ if an up move occurs and $X(i + 1, n + 1)$ if a down move occurs equals $KX(i, n)/R_f$, where R_f denotes the return on one-period risk-free bonds. We assume that R_f is constant.

6.2.2 Valuation without the Suspension Option

We begin by considering the case when the factory must be operated continuously until date 5, when it shuts down permanently. The main reason for looking at this case is that it provides a benchmark we can use to show how much value the suspension option contributes to the factory. In this case we denote the market value of the factory at node (i, n) by $V'(i, n)$.

The simplest approach to valuing the factory in this case is to use the annuity formulae from Section 4.3.3. The factory produces one unit of output per period from dates 0 to 5 inclusive, generating a cash flow of $X(\cdot, n) - C$ at each node $(\cdot, n)$ for $n = 0, 1, \ldots, 5$. Because the two components—revenue and operating cost—have different risk characteristics, we separate out the revenue from the operating cost and value the two streams individually. The stream of operating costs is risk free, so that equation (4.13) implies its market value equals

$$C + \left(1 - \left(\frac{1}{R_f}\right)^5\right)\frac{C}{R_f - 1} = \left(1 - \left(\frac{1}{R_f}\right)^6\right)\frac{R_f C}{R_f - 1}.$$

The revenue stream is risky, so we use equation (4.15) to show that its current market value is

$$X(0,0) + \left(1 - \left(\frac{K}{R_f}\right)^5\right)\frac{KX(0,0)}{R_f - K} = \left(1 - \left(\frac{K}{R_f}\right)^6\right)\frac{R_f X(0,0)}{R_f - K}.$$

The firm is therefore worth

$$V'(0,0) = \left(1 - \left(\frac{K}{R_f}\right)^6\right)\frac{R_f X(0,0)}{R_f - K} - \left(1 - \left(\frac{1}{R_f}\right)^6\right)\frac{R_f C}{R_f - 1} \qquad (6.1)$$

at date 0 in the special case that its manager cannot suspend production.

Alternatively, we can value the factory using backward induction. This involves more calculations than the method we have just used, but it is useful later on when we compare the value of the factory with and without the suspension option. We begin by building a binomial tree for the state variable, starting at node $(0,0)$ and filling in the tree from left to right. The next step is to build a binomial tree for the factory's market value. From date 6 onwards the factory will be worthless, since no future production is possible. This gives us the terminal condition

$$V'(i,6) = 0, \qquad (6.2)$$

which holds for all $i = 0, 1, \ldots, 6$. At any node (i,n) prior to date 6, the factory produces one unit of output, generating a cash flow of $Y'(i,n) = X(i,n) - C$. One period later the factory will be worth $V'(i, n+1)$ if an up move occurs and $V'(i+1, n+1)$ if a down move occurs. The market value of the factory is therefore

$$V'(i,n) = \underbrace{X(i,n) - C}_{\text{cash flow at date } n} + \underbrace{\frac{\pi_u(i,n)V'(i, n+1) + \pi_d(i,n)V'(i+1, n+1)}{R_f}}_{\text{cash flows from date } n+1 \text{ onwards}},$$

$$\qquad (6.3)$$

which holds for all dates $n = 5, \ldots, 1, 0$. The first term in (6.3) gives the cash flow to be received at date n, while the second term gives the market value at date n of all cash flows to be received from date $n+1$ onwards. We use the terminal condition (6.2) to fill in the final column of the tree and fill the rest in, working from right to left, using the recursive equation (6.3). This procedure will be demonstrated in Section 6.2.4.

This analysis assumes that the factory must produce at all dates up to and including date 5. If the output price falls sufficiently in the future, the manager of the factory will want to suspend production and only resume production once the output price returns to a suitably high level. When such a suspension option is available to the manager, any evaluation of the factory should allow the manager to operate it in a way that reflects movements in the factory's output price. We do exactly this in the next section.

6.2.3 Valuation with the Suspension Option

In any situation where we allow the manager of a firm some degree of choice in the future we should start by building a decision tree for the problem being analyzed. The decision tree for the production-suspension problem is particularly simple. At date 0, the manager of the firm must do one of two things: suspend production or operate the factory at full capacity. These are represented by the actions labeled S ("suspend") and O ("operate") in the decision tree shown in Figure 6.2. Regardless of which action she takes at date 0, one period later she must once again choose between suspending production and producing at full capacity. This process continues until date 5, when the manager makes her final production decision. No more production is possible after this date, so that the decision tree ends at date 6, when the firm is worthless.

Now we have exhausted all possibilities, so that the decision tree, shown in Figure 6.2, is complete. The empty circles indicate the manager's decision nodes, while the filled circle indicates the sole terminal node.

The defining feature of the problems in this chapter is that the choices that the decision maker makes at date n have no effect on the market value of the firm from date $n + 1$ onwards. For instance, the same choices are available, and the same payoffs result from these choices, regardless of what the manager decided to do at date n. This is evident from Figure 6.2—all we need to know in order to estimate the factory's market value at date n is the number of down moves that have occurred since date 0. In particular, we do *not* need to know what actions the decision maker has taken at dates $0, 1, \ldots, n - 1$.[6] Therefore, we need to build

$$n = 0 \quad n = 1 \quad n = 2 \quad n = 3 \quad n = 4 \quad n = 5 \quad n = 6$$

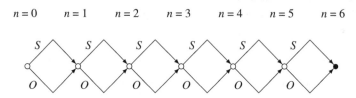

Figure 6.2. Decision tree for the production-suspension problem

---

6. However, this will not be the case if suspending production involves expenditure that cannot be recovered when production resumes—that is, when there is an element of irreversibility about the production-suspension decision. We analyze such a situation in Chapter 10.

one binomial tree for the state variable and one tree for the market value of the factory. We denote the market value of the factory at node (i, n) by $V(i, n)$.

From date 6 onwards the factory will be worthless, since no future production is possible. This gives us the terminal condition

$$V(i, 6) = 0, \tag{6.4}$$

which holds for all $i = 0, 1, \ldots, 6$.

At any time prior to date 6, the manager must either produce one unit of output or (perhaps temporarily) close the factory. If the manager decides to close the factory at node (i, n), then there is no immediate cash flow and after one period elapses the factory will be worth $V(i, n + 1)$ if an up move occurs and $V(i + 1, n + 1)$ if a down move occurs. The payoff from this action is therefore

$$\frac{\pi_u(i, n)V(i, n + 1) + \pi_d(i, n)V(i + 1, n + 1)}{R_f}.$$

Alternatively, if the manager decides to keep the factory open, then it generates an immediate cash flow of $X(i, n) - C$ and, as in the first case, after one period elapses the factory will be worth $V(i, n + 1)$ if an up move occurs and $V(i + 1, n + 1)$ if a down move occurs. The payoff from this action is

$$X(i, n) - C + \frac{\pi_u(i, n)V(i, n + 1) + \pi_d(i, n)V(i + 1, n + 1)}{R_f}.$$

The manager chooses whichever action has the greater payoff, implying the recursive equation

$$V(i,n) = \max \left\{ \frac{\pi_u(i,n)V(i,n+1) + \pi_d(i,n)V(i+1,n+1)}{R_f}, \right.$$
$$\left. X(i,n) - C + \frac{\pi_u(i,n)V(i,n+1) + \pi_d(i,n)V(i+1,n+1)}{R_f} \right\} \tag{6.5}$$

for dates $n = 5, \ldots, 1, 0$.

We use the terminal condition (6.4) to fill in the final column of the tree for the factory's market value and fill the rest in, working from right to left, using the recursive equation (6.5).

Before we demonstrate this procedure, it is worthwhile taking a closer look at (6.5). It says that the market value of the factory at node (i, n) is the greater of (i) the market value of the right to all the cash flows that it generates from date $n + 1$ onwards, and (ii) the sum of net revenue at date n and the market value of the right to all the cash flows that it generates from date $n + 1$ onwards. The only difference between these two payoffs is that the second one includes the net revenue from operating at date n whereas the first one does not.

Therefore, the recursive equation can be simplified to

$$
V(i, n) = \underbrace{\max\{0, X(i, n) - C\}}_{\text{cash flow at date } n} + \underbrace{\frac{\pi_u(i, n)V(i, n + 1) + \pi_d(i, n)V(i + 1, n + 1)}{R_f}}_{\text{cash flows from date } n + 1 \text{ onwards}}.
$$

(6.6)

If net revenue is positive then $V(i, n)$ equals the second term inside the brackets in (6.5); if it is negative then $V(i, n)$ equals the first term instead.

As equation (6.6) makes clear, we can analyze the suspension option by simply setting the cash flow at node (i, n) equal to $Y(i, n) = \max\{0, X(i, n) - C\}$. However, this reduction works only because the two actions available to the manager do not affect the future state of the project, so that the market value of the right to all the cash flows that the factory generates from date $n + 1$ onwards is the same regardless of which action is taken at date n. This is not the case for the other real options problems we look at in Part II—in those examples, the actions taken by the decision maker have potentially long-lasting effects on future cash flows and allowable actions.

6.2.4 A Numerical Example

We suppose that the current level of the output price is $X_0 = 10$ and that it is equally likely to grow by a factor of either $U = 1.2500$ or $D = 1/U = 0.8000$ each period. The output price at node (i, n), by which time i down moves and $n - i$ up moves will have occurred, is $X(i, n) = X_0 D^i U^{n-i}$. The resulting binomial tree for the output price is shown in Table 6.1. The risk-adjusted growth factor is $K = 0.9800$, so that equation (3.8) implies that the risk-neutral probability of an up move equals

$$
\pi_u = \frac{K - D}{U - D} = \frac{0.9800 - 0.8000}{1.2500 - 0.8000} = 0.4000
$$

at every node. The risk-neutral probability of a down move is therefore $\pi_d = 1 - \pi_u = 0.6000$. It costs $C = 8.5$ to produce each unit of output and the one-period risk-free interest rate equals 5%, so that $R_f = 1.05$.

Table 6.1. Output Price

$X(i, n)$	0	1	2	3	4	5	6
0	10.00	12.50	15.63	19.53	24.41	30.52	38.15
1		8.00	10.00	12.50	15.63	19.53	24.41
2			6.40	8.00	10.00	12.50	15.63
3				5.12	6.40	8.00	10.00
4					4.10	5.12	6.40
5						3.28	4.10
6							2.62

Table 6.2. Valuing the Factory Without the Suspension Option

$Y'(i, n)$	0	1	2	3	4	5	6
0	1.50	4.00	7.13	11.03	15.91	22.02	0.00
1		−0.50	1.50	4.00	7.13	11.03	0.00
2			−2.10	−0.50	1.50	4.00	0.00
3				−3.38	−2.10	−0.50	0.00
4					−4.40	−3.38	0.00
5						−5.22	0.00
6							0.00

$V'(i, n)$	0	1	2	3	4	5	6
0	5.55	16.06	24.88	30.47	30.61	22.02	0.00
1		−3.63	4.53	10.75	13.61	11.03	0.00
2			−8.50	−1.87	2.74	4.00	0.00
3				−9.95	−4.22	−0.50	0.00
4					−8.68	−3.38	0.00
5						−5.22	0.00
6							0.00

Step 1: Fill in final column using equation (6.2)

Step 2: Fill in remaining columns using equation (6.3)

Valuation of the factory when there is no suspension option is summarized in Table 6.2. The top panel describes the cash flow stream, while the bottom panel shows how the factory's market value evolves. Although it is not actually needed to value the factory, the top panel is included here because it will help us understand the source of the suspension option's value. The bottom panel, however, is crucial. We fill in the final column using the terminal condition (6.2) and then use the recursive equation (6.3) to fill in the remaining columns, working from right to left.

Table 6.3 repeats this information for the situation when the project does have the suspension option, with the shaded cells in the top panel showing nodes where the manager chooses to suspend production. Notice from the top panel that the only difference from Table 6.2 is to replace all negative cash flows with zero. This is consistent with the recursive equation when it is written in the simpler form (6.6). The bottom panel shows how the factory's market value evolves. We see that introducing the suspension option raises the market value from 5.55 to 9.54; the suspension option is worth 3.99 to the factory's owner, increasing its value by more than 70%. This increase in value comes solely from the option to avoid the negative cash flows that occur in the bottom part of the binomial tree in the top panel of Table 6.2.

6.2.5 Can we Use Static DCF Analysis to Examine this Problem?

Now that we have seen how to value the factory using the risk-neutral pricing formula—with and without the suspension option—we consider the extent to which it can be valued using static DCF analysis.

Table 6.3. Valuing the Factory With the Suspension Option

$Y(i, n)$	0	1	2	3	4	5	6
0	1.50	4.00	7.13	11.03	15.91	22.02	0.00
1		0.00	1.50	4.00	7.13	11.03	0.00
2			0.00	0.00	1.50	4.00	0.00
3				0.00	0.00	0.00	0.00
4					0.00	0.00	0.00
5						0.00	0.00
6							0.00

$V(i, n)$	0	1	2	3	4	5	6
0	9.54	17.12	24.97	30.47	30.61	22.02	0.00
1		2.66	6.32	10.91	13.61	11.03	0.00
2			0.44	1.15	3.02	4.00	0.00
3				0.00	0.00	0.00	0.00
4					0.00	0.00	0.00
5						0.00	0.00
6							0.00

We begin in the top panel of Table 6.4 by showing how static DCF analysis would value the factory when there is no suspension option. Since the factory's revenue and operating expenditure have different risk characteristics, it is easiest to value them separately. Revenue is initially 10.00, and is expected to grow by a factor of

$$1 + g = \frac{1}{2}U + \frac{1}{2}D = 0.5 \times 1.25 + 0.5 \times 0.8 = 1.025,$$

or 2.5%, per period. Thus, expected revenue at date n equals $(1 + g)^n X_0$. By date 5, expected revenue is 11.31. From equation (4.11), the RADR for revenue risk, ρ, satisfies

$$\frac{K}{R_f} = \frac{1 + g}{1 + \rho},$$

so that

$$\rho = \frac{(1 + g)R_f}{K} - 1 = \frac{1.025 \times 1.05}{0.98} - 1 = 0.0982,$$

or 9.82% per period. The present value of revenue to be received at date n is therefore equal to

$$\frac{(1 + g)^n X_0}{(1 + \rho)^n},$$

Table 6.4. Presenting the Results in a DCF-friendly Format

n	0	1	2	3	4	5
Without suspension option: DCF analysis						
Revenue						
$E[c/f]$	10.00	10.25	10.51	10.77	11.04	11.31
RADR	–	0.0982	0.0982	0.0982	0.0982	0.0982
PV	10.00	9.33	8.71	8.13	7.59	7.08
Total	50.85					
Operating expenditure						
$E[c/f]$	8.50	8.50	8.50	8.50	8.50	8.50
RADR	–	0.0500	0.0500	0.0500	0.0500	0.0500
PV	8.50	8.10	7.71	7.34	6.99	6.66
Total	45.30					
Difference	5.55					
Without suspension option: Real options analysis						
$E[c/f]$	1.50	1.75	2.01	2.27	2.54	2.81
RADR	–	0.4135	0.4155	0.4228	0.4369	0.4612
PV	1.50	1.24	1.00	0.79	0.60	0.42
Total	5.55					
With suspension option: Real options analysis						
$E[c/f]$	1.50	2.00	2.53	2.88	3.34	3.66
RADR	–	0.3125	0.2249	0.2150	0.1905	0.1857
PV	1.50	1.52	1.69	1.61	1.66	1.56
Total	9.54					

and is reported in the third row of the top panel. The present value of the entire revenue stream is 50.85. The stream of operating expenditure is valued in the same way, but because the factory's operating cost is constant, the expected growth rate is zero and the RADR is the risk-free interest rate of 5% per annum. The present value of the entire operating expenditure stream is 45.30, which implies the factory is worth $50.85 - 45.30 = 5.55$, as in Table 6.2. Clearly, when there is no suspension option static DCF analysis offers a straightforward way of valuing the factory.

The second panel of Table 6.4 summarizes the results of using the risk-neutral pricing formula and backward induction to value the factory when there is no suspension option. We are not using this panel to actually calculate the market value—all the calculations occur in Table 6.2. Rather, we are using it to present a different way of reporting the results of those calculations. This is why we show the rows in a different order from that in which they are constructed. The order we use is the natural one from the perspective of static DCF analysis: as in the top panel, we report expected cash flows, RADRs, and then present values.

We begin by filling in the first row, which shows the expected value of the cash flow at each date. It is constructed using the cash flows in the top panel of Table 6.2

and the *actual probabilities* of up and down moves.[7] For example, the expected
value of the cash flow generated at date 2 is

$$\theta_u^2 Y'(0, 2) + 2\theta_u \theta_d Y'(1, 2) + \theta_d^2 Y'(2, 2)$$

$$= 0.5000^2 \times 7.13 + 2 \times 0.5000 \times 0.5000 \times 1.50 + 0.5000^2 \times (-2.10)$$

$$= 2.01,$$

where θ_u and θ_d are the actual probabilities of up and down moves respectively.
The next step is to calculate the third row, which we do by applying the valuation
formula in equation (4.9) to each cash flow in turn.[8] For example, the market value
of the cash flow generated at date 2 is

$$\frac{1}{R_f^2} \left(\pi_u^2 Y'(0, 2) + 2\pi_u \pi_d Y'(1, 2) + \pi_d^2 Y'(2, 2) \right)$$

$$= \frac{1}{1.05^2} \left(0.4000^2 \times 7.13 + 2 \times 0.4000 \times 0.6000 \times 1.50 + 0.6000^2 \times (-2.10) \right)$$

$$= 1.00.$$

Finally, we construct the second row, which shows the RADRs implied by the
expected value and the market value of each cash flow. For example, the RADR
for the cash flow generated at date 2 is

$$\left(\frac{E[c/f]}{PV} \right)^{1/2} - 1 = \left(\frac{2.01}{1.00} \right)^{1/2} - 1 = 0.4155,$$

or 41.55% per period. Notice the dramatic effect of the factory's operating
leverage: it turns a revenue-RADR of 9.82% into a net-revenue-RADR of
41.55%.

Unlike their counterparts in the top panel of Table 6.4, the RADRs in the middle
panel are outputs of the risk-neutral pricing formula, not inputs into a valuation
procedure. However, if we could somehow calculate these RADRs independently
of the risk-neutral pricing formula, then we could use them to discount expected
revenue in the conventional way and get the correct market value for the stream of
net revenue. If, moreover, the RADRs took the same value for all future dates n,
then we could value the stream of net revenue using a constant RADR—that is,
static DCF valuation would be feasible. But these RADRs are not constant with
respect to the time until the cash flow is generated. This reflects the fact that
net revenue is a mix of cash flows—revenue and operating expenditure—with
different risk profiles and therefore different RADRs. The composition of this

---

7. Notice that in each case the expected value of net revenue is equal to the value implied by
   expected revenue and operating expenditure in the top panel of Table 6.4.

8. The market value of net revenue is equal to the value implied by the present values of revenue
   and operating expenditure in the top panel of Table 6.4.

mix varies with the date on which the cash flows are generated, and this variation is reflected in the different RADRs for net revenue. As a result of this variation, we cannot correctly value the entire net revenue stream by discounting each expected net revenue at a *common* RADR.

The only way that we can use static DCF techniques to value the factory in this example is to split net revenue into two separate components, each of which *does* have a constant RADR. Thus, we can apply the static DCF technique to the factory's revenue, apply it again to the factory's operating expenditure, and then calculate the difference between the two present values.

The third panel of Table 6.4 repeats the information contained in the second one, but for the situation where the factory has a suspension option. The procedure for calculating the three rows in this panel is exactly the same as for the second panel, except that we use the cash flows in the top panel of Table 6.3 in place of those in Table 6.2. The third panel of the table shows that net-revenue risk is also not constant over time in this case, so that we cannot use static DCF valuation techniques to value the stream of net revenue. If we want to value net revenue, we need to use the risk-neutral pricing formula. Moreover, as we show in Problem 6.1, in this case revenue and operating costs cannot be valued separately using static DCF analysis, because the RADRs for revenue and operating expenditure are not constant over the cash flow horizon. Thus, once we introduce the suspension option we have no choice but to use the risk-neutral pricing formula.

One useful by-product of reporting the information in the third panel of Table 6.4 is that it helps identify the contribution that the suspension option makes to the factory's value in a format that will be familiar to DCF-aware decision makers. Specifically, the suspension option makes the factory more valuable because it increases the expected value of future net revenue and reduces the risk (and hence the RADR) of net revenue. The expected net revenue is higher for each future cash flow than in the corresponding entry in the second panel of Table 6.4, reflecting the fact that the manager is able to replace the negative net revenues in the top panel of Table 6.2 with zero by suspending operations that period. Secondly, and more subtly, the RADR is lower for each period than in the second panel. When suspension is impossible, a shock to the output price feeds into net revenue one-for-one, for both positive and negative values of net revenue. In contrast, when suspension is possible output-price shocks have no effect on net revenue when the output price is less than the factory's operating cost: production is suspended, so that net revenue remains at zero except when the shock is positive and sufficiently large that the factory resumes production. Thus, net revenue's sensitivity to output-price risk is reduced, so that a lower RADR is appropriate.

Although we cannot correctly value the factory (with the suspension option) using static DCF analysis, presenting the results of our valuation using the format in the third panel of Table 6.4 might make it easier for decision makers unfamiliar with real options analysis to understand our results. The suspension option's contribution to the project's value can still be discussed at an intuitive level, but its quantitative effect on market value will be reported in a format that will be quite familiar to decision makers. They can concentrate on understanding the intuition and not have to worry about the intricacies of the risk-neutral pricing formula. However, the DCF-friendly format in the third panel of Table 6.4 is only a presentational tool: the valuation procedure will still require use of the risk-neutral pricing formula. From the perspective of the decision makers, the "black box" that is risk-neutral pricing is not eliminated. However, by thinking carefully about how we present the output of the black box, we can at least offer decision makers a greater understanding of what the output from the black box means.

6.3 SOLVING PROBLEMS INVOLVING OPTIONS THAT DO NOT AFFECT THE STATE OF A PROJECT

In this chapter we have looked at one particular example of a real option that affects short-term cash flows but has no effect on future cash flows or project values. The general real options problem of this type can be described as follows. There are M distinct actions that the manager can take at each node, which we label $m = 1, 2, \ldots, M$.[9] We denote the (cum dividend) market value of the project at node (i, n) by $V(i, n)$. For the particular problem we are studying we need to be able to identify the cash flow that will occur at node (i, n) if the manager of the project takes action m at that node, for each possible value of m. We denote this cash flow by $Y_m(i, n)$.

The first step in analyzing this problem is to build the decision tree and use it to identify the actions that can be taken at each node. Once that is complete, we construct the binomial trees for the state variable and the market value of the project. We start the construction of the latter by using the appropriate terminal condition to fill in the terminal nodes of the tree, before using backward induction to fill in the remaining entries.

Suppose we are currently at node (i, n). The manager must choose one of the actions $m = 1, 2, \ldots, M$. If action m is chosen then the project generates a cash flow of $Y_m(i, n)$ immediately and, after one period, will be worth $V(i, n + 1)$ if an up move occurs and $V(i + 1, n + 1)$ if a down move occurs. The payoff from this action is therefore[10]

$$Y_m(i, n) + \frac{\pi_u(i, n)V(i, n + 1) + \pi_d(i, n)V(i + 1, n + 1)}{R_f}.$$

---

9. In some cases the actions available to the manager will vary with the date. For example, the manager might have more actions to choose from at date 1 than at date 2. We ignore this possibility here only to keep the notation as simple as possible. The extension to date-dependent choice sets is straightforward.

10. Notice that the future market value of the project is independent of the action taken by the manager. That is, the payoff from taking action m' at node (i, n) is identical, except that the immediate cash flow term $Y_m(i, n)$ is replaced by $Y_{m'}(i, n)$.

Table 6.5. Fitting the Example into the General Approach

	Production-suspension Problem
State variable	Output price
Number of actions	$M = 2$
Allowable actions	$1 = \text{operate}$
	$2 = \text{suspend}$
Cash flows	$Y_1(i, n) = X(i, n) - C$
	$Y_2(i, n) = 0$

Since the manager can choose any action m, and since the objective is to maximize market value, the value of the project at node (i, n) is

$$V(i, n) = \max_{m=1,2,\dots,M} \left\{ Y_m(i, n) + \frac{\pi_u(i, n)V(i, n + 1) + \pi_d(i, n)V(i + 1, n + 1)}{R_f} \right\}.$$

As in Section 6.2.3, we can simplify this recursive equation to

$$V(i, n) = \max_{m=1,2,\dots,M} \{Y_m(i, n)\} + \frac{\pi_u(i, n)V(i, n + 1) + \pi_d(i, n)V(i + 1, n + 1)}{R_f}.$$

$$(6.7)$$

By the time we complete the backward induction procedure, we will have determined the current market value of the project together with the optimal action to take at each node of the binomial tree.

The solution process can be summarized as follows:

1. Build the decision tree and use it to identify the actions that can be taken at each node.
2. Build a tree for the state variable.
3. Build a tree for the market value of the project.

   (a) Start by using the terminal condition to fill in the final column of the tree.
   (b) Fill in the remaining nodes of the tree, working from right to left, using the recursive formula in equation (6.7).

Table 6.5 summarizes how the example considered in this chapter fits into this general scheme.

6.4 PROBLEMS

6.1. **(Demonstration)** This problem will demonstrate that when there is suspension flexibility, even decomposing net revenue into its two components does not allow us to use static DCF techniques.

    (a) Assuming that the factory follows the optimal production policy, what is its revenue at nodes $(0, 1)$, $(1, 1)$, $(0, 2)$, $(1, 2)$, and $(2, 2)$?

    (b) Calculate the expected value (using the actual probabilities) at date 0 of the date 1 revenue. Repeat these calculations for the date 2 revenue.

    (c) Calculate the market value at date 0 of the date 1 revenue. Repeat these calculations for the date 2 revenue.

    (d) Calculate the RADR for date 1 revenue. Repeat these calculations for the date 2 revenue.

    (e) Discuss the results.

6.2. **(Demonstration)** In this problem we reevaluate the numerical example in Section 6.2.4 for several different values of U and use the results to assess the role that output-price volatility plays in determining the market value of the factory. We consider the following values of U: 1.05, 1.10, 1.15, ..., 1.45, 1.50. In each case we set $D = 1/U$ and keep all other aspects of the model unchanged.

    (a) Calculate the values of g and ρ for each value of U.

    (b) Calculate the market value of the factory at date 0, with and without the suspension option, for each value of U.

    (c) Discuss the results.

6.3. **(Practice)** Suppose that the factory in Section 6.2.4 incurs expenditure of $C' = 2$ at each date when it does not produce output. All other aspects of the model are unchanged.

    (a) Derive the recursive equations needed to calculate the market value of the factory with the suspension option.

    (b) How much is the factory worth at date 0 with the suspension option? What is the value-maximizing production policy?

    (c) How do these results differ from the case where $C' = 0$, and why?

6.4. **(Practice)** Suppose that at each date the factory in Section 6.2.4 can suspend production or produce one unit of output at a cost of $C = 8.5$ or produce two units of output at a cost of $C' = 11$ per unit. All other aspects of the model are unchanged.

    (a) Derive the recursive equations needed to calculate the market value of the factory when it is able to produce zero, one, or two units of output at each date up to and including date 5.

    (b) How much is the factory worth at date 0? What is the value-maximizing production policy?

6.5. **(Practice)** Suppose that production of each unit of output in Section 6.2.4 takes one period. That is, if the manager decides to operate the firm at date n then the firm incurs an operating cost of C at date n and receives $X(\cdot, n + 1)$ at date $n + 1$; if she decides not to operate at date n then the firm incurs no operating costs at date n and produces no output at date $n + 1$. The latest that output can be produced is now date 6. All other aspects of the model are unchanged.

    (a) Derive the recursive equations needed to calculate the market value of the factory with and without the suspension option.

(b) How much is the factory worth at date 0 with and without the suspension option? What is the value-maximizing production policy?

6.6. **(Application: Regulation of telecommunications networks)** A firm (called the access-seeker) is allowed to access a telecommunications network (called the access-provider) for a fixed fee of L per period, at any time between dates 0 and 10 inclusive. The access-seeker needs to pay this fee only when it accesses the network. The access-provider paid $I = 45$ at date 0 to build the facilities the access-seeker will use; these facilities are worthless from date 11 onwards. If it accesses the network at node (i, n) then the access-seeker receives net revenue of $X(i, n) - L$, where $X(i, n)$ evolves according to $X(i, n) = X_0 D^i U^{n-i}$. We set $X_0 = 10$, $U = 1.1$, and $D = 1/U$. The risk-adjusted growth factor is $K = 0.99$ and the one-period return on risk-free bonds is $R_f = 1.04$.

(a) Find the level of L such that the access-provider recovers the cost of building the facilities, assuming that the access-seeker pays L at *all* dates from 0 to 10 inclusive.

(b) Calculate the market value of the access-seeker at date 0, together with its optimal access policy, in the special case where $L = 4$.

(c) Calculate the date 0 market value of the stream of fees received by the access-provider, assuming that the access-seeker follows the optimal access policy in the special case where $L = 4$.

(d) Find the level of L such that the access-provider recovers the cost of building the facilities, assuming that the access-seeker follows the optimal access policy. (Use the numerical search routine in the software being used to carry out the valuation.)

7

Simple Timing Options

In 1974, Sony demonstrated its Betamax videocassette recorder (VCR) to other electronics manufacturers, hoping that Betamax would be adopted as the industry standard. However, JVC subsequently developed its own VCR format, known as VHS, and thus began a classic format war. Sony's Betamax machines entered the market in 1975, with JVC's VHS machines entering in 1977.[1]

The left-hand graph in Figure 7.1 plots annual production of VCRs using Betamax (the solid curve) and VHS (the dashed curve), measured in millions of units. The right-hand graph plots cumulative production, again in millions of units. Despite the fact that JVC entered the market two years after Sony, production of VHS-format VCRs quickly overtook the Betamax format. Indeed, almost twice as many VHS machines as Betamax ones were produced in 1980 and the ratio of VHS production to Betamax production increased during the entire period. Betamax production peaked at six million units in 1984, a year in which more than 23 million VHS units were produced. One year later, Betamax production had fallen by 44%, while VHS production had grown by 75%.

It was clear from the early 1980s that Betamax was losing the format war. Faced with this situation, what should Sony have done? It could have admitted defeat and begun producing its own VCRs using the VHS format. This would have increased its share of the market for VCRs but would also have killed off any chance that Betamax would become the dominant format—potential future

---

1. See Cusumano et al. (1992) for a detailed account of the format war between Betamax and VHS.

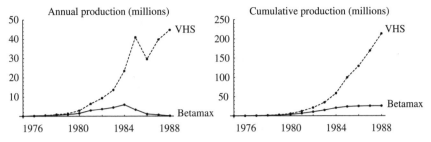

Figure 7.1. Market share of the VCR market

Note: Annual and cumulative production of VCRs using Betamax (solid curves) and VHS (dashed curves), as reported by Cusumano et al. (1992).

Betamax customers and suppliers would surely have adopted the new format along with Sony. Moreover, this decision would have been almost impossible to reverse. An alternative strategy would have been to wait, because by continuing to back its Betamax format Sony kept alive the possibility that the trend would be reversed and consumers would start switching away from VHS. If this happened, Betamax would become the dominant format and Sony would benefit accordingly; if it did not then Sony could still adopt VHS at a later date. The cost of keeping this possibility alive was the lost potential sales of VHS-format VCRs.

Sony decided to wait, taking until 1988 to exercise its timing option and market its own VHS machines. Although Sony continued producing VCRs using the Betamax format until 2002 (mainly for markets in Japan and parts of South America), its decision to adopt the VHS format in 1988 effectively ended the VCR format war.

Sony's problem in deciding when to concede defeat in the VCR format war is an example of a firm choosing when to exercise a timing option. In this chapter we feature three such situations: choosing an optimal time to invest in a new project; choosing an optimal time to abandon an existing one; and choosing an optimal strategy for undertaking R&D. We introduce these applications in Section 7.1 and analyze each of them in detail in Sections 7.2–7.4. By the time we have worked through these examples we will be in a strong position to analyze any problem involving a simple timing option. We outline the general technique for analyzing such a problem in Section 7.5.

7.1 EXAMPLES OF SIMPLE TIMING OPTIONS

7.1.1 The Optimal Time to Invest

The most commonly discussed example of a simple timing option is the option to invest in a new asset. It could be something as simple as an option to invest in a new factory or to adopt a new technology. It could be an option to develop a piece of land. It could be an option to expand an existing production process. But in each case there is an initial (usually relatively substantial) outflow of cash, followed by a much longer lasting inflow of cash. The decision maker hopes that the cash inflow will be sufficiently valuable to justify funding the initial cash outflow.

In the simple timing option considered in this chapter, the sole choice variable of the decision maker is the date at which the initial investment is made. Other considerations—such as the size of the factory, the type of new technology, or the extent of land development—are not considered here, although they will be in Chapter 9.

There are many examples of such investment timing options.

Expansion of Capacity A firm currently operates a factory and has the option to expand its capacity by installing additional machinery. Expansion requires the purchase and installation of the additional machinery, which will increase the firm's revenue (and probably its operating costs). When attention is restricted to the incremental cash flows—the one-off cost of expanding capacity, followed by the change in net revenue due to expansion—this is almost identical to the standard investment timing problem described above.

Land Development The owner of a piece of land has the right to develop the land, which expires at a fixed date in the future. The land may generate rental income prior to being developed, but will (hopefully) generate higher rental income once development is complete. The costs of developing the land might include planning and marketing costs as well as construction costs and other direct expenditure.

Resource Extraction A so-called proven undeveloped reserve of oil and gas requires drilling new wells, installing gas compression equipment, and similar investments before the oil and gas can be extracted.[2] The extraction process will be carried out by the owner of a lease to exploit the reserve, which typically expires after a finite period of time has elapsed. Once production begins, which may involve a lag after the decision is made, the owner of the lease receives a cash flow equal to the revenue from selling the extracted resource less the extraction costs.

Each of these cases is simplified to fit into our categorization of simple timing options. For example, some land development can be reversed (perhaps at considerable cost) and subsequent development of the land may be possible. Nevertheless, the descriptions given here contain the most important features of the various situations considered.[3]

---

2. The defining feature of a proven undeveloped reserve, as opposed to an unproven one, is that there is relatively little uncertainty about the quantity of oil and gas that can be extracted. The more difficult case where the quantity of the reserve is unknown is considered in Chapter 11, where we discuss learning options.

3. Some variations, such as construction lags, are easily handled within the framework described here, as we see later in this chapter.

7.1.2 The Optimal Time to Abandon

A closely related simple timing option is the option to abandon an existing project. Typically this project is currently generating a cash flow stream that can be terminated upon abandonment. The cost of abandoning the project, such as expenditure on cleaning up an industrial site, may be offset by the salvage value of any plant and machinery that can be recovered. If the salvage value of the plant is sufficiently high, then the initial cash flow may actually be a net inflow. Once abandonment is complete, the project's cash flow will be zero.

When only the incremental cash flows are considered, abandonment is similar to the standard investment option described in Section 7.1.1. Rather than spending funds building new factories at investment time, now the firm will be spending funds cleaning up the site, making severance payments to workers, and so on. Thus, as in the investment case, abandonment may require substantial cash outflows for a short period of time. The subsequent incremental cash flow from abandoning operations is the amount of the avoided ongoing losses that would have been generated had the firm continued to operate. If, as will often be the case, the net revenue from continuing to operate would have been negative, then this incremental cash flow from abandoning operations is in fact positive, as in the typical investment case.

Abandonment timing options can take many forms.

Contraction of Capacity A firm currently operates a factory and has the option to reduce its capacity by selling some machinery. Contraction involves the decommissioning and sale of the machinery, which will reduce both the firm's future revenue and its operating costs. When attention is restricted to the incremental cash flows—the one-off cost of reducing capacity, followed by the change in net revenue due to contraction—this is almost identical to the standard abandonment timing problem described above.

Shareholders' Default Option A firm has issued debt that obliges it to make a series of payments to bondholders. Shareholders have the option to default on these repayments, in which case the bondholders take ownership of the firm's assets. Prior to default, shareholders receive a flow of dividends (which may be negative if cash injections are used to keep the firm afloat); after default, shareholders' cash flow is zero.

Unlike the abandonment option described above, the firm's assets will often continue to be operated after default. However, the ownership of the assets passes from shareholders to bondholders. Default can be a strategic choice by shareholders—they are protected by limited liability—and this option contributes to the value of the firm's equity.

Lease Agreements with a Cancelation Clause A retailer wishes to lease rental space for ten years but requires the right to cancel the lease after five years. The lessee must make fixed rent payments for as long as it leases the retail space. If it exercises the cancelation option, the lessee will have to incur the costs associated with moving to new premises, where it will pay rent at a market-determined level for the second five-year period.

7.1.3 The Optimal Time to Act when Success is Uncertain

In the examples described above, once the decision maker decides to change the condition of the project, that change is certain to occur. However, there are many situations in which the decision maker cannot be certain that the change will actually occur. These are situations where there is a prominent role for project-specific risk, such as the technical risk that is associated with R&D projects.[4] Project-specific risk arises in numerous situations.

Research and Development (R&D) A firm can expend resources in attempting to develop a new product. If development is successful, the firm will be able to license the product for an amount that depends on market-wide conditions, so that the payoff from successful development is exposed to market risk. However, whether or not the development attempt succeeds involves project-specific risk.

Exploration for Natural Resources A firm has acquired the right to explore a specific location for oil and gas for a certain period. If exploration is successful the firm effectively receives a proven undeveloped reserve of the type described in Section 7.1.1, the market value of which will depend on market-wide factors such as the price of oil. However, provided the potential size of the reserve is small relative to the market as a whole, the success or failure of exploration will have a negligible effect on market prices. Thus, the exploration risk (only) can be regarded as being unique to this project.

Launching a Hostile Takeover Bid A firm incurs costs in identifying a suitable target for a hostile takeover bid and then in launching the bid. If it is successful then the firm gains ownership of the target at a cost determined by the terms of the bid itself. Whether the bid is successful or not is uncertain and may depend on factors that have little to do with market-wide conditions. However, the payoff of the bid, conditional on its succeeding, will generally depend on market-wide conditions.

7.1.4 The General Simple Timing Option Problem

The real options problems described above share a common underlying structure. In each case a project starts out in one state and—at a time determined by the decision maker—changes into another state. The change from the first state to the second is completely irreversible, and no further changes to the project are possible. Depending on the particular application, there may be restrictions on

---

4. Since such project-specific risk cannot possibly be spanned by the prices of securities currently being traded in financial markets, we need to modify the valuation framework that we introduced in Chapter 2. We show how this can be done in Section 7.4.

when the decision maker can attempt to change the state of the project. For example, the change may have to occur before a particular date; in some cases the decision maker may be allowed to leave the project in its initial state indefinitely. The project generates one cash flow stream as long as it is in the first state, and generates an alternative cash flow stream when it is in the second one. The decision maker receives (or, typically, incurs) a one-off cash flow when attempting to change the state of the project.

7.2 SOLVING THE INVESTMENT TIMING PROBLEM

7.2.1 Setting Up the Investment Timing Problem

An individual owns the right to invest in a project. Construction lasts one period and costs I. Construction costs are paid in advance and are sunk as soon as they are incurred—that is, investment is irreversible. The rights to the project are lost if construction is not completed on or before date 5. Equivalently, construction must begin on or before date 4 or the opportunity to invest will be lost altogether.

We define the state variable $X(i, n)$ to be the market value of the completed project at node (i, n). The risk-adjusted growth factor associated with X equals the constant K. This means that the market value at node (i, n) of the claim to a cash flow at date $n + 1$ that will equal $X(i, n + 1)$ if an up move occurs and $X(i + 1, n + 1)$ if a down move occurs is $KX(i, n)/R_f$, where R_f equals the return on one-period risk-free bonds.

7.2.2 Analyzing the Investment Timing Problem

The first step in analyzing this problem is to construct the decision tree. At date 0, the owner of the project rights must do one of two things: she can invest in the project or she can wait. These are represented by the actions labeled I and W in the decision tree shown in Figure 7.2. If she chooses to invest, then at date 1 she owns a completed project that, without loss of generality, we assume she sells immediately. Thus, if she chooses to invest at date 0 she will pay I at date 0, receive a lump-sum cash flow of $X(\cdot, 1)$ at date 1, and then the decision tree will terminate.

If, instead, the owner chooses to wait at date 0, she then moves to date 1 in the decision tree, where she must choose from the same two actions: she can invest

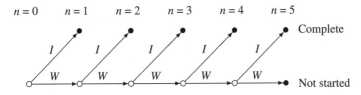

Figure 7.2. Decision tree for the investment timing problem when construction takes one period

in the project or she can wait. If she decides to invest (action I) then she will pay I at date 1, receive a lump-sum cash flow of $X(\cdot, 2)$ at date 2, and then the decision tree will terminate. If she decides to wait (action W) then she moves to date 2 in the decision tree and the situation repeats itself.

This process continues until date 5, when the investment option has expired. The owner cannot invest in the project. In fact, the investment option is now worthless, so that the payoff is zero.

This exhausts all possibilities, completing the decision tree shown in Figure 7.2. The empty circles indicate the owner's decision nodes, whereas the filled circles indicate terminal nodes. The next step is to use the decision tree to identify the market-value trees that need to be constructed and derive the equations that we use to calculate the entries in these trees.

At any point in time the project will be in one of two possible states— "not started" and "complete"—corresponding to before and after investment respectively. We let $V_b(i, n)$ denote the market value of the project rights at node (i, n) before investment begins and $V_a(i, n)$ denote their market value immediately after it is completed. Because we are assuming that the project will be sold as soon as construction is completed, we must have $V_a(i, n) = X(i, n)$. That is, immediately after construction is completed, the project rights are worth whatever the owner will receive from the imminent sale of the completed project.

This leaves us with the problem of calculating the market value, $V_b(i, n)$, of the project rights before investment occurs. Since the investment option expires at date 5, the project rights will be worthless at this date, leading to the terminal condition

$$V_b(i, 5) = 0, \qquad (7.1)$$

for $i = 0, 1, \ldots, 5$. The decision tree in Figure 7.2 shows that at all earlier dates $n \le 4$ the owner chooses between investing and waiting. If the owner invests at node (i, n), she pays I immediately and at date $n + 1$ she will (briefly) own a completed project worth $V_a(i, n + 1) = X(i, n + 1)$ if an up move occurs and $V_a(i + 1, n + 1) = X(i + 1, n + 1)$ if a down move occurs. In general we can write the market value of this cash flow stream as

$$-I + \frac{\pi_u(i, n)V_a(i, n + 1) + \pi_d(i, n)V_a(i + 1, n + 1)}{R_f}.$$

However, in this particular case we can use (4.10) to show that the revenue from selling the completed project at date $n + 1$ is worth

$$\frac{KX(i, n)}{R_f}$$

at date n, so that the payoff from investing equals

$$\text{payoff}_{\text{invest}}(i, n) = -I + \frac{KX(i, n)}{R_f}.$$

If the owner waits at node (i, n), she pays nothing immediately; at date $n + 1$ she will own an asset that is worth $V_b(i, n + 1)$ if an up move occurs and $V_b(i + 1, n + 1)$

if a down move occurs. This asset is worth

$$\frac{\pi_u(i, n)V_b(i, n+1) + \pi_d(i, n)V_b(i+1, n+1)}{R_f}$$

at date n, so that the payoff from waiting equals

$$\text{payoff}_{\text{wait}}(i, n) = \frac{\pi_u(i, n)V_b(i, n+1) + \pi_d(i, n)V_b(i+1, n+1)}{R_f}.$$

Since the owner seeks to maximize the market value of the project rights, the market value at node (i, n) must equal the maximum of the payoff from investing and the payoff from waiting. Thus,

$$V_b(i, n) = \max\left\{ -I + \frac{KX(i, n)}{R_f}, \frac{\pi_u(i, n)V_b(i, n+1) + \pi_d(i, n)V_b(i+1, n+1)}{R_f} \right\}$$

$$(7.2)$$

for all $n = 4, \ldots, 1, 0$. This recursive equation, together with the terminal condition (7.1), completely determines the market value of the project rights before investment, as well as the optimal investment policy.

The recursive equation reveals an important property of optimal investment in the presence of timing options. It is optimal to invest at date n if and only if the payoff from investing exceeds the payoff from waiting; that is, we require

$$-I + \frac{KX(i, n)}{R_f} = \text{payoff}_{\text{invest}}(i, n) > \text{payoff}_{\text{wait}}(i, n). \qquad (7.3)$$

In particular, it is not generally sufficient for the standard NPV (in this case, $KX(i, n)/R_f - I$) to be greater than zero. Rather, it must be greater than the market value of keeping the investment option alive, commonly known as the value of waiting.

The rule for optimal investment, (7.3), can be rewritten as

$$\frac{KX(i, n)}{R_f} > I + \text{payoff}_{\text{wait}}(i, n).$$

The left-hand side is the market value of the asset that will be created by the investment. The right-hand side can be interpreted as the opportunity cost of investing capital in the project. To see why, recall that the opportunity cost is the cost of passing up the best alternative choice—it equals the market value of the most valuable alternative project that the capital could have been used to finance. What is the opportunity cost of investing in this case? If the owner invests in the project now, then she cannot invest the funds spent on the project in financial securities. Nor can she invest in the project at a later, perhaps more profitable, date. These are the two opportunities she foregoes when she invests in the project. Their market values make up the two components of the opportunity cost of investing.

- The first component, I, is the market value of the funds invested in the project if they were instead invested in securities traded in (efficient) financial markets.

- The second component, payoff$_{wait}(i, n)$, is the market value of the option to delay investment in the project until some future date.

Investing in the project now destroys the option to wait and invest in the project at some future date when the investment climate might be more attractive. The firm must be compensated for the lost ability to invest the funds in traded securities and the loss of this option. The standard NPV calculation allows for the first component but not the second.

7.2.3 A Numerical Example

In this example we analyze the real option to invest in the project described above. Construction costs $I = 102$ and takes one period. If it is not completed on or before date 5 then the option is lost forever. The completed project would have market value $X_0 = 100$ if it were available for sale immediately. Each period this market value is equally likely to grow by a factor of $U = 1.2500$ or $D = 1/U = 0.8000$. Therefore the market value of the completed project at node (i, n), by which time there will have been i down moves and $n - i$ up moves, is $X(i, n) = X_0 D^i U^{n-i}$. The corresponding binomial tree is shown in the top panel of Table 7.1. The risk-adjusted growth factor is $K = 0.9000$, so that equation (3.8) implies that the risk-neutral probabilities of up and down moves are $\pi_u = 0.2222$ and $\pi_d = 0.7778$, respectively, throughout the tree. The one-period risk-free interest rate equals 5% per period, so that $R_f = 1.05$.

If the owner of the investment option exercises it at node (i, n), she pays the investment outlay of I immediately, and one period later receives a completed project worth either $1.2500X(i, n)$ (if an up move occurs) or $0.8000X(i, n)$

Table 7.1. Analysis of the Option to Invest in a Project when Construction Takes One Period

$X(i, n)$	0	1	2	3	4	5	
0	100.00	125.00	156.25	195.31	244.14	305.18	
1		80.00	100.00	125.00	156.25	195.31	Step 1: Construct binomial
2			64.00	80.00	100.00	125.00 ←	tree for the state variable
3				51.20	64.00	80.00	
4					40.96	51.20	
5						32.77	

$V_b(i, n)$	0	1	2	3	4	5	
0	1.88	7.82	31.93	65.41	107.26	0.00	Step 2: Fill in final column
1		0.30	1.43	6.76	31.93	0.00 ←	using equation (7.1)
2			0.00	0.00	0.00	0.00	
3				0.00	0.00	0.00	Step 3: Fill in remaining
4					0.00	0.00 ←	columns using equation (7.2)
5						0.00	

(if a down move occurs). Her investment payoff is therefore

$$\frac{KX(i, n)}{R_f} - I = \frac{0.9000X(i, n)}{1.05} - 102 = \frac{6}{7}X(i, n) - 102.$$

Note that the break-even value of $X(i, n)$ is therefore $(7/6) \times 102 = 119$. Thus, the standard NPV rule would say to invest now if and only if the value of an identical (completed) project exceeds 119. Since $X(0, 0) < 119$, the payoff from investing immediately is negative. Therefore, if investment could not be delayed the project rights would be worthless.

However, investment can be delayed, so that we need to use the approach in Section 7.2.2 to determine an optimal investment policy. The market value of the project rights in the case that construction has not yet begun is shown in the bottom panel of Table 7.1. The shaded cells indicate nodes of the binomial tree where it is optimal to begin construction of the project. It is not optimal to invest immediately. In fact, the earliest that investment will occur is at date $n = 2$, and then only if the first two moves are up.

Construction of the table begins by using the terminal condition (7.1) to fill in the column corresponding to date 5. The investment option is worthless because of our assumptions that construction takes one period and that construction must be completed on or before date 5.

We then move back to date 4 and use equation (7.2) with $n = 4$. At a typical node in this column, say $(i, 4)$, the payoff from immediate investment equals $\frac{6}{7}X(i, 4) - 102$, while the payoff from waiting is

$$\frac{\pi_u V_b(i, 5) + \pi_d V_b(i + 1, 5)}{R_f} = \frac{0.2222 \times 0 + 0.7778 \times 0}{1.05} = 0.$$

Therefore, the market value of the project rights equals $\frac{6}{7}X(i, 4) - 102$ whenever that number is positive, and is otherwise equal to zero. Consequently, if investment has not already begun, the owner should invest if and only if $X(i, 4)$ lies above the break-even threshold of 119. In other words, when investment cannot be delayed any longer the standard NPV rule is optimal.[5]

The construction is only slightly more complicated when we apply equation (7.2) to the column representing date 3, with the complication arising from the possibility that the payoff from waiting will no longer always be zero. For example, at node $(0, 3)$ the payoff from waiting equals

$$\frac{\pi_u V_b(0, 4) + \pi_d V_b(1, 4)}{R_f} = \frac{0.2222 \times 107.26 + 0.7778 \times 31.93}{1.05} = 46.35,$$

---

5. This is consistent with our discussion in Section 2.1.2, where we showed that using the standard NPV rule maximizes the market value of a firm's existing equity in the special case of a now-or-never investment opportunity.

while at node $(1, 3)$ it equals

$$\frac{\pi_u V_b(1, 4) + \pi_d V_b(2, 4)}{R_f} = \frac{0.2222 \times 31.93 + 0.7778 \times 0}{1.05} = 6.76.$$

In the first case, the investment payoff equals

$$-102.00 + \frac{6}{7} X(0, 3) = 65.41 > 46.35,$$

so that immediate investment is optimal; in the second case, the investment payoff equals

$$-102.00 + \frac{6}{7} X(1, 3) = 5.14 < 6.76,$$

so that waiting is optimal.

We continue like this, working backwards through the tree and applying equation (7.2) at each step. For example, at node $(0, 1)$ the payoff from waiting equals

$$\frac{\pi_u V_b(0, 2) + \pi_d V_b(1, 2)}{R_f} = \frac{0.2222 \times 31.93 + 0.7778 \times 1.43}{1.05} = 7.82,$$

while the investment payoff equals

$$-102.00 + \frac{6}{7} X(0, 1) = 5.14 < 7.82.$$

That is, it is not optimal to invest at node $(0, 1)$, even though the payoff from investing at that node is positive.

We finally calculate the market value of the project rights at node $(0, 0)$, which equals $V_b(0, 0) = 1.88$. Despite the fact that the standard NPV from investing immediately is negative, the market value is positive. This is due to the positive probability that the investment option will be exercised, for a positive payoff, at some time in the future. This possibility is not considered in standard NPV analysis.

An important step towards getting real options analysis accepted by decision makers is to facilitate the comparison between the results of real options analysis and those of techniques with which they may be more familiar. One way to do this is to show where standard NPV analysis fits within the real options framework. In the context of the situation considered in this section, standard NPV analysis assumes that investment is now-or-never. Specifically, construction must be completed by date 1 or the opportunity is lost forever. The fundamental difference between standard NPV analysis and real options analysis is that the latter relaxes this restrictive assumption and allows the decision maker to delay investment whenever this is in the best interests of the firm's owner.

One way to demonstrate this to managers is to calculate the market value of the project rights for a range of degrees of flexibility, with the standard NPV case

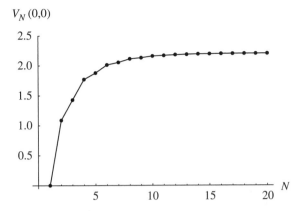

Figure 7.3. The effect of timing flexibility on the market value of the option to invest in a project when construction takes one period

lying at one extreme. This is demonstrated in Figure 7.3, which plots the current market value of the project rights, denoted $V_N(0, 0)$, when construction must be completed by date N or the investment opportunity is lost forever.[6] Standard NPV analysis corresponds to the first point, where $N = 1$. Relaxing the standard NPV constraint by one period raises the market value of the project rights by 1.09 because, as can be seen in Table 7.1, the market value of the completed project climbs above the break-even threshold if an up move occurs; thus, allowing investment to be delayed until date 1 means that profitable investment can take place if an up move occurs. Relaxing the constraint further leads to additional increases in value, although beyond eight periods the increases are relatively minor.

7.2.4 Asymmetric Risk and the Value of Waiting

As well as correctly valuing the project rights, real options analysis has identified the optimal investment policy. Most importantly, it has incorporated the value of waiting into the investment decision at every node of the tree. It is not optimal to invest as soon as the standard NPV is positive. Instead, as discussed earlier, the standard NPV from investing must exceed the value of keeping the investment option alive for future exercise.

An important source of the value of waiting is an asymmetry between the upside and downside risks faced by the owner. For example, consider the situation at node $(0, 1)$, where it is optimal to wait and, after one period, invest if the next move is up and continue to wait if the next move is down. If the owner invested immediately,

---

6. Only the detailed calculations for the case $N = 5$ have been included in this section. However, the other cases follow exactly the same procedure, with the exception that the terminal condition (7.1) is now $V_N(i, N) = 0$ for the appropriate value of N.

instead of waiting, her payoff would be

$$-I + \frac{KX(0, 1)}{R_f} = -102.00 + \frac{0.9000 \times 125.00}{1.05} = 5.14.$$

However, rather than invest immediately and receive a payoff of 5.14, the owner waits. If the next move is up, she will invest at date 2 and receive a payoff of

$$-I + \frac{KX(0, 2)}{R_f} = -102.00 + \frac{0.9000 \times 156.25}{1.05} = 31.93,$$

but if the next move is down she will wait again and the project rights will be worth $V_b(1, 2) = 1.43$. That is, by waiting at node $(0, 1)$ (rather than investing immediately) she receives a payoff that is $31.93 - 5.14 = 26.79$ higher if an up move occurs and is just $5.14 - 1.43 = 3.71$ lower if a down move occurs. It is this asymmetry that gives the owner the incentive to wait at node $(0, 1)$.

The source of this asymmetry is the owner's ability to respond to new information as it becomes available. This allows her to mitigate the effects of bad news.[7] For instance, if at node $(0, 1)$ the owner had to commit to investing at date 2, the payoff after an up move would continue to be 31.93 whereas the payoff from a down move would become

$$-I + \frac{KX(1, 2)}{R_f} = -102.00 + \frac{0.9000 \times 100.00}{1.05} = -16.29.$$

With this arrangement, by waiting at node $(0, 1)$ (rather than investing immediately) the owner receives a payoff that is $31.93 - 5.14 = 26.79$ higher if an up move occurs and is $5.14 - (-16.29) = 21.43$ lower if a down move occurs. The asymmetry has largely disappeared and she now faces substantial downside risk. Indeed, under this scenario the payoff from waiting would be

$$\frac{\pi_u \times 31.93 + \pi_d(-16.29)}{R_f} = \frac{0.2222 \times 31.93 + 0.7778 \times (-16.29)}{1.05} = -5.31,$$

so that the owner would be better off investing at node $(0, 1)$. The option to base her date 2 investment decision on all information available at that time reduces the downside risk from 21.43 to 3.71, increasing the value of waiting by enough for delay to be optimal.

In summary, by waiting at node $(0, 1)$ the owner retains the ability to benefit from good news and acquires the ability to mitigate the effects of bad news. If the project underlying the investment rights increases in value, she can still invest in the future—the only cost is that receipt of the investment payoff is delayed. If the project falls in value, she can insulate herself from the consequences by simply not investing. It is this asymmetry that makes waiting valuable.

---

7. In some situations, waiting gives decision makers the ability to accentuate the effects of good news. This also introduces an asymmetry between upside and downside risk that contributes to the value of waiting.

7.2.5 Extension: Construction Takes Multiple Periods

One simplifying assumption we made when setting up the model in this section was to suppose that construction of the project takes one period. In practice, many of the investment projects for which real options analysis is used will have lengthy construction schedules. Moreover, the accuracy of real options analysis is greatest when the length of time represented by each period is small. Thus, even for relatively straightforward projects construction may last for more than one of the periods used to construct the binomial trees. In this section we describe how to modify the model above by supposing that construction takes more than one period to complete.

Suppose, for example, that construction of the project takes two periods. We assume that the firm incurs a cost of J_1 as soon as it begins construction, that it incurs an additional cost of J_2 one period later, and that there is no possibility of abandonment before the project is completed.[8] That is, once the owner starts to invest there is no pulling out. We continue to suppose that construction must be completed by date 5 or the investment opportunity is lost (so that now the first stage must be undertaken no later than date 3). As before, investment is irreversible.

The modified decision tree is shown in Figure 7.4. The only substantive change in the tree's structure occurs at date 4, where (due to the longer construction time) the owner now has no choice but to wait. As a result of this change in structure, we have the recursive equation

$$V_b(i, 4) = \frac{\pi_u(i, 4)V_b(i, 5) + \pi_d(i, 4)V_b(i, +1, 5)}{R_f}$$

at date 4. At each earlier date, the decision maker must still choose between investing (action I) and waiting (action W); the only difference is that it takes two periods rather than one for the project to be completed. All that is left to do in order to correctly value the project rights for the situation summarized in Figure 7.4 is to derive the recursive equation for $V_b(i, n)$ at these earlier dates.

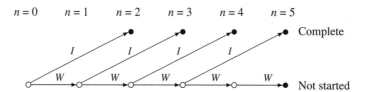

Figure 7.4. Decision tree for the investment timing problem when construction takes two periods

---

8. Inclusion of a mid-construction abandonment (or delay) option takes us into the realm of compound timing options. These are considered in Chapter 8, where a modified version of the investment timing problem treated here is one of the examples we discuss in detail.

If the owner invests at node (i, n) then there will be cash flows of $-J_1$ at date n and $-J_2$ at date $n + 1$, followed by the sale of the completed project at date $n + 2$. The investment payoff therefore equals

$$-J_1 - \frac{J_2}{R_f} + \left(\frac{K}{R_f}\right)^2 X(i, n),$$

where we have used (4.10) to calculate how much the proceeds from selling the completed project at date $n + 2$ are worth at date n.[9,10] The recursive formula for the market value of the project rights is therefore

$$V_b(i, n) = \max\left\{-J_1 - \frac{J_2}{R_f} + \left(\frac{K}{R_f}\right)^2 X(i, n),\right.$$

$$\left.\frac{\pi_u(i, n)V_b(i, n + 1) + \pi_d(i, n)V_b(i + 1, n + 1)}{R_f}\right\}$$

for all $n = 3, 2, 1, 0$. When combined with the new terminal conditions, this equation completely determines the market value of the project rights and the optimal investment policy.

Table 7.2 shows the results of applying this procedure to the investment timing problem analyzed in Section 7.2.3, modified such that construction lasts two periods and involves expenditure of $J_1 = 6$ and $J_2 = 84$. The total construction cost is lower than in the first case (90, compared with 102 in the earlier example) and is even lower when expressed in present value terms ($6 + 84/1.05 = 86$ compared with 102), which increases the market value of the project rights. However, offsetting this is the fact that, since construction takes twice as long, receipt of the revenue from selling the completed project is delayed one period. The table shows that the market value of the project rights in the case that construction has not yet begun is initially equal to $V_b(0, 0) = 1.68$, lower than in Section 7.2.3. Thus, in this example the delay in selling the completed project dominates the gain in value due to the lower construction costs.

The shaded cells in Table 7.2 indicate the nodes of the binomial tree where it is optimal to begin construction of the project. Construction will only occur if at least two of the first three moves are up. In contrast, in the one-period case in Table 7.1,

---

9. The investment payoff function makes it clear that all we need to know about J_1 and J_2 is their present value, $J_1 + J_2/R_f$. Different combinations with the same present value would lead to the same optimal investment policy and the same market value for the project rights. However, we will see in Section 8.2.4 that the expenditure profile can be crucial when the firm has a mid-construction abandonment (or delay) option.

10. If K is not constant throughout the tree then we cannot use (4.10) to calculate the investment payoff. Instead, we must value the project rights separately for the cases when investment is half-complete and when it has not begun. This is similar to the approach we adopt in Chapter 8 and is the one we use in Chapter 17.

Table 7.2. Analysis of the Option to Invest in a Project
when Construction Takes Two Periods

$V_b(i, n)$	0	1	2	3	4	5
0	1.68	7.01	28.80	57.49	0.00	0.00
1		0.26	1.24	5.84	0.00	0.00
2			0.00	0.00	0.00	0.00
3				0.00	0.00	0.00
4					0.00	0.00
5						0.00

an initial down move had to be followed by three up moves for construction to
occur. The longer construction time and lower cost mean that only two further up
moves, not three, are required to trigger investment.

7.3 SOLVING THE ABANDONMENT TIMING PROBLEM

7.3.1 Setting Up the Abandonment Timing Problem

A firm is currently operating a production process that produces one unit of output
each period. Production is instantaneous and costs C per unit of output. The firm
has the option to pay clean-up costs of S and permanently shut down the production
process at any time up to and including date 4. If the firm has not shut down by
then, it must continue to operate indefinitely.

The state variable $X(i, n)$ is the price of one unit of the project's output at node
(i, n). The associated risk-adjusted growth factor equals the constant K and the
return on one-period risk-free bonds equals the constant R_f.

7.3.2 Valuing the Project when Production Cannot be Abandoned

In this section we ignore the abandonment option and value the project as though
it will operate indefinitely. This will subsequently allow us to isolate the value
of the abandonment option to the firm. If abandonment is not possible, then
the firm's owners receive a perpetual cash flow that equals $X(\cdot, n) - C$ at date
n for each $n \geq 0$. The simplest way to value the project in this situation is to
use the portfolio approach of Section 4.3 and value the revenue and operating
costs separately. From (4.14), the market value of the operating cost stream
equals

$$C + \frac{C}{R_f - 1} = \frac{R_f C}{R_f - 1},$$

where the first term on the left-hand side equals the operating cost at date 0 and
the second term on the left-hand side equals the market value of all subsequent
operating costs. Our assumption that the risk-adjusted growth factor is constant
throughout the tree allows us to use (4.16) to show that the revenue stream is

currently worth

$$X(0, 0) + \frac{KX(0, 0)}{R_f - K} = \frac{R_f X(0, 0)}{R_f - K}.$$

It follows that the project is worth

$$V'(0, 0) = \frac{R_f X(0, 0)}{R_f - K} - \frac{R_f C}{R_f - 1} \qquad (7.4)$$

when abandonment is impossible. Recalling our discussion in Section 4.3.3, we are effectively discounting expected future revenues using a risk-adjusted discount rate, while discounting the risk-free operating costs using the risk-free interest rate. This is exactly what we should be doing with a properly conducted static DCF analysis of the problem.

We will find it useful to know the market value of the project at any node (i, n). This is easily achieved, because all we have to do is replace the initial output price, $X(0, 0)$, in equation (7.4) with its level at node (i, n). That is, assuming that the project will operate indefinitely, its market value at node (i, n) equals

$$V'(i, n) = \frac{R_f X(i, n)}{R_f - K} - \frac{R_f C}{R_f - 1}. \qquad (7.5)$$

7.3.3 Valuing the Project when Production Can be Abandoned

Now we describe how real options analysis can be used to simultaneously value the firm and derive an optimal abandonment policy. The first step in this process is to construct the decision tree.

At date 0, the manager of the firm must either shut the project down or continue to operate it for at least one more period. These alternatives are represented by the actions labeled A (for "abandon") and O (for "operate") in the decision tree shown in Figure 7.5. If he chooses to shut the project down, the firm pays S at date 0 and the decision tree terminates. If, instead, the manager chooses to continue production at date 0, the project generates net revenue of $X(0, 0) - C$ at date 0, after which we move to date 1 in the decision tree.

The manager must then choose from the same two actions: shut the project down or continue to operate it. If he chooses to shut the project down (action A), the firm pays S at date 1 and the decision tree terminates. If he decides to continue production (action O), the project generates net revenue of $X(\cdot, 1) - C$

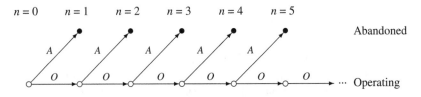

Figure 7.5. Decision tree for the abandonment timing problem

at date 1, after which we move to date 2 in the decision tree, where the situation repeats itself. This process continues until date 4, when the manager has his last opportunity to shut the project down. The firm either pays the clean-up cost of S at date 4 and the decision tree terminates, or the manager commits to continue production indefinitely, in which case the project generates a perpetual cash flow of $X(\cdot, n) - C$ for all $n \geq 4$.

Now we have exhausted all possibilities, so that the decision tree shown in Figure 7.5 is complete. At any point in time the project will be in one of two possible states—"operating" and "abandoned"—corresponding to before and after abandonment respectively. We let $V_b(i, n)$ denote the market value of the project at node (i, n) before abandonment and $V_a(i, n)$ denote its market value immediately after abandonment has been completed. Because abandonment is permanent, we must have $V_a(i, n) = 0$.

This leaves us with the problem of calculating the market value, $V_b(i, n)$, of the project before abandonment occurs. Since a project still operating at date 5 must operate indefinitely, we can actually use the valuation at that node from Section 7.3.2. This gives us the terminal condition

$$V_b(i, 5) = \frac{R_f X(i, 5)}{R_f - K} - \frac{R_f C}{R_f - 1},$$

which we need in order to begin the backward induction procedure. The decision tree in Figure 7.5 shows that at all earlier dates $n \leq 4$, the manager chooses between shutting down and waiting. If the manager decides to shut the project down, the firm pays S immediately and at date $n + 1$ the project will be worth $V_a(i, n + 1)$ if an up move occurs and $V_a(i + 1, n + 1)$ if a down move occurs. In general we can write the market value of this cash flow stream as

$$-S + \frac{\pi_u(i, n)V_a(i, n + 1) + \pi_d(i, n)V_a(i + 1, n + 1)}{R_f},$$

but for this particular problem the market value of the project after abandonment is zero, so that the abandonment payoff at node (i, n) equals $-S$. Similarly, the payoff from waiting at this node equals the sum of the net cash flow at that date, $X(i, n) - C$, and the market value of the firm's claim to the project's future cash flows,

$$\frac{\pi_u(i, n)V_b(i, n + 1) + \pi_d(i, n)V_b(i + 1, n + 1)}{R_f}.$$

The payoff from waiting is therefore

$$X(i, n) - C + \frac{\pi_u(i, n)V_b(i, n + 1) + \pi_d(i, n)V_b(i + 1, n + 1)}{R_f}.$$

Since the manager seeks to maximize the market value of the project, the market value at node (i, n) must equal

$$V_b(i,n) = \max\left\{ -S, X(i,n) - C + \frac{\pi_u(i,n)V_b(i,n+1) + \pi_d(i,n)V_b(i+1,n+1)}{R_f} \right\}$$

(7.6)

for all $n = 4, \ldots, 1, 0$. This recursive equation, together with the terminal condition above, completely determines the market value of the project, as well as the optimal abandonment policy.

7.3.4 A Numerical Example

In this section we suppose that the output price is currently $X_0 = 1.40$ and that it is equally likely to change by a factor of $U = 1.1000$ or $D = 1/U = 0.9091$ each period, so that the output price at node (i, n) is $X(i, n) = X_0 D^i U^{n-i}$. The resulting tree of output prices in shown in the top panel of Table 7.3. The risk-adjusted growth factor is $K = 0.9900$, so that equation (3.8) implies the risk-neutral probabilities of up and down moves are $\pi_u = 0.4238$ and $\pi_d = 0.5762$, respectively, throughout the tree. The return on one-period risk-free bonds is $R_f = 1.04$, the operating cost for the production process is $C = 1.18$ per unit, and the firm must pay clean-up costs of $S = 2$ as soon as it shuts the production process down.

We can use equation (7.5) to calculate the market value of the project at each node in the tree when abandonment is impossible. These market values are reported in the middle panel of Table 7.3, which shows that the current market value of the project is -1.56 when abandonment is impossible. Notice that there are six nodes between dates 0 and 4 where the market value of the project is less than -2 (which is the market value of the project rights if abandonment occurred at those nodes). However, if abandonment is possible it will not necessarily be the case that abandonment is optimal at each of these six nodes. To find the optimal abandonment policy, and correctly value the project when abandonment is possible, we need to use the approach described in Section 7.3.3.

The bottom panel of Table 7.3 shows how the market value of the project evolves when the firm's manager adopts a value-maximizing abandonment policy. The shaded cells correspond to the nodes where abandonment takes place. We see that the project will be abandoned

- at date 3 if the first three moves in the output price are down;
- at date 4 if two of the first three moves, and the fourth, are down.

The existence of the abandonment option has allowed the manager of the firm to put a floor under the project's market value equal to -2. He still continues to operate the project when the net revenue from doing so is negative (see node (2, 2)), but he never operates when doing so would drive the market value of the project below -2. As a result of following this policy, the manager is able to increase the project's current market value from -1.56 to 0.56. If we ignored the value added by the real option to abandon the project early, we would

Table 7.3. Analysis of the Option to Abandon Production

$X(i, n)$	0	1	2	3	4	5
0	1.40	1.54	1.69	1.86	2.05	2.25
1		1.27	1.40	1.54	1.69	1.86
2			1.16	1.27	1.40	1.54
3				1.05	1.16	1.27
4					0.96	1.05
5						0.87

$V'(i, n)$	0	1	2	3	4	5
0	−1.56	1.35	4.56	8.08	11.95	16.22
1		−4.21	−1.56	1.35	4.56	8.08
2			−6.61	−4.21	−1.56	1.35
3				−8.80	−6.61	−4.21
4					−10.79	−8.80
5						−12.60

$V_b(i, n)$	0	1	2	3	4	5
0	0.56	2.14	4.56	8.08	11.95	16.22
1		−0.97	−0.14	1.35	4.56	8.08
2			−1.80	−1.65	−1.56	1.35
3				−2.00	−2.00	−4.21
4					−2.00	−8.80
5						−12.60

attach a negative market value to a project that actually has a positive market value.

With a view toward explaining the difference between the two valuations to decision makers, Figure 7.6 plots the current market value of the project for a range of different levels of operating flexibility.[11] For the indicated value of N, the height of the curve gives the market value of the project at date 0 assuming that the manager has complete freedom to shut down production at any time up to and including date N.[12] Thus, the first point corresponds to the situation where abandonment occurs now or never. Allowing the manager to shut the project down

---

11. When we evaluate projects such as these in practice we generally fit many more time steps into a given time period, which has the effect of smoothing the occasional substantial jumps apparent in Figure 7.6.

12. Only the detailed calculations for the case $N = 4$ have been included in this section. However, the other cases follow exactly the same procedure, with the exception that the recursive equation (7.6) is used for all $n \leq N$, while equation (7.5) is used for $n = N + 1$.

$V_N\,(0,0)$

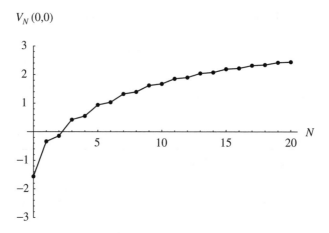

Figure 7.6. The effect of timing flexibility on the project's market value

at date 3 is sufficient for it to have a positive market value. Allowing even later abandonment—again, if the situation demands it—raises the market value further.

7.3.5 Extension: Abandonment Takes Multiple Periods

Shutting down the production process is instantaneous in the example analyzed above. However, in practice there can be lags in the shut-down process. For example, production might cease immediately but, because of the time taken to clean up the site, the clean-up costs might be incurred over the next k periods. If the clean-up costs each period are S_0, S_1, ..., S_k (which we assume are known with certainty), then the abandonment payoff equals

$$-S_0 - \frac{S_1}{R_f} - \cdots - \frac{S_k}{R_f^k}.$$

The recursive formula, equation (7.6), becomes

$$V_b(i, n) = \max\left\{-S_0 - \frac{S_1}{R_f} - \cdots - \frac{S_k}{R_f^k},\right.$$

$$\left. X(i, n) - C + \frac{\pi_u(i, n)V_b(i, n+1) + \pi_d(i, n)V_b(i+1, n+1)}{R_f}\right\}.$$

The case when the project continues to generate some output during the shut-down process is more complicated, but can be solved using the multi-period valuation approach described in Section 4.2.2. Suppose, for example, that it takes one period to shut the project down, that production continues at the normal rate during this period, and that a single clean-up cost of S is paid on completion of the shut-down process. If the shut-down process begins at node (i, n) then the firm's owner will receive a cash flow of $X(i, n) - C$ immediately, followed by an outflow of S after one period, so that the abandonment payoff equals

$$X(i, n) - C - \frac{S}{R_f}.$$

The recursive formula must be replaced by

$$V_b(i, n) = \max \left\{ X(i, n) - C - \frac{S}{R_f}, \right.$$

$$\left. X(i, n) - C + \frac{\pi_u(i, n)V_b(i, n+1) + \pi_d(i, n)V_b(i+1, n+1)}{R_f} \right\}.$$

Suppose, instead, that it takes two periods to shut the project down, that production continues at the normal rate during these two periods, and that a single clean-up cost of S is paid on completion of the shut-down process. If the shut-down process begins at node (i, n) then the firm's owner will receive a cash flow of $X(i, n) - C$ immediately, one of either $X(i, n+1) - C$ or $X(i+1, n+1) - C$ after one period (corresponding to up and down moves, respectively), followed by an outflow of S after one further period. The abandonment payoff therefore equals

$$X(i, n) - C + \frac{KX(i, n) - C}{R_f} - \frac{S}{R_f^2},$$

so that the recursive formula becomes

$$V_b(i, n) = \max \left\{ X(i, n) - C + \frac{KX(i, n) - C}{R_f} - \frac{S}{R_f^2}, \right.$$

$$\left. X(i, n) - C + \frac{\pi_u(i, n)V_b(i, n+1) + \pi_d(i, n)V_b(i+1, n+1)}{R_f} \right\}.$$

Longer shut-down processes can be treated in a similar way.

7.4 SOLVING THE R&D TIMING PROBLEM

7.4.1 Setting Up the R&D Timing Problem

An individual owns the right to attempt development of a project. Each development attempt costs I, lasts one period, and succeeds with probability q for some constant q between 0 and 1.[13] Development costs are paid in advance.

---

13. The assumption that q is constant can be relaxed. For example, we might allow development attempted at date n to succeed with probability q_n, where q_n grows over time to reflect technological progress. This could be analyzed using the techniques developed in this section. We could also allow for "learning by doing", meaning that q rises with each development attempt as the firm learns more about the development process. However, because the market value of the development rights depends on the number of development attempts in this case, we would need to use the techniques developed in Chapter 8 to deal with compound timing options.

The development rights to the project are lost if development is not completed on or before date 4.

We define the state variable $X(i, n)$ to be the market value of the developed project at node (i, n). As for the other examples in this chapter, the risk-adjusted growth factor associated with X equals the constant K and the return on one-period risk-free bonds equals the constant R_f.

In order to complete the description of the problem, we need to specify how investors are compensated for bearing the technical risk surrounding whether or not the attempted development is successful. The risk cannot be spanned by the prices of securities currently traded in financial markets, because the success or failure of each development attempt is specific to this project. Thus, the valuation framework motivated in Chapter 2 and implemented in Chapter 3 is not directly applicable. However, provided the project is small compared with the market as a whole it seems reasonable to assume that success or failure of this particular project will have a negligible effect on the prices of other securities, in which case it affects investors' consumption and investment opportunities only through its impact on their personal wealth. If investors are able to hold diversified portfolios, we can reasonably assume that the project-specific risk can be diversified away, in which case it will not attract any risk premium.[14] With these assumptions in place, all that we need to know about an asset in order to calculate its market value is the expected value of its cash flow at each node of the binomial tree.

7.4.2 Analyzing the R&D Timing Problem

The real options analysis of this problem simultaneously values the development rights and derives an optimal R&D policy. As always, the first step is to construct the decision tree.

At date 0, the owner of the development rights must either attempt to develop the project or wait. These are represented by the actions labeled A (for "attempt development") and W (for "wait") in the decision tree shown in Figure 7.7. If the owner chooses a development attempt, then at date 1 she owns a developed project with probability q and owns an undeveloped project with probability $1 - q$. As for the investment timing problem analyzed in Section 7.2, the easiest way to approach the problem is to imagine that the project is sold immediately after it is successfully developed. Thus, if the owner chooses to attempt development at date 0 then she will pay I at date 0 and either receive a lump-sum cash flow of $X(\cdot, 1)$ at date 1 (which occurs with probability q), after which the decision tree terminates, or continue to own the undeveloped project (which occurs with probability $1 - q$).

If the owner chooses to wait at date 0 or she makes an unsuccessful development attempt at date 0 then we move to date 1 in the decision tree where she must choose

---

14. The alternative is to assume that investors cannot diversify the project-specific risk away, in which case decision making involves maximizing the decision maker's expected utility function. However, this approach (which is described by Mello and Pyo (2002)) rests on its own set of assumptions, including the specific form of the utility function.

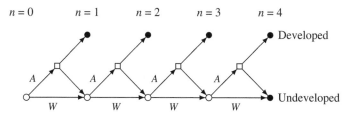

Figure 7.7. Decision tree for the R&D timing problem

from the same two actions: attempt to develop the project or wait. If she decides to attempt development (action A) then she will pay I at date 1 and either receive a lump-sum cash flow of $X(\cdot, 2)$ at date 2 (which occurs with probability q), after which the decision tree terminates, or continue to own the undeveloped project (which occurs with probability $1 - q$). If she decides to wait (action W) then we move to date 2 in the decision tree and the situation repeats itself.

This process continues until date 4, when the development option has expired and the development rights are worthless. Now we have exhausted all possibilities, so that the decision tree shown in Figure 7.7 is complete.

At any point in time the project will be in one of two possible states—"undeveloped" and "developed"—corresponding to before and after successful development respectively. We let $V_b(i, n)$ denote the market value of the development rights at node (i, n) before development and $V_a(i, n)$ denote their market value immediately after successful development. Because we are assuming that the project will be sold as soon as development is completed, we must have $V_a(i, n) = X(i, n)$.

This leaves us with the problem of calculating the market value, $V_b(i, n)$, of the development rights before development occurs. Since the development option expires at date 4, the development rights will be worthless at this date, leading to the terminal condition

$$V_b(i, 4) = 0.$$

The decision tree in Figure 7.7 shows that at all earlier dates $n \leq 3$, the owner chooses between attempting development and waiting. We consider the two actions separately.

If the owner does not attempt development then there is no immediate cash flow and, after one period elapses, the development rights will be worth $V_b(i, n + 1)$ if an up move occurs and $V_b(i + 1, n + 1)$ if a down move occurs. The payoff from waiting at this node is therefore equal to

$$\text{payoff}_{\text{wait}}(i, n) = \frac{\pi_u(i, n)V_b(i, n + 1) + \pi_d(i, n)V_b(i + 1, n + 1)}{R_f}.$$

Suppose, instead, that the owner attempts development, which involves an immediate cash outflow of I. If an up move occurs then one of two things will happen: either the trial succeeds and she (briefly) owns a completed project worth $V_a(i, n+1) = X(i, n+1)$, or it fails and the development rights are worth $V_b(i, n+1)$. We have assumed that the risk associated with success or failure is diversifiable, so that all we need to know about the market value of the development rights in the up state is its expected value. Since the development attempt succeeds with probability q, this expected value is

$$qX(i, n+1) + (1-q)V_b(i, n+1).$$

Similarly, if a down move occurs the expected market value of the development rights at date $n+1$ equals

$$qX(i+1, n+1) + (1-q)V_b(i+1, n+1).$$

The payoff from attempting development is therefore equal to

$$\text{payoff}_{\text{attempt}}(i, n) = -I + \frac{1}{R_f}\left(\pi_u(i, n)\left(qX(i, n+1) + (1-q)V_b(i, n+1)\right)\right.$$
$$\left. + \pi_d(i, n)\left(qX(i+1, n+1) + (1-q)V_b(i+1, n+1)\right)\right),$$

which we can rewrite as

$$\text{payoff}_{\text{attempt}}(i, n) = -I + q\frac{\pi_u(i, n)X(i, n+1) + \pi_d(i, n)X(i+1, n+1)}{R_f}$$
$$+ (1-q)\frac{\pi_u(i, n)V_b(i, n+1) + \pi_d(i, n)V_b(i+1, n+1)}{R_f}$$
$$= -I + q\frac{KX(i, n)}{R_f}$$
$$+ (1-q)\frac{\pi_u(i, n)V_b(i, n+1) + \pi_d(i, n)V_b(i+1, n+1)}{R_f}.$$

Since the owner seeks to maximize the market value of the development rights, the market value at node (i, n) must equal the maximum of the payoff from waiting and the payoff from attempting development; that is,

$$V_b(i, n) = \max\left\{\frac{\pi_u(i,n)V_b(i,n+1) + \pi_d(i,n)V_b(i+1,n+1)}{R_f},\right.$$
$$\left. -I + q\frac{KX(i,n)}{R_f} + (1-q)\frac{\pi_u(i,n)V_b(i,n+1) + \pi_d(i,n)V_b(i+1,n+1)}{R_f}\right\}$$

for all $n = 3, 2, 1, 0$. This recursive equation, together with the terminal condition above, completely determines the market value of the development rights as well as the optimal development policy.

7.4.3 A Numerical Example

In this example we analyze the real option to attempt development of the project described above. Each development attempt costs $I = 50$ and succeeds with probability $q = 0.5800$. If development is not completed on or before date 4 then the option is lost forever. The completed project would have market value $X_0 = 100$ if it were available for sale immediately. Each period this market value is equally likely to grow by a factor of $U = 1.2000$ or $D = 1/U = 0.8333$, so that the market value of the completed project at node (i, n) is $X(i, n) = X_0 D^i U^{n-i}$. The binomial tree for the state variable is shown in the top panel of Table 7.4. The risk-adjusted growth factor is $K = 0.9800$, so that equation (3.8) implies that the risk-neutral probabilities of up and down moves are $\pi_u = 0.4000$ and $\pi_d = 0.6000$, respectively, at every node. The one-period risk-free interest rate equals 5% per period, so that $R_f = 1.05$.

The market value of the development rights evolves as described in the bottom panel of Table 7.4, which is constructed by filling in the final column using the terminal condition and then working from right to left, using the recursive equation to complete each column in turn. The shaded cells correspond to the nodes where attempting development is optimal.

Consider, for example, the situation facing the owner of the development rights at node $(0, 0)$. Suppose she attempts to develop the project, paying the development cost of 50 immediately. If an up move occurs, then either the trial succeeds and she can sell the completed project for 120.00 or it fails and the development rights are worth 22.69. Since the development attempt succeeds with probability 0.5800, the expected value is

$$Y_u = qX(0, 1) + (1 - q)V_b(0, 1) = 0.5800 \times 120.00 + 0.4200 \times 22.69 = 79.13.$$

Table 7.4. Analysis of the Option to Conduct R&D

$X(i, n)$	0	1	2	3	4
0	100.00	120.00	144.00	172.80	207.36
1		83.33	100.00	120.00	144.00
2			69.44	83.33	100.00
3				57.87	69.44
4					48.23

$V_b(i, n)$	0	1	2	3	4
0	10.06	22.69	38.51	43.54	0.00
1		2.49	6.53	14.96	0.00
2			0.00	0.00	0.00
3				0.00	0.00
4					0.00

If a down move occurs, then either the trial succeeds and she can sell the completed project for 83.33 or it fails and the development rights are worth 2.49; the expected market value of the development rights will be

$$Y_d = qX(1, 1) + (1 - q)V_b(1, 1) = 0.5800 \times 83.33 + 0.4200 \times 2.49 = 49.38.$$

The payoff from a development attempt at node $(0, 0)$ is therefore

$$\text{payoff}_{\text{attempt}}(0, 0) = -I + \frac{\pi_u Y_u + \pi_d Y_d}{R_f}$$

$$= -50.00 + \frac{0.4000 \times 79.13 + 0.6000 \times 49.38}{1.05}$$

$$= 8.36.$$

If the owner does not attempt to develop the project at node $(0, 0)$, after one period elapses she will be left with project rights worth 22.69 if an up move occurs and 2.49 if a down move occurs, a payoff that is currently worth

$$\text{payoff}_{\text{wait}}(0, 0) = \frac{\pi_u V_b(0, 1) + \pi_d V_b(1, 1)}{R_f} = \frac{0.4000 \times 22.69 + 0.6000 \times 2.49}{1.05}$$

$$= 10.06.$$

Since the payoff from waiting exceeds the payoff from attempting development, the optimal policy is to not attempt development of the project at node $(0, 0)$, so that the development rights are currently worth

$$V_b(0, 0) = \max\{\text{payoff}_{\text{attempt}}(0, 0), \text{payoff}_{\text{wait}}(0, 0)\} = 10.06.$$

The shaded cells in the bottom panel of Table 7.4 show that it is optimal to attempt development of the project only if the market value of a developed project is sufficiently high. At date 0, a market value of $X_0 = 100$ is not high enough for development to be attempted, but if the first move is up then development should be attempted at date 1. If the first move is down, instead, then development may still be optimal, but only at date 2 and then only if the second move is up. Two interesting points emerge from consideration of the optimal development policy.

First, the development threshold depends on the length of time left before the development rights expire. For example, if the market value of a developed project is 100, then development is not optimal at date 0 (where $X(0, 0) = 100$) but it is optimal at date 2 (where $X(1, 2) = 100$). The reason for the different behavior is that the value of waiting is higher in the first case than in the second—the option has longer to run—and development is optimal only if the payoff from a development attempt exceeds the value of waiting. In the first case the payoff from attempting development is less than the relatively high value of waiting, while in the second case it is greater than the relatively low value of waiting.

Second, although the risk surrounding the outcome of a given development attempt is diversifiable, the timing of the attempts exposes the owner of the development rights to market risk. For example, when viewed from date 0, a successful development is much more likely to occur if the next move in the state variable is up than if it is down. Indeed, if the first move is down, development will not be attempted at date 1, so that there is no possibility of successful development at that date. In contrast, if the first move is up then development will be attempted and will be successful with probability 0.5800. Since up and down moves are equally likely, the unconditional probability of successful development at date 1 equals $0.5000 \times 0.5800 = 0.2900$. However, this unconditional probability tells only part of the story—it hides the fact that successful development is heavily skewed toward situations where the market value of a developed project is high.

7.5 SOLVING PROBLEMS INVOLVING SIMPLE TIMING OPTIONS

Now that we have gained experience in analyzing particular instances of simple timing options, we can formulate a procedure for analyzing the general problem of this type. Recall that in the general problem a project starts out in one state and—at a time determined by the manager—changes into another. The change is completely irreversible and no further changes to the project are possible. The project generates a cash flow stream prior to the change in state, which we suppose equals $Y(i, n)$ at node (i, n). Attempting to change the project's state at node (i, n) generates an immediate cash flow of $A(i, n)$. Each attempt is successful with probability q, and the market value of the project in its final state equals $B(i, n)$ at node (i, n). We denote the market value of the project before the change has occurred by $V(i, n)$.

We begin by building the decision tree and using it to identify the nodes where the manager is allowed to attempt to change the project's state. Once that is complete, we construct the binomial tree for the state variable. The next step is to build a binomial tree for $V(i, n)$, starting with the terminal condition that is appropriate for the specific valuation problem being analyzed, and then filling in the remainder of the tree using backward induction.

At some nodes (i, n), the manager may not be allowed to try and change the project's state: waiting is the only available action. The project generates a cash flow of $Y(i, n)$ and, after one period elapses, it will be worth $V(i, n + 1)$ if an up move occurs and $V(i + 1, n + 1)$ if a down move occurs. The market value of the project at such a node therefore equals

$$V(i, n) = Y(i, n) + \frac{\pi_u(i, n)V(i, n + 1) + \pi_d(i, n)V(i + 1, n + 1)}{R_f}. \tag{7.7}$$

However, if attempting to change the project's state is permitted, then the manager must do one of two things: attempt to change the state of the project or wait. The payoff from waiting is

$$Y(i, n) + \frac{\pi_u(i, n)V(i, n + 1) + \pi_d(i, n)V(i + 1, n + 1)}{R_f},$$

as in (7.7). Suppose the manager attempts to change the state of the project instead. If an up move occurs, then one of two things will happen: either the attempt succeeds, so that the project is worth $B(i, n + 1)$, or it fails and the project is worth $V(i, n+1)$. Provided that the risk associated with success or failure is diversifiable, all we need to know about the market value of the project in the up state is its expected value,

$$qB(i, n + 1) + (1 - q)V(i, n + 1).$$

Similarly, if a down move occurs, the expected market value of the project at date $n + 1$ equals

$$qB(i + 1, n + 1) + (1 - q)V(i + 1, n + 1).$$

Since there is an immediate cash flow of $A(i, n)$, the payoff from attempting to change the project's state equals

$$A(i, n) + \frac{1}{R_f} \left(\pi_u(i, n) \Big(qB(i, n + 1) + (1 - q)V(i, n + 1) \Big) \right.$$
$$\left. + \pi_d(i, n) \Big(qB(i + 1, n + 1) + (1 - q)V(i + 1, n + 1) \Big) \right).$$

The market value of the project therefore equals

$$V(i, n) = \max \left\{ Y(i, n) + \frac{\pi_u(i, n)V(i, n + 1) + \pi_d(i, n)V(i + 1, n + 1)}{R_f} , \right.$$
$$A(i, n) + \frac{1}{R_f} \left(\pi_u(i, n) \Big(qB(i, n + 1) + (1 - q)V(i, n + 1) \Big) \right.$$
$$\left. \left. + \pi_d(i, n) \Big(qB(i + 1, n + 1) + (1 - q)V(i + 1, n + 1) \Big) \right) \right\}.$$

$$(7.8)$$

By the time we have completed the backward induction procedure, we will have determined the current market value of the project, $V(0, 0)$, together with an optimal policy for exercising the simple timing option.

The solution process can be summarized as follows:

1. Build the decision tree and use it to identify the nodes where the manager is allowed to attempt to change the project's state.
2. Build a tree for the state variable.
3. Build a tree for the market value of the project in its initial state.

   (a) Start with the terminal condition.
   (b) Fill in the remainder of the tree, working from right to left, using the recursive formula in equations (7.7) and (7.8) as appropriate.

Table 7.5. Fitting the Examples into the General Approach

	Optimal Time to Invest	Optimal Time to Abandon	Optimal R&D
State variable	Market value of the completed project	Output price	Market value of the developed project
Cash flow before action	None	Net revenue	None
Cash flow at time of action	Investment expenditure	Clean-up costs	Development expenditure
Cash flow after action	Revenue from selling the completed project	None	Revenue from selling the developed project
Cash flow before action	$Y(i, n) = 0$	$Y(i, n) = X(i, n) - C$	$Y(i, n) = 0$
Cash flow at time of action	$A(i, n) = -I$	$A(i, n) = -S$	$A(i, n) = -I$
Probability of successfully changing state	$q = 1$	$q = 1$	$q =$ arbitrary
Cash flow after action	$B(i, n) = X(i, n)$	$B(i, n) = 0$	$B(i, n) = X(i, n)$
Terminal condition	$V(i, N) = 0$	$V(i, N) = \frac{R_f X(i,N)}{R_f - K} - \frac{R_f C}{R_f - 1}$	$V(i, N) = 0$

Table 7.5 summarizes how each of the three situations considered in this chapter fits into this general scheme.

7.6 PROBLEMS

7.1. **(Practice)** Reevaluate the numerical example in Section 7.2.3 for the following parameter values: $X_0 = 50$, $U = 1.15$, $D = 1/U$, $K = 0.96$, $R_f = 1.03$, $I = 50$. Suppose that the project rights are lost if construction is not completed on or before date 8. All other aspects of the problem are unchanged.

7.2. **(Demonstration)** Reevaluate the numerical example in Section 7.2.3 for the following values of U: 1.15, 1.20, 1.25, ... , 1.45, 1.50. In each case set $D = 1/U$. Investment costs $I = 80$, but all other aspects of the model are unchanged. Calculate the market value of the project rights at date 0 for each value of U, as well as the payoff from immediate investment and the optimal investment policy. Discuss the results.

7.3. **(Practice)** Suppose that the latest time construction can begin in Section 7.2.3 is date 12. All other aspects of the problem are unchanged.
   (a) Calculate the market value of the project rights, and identify an optimal investment policy.

(b) Repeat, assuming investment can occur only at date 0, 2, 4, 6, 8, 10, or 12.

(c) Repeat, assuming investment can occur only at date 0, 4, 8, or 12.

(d) Repeat, assuming investment can occur only at date 0 or 12.

(e) Discuss the results.

7.4. **(Application: Building a sports stadium)** A firm has won the contract to build a new sports stadium. Construction takes one period and must be completed on or before date 4. If construction begins at node (i, n) then the immediate lump-sum expenditure required to build the stadium is $X(i, n)$. The risk-adjusted growth factor equals the constant K and the return on one-period risk-free bonds is the constant R_f. The firm receives a payment of P as soon as the stadium is complete. The manager of the firm wishes to identify a construction policy that maximizes the market value of the construction rights.

(a) Draw the decision tree for this problem.

(b) Derive the terminal conditions and recursive equations needed to calculate the market value of the construction rights.

(c) How does this situation compare with the one in Section 7.2?

(d) Calculate the market value of the construction rights and an optimal construction policy for the following parameter values: $X_0 = 50$, $U = 1.25, D = 1/U, K = 0.99, R_f = 1.05, P = 70$.

(e) Discuss the form of the optimal construction policy. What is the intuitive reason for waiting? Does the answer depend on whether the construction firm is going to make a profit or a loss?

7.5. **(Practice)** Reevaluate the numerical example in Section 7.3.4 for the following parameter values: $X_0 = 2.95, U = 1.12, D = 1/U, K = 1.00$, $R_f = 1.04, C = 2.75, S = 5$. Suppose that the option to shut down is lost if it is not exercised on or before date 8. All other aspects of the problem are unchanged.

7.6. **(Practice)** Suppose that shutting down the production process in Section 7.3 must occur gradually. Specifically, if the manager shuts down production at date n then one unit of output is produced at date n (costing C), 0.3 units are produced at date $n + 1$ (costing $0.3C$), and no units are produced from date $n + 2$ onwards. There are no clean-up costs. The shut-down process cannot begin after date 8, but otherwise all other aspects of the situation are unchanged.

(a) Draw the decision tree for the problem facing the firm's manager.

(b) Derive the terminal conditions and recursive equations needed to calculate the market value of the firm.

(c) Calculate the market value of the firm and an optimal construction policy for the following parameter values: $X_0 = 2.95, U = 1.12$, $D = 1/U, K = 1.00, R_f = 1.04, C = 2.75$.

7.7. (**Discussion**) A firm produces a single type of good. Its price is forecast to be less in the future than what it costs the firm to produce each unit of output, yet the market value of the firm is currently positive. Explain what might be happening here, using the language of real options.

7.8. (**Application: Investment timing**) Suppose that an individual owns the right to invest in a project provided that construction is completed on or before date 10. Construction lasts one period and costs I. Construction costs are paid in advance and are sunk as soon as they are incurred. As soon as construction is completed, the project begins to generate a perpetual net cash flow that equals $X(i, n)$ at node (i, n). The risk-adjusted growth factor associated with X equals the constant K and the return on one-period risk-free bonds equals the constant R_f.

    (a) Draw the decision tree for this problem.

    (b) Derive the terminal condition and the recursive equation needed to calculate the market value of the project rights.

    (c) How does this situation compare with the one in Section 7.3?

    (d) How do the terminal condition and the recursive equation change if construction takes three periods (and cannot be interrupted)?

    (e) How does the recursive equation change if the completed project generates cash flow for only 15 periods?

    (f) How does the recursive equation change if the completed project generates cash flow only until date 15 (regardless of when construction occurs)?

7.9. (**Practice**) Reevaluate the numerical example in Section 7.4.3 for the following parameter values: $X_0 = 11$, $U = 1.1$, $D = 1/U$, $K = 0.97$, $R_f = 1.05$, $I = 8$, $q = 0.8$. Suppose that the development rights are lost if development is not completed on or before date 8. All other aspects of the problem are unchanged.

7.10. (**Practice**) Suppose that each development attempt in Section 7.4 has three possible outcomes: failure, partial success, complete success. The respective probabilities are $q_1 = 0.5$, $q_2 = 0.3$, $q_3 = 0.2$. Successful attempts are final—that is, if development is a partial success the owner cannot attempt development again to try for complete success. The market value of a developed project at node (i, n) is $X(i, n)$ for a partial success and $2X(i, n)$ for a complete success. All other aspects of the situation are unchanged.

    (a) Draw the decision tree for the problem facing the owner.

    (b) Derive the terminal conditions and recursive equations needed to calculate the market value of the development rights.

    (c) Calculate the market value of the development rights and an optimal construction policy for the following parameter values: $X_0 = 7$, $U = 1.15$, $D = 1/U$, $K = 0.95$, $R_f = 1.05$, $I = 4$.

7.11. (**Application: A bird in the hand…**) Suppose that each period that the individual in Section 7.2 does not begin construction there is a constant probability q that the option to invest in the project will be lost; this risk is project-specific. All other aspects of the model are unchanged. In particular, if construction is not completed on or before date 5 then the investment option is lost forever.

(a) Describe some reasons why the investment option might be lost if investment is delayed.

(b) Draw the decision tree for this problem.

(c) Derive the terminal condition and the recursive equation needed to calculate the market value of the project rights.

(d) How does this situation compare with the one in Section 7.4?

(e) Calculate the market value of the project rights and an optimal investment policy for the following values of q: $0.0, 0.1, \ldots, 0.9, 1.0$. Use the following parameter values: $X_0 = 60$, $U = 1.25$, $D = 1/U$, $K = 0.9$, $R_f = 1.05$, $I = 50$. Discuss the results.

8

Compound Timing Options

The deregulation of the US electricity sector at the end of the twentieth century created a new type of firm—the merchant generator. These firms, which did not have their own retail customers, owned plants that generated electricity for sale in wholesale markets. The growth of merchant generation is seen in Figure 8.1, which plots the total net summer capacity of utility-owned power plants (the light gray bars) and of plants owned by non-utilities (the dark gray bars). Approximately half of the growth in non-utility capacity is at the expense of utility-owned capacity, reflecting the latter's forced divestiture of generation in many states. However, the graph shows that there was also very substantial investment in new capacity by non-utilities.

Duke Energy is a North Carolina-based energy company that, amongst other things, operates an integrated electricity business in various regions in the US. As electricity markets deregulated, Duke Energy developed its own merchant generation unit.[1] As part of this expansion, Duke Energy began constructing a 1160 MW natural gas-fueled power plant at Moapa, 20 miles northeast of Las Vegas, in October 2001. The plant was to cost $600 million and to begin supplying electricity to the wholesale market by summer 2003. Duke Energy intended to export the plant's output to California when the price there was sufficiently high and otherwise sell it for consumption in Las Vegas. However, in August 2002 Duke Energy slowed construction at the Moapa site

---

1. Two articles in *Fortune* magazine, Schwartz (2002) and Stires (2004), describe Duke Energy's experiences with merchant generation.

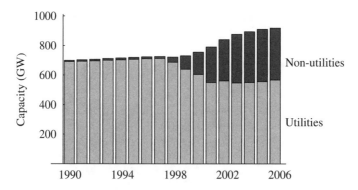

Figure 8.1. Existing net summer capacity

Note: Total net summer capacity of utility-owned power plants (light gray bars) and of plants owned by non-utilities (dark gray bars), as reported in various issues of US Department of Energy, Energy Information Administration, Electric Power Annual.

and, one month later, announced that it was ceasing construction altogether due to the declining regional wholesale electricity market. Construction of the facility was reported to be approximately 50% complete. The firm retained just enough staff to provide security and stop the equipment already installed from deteriorating.

Duke Energy announced the sale of the partially completed Moapa plant to Nevada Power Company for $182 million in June 2004. Construction was to resume immediately, and the purchaser estimated that completing the plant would cost approximately $376 million. The sale was completed in October 2004 and 18 months later, in April 2006, the facility (renamed the Chuck Lenzie Generating Station) became fully operational—approximately three years later than originally forecast.

The owners of the plant exercised several real options during its construction. First, in October 2001 they exercised the option to begin construction, in the process destroying the option to delay investment. However, the investment decision also created a real option, the option to suspend construction in the future. They subsequently exercised this option in September 2002, when they also destroyed the option to delay suspension any longer. By ensuring security and maintenance of the installed equipment, Duke Energy created the option to subsequently resume construction. Finally, in June 2004, this option was exercised. The suspension option that was created then was not exercised, so that the project was ultimately completed.

It would be optimal for Duke Energy to suspend construction only when the payoff from doing so (the avoided capital expenditure plus the value of the real option created by suspending investment) exceeded the value of the delay option destroyed by suspension. Depending on the relative values of the real options created and destroyed by suspension, the standard NPV from suspension could be positive or negative at the optimal suspension date. Likewise, the timing of the decision to resume construction depends crucially on the values of the options created and destroyed by resumption.

Real options analysis is ideally suited for analyzing investment decisions involving major capital projects such as power plant construction, which, even if it is not interrupted, will take several years to complete. It is essential if value-maximizing investment decisions are to be made. Moreover, when changes of ownership occur in the middle of construction, as they did with the Moapa project, real options analysis can give valuable guidance as to a suitable purchase price.

There are many problems, like the construction of a power plant, that involve a sequence of stages that must be completed, in order, before some overall goal is accomplished. We consider three examples in this chapter: choosing when to start (and deciding how quickly to finish) investment in a new project; choosing how quickly to extract copper from a mine; and choosing an optimal strategy for completing a multi-stage R&D program. We introduce these applications in Section 8.1 and analyze each of them in detail in Sections 8.2–8.4. The tools we acquire along the way will allow us to analyze quite general problems involving compound timing options. We outline the general technique for analyzing such problems in Section 8.5.

8.1 EXAMPLES OF COMPOUND TIMING OPTIONS

8.1.1 Sequential Investment

Problems involving compound timing options are frequently encountered when considering firms that are investing in new projects. Although we might think of a firm as making a single investment, in practice it will actually be making a sequence of decisions and incurring a series of cash outflows. At many points during the construction process the firm may have the ability to alter its plans—for example, to halt construction and only resume when market conditions improve. Such flexibility cannot be dealt with using the techniques in Chapter 7, which allow for only a single decision to be made.

Even if we might think of the project as involving a single construction decision, in order to improve the accuracy of our analysis we generally try to divide the lifetime of an option into a large number of small time steps. As a result, even relatively simple investment programs will be spread over several periods. The crucial aspect will be whether or not the decision maker can halt the investment program once it begins. If this is possible, then we need to analyze the situation using the compound option formulation developed in this chapter. If not, then we might be able to use the simpler approach described in Section 7.2.5.

There are many situations where a firm's investment program can best be thought of as involving several stages.

Sequential Investment A firm has the right to build a new factory on a particular site. Investment will involve completing a number of distinct stages in a specific order. Construction can be interrupted between each stage, but some expenditure may be required during periods when construction is idle. The factory will not be able to operate until all stages are completed.

Gradual Expansion of Capacity A firm is currently operating a production facility and has the option to gradually expand its capacity in the future. Like the sequential investment problem, this involves a series of investments. However, it differs in two important ways. First, the facility continues to operate during the expansion process, so that the firm does not need to wait until the end of the sequence of investments before it receives a payoff. Second, it is not necessary for the firm to complete all of the steps. For instance, the firm may choose to expand to a level somewhere less than the maximum level it might have achieved.

Investment, with the Option to Subsequently Abandon A firm has the right to invest in a new project and, once the project is complete, to subsequently abandon it. Thus, the sequence of investment steps does not need to finish with an operational facility as in the first two examples. Rather, the first few stages could see a new factory being built, while the last few stages of the "investment" process actually involve shutting the factory down, either when it reaches the end of its physical life or when market conditions make its continued operation uneconomic.

8.1.2 Resource Extraction

Much of the development of real options analysis occurred within the context of the natural resources sector. One of the main applications has been to the problem of optimally extracting a natural resource when prices are volatile and extraction is irreversible. A firm that owns the right to extract a resource over a specified period of time is faced with the problem of choosing the timing of the extraction to maximize the market value of the associated cash flows. The aim is to keep the resource in the ground while prices are low and extract it for sale when they are high. However, if (as is typical) the extraction rights have a finite life, delaying extraction early in the life of the lease will reduce flexibility later.

It is natural to describe the state of the project in this problem by the quantity of the resource remaining to be extracted. Each time extraction occurs the project state changes. The manager of the firm decides when extraction occurs, and thus determines how quickly the project moves through the various stages. Thus, this is a special case of the sequential investment problem described in Section 8.1.1. However, we discuss it here separately—and study it in detail in Section 8.3— because it is one of the most important uses of real options analysis.

8.1.3 Sequential Actions when Success is Uncertain

In all of the examples considered so far in this chapter, the decision maker has complete control over how rapidly the project moves through the series of steps. However, there are many circumstances where the decision maker can influence the timing, but not necessarily control it—such as when the decision maker can attempt to move from one step to the next but the success of the attempt is uncertain. In these situations there is a prominent role for project-specific risk, such as the technical risk that is an essential part of an R&D project.

Multi-stage R&D Programs A firm is attempting to develop a new product, which will require successful completion of a series of steps. Each step requires expenditure on R&D and is not guaranteed to be successful. The firm has the option to (permanently or temporarily) halt development, which it may exercise in circumstances where the demand for a successfully developed product would be relatively low. We discuss this problem in detail in Section 8.4.

Single-stage R&D with Learning A firm needs to complete a single stage of R&D, but many attempts may be needed before development is successful. However, each time the firm attempts to develop the project it learns more about what is needed for development to succeed. That is, the probability of success increases with each development attempt. In this case we can think of the project as moving through a series of steps, ceasing when either a development attempt succeeds or the development rights expire.

Construction Cost Uncertainty Investment programs often experience budget overruns. Even if they are completed under-budget, at the time construction begins there will often be considerable uncertainty about just how much expenditure will ultimately be required. A simple way of modeling this situation is to suppose that construction of the project requires successful completion of a number of steps in much the same way as a multi-stage R&D program.[2] We adopt this approach in Chapter 16 when we analyze the problem of when and how to develop a natural gas field.

8.1.4 The General Compound Timing Option Problem

All of these situations involve a project that starts out in one state and moves through a specified sequence of states. The order in which these changes occur is fixed, but the dates at which they occur are influenced by the decision maker. The change from the first state to the second is completely irreversible, and (if success is certain) occurs when the decision maker chooses. Likewise, the subsequent change from the second state to the third is completely irreversible, and occurs when the decision maker chooses. The project generates one cash flow stream as long as it is in the first state, another as long as it is in the second state, and so on. The project generates one-off cash flows each time the decision maker tries to change it from one state to the next.

---

2. However, in practice the manager of the project may learn information about the required expenditure gradually over time in a way that would make the techniques developed in Chapter 11 more suitable.

8.2 SOLVING THE SEQUENTIAL INVESTMENT PROBLEM

The situation we consider in this section is based on the investment timing problem analyzed in Section 7.2, especially the extension discussed in Section 7.2.5. However, whereas previously we required that the investment program had to be completed as soon as possible after it began, now we allow the decision maker to delay completion or even abandon the project altogether.

8.2.1 Setting Up the Sequential Investment Problem

An individual owns the right to invest in a project. Investment involves two stages that must be undertaken before construction is complete. At most one stage can be completed each period. The two stages cost J_1 and J_2 to complete. Construction costs are paid in advance and are sunk as soon as they are incurred—that is, each stage of investment is irreversible. The rights to the project are lost if construction is not completed on or before date 5, so that construction of the first stage must begin on or before date 3 or the opportunity to invest will be lost altogether.

As in Section 7.2, we define the state variable $X(i, n)$ to be the market value of the completed project at node (i, n). We suppose that the risk-adjusted growth factor associated with X equals the constant K. This means that the market value at node (i, n) of the right to a cash flow at date $n + 1$ that will equal $X(i, n + 1)$ if an up move occurs and $X(i + 1, n + 1)$ if a down move occurs is $KX(i, n)/R_f$, where the constant R_f is the return on one-period risk-free bonds.

8.2.2 Analyzing the Sequential Investment Problem

One of the issues we are interested in is how much value is added by the real options embedded in the project rights—that is, the options to delay starting and to delay completing construction. Therefore we start our analysis by calculating the market value of the project rights when these real options are not present. We subsequently compare this with the market value when they are present.

When the owner has no investment timing flexibility, she starts construction immediately and finishes it as soon as possible. In this case the owner of the firm pays J_1 at date 0, pays J_2 at date 1, and then receives a completed project at date 2 that is worth $X(i, 2)$, where i is the number of down moves that occur between dates 0 and 2. Because K is constant throughout the tree, we can use (4.10) to show that this cash flow stream is worth

$$-J_1 - \frac{J_2}{R_f} + \left(\frac{K}{R_f}\right)^2 X(0, 0)$$

at date 0. This is the market value of the investment opportunity for the case where construction is completed as quickly as possible.[3]

---

3. The slightly more complicated case, where the owner of the project rights can delay starting investment but must then complete construction as quickly as possible, was considered in

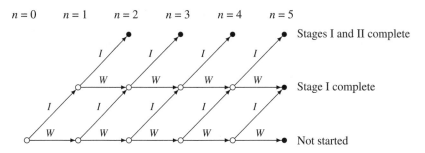

Figure 8.2. Decision tree for the sequential investment problem

We start our analysis of the situation with maximal flexibility by constructing the decision tree, and begin its construction by considering the owner's problem at date 0. Since both construction stages are still to be undertaken, the owner must either wait or undertake Stage I of the construction program, as shown in the decision tree drawn in Figure 8.2. If she waits, there is zero cash flow at date 0 and when date 1 arrives she will still not have begun construction. This action corresponds to the arrow labeled W (for "wait") in the decision tree. In contrast, if she builds Stage I there is cash flow of $-J_1$ at date 0 and after one period elapses she will have just one construction stage remaining. This action is represented by the arrow labeled I (for "invest") in the decision tree.

Thus, at date 1 the project will be in one of two states: either Stage I will be completed or it will not be. We need to consider each possibility separately. If Stage I has not been completed, then the situation is the same as at date 0: the owner must either wait or undertake Stage I. If Stage I has been completed, then she must either wait or undertake Stage II of the construction program. If she waits, there is zero cash flow at date 1 and after one period elapses she will still have completed just one construction stage. In contrast, if the owner undertakes Stage II she incurs capital expenditure of J_2 at date 1 and she will be able to sell the completed project at date 2.

From date 2 onwards the project will be in one of three states: neither stage will be completed, or just Stage I will be completed, or Stages I and II will be completed. Prior to date 5, the owner must either wait or undertake Stage I in the first case, while she must either wait or undertake Stage II in the second case; we do not need to consider the owner's actions in the third case since here the investment program is complete. From date 5 onwards she can do nothing because the investment rights have expired.

This completes the construction of the decision tree shown in Figure 8.2. The remaining steps are to identify the binomial trees that are needed and to complete

---

Section 7.2.5. Relative to that case, the key feature that we are adding in this chapter is the option to interrupt construction after it has begun.

their construction. At any point in time the project will be in one of three possible states. We let $V_m(i, n)$ denote the market value of the project rights at node (i, n) when there are m stages of the investment program remaining to be completed; we need to consider $m = 0, 1, 2$. Immediately after construction is completed, the project rights are worth whatever the owner will receive from the imminent sale of the completed project. Therefore $V_0(i, n) = X(i, n)$. As a result, we need to build only two market-value trees, one for the project rights in the "Stage I complete" state ($m = 1$), and another for the project rights in the "not started" state ($m = 2$).

Since the project rights are lost if investment is not completed on or before date 5, it follows that

$$V_1(i, 5) = V_2(i, 5) = 0 \qquad (8.1)$$

for all $i = 0, 1, \ldots, 5$. These are the terminal conditions that we use to begin filling in the binomial trees for V_1 and V_2.

Consistent with the notion of backward induction, we start at the end of the project investment process and work backwards in time. Thus we begin by analyzing the case when the owner has already completed Stage I of the investment program. Consider her situation at node (i, n). She must either wait or undertake Stage II of the construction program. If she waits, then there is zero cash flow now and after one period elapses the project will still have just Stage II remaining: if an up move occurs the project rights will be worth $V_1(i, n + 1)$, whereas if a down move occurs they will be worth $V_1(i + 1, n + 1)$. The payoff from waiting therefore equals

$$\frac{\pi_u(i, n)V_1(i, n + 1) + \pi_d(i, n)V_1(i + 1, n + 1)}{R_f}.$$

In contrast, if the owner undertakes Stage II immediately, then there is cash flow of $-J_2$ now and after one period elapses she will be able to sell the completed project: if an up move occurs she will be able to sell it for $V_0(i, n + 1) = X(i, n + 1)$, whereas if a down move occurs the sale price will be $V_0(i + 1, n + 1) = X(i + 1, n + 1)$. Using (4.10), the market value at node (i, n) of the sales revenue equals $KX(i, n)/R_f$, so that the payoff from undertaking Stage II equals

$$-J_2 + \frac{KX(i, n)}{R_f}.$$

The owner will choose the action that maximizes the market value of the project rights, which must therefore equal

$$V_1(i,n) = \max \left\{ \frac{\pi_u(i,n)V_1(i,n+1) + \pi_d(i,n)V_1(i+1,n+1)}{R_f}, -J_2 + \frac{KX(i,n)}{R_f} \right\}.$$

$$(8.2)$$

Now we turn to the remaining tree, for the case when the owner has not begun the first investment stage. Consider her situation at node (i, n). She must either wait or undertake Stage I of the construction program. If she waits, then there is zero cash flow now and after one period elapses she will still not have begun construction: if an up move occurs the project rights will be worth $V_2(i, n + 1)$, whereas if a down move occurs they will be worth $V_2(i + 1, n + 1)$. The corresponding payoff equals

$$\frac{\pi_u(i, n)V_2(i, n + 1) + \pi_d(i, n)V_2(i + 1, n + 1)}{R_f}.$$

In contrast, if the owner undertakes Stage I immediately, then there is cash flow of $-J_1$ now and after one period elapses the firm will have just one construction stage to go: if an up move occurs the project rights will be worth $V_1(i, n + 1)$, whereas if a down move occurs they will be worth $V_1(i + 1, n + 1)$. The payoff from undertaking Stage I is therefore

$$-J_1 + \frac{\pi_u(i, n)V_1(i, n + 1) + \pi_d(i, n)V_1(i + 1, n + 1)}{R_f}.$$

The owner will choose the action that maximizes the market value of the project rights, which are therefore worth

$$V_2(i, n) = \max \left\{ \frac{\pi_u(i, n)V_2(i, n + 1) + \pi_d(i, n)V_2(i + 1, n + 1)}{R_f}, \right.$$
$$\left. -J_1 + \frac{\pi_u(i, n)V_1(i, n + 1) + \pi_d(i, n)V_1(i + 1, n + 1)}{R_f} \right\}.$$

$$(8.3)$$

We now have all the information we need to calculate the market value of the project rights and determine an optimal investment policy. The following numerical example demonstrates the procedure.

8.2.3 A Numerical Example

We continue our analysis of the investment timing problem begun in Section 7.2. Recall that the investment option is lost forever if construction is not completed on or before date 5. We supposed that if the completed project were available for sale immediately it would have market value $X_0 = 100$ and that in each period this market value is equally likely to grow by a factor of either $U = 1.2500$ or $D = 1/U = 0.8000$. The resulting binomial tree for the market value of the completed project was shown in the top panel of Table 7.1 and it is repeated in the top panel of Table 8.1. The risk-adjusted growth factor is $K = 0.9000$, so that equation (3.8) implies that the risk-neutral probabilities of up and down moves are $\pi_u = 0.2222$ and $\pi_d = 0.7778$, respectively, throughout the tree. The one-period risk-free interest rate equals 5%, so that $R_f = 1.05$.

Construction takes two periods and, as in our earlier example, requires cash outlays of $J_1 = 6$ and $J_2 = 84$. We start by considering the two cases with restricted flexibility that we discussed earlier. First, if the owner must start construction immediately and finish it as soon as possible, then the market value of the

Table 8.1. Analysis of the Option to Invest in a Project when Construction Takes Two Periods and Can be Interrupted

$X(i, n)$	0	1	2	3	4	5	
0	100.00	125.00	156.25	195.31	244.14	305.18	
1		80.00	100.00	125.00	156.25	195.31	
2			64.00	80.00	100.00	125.00←	Step 1: Construct binomial
3				51.20	64.00	80.00	tree for the state variable
4					40.96	51.20	
5						32.77	

$V_1(i, n)$	0	1	2	3	4	5	
0	5.75	23.14	49.93	83.41	125.26	0.00	
1		1.15	5.17	23.14	49.93	0.00←	Step 2a: Fill in final column
2			0.08	0.36	1.71	0.00	using equation (8.1)
3				0.00	0.00	0.00	
4					0.00	0.00←	Step 2b: Fill in remaining
5						0.00	columns using equation (8.2)

$V_2(i, n)$	0	1	2	3	4	5	
0	1.97	8.39	28.80	57.49	0.00	0.00	
1		0.26	1.24	5.84	0.00	0.00←	Step 3a: Fill in final column
2			0.00	0.00	0.00	0.00	using equation (8.1)
3				0.00	0.00	0.00	
4					0.00	0.00←	Step 3b: Fill in remaining
5						0.00	columns using equation (8.3)

project rights is

$$-J_1 - \frac{J_2}{R_f} + \left(\frac{K}{R_f}\right)^2 X(0, 0) = -6 - \frac{84}{1.05} + \left(\frac{0.9000}{1.05}\right)^2 100 = -12.53.$$

The second case, where the initial investment can be delayed until date 3 but the second stage must occur immediately after the first is complete, was considered in Section 7.2.5. The market value of the project rights evolved according to the binomial tree shown in Table 7.2, showing that the project rights were initially worth 1.68.

Now we suppose that the construction program can be interrupted without cost. Table 8.1 shows how the market value of the project evolves in this case. The top panel shows the binomial tree for the market value of the completed project. The middle panel describes $V_1(i, n)$, the market value of the project rights when one stage has already been completed, while the bottom panel describes $V_2(i, n)$, the market value of the project rights when construction has not yet begun.[4] The shaded cells in the middle panel indicate nodes at which the second construction stage is undertaken, while those in the bottom panel indicate nodes where it is optimal to begin the first stage of construction. Comparison with Table 7.2 shows that flexibility has value in this case: the project rights have increased in value from 1.68 to 1.97.

In the case considered here the tree is reasonably small, which allows us to list the various outcomes that are possible. For instance, if the first two moves are up, the owner will invest in Stage I at date 1 and invest in Stage II at date 2; the market value of the project rights will take the values 1.97, 8.39, and 49.93 over the interval from date 0 to date 2. In contrast, if the first two moves are down, the owner will never invest in either stage of the project and the market value of the project rights will fall from 1.97 to 0.26 and then to 0.00. For the example considered in this section the full list of possible outcomes is as follows (where the labels indicate the moves that occur, in the order that they occur):

- UU: invest at dates 1 and 2.
- UDU: invest at dates 1 and 3. That is, the project is eventually completed, but only after investment is interrupted at date 2.
- UDDU: invest at dates 1 and 4.
- UDDD: invest at date 1 but do not complete the project.
- DUU: invest at dates 3 and 4.
- DUD: do not invest at all.
- DD: do not invest at all.

Given that up and down moves are equally likely, it follows that the project is completed with probability 9/16, abandoned after Stage I with probability 1/16, and abandoned without any investment whatsoever with probability 6/16. These results make it clear that it can be optimal to exploit the flexibility afforded by the options to delay starting investment and to delay completing it. For instance, it is always optimal to delay starting construction in this example. Furthermore, it can be optimal to temporarily halt construction in some cases (such as path UDU) or abandon a partly completed project altogether (such as path UDDD).

In the case where investment could not be interrupted, the owner of the project rights destroyed the option to wait when she invested. The payoff from investing therefore had to be sufficiently high to compensate the owner for the destruction of this option if investment was to be optimal. Now, however, while investment in Stage I still destroys the option to wait and invest in Stage I at a later date, it also creates the option to delay (or avoid altogether) undertaking Stage II. This makes investment in Stage I more attractive. For example, Table 7.2 shows that it

---

4. Since we assume that construction has not begun prior to date 0, it makes little sense to report $V_1(0, 0)$, but we include the information in the table for completeness. It can sometimes be useful to know what the project rights would be worth at various stages, as we demonstrate in Section 8.3.

is optimal to wait at node (0, 1) when investment cannot be interrupted, whereas Table 8.1 shows that investment is optimal there when the construction program can be interrupted—but note that Stage II will be completed only if at least one of the next three moves is up. It is this extra flexibility not to go on and finish the project immediately that makes investment at node (0, 1) attractive to the owner. Without it, she would not be willing to invest at node (0, 1). The creation of the suspension option has been enough to lift the payoff from investing above the payoff from waiting at that node.

8.2.4 Determinants of Option Value: Capital Expenditure Profile

In the two-period investment problem in Section 7.2.5, all we needed to know about J_1 and J_2 was their combined present value, $J_1 + J_2/R_f$. Different combinations of capital expenditure with the same present value would lead to the same optimal investment policy and the same market value for the project rights. However, the expenditure profile can be crucial when the owner has a mid-construction suspension option.

We investigate this issue using Figure 8.3, which plots the market value of the project rights at date 0 as a function of J_1, where J_2 is chosen so that the present value of J_1 and J_2 equals 86 (the same as for the base case considered in Section 8.2.3). That is, for each value of J_1 we set J_2 such that

$$J_1 + \frac{J_2}{R_f} = 86 \quad \Leftrightarrow \quad J_2 = (86 - J_1)R_f = 90.3 - 1.05J_1.$$

The solid curve shows the market value when investment can be suspended after the first stage is complete, while the dashed curve corresponds to the case that the owner must undertake the second stage immediately after the first one is complete.

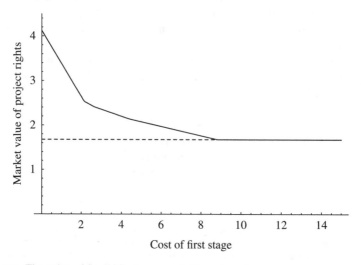

Figure 8.3. The value of flexibility in sequential investment

Since we have chosen J_1 and J_2 so that the stream of capital expenditure has a present value of 86 (assuming that Stage II is undertaken as soon as Stage I is complete), the market value of the project rights will take the same value for all cases when we impose the restriction that investment cannot be suspended. This is consistent with the fact that the dashed curve in Figure 8.3 traces out a horizontal straight line. Figure 8.3 also shows that for sufficiently large values of J_1 the project rights have the same value whether or not investment can be suspended after Stage I. For these values, the cost of Stage II is so low that it is always optimal to undertake Stage II as soon as Stage I is complete—the suspension option has no value because it will never be exercised. However, for lower values of J_1 we must have a relatively high value of J_2 for the present value of all capital expenditure to equal 86. When Stage II is expensive it may be optimal to suspend the investment program after Stage I is complete, so that the suspension option will be valuable. Again, this is consistent with Figure 8.3, which shows that the value of the project rights (and therefore the value of the suspension option) grows larger as J_1 falls (and J_2 rises). That is, holding the present value of (uninterrupted) capital expenditure constant, the suspension option is more valuable when the capital expenditure grows more steeply during the investment program.

8.3 SOLVING THE RESOURCE EXTRACTION PROBLEM

In this section we analyze the resource extraction problem. Although the analysis below will look different from that in Section 8.2, the underlying mathematical structure is the same.

8.3.1 Setting Up the Resource Extraction Problem

A firm owns a lease that gives it the right to extract up to four units of copper from a mine at the rate of at most one unit per period. Extraction is instantaneous, costs C per unit, and can be suspended or resumed without cost.[5] However, no further extraction is allowed after date 5. No clean-up costs are incurred when extraction ends.

We analyze this problem using a model that defines the state variable $X(i, n)$ to be the spot price of copper at node (i, n). We suppose that the risk-adjusted growth factor for the copper price equals the constant K and that the return on a one-period risk-free bond equals the constant R_f.

8.3.2 Analyzing the Resource Extraction Problem

We start by valuing the copper mine when there is no flexibility regarding the timing for extraction. Later we compare this value to the case where the manager has full flexibility in order to determine the value of the real option embedded in

---

5. It might be more realistic to assume that sunk costs are incurred whenever suspending or resuming extraction, in which case we need to use the techniques described in Chapter 10.

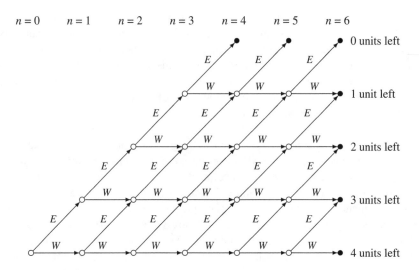

Figure 8.4. Decision tree for the resource extraction problem

the stored copper—that is, the option to keep it in the ground to sell when the spot price of copper is high.

If the firm's manager starts extracting copper immediately and continues until the mine is exhausted, it would produce one unit of copper per period from dates 0 to 3 inclusive. Thus the firm would generate a cash flow of $X(\cdot, n) - C$ at each node $(\cdot, n)$ for $n = 0, 1, 2, 3$. The simplest way to value this cash flow is to separate out the revenue from the extraction cost and then value the two streams separately. We can repeat the calculations described in Section 6.2.2 to show that the mine is worth

$$\left(1 - \left(\frac{K}{R_f}\right)^4\right) \frac{R_f X(0, 0)}{R_f - K} - \left(1 - \left(\frac{1}{R_f}\right)^4\right) \frac{R_f C}{R_f - 1}$$

at date 0 when there is no ability to delay extraction.

The first step in analyzing the real options associated with resource extraction is to construct the decision tree. At date 0, the manager must either wait or extract one unit of copper. These are represented by the actions labeled W (for "wait") and E (for "extract") in the decision tree shown in Figure 8.4. If he chooses to wait, then at date 1 he will still have the right to extract at most four units of copper, but the remaining lifetime of the lease will be one period shorter. If, instead, the manager chooses to extract at date 0, then he will pay the extraction cost and receive one unit of copper immediately; at date 1 he will have the right to extract at most three units of copper, and again the remaining lifetime of the lease will be one period shorter.

Therefore, the project will be in one of two states at date 1, depending on how many units of copper can still be extracted, and the manager must choose from the same two actions as before. If he chooses to wait, then at date 2 he will still have the right to extract the same number of units of copper as at date 1, but the remaining lifetime of the lease will be one period shorter. If, instead, he chooses to extract at date 1, then he will pay the extraction cost and receive one unit of copper immediately; at date 2 he will have the right to extract one less unit of copper than before, and again the remaining lifetime of the lease will be one period shorter.

By the time we get to date 2 the project will be in one of three states: there will be two, three, or four units of copper remaining to be extracted. Repeating the arguments in the preceding paragraph, at date 3 the project will be in one of four states—there will be one, two, three, or four units of copper remaining to be extracted—and the manager's problem is of the type described above: either extract one unit of copper or wait. The decision tree continues to evolve in this way until either of two things happens: the term of the lease expires, or no more copper can be extracted. At that point there is nothing more for the manager to do and all future cash flows are zero.

As the decision tree in Figure 8.4 makes clear, we need to build a tree for the market value of the mine for each possible value of m, where m equals the number of units of copper still to be extracted. Let $V_m(i, n)$ denote the (cum dividend) market value of the mine at node (i, n) when there are m units of copper still available.

If the mine is empty then it has no value, so that

$$V_0(i, n) = 0 \qquad (8.4)$$

at all nodes (i, n).

Now consider the more interesting case where the mine contains $m > 0$ units of copper. From date 6 onwards the lease is worthless because the right to extract copper has expired. Therefore

$$V_m(i, 6) = 0 \qquad (8.5)$$

for all $i = 0, 1, \ldots, 6$. At each earlier date, the manager must either wait or extract one unit of copper. If he decides to wait, then there is no cash flow at date n, but at date $n + 1$ the mine (still containing m units of copper) will be worth $V_m(i, n + 1)$ if an up move occurs and $V_m(i + 1, n + 1)$ if a down move occurs. The payoff from waiting is therefore

$$\frac{\pi_u(i, n)V_m(i, n + 1) + \pi_d(i, n)V_m(i + 1, n + 1)}{R_f}.$$

In contrast, if he extracts one unit of copper, he pays C and immediately receives one unit of copper worth $X(i, n)$; at date $n + 1$ the mine (containing only $m - 1$ units of copper) will be worth $V_{m-1}(i, n + 1)$ if an up move occurs and $V_{m-1}(i + 1, n + 1)$ if a down move occurs. The payoff from extracting copper is therefore

$$X(i, n) - C + \frac{\pi_u(i, n)V_{m-1}(i, n + 1) + \pi_d(i, n)V_{m-1}(i + 1, n + 1)}{R_f}.$$

The manager should adopt whichever action has the higher payoff, so that the market value of the mine at node (i, n) equals

$$V_m(i,n) = \max \left\{ \frac{\pi_u(i,n)V_m(i,n+1)+\pi_d(i,n)V_m(i+1,n+1)}{R_f} , \right.$$

$$\left. X(i,n)-C+\frac{\pi_u(i,n)V_{m-1}(i,n+1)+\pi_d(i,n)V_{m-1}(i+1,n+1)}{R_f} \right\}.$$

$$(8.6)$$

This equation, together with the terminal conditions (8.4) and (8.5), completely determines the market value of the mine at date 0.

8.3.3 A Numerical Example

The mine contains four units of copper, which can be extracted at the rate of one unit per period at a cost of $C = 98$ per unit. No extraction is allowed after date 5. The spot price of copper is currently $X_0 = 100$ and is equally likely to grow by a factor of $U = 1.1100$ or $D = 1/U = 0.9009$ each period, so that the spot price at node (i, n) is $X(i, n) = X_0 D^i U^{n-i}$. The binomial tree is shown in the top panel of Table 8.2. The risk-adjusted growth factor is $K = 0.9500$, so that equation (3.8) implies that the risk-neutral probabilities of up and down moves are $\pi_u = 0.2348$ and $\pi_d = 0.7652$, respectively, throughout the tree. The one-period risk-free interest rate equals 5% per period, so that $R_f = 1.05$.

The remaining panels of Table 8.2 show the market value of the copper mine for various levels of reserves, with the shaded cells indicating nodes when immediate extraction of one unit of copper is optimal. For instance, the second panel shows the mine's market value when there is just one unit of copper left. We start by using (8.5) to fill in the final column, and then use (8.6), together with (8.4), to fill in the remaining entries. Once this panel of the table is complete, we move on to the third panel, which shows the mine's market value when it contains two units of copper. Again, we start by filling in the final column using (8.5). We then work from right to left, filling in the rest of the panel using (8.6) together with the market values in the second panel. This procedure is repeated until we have filled in the bottom panel of the table, which gives us our estimate of the mine's market value, $V_4(0, 0) = 9.31$.

The arrangement of the shaded cells in the bottom four panels of Table 8.2 shows that extraction becomes less aggressive as the amount left in the mine falls. For instance, at node $(0, 0)$ it is optimal to extract one unit of copper immediately if the mine currently contains three or more units of copper, but it is optimal to wait if the mine contains two or less units. More generally, if it is optimal to extract when there are m units of copper left in the mine then it will also be optimal to extract when there are $m + 1$ units of copper left. However, in some cases where it is optimal to wait when there are m units of copper left in the mine, it will actually be optimal to extract when there are $m + 1$ units of copper left. The cause of this behavior is explained in the next section, where we consider the effect of timing options on the market value of copper reserves.

Table 8.2. Analysis of the Resource Extraction Problem

$X(i, n)$	0	1	2	3	4	5	6
0	100.00	111.00	123.21	136.76	151.81	168.51	187.04
1		90.09	100.00	111.00	123.21	136.76	151.81
2			81.16	90.09	100.00	111.00	123.21
3				73.12	81.16	90.09	100.00
4					65.87	73.12	81.16
5						59.35	65.87
6							53.46

$V_1(i, n)$	0	1	2	3	4	5	6
0	3.54	13.00	25.21	38.76	53.81	70.51	0.00
1		0.86	3.38	13.00	25.21	38.76	0.00
2			0.15	0.65	2.91	13.00	0.00
3				0.00	0.00	0.00	0.00
4					0.00	0.00	0.00
5						0.00	0.00
6							0.00

$V_2(i, n)$	0	1	2	3	4	5	6
0	5.74	21.10	43.35	69.17	97.82	70.51	0.00
1		1.40	5.44	20.76	43.35	38.76	0.00
2			0.25	1.10	4.91	13.00	0.00
3				0.00	0.00	0.00	0.00
4					0.00	0.00	0.00
5						0.00	0.00
6							0.00

$V_3(i, n)$	0	1	2	3	4	5	6
0	7.74	26.66	55.80	92.23	97.82	70.51	0.00
1		1.84	7.44	26.27	43.35	38.76	0.00
2			0.25	1.10	4.91	13.00	0.00
3				0.00	0.00	0.00	0.00
4					0.00	0.00	0.00
5						0.00	0.00
6							0.00

$V_4(i, n)$	0	1	2	3	4	5	6
0	9.31	30.90	64.98	92.23	97.82	70.51	0.00
1		2.12	8.67	26.27	43.35	38.76	0.00
2			0.25	1.10	4.91	13.00	0.00
3				0.00	0.00	0.00	0.00
4					0.00	0.00	0.00
5						0.00	0.00
6							0.00

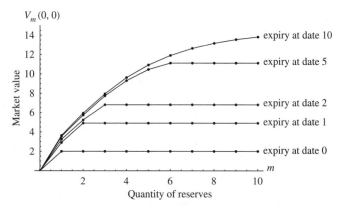

Figure 8.5. The effect of flexibility on the market value of a lease on a copper mine

8.3.4 Valuing Copper Reserves

In the course of calculating the market value of a mine containing four units of copper we also calculate the market values of mines holding smaller levels of reserves. For example, Table 8.2 shows that a lease expiring at date 5 on a mine holding one unit of copper is worth 3.54, while an identical lease on a mine holding two units of copper is worth 5.74. If we applied exactly the same techniques as above to a smaller or larger binomial tree we would be able to value a lease with a shorter or longer time, respectively, until expiry. The results of such calculations are summarized in Figure 8.5, which plots the market value of the lease as a function of the amount of the resource left in the ground for different lengths of time until the lease expires.

For a given lease (that is, a given curve in the graph), the market value of the reserve is an increasing function of the reserve's size, but the marginal market value is decreasing. In fact, the marginal market value eventually falls to zero. For a given reserve size (m), the reserve becomes more valuable as the length of the lease increases—that is, the curves in the graph shift upwards as the lease lengthens.

The diminishing marginal market value of copper reserves evident in Figure 8.5 can be explained by the timing option embedded in each unit of copper stored in the mine. If the mine contained just one unit of copper, then it could be extracted at the date that maximizes the market value of the firm. However, if the mine contains two units instead, only one unit can be extracted at this date—the second unit can only be extracted at any *other* date.[6] The second unit cannot contribute more value to the firm than the first—if it did, then a lessee entitled to extract just one

---

6. Note that we are not ranking the two units according to when they are extracted, but rather according to their contribution to the lessee's market value. That is, the "first" unit need not be extracted before the "second" unit.

unit should actually follow the policy for extracting the second unit here, rather than the first one—and may actually contribute less.[7] Similarly, a third unit of copper cannot contribute more value to the firm than the second and may actually contribute less. This explains why the marginal value of copper reserves falls as the quantity of the reserve rises.

Our numerical example shows that the marginal value of copper reserves can be greater than, equal to, or less than the net revenue from immediate extraction. The second panel of Table 8.2 shows that a lease expiring at date 5 on a mine holding just one unit of copper is currently worth 3.54, whereas the third panel shows that the market value of a mine holding two units of copper is 5.74. The marginal value of the first unit is therefore 3.54, whereas that of the second unit is just 2.20. Inspection of the remaining panels shows that the marginal values of the third and fourth units are 2.00 and 1.57 respectively.

The existence of timing options can explain the difference between the marginal value of copper reserves and the net revenue from immediate extraction. There are two distinct cases to consider, depending on whether or not immediate extraction is optimal.

In the first case, the size of the reserve is sufficiently low that it is not currently optimal to extract copper. Thus, if the reserve was found to be one unit larger we could extract the additional copper immediately without affecting the extraction of the remaining copper, so that we benefit by an amount at least as great as the net revenue from immediate extraction. This is not necessarily the optimal way to manage the additional reserve, so the market value of the additional unit of copper may actually exceed the net revenue. However, we can say with certainty that the marginal value cannot be less than the net revenue from immediate extraction.

We can easily show this formally. Since it is not optimal to extract immediately from the original mine, we have

$$V_m(0, 0) = \frac{\pi_u(0, 0)V_m(0, 1) + \pi_d(0, 0)V_m(1, 1)}{R_f}.$$

This follows from (8.6) when waiting is optimal. The market value of the additional unit of copper therefore equals

$V_{m+1}(0, 0) - V_m(0, 0)$

$= V_{m+1}(0, 0) - \dfrac{\pi_u(0, 0)V_m(0, 1) + \pi_d(0, 0)V_m(1, 1)}{R_f}$

---

7. We have discussed similar behavior in other parts of this book. For example, in Section 2.3 we noted that real options analysis leads to higher (or, more precisely, not lower) market values than static DCF analysis because it allows managers more policies to choose from.

$$\underbrace{= X(0, 0) - C}_{\text{net revenue}}$$

$$+ V_{m+1}(0, 0) - \underbrace{\left(X(0, 0) - C + \frac{\pi_u(0, 0)V_m(0, 1) + \pi_d(0, 0)V_m(1, 1)}{R_f} \right)}_{\text{market value of the option to delay extracting the additional unit of copper}},$$

where all we have done is add and subtract the net revenue from immediate extraction on the right-hand side. The first term is the net revenue from immediately extracting the additional unit of copper from the mine. The second term is the amount by which the market value of the larger mine exceeds the payoff from extracting one unit of copper from that mine immediately—that is, it is the market value of the option to *not* extract copper immediately.

Consider, for example, the situation when $m = 1$. The second and third panels of Table 8.2 show that it is optimal to delay extraction from mines containing $m = 1$ and $m + 1 = 2$ units of copper. Indeed, when the mine holds two units of copper, the payoff from waiting is $V_2(0, 0) = 5.74$, whereas the payoff from extracting copper immediately is

$$X(0, 0) - C + \frac{\pi_u(0, 0)V_1(0, 1) + \pi_d(0, 0)V_1(1, 1)}{R_f} = 5.54.$$

Thus, the option to delay extracting copper from the enlarged mine is worth $5.74 - 5.54 = 0.20$. The discussion above indicates that the market value of the second unit of copper in the mine equals the net revenue (2.00) plus this option value (0.20), which equals the figure of 2.20 that we found earlier.

In the second case, the size of the reserve is sufficiently high that it is optimal to extract copper from the enlarged reserve. However, while the owner receives the net revenue from extracting the additional unit of copper immediately, this is partly offset by the reduced timing flexibility for exploiting the original copper reserve. Thus, the marginal value of copper will be less than or equal to the net revenue from immediate extraction of one unit of copper.

As in the first case, we can show this formally. Since it is now optimal to extract copper immediately, we have

$$V_{m+1}(0, 0) = X(0, 0) - C + \frac{\pi_u(0, 0)V_m(0, 1) + \pi_d(0, 0)V_m(1, 1)}{R_f}.$$

The marginal value of copper therefore equals

$$V_{m+1}(0, 0) - V_m(0, 0)$$

$$= X(0, 0) - C + \frac{\pi_u(0, 0)V_m(0, 1) + \pi_d(0, 0)V_m(1, 1)}{R_f} - V_m(0, 0)$$

$$= \underbrace{X(0, 0) - C}_{\text{net revenue}} - \underbrace{\left(V_m(0, 0) - \frac{\pi_u(0, 0)V_m(0, 1) + \pi_d(0, 0)V_m(1, 1)}{R_f} \right)}_{\text{market value of the option to extract copper immediately}}.$$

As in the first case we considered, the first term is the net revenue from extracting the additional unit of copper from the mine. Now, however, we subtract the second term, which equals the amount by which the market value of the original mine exceeds the payoff from leaving all the copper in the mine until at least date 1— that is, it is the market value of the option to extract copper from the original mine at date 0. It follows that in this case the marginal value of copper reserves equals the net revenue from immediate extraction minus the value of the option to immediately extract copper from the original mine.

Consider the situation when $m = 2$. The fourth panel of Table 8.2 shows that immediate extraction is optimal when the mine contains $m + 1 = 3$ units of copper, so this example corresponds to the case just discussed. However, the third panel shows that delay is optimal when the mine contains $m = 2$ units, and that $V_2(0, 0) = 5.74$. This can also be seen directly by noting that the payoff from delaying copper extraction in this case is

$$\frac{\pi_u(0, 0)V_2(0, 1) + \pi_d(0, 0)V_2(1, 1)}{R_f} = 5.74.$$

Thus, the option to *immediately* extract copper from the original mine is worthless. The discussion above indicates that the marginal value of copper reserves for this mine equals the net revenue (2.00) minus this option value (0.00), which equals the figure of 2.00 that we found earlier—the marginal value of additional copper reserves equals net revenue because the option to immediately extract copper is worthless.

The situation when $m = 3$ is slightly different. The bottom panel of Table 8.2 shows that immediate extraction is optimal when the mine contains $m + 1 = 4$ units of copper, so this example also corresponds to the case just discussed. The fourth panel of the table shows that immediate extraction is also optimal when the mine contains just $m = 3$ units of copper, with $V_3(0, 0) = 7.74$. Indeed, if the lessee decided not to extract copper from this mine at date 0 then the market value of the mine would equal

$$\frac{\pi_u(0, 0)V_3(0, 1) + \pi_d(0, 0)V_3(1, 1)}{R_f} = 7.31.$$

Thus, the option to immediately extract copper from the original mine is worth $7.74 - 7.31 = 0.43$. The marginal value of copper reserves for this mine therefore equals the net revenue (2.00) minus this option value (0.43), which equals the figure of 1.57 that we found earlier.

In summary, when reserves are so low that the mine is currently inactive, the value of each additional unit of reserves equals net revenue *plus* the value of the real option to *delay extraction* of the additional unit. This reflects the fact that the additional reserves come with their own timing flexibility. In contrast, when reserves are so high that a larger mine would currently be active, the value of each additional unit of reserves equals net revenue *minus* the value of the real option to *immediately extract* copper from the original mine. This reflects the fact that the discovery of additional reserves destroys some of the timing flexibility associated with managing the original mine.

8.4 SOLVING THE MULTI-STAGE R&D TIMING PROBLEM

The final example considered in this chapter features an R&D program that contains more than one stage to be completed. We base our discussion of this problem on an extension of the model analyzed in Section 7.4 that is designed to handle the case where there are several stages to the R&D program.[8]

8.4.1 Setting Up the R&D Timing Problem

An individual owns the right to attempt development of a project. There are three distinct stages of development. Each development attempt costs I, lasts one period, and succeeds in moving the project to the next stage with some constant probability q between 0 and 1. The development rights to the project are lost if all three stages are not successfully completed on or before date 6.

We define the state variable $X(i, n)$ to be the market value of the developed project at node (i, n). Given that the project has not been developed yet, its market value cannot be directly observed. However, we assume that the owner of the development rights is able to estimate the market value the project would have today if development were already complete. We continue to assume that the risk-adjusted growth factor, K, and the return on one-period risk-free bonds, R_f, are constant. Finally, as in Section 7.4, we assume that the technical risk surrounding whether or not any particular development attempt is successful can be diversified away. Thus, in order to value any cash flow containing technical risk, all we need to know about the cash flow is its expected value at each node of the binomial tree.

8.4.2 Analyzing the R&D Timing Problem

We begin by constructing the decision tree for this problem. At date 0, the owner of the development rights must either attempt to develop the first stage of the project or wait. These options are represented by the actions labeled A (for "attempt") and W (for "wait") in the decision tree shown in Figure 8.6. If she chooses a development attempt, she pays I at date 0 and then one of two things will happen: the attempt succeeds (with probability q) and at date 1 there will be just two stages remaining to be developed; or the attempt fails (with probability $1 - q$) and the project still has three stages remaining at date 1. If she chooses to wait, there is no cash flow at date 0 and at date 1 there will still be three stages remaining to be developed.

Thus, at date 1 the project will be in one of two states: either there will be three stages remaining to be completed or there will be two stages. In the first case the situation facing the owner of the development rights is exactly the same

---

8. The extended model is a simplified version of the one that Berk et al. (2004) use to analyze the risk premia associated with multi-stage R&D projects.

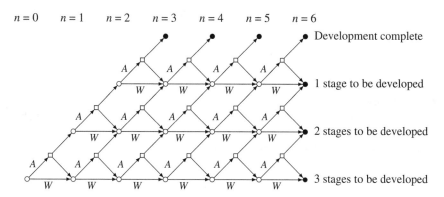

Figure 8.6. Decision tree for the multi-stage R&D timing problem

as at date 0. In the second case, the owner must either attempt to develop the second stage of the project or wait. If she chooses a development attempt, she pays I at date 1 and then one of two things will happen: the attempt succeeds (with probability q) and at date 2 there will be just one stage remaining to be developed; or the attempt fails (with probability $1 - q$) and the project still has two stages remaining at date 2. If she chooses to wait, there is no cash flow at date 1 and at date 2 there will still be two stages remaining to be developed.

The project will be in one of three states by the time we get to date 2: there will be one, two, or three stages remaining to be completed. Whenever there are any stages remaining the owner's problem is of the type described above: she must either attempt to develop the next stage of the project or wait. However, when there is just one stage remaining the treatment of a development attempt is slightly different. Now, if she chooses a development attempt, she pays I and then one of two things will happen: the attempt succeeds (with probability q) and at the next date she sells the developed project, receiving the sales price as a cash inflow, and the decision tree terminates; or the attempt fails (with probability $1 - q$) and the project still has one stage remaining.

We continue like this, building the decision tree out as far as date 5. Finally, at date 6 the development rights are lost, so that the rights are worthless and the decision tree terminates. This completes the construction of the decision tree shown in Figure 8.6. The remaining steps are to identify the binomial trees that are required and to complete their construction. We need to build a tree for the market value of the development rights for each possible value of m, where m equals the number of stages still to be completed. Let $V_m(i, n)$ denote the (cum dividend) market value of the rights at node (i, n) when there are m stages still to complete.

If the R&D program has just been completed successfully then the development rights are worth the same as a completed project, so that

$$V_0(i, n) = X(i, n) \tag{8.7}$$

at all nodes (i, n).

Now consider the more interesting case where there are still $m > 0$ stages remaining. Development rights that have expired are worthless, so that

$$V_m(i, 6) = 0 \tag{8.8}$$

for all $i = 0, 1, \ldots, 6$. At each earlier date, the owner of the development rights must do one of two things: wait or attempt to complete the current stage. If she decides to wait then there is no cash flow at date n, but at date $n + 1$ the rights (still with m stages remaining) will be worth $V_m(i, n + 1)$ if an up move occurs and $V_m(i + 1, n + 1)$ if a down move occurs. The payoff from waiting is therefore

$$\text{payoff}_{\text{wait}}(i, n) = \frac{\pi_u(i, n)V_m(i, n + 1) + \pi_d(i, n)V_m(i + 1, n + 1)}{R_f}.$$

Suppose, instead, that the owner attempts development. If an up move occurs, then either the attempt succeeds and the development rights are worth $V_{m-1}(i, n+1)$, or it fails and they are worth $V_m(i, n + 1)$. Because the risk associated with success or failure is diversifiable, all we need to know about the market value of the development rights in the up state is its expected value. Since the development attempt succeeds with probability q, this expected value is

$$qV_{m-1}(i, n + 1) + (1 - q)V_m(i, n + 1).$$

Similarly, if a down move occurs the expected market value of the development rights at date $n + 1$ equals

$$qV_{m-1}(i + 1, n + 1) + (1 - q)V_m(i + 1, n + 1).$$

The payoff from attempting development is therefore equal to

$$\text{payoff}_{\text{attempt}}(i, n) = -I + \frac{1}{R_f}\left(\pi_u(i, n)\left(qV_{m-1}(i, n + 1) + (1 - q)V_m(i, n + 1)\right)\right.$$

$$\left. + \pi_d(i, n)\left(qV_{m-1}(i + 1, n + 1) + (1 - q)V_m(i + 1, n + 1)\right)\right).$$

Now that we have constructed the payoff functions for the owner's two possible actions, we can derive the recursive equation that drives the backward induction process. Since the owner of the development rights will take whichever action has the higher payoff, their market value at node (i, n) equals

$$V_m(i, n) = \max\left\{ \frac{\pi_u(i, n)V_m(i, n + 1) + \pi_d(i, n)V_m(i + 1, n + 1)}{R_f}, \right.$$

$$-I + \frac{1}{R_f}\left(\pi_u(i, n)\left(qV_{m-1}(i, n + 1) + (1 - q)V_m(i, n + 1)\right)\right.$$

$$\left.\left. + \pi_d(i, n)\left(qV_{m-1}(i + 1, n + 1) + (1 - q)V_m(i + 1, n + 1)\right)\right)\right\}. \tag{8.9}$$

When this equation is combined with the two different terminal conditions, (8.7) and (8.8), we can completely determine the market value of the development rights at date 0, as we now demonstrate.

8.4.3 A Numerical Example

In this example we analyze the real option to invest in the project described above. Each development attempt costs $I = 12$ and succeeds with probability $q = 0.5000$. If development is not completed on or before date 6 then the option is lost forever. The completed project would be worth $X_0 = 100$ if it were available for sale immediately. Each period this market value is equally likely to grow by a factor of $U = 1.2500$ or $D = 1/U = 0.8000$, so that the market value of the completed project at node (i, n) is $X(i, n) = X_0 D^i U^{n-i}$. The binomial tree is shown in the top panel of Table 8.3. The risk-adjusted growth factor is $K = 0.9800$, so that equation (3.8) implies that the risk-neutral probabilities of up and down moves are $\pi_u = 0.4000$ and $\pi_d = 0.6000$, respectively, at every node. The one-period risk-free interest rate equals 4% per period, so that $R_f = 1.04$.

Having constructed the binomial tree for the state variable, the next step is to construct the market value of the development rights when there is just one stage remaining. This is shown in the second panel of Table 8.3 and is constructed by first using (8.8) to complete the final column and then using (8.7) and (8.9) to fill in the remainder of the tree from right to left. We continue by constructing the tree for the market value of the development rights when there are two stages remaining. This is shown in the third panel of Table 8.3 and is constructed by first using (8.8) to complete the final column and then using (8.9) and the values in the second panel to fill in the remainder of the tree from right to left. Continuing in this way, we complete the bottom panel of the table, which shows the tree for the market value of the development rights when there are three stages remaining.

The shaded cells in each panel of Table 8.3 show nodes where development should be attempted. For example, the bottom panel shows that the earliest that development should be attempted is at date 1 and then only if the first move is up. If that attempt fails then at most one further development attempt should be made, at date 2, but only if the second move is up. In contrast, inspection of the third panel of Table 8.3 shows that if the first development attempt is successful, then it is optimal to attempt the second stage of development at date 2 whether the second move is up or down.

8.5 SOLVING PROBLEMS INVOLVING COMPOUND TIMING OPTIONS

The examples considered in Sections 8.2–8.4 are all particular instances of compound timing options. Now that we have worked through the procedure for analyzing these examples, we can formulate a procedure for dealing with the general compound timing option problem described at the beginning of this chapter. Recall that in the general problem a project starts out in one state and goes

Table 8.3. Analysis of the Multi-stage R&D Timing Problem

$X(i, n)$	0	1	2	3	4	5	6
0	100.00	125.00	156.25	195.31	244.14	305.18	381.47
1		80.00	100.00	125.00	156.25	195.31	244.14
2			64.00	80.00	100.00	125.00	156.25
3				51.20	64.00	80.00	100.00
4					40.96	51.20	64.00
5						32.77	40.96
6							26.21

$V_1(i, n)$	0	1	2	3	4	5	6
0	65.29	86.26	110.47	135.26	151.45	131.78	0.00
1		47.10	62.82	79.17	90.53	80.02	0.00
2			32.33	43.28	51.54	46.89	0.00
3				20.30	26.59	25.69	0.00
4					10.62	12.12	0.00
5						3.44	0.00
6							0.00

$V_2(i, n)$	0	1	2	3	4	5	6
0	30.93	44.31	54.61	55.13	36.43	0.00	0.00
1		14.69	22.34	24.81	16.92	0.00	0.00
2			3.42	6.43	4.43	0.00	0.00
3				0.00	0.00	0.00	0.00
4					0.00	0.00	0.00
5						0.00	0.00
6							0.00

$V_3(i, n)$	0	1	2	3	4	5	6
0	2.33	6.05	5.76	0.00	0.00	0.00	0.00
1		0.00	0.00	0.00	0.00	0.00	0.00
2			0.00	0.00	0.00	0.00	0.00
3				0.00	0.00	0.00	0.00
4					0.00	0.00	0.00
5						0.00	0.00
6							0.00

through a series of changes. The order in which these changes occur is fixed, but the dates on which they occur are influenced by the manager. We label these states by the number of changes that must occur before we reach the final state; that is, the project starts in state M, then moves to state $M - 1$, then to state $M - 2$, and so on until it reaches state 0.

Suppose the project is in state m when it arrives at node (i, n). We denote the (cum dividend) market value of the project by $V_m(i, n)$. We suppose that the project generates a cash flow of $Y_m(i, n)$ at node (i, n) if the manager does not attempt to change the state at that node and a cash flow of $A_m(i, n)$ at that node if an attempt to change the state from m to $m - 1$ is made. The attempt is assumed to succeed with probability q.

We begin by building the decision tree and using it to identify the nodes where the manager is allowed to change the project's state. After building a binomial tree for the state variable, the next step is to build a tree for the market value of the project in its final state $(m = 0)$. The procedure for doing this will depend on the particular problem being analyzed, but $V_0(i, n)$ needs to be a known function of the state variable at each node (i, n). For example, it might equal the state variable itself (as in Sections 8.2 and 8.4) or it might equal zero (as in Section 8.3), in which case we may not bother building a separate tree for V_0. In other cases the market value will be a more complicated function of the state variable, so building a separate tree for V_0 may be worthwhile.

We continue by building a binomial tree for $V_m(i, n)$ for the case when the project is in state $m = 1$, starting with the terminal condition that is appropriate for the specific problem being analyzed, and then filling in the remainder of the tree using backward induction.

The manager may not be allowed to change the project's state at some nodes. Waiting is the only option at such nodes. The project immediately generates a cash flow of $Y_m(i, n)$ and, after one period elapses, it will be worth $V_m(i, n + 1)$ if an up move occurs and $V_m(i + 1, n + 1)$ if a down move occurs. The market value of the project at such a node therefore equals

$$V_m(i, n) = Y_m(i, n) + \frac{\pi_u(i, n)V_m(i, n + 1) + \pi_d(i, n)V_m(i + 1, n + 1)}{R_f}. \quad (8.10)$$

At nodes where changing the project's state is permitted, the manager must either attempt to change the state of the project or wait. If the manager waits then the payoff equals the expression on the right-hand side of (8.10). Suppose the manager attempts to change the state of the project instead. If an up move occurs, then one of two things will happen: either the trial succeeds, so that the project is worth $V_{m-1}(i, n + 1)$, or it fails and the project is worth $V_m(i, n + 1)$. Because the risk associated with success or failure is diversifiable, all we need to know about the market value of the project in the up state is its expected value,

$$qV_{m-1}(i, n + 1) + (1 - q)V_m(i, n + 1).$$

Similarly, if a down move occurs, the expected market value of the project at date $n + 1$ equals

$$qV_{m-1}(i + 1, n + 1) + (1 - q)V_m(i + 1, n + 1).$$

The payoff from attempting to change the project's state is thus

$$A_m(i, n) + \frac{1}{R_f} \left(\pi_u(i, n) \left(q V_{m-1}(i, n+1) + (1-q) V_m(i, n+1) \right) \right.$$

$$\left. + \pi_d(i, n) \left(q V_{m-1}(i+1, n+1) + (1-q) V_m(i+1, n+1) \right) \right).$$

The market value of the project therefore equals

$$V_m(i, n)$$

$$= \max \left\{ Y_m(i, n) + \frac{\pi_u(i, n) V_m(i, n+1) + \pi_d(i, n) V_m(i+1, n+1)}{R_f}, \right.$$

$$A_m(i, n) + \frac{1}{R_f} \left(\pi_u(i, n) \left(q V_{m-1}(i, n+1) + (1-q) V_m(i, n+1) \right) \right. \qquad (8.11)$$

$$\left. \left. + \pi_d(i, n) \left(q V_{m-1}(i+1, n+1) + (1-q) V_m(i+1, n+1) \right) \right) \right\}.$$

By the time we have completed the backward induction procedure, we will have determined the market value of the project in state 1, $V_1(0, 0)$.

We then repeat the whole procedure, but this time for state $m = 2$, so that we obtain a binomial tree for $V_2(i, n)$. We continue doing this, increasing m by one each time, until eventually we have completed construction of the binomial tree for $V_M(i, n)$.

The solution process can be summarized as follows:

1. Build the decision tree and use it to identify the nodes where the decision maker is allowed to change the project's state.
2. Build a tree for the state variable.
3. Build a tree for the market value of the project in its final state, $m = 0$.
4. Build a tree for the market value of the project in its second-to-last state.

   (a) Start with the terminal condition.
   (b) Fill in the remainder of the tree, working from right to left, using the recursive formula in equations (8.10) and (8.11) as appropriate, with $m = 1$.

5. Repeat this process for $m = 2, 3, \ldots, M$ until we have built the tree for the market value of the project in its initial state, $m = M$.

Table 8.4 summarizes how each of the three situations considered in this chapter fits into this general scheme.

8.6 PROBLEMS

8.1. **(Practice)** Reevaluate the numerical example in Section 8.2.3 for the following parameter values: $X_0 = 100$, $U = 1.15$, $D = 1/U$, $K = 0.99$, $R_f = 1.05$, $J_1 = 30$, $J_2 = 50$. Suppose that the project rights are lost if

Table 8.4. Fitting the Examples into the General Approach

	Sequential Investment Timing	Resource Extraction	Optimal R&D
State variable	Market value of the completed project	Copper price	Market value of the developed project
Cash flow while waiting	None	None	None
Cash flow while attempting to change state	Investment expenditure	Net revenue	Development expenditure
Value of project rights in final state	Revenue from selling the completed project	None	Revenue from selling the developed project
Value of project rights when rights expire	None	None	None
Cash flow while waiting	$Y_m(i,n) = 0$	$Y_m(i,n) = 0$	$Y_m(i,n) = 0$
Cash flow while attempting to change state	$A_m(i,n) = -J_1 \text{ or } -J_2$	$A_m(i,n) = X(i,n) - C$	$A_m(i,n) = -I$
Probability of successfully changing state	$q = 1$	$q = 1$	$q = $ arbitrary
Value of project rights in final state	$V_0(i,n) = X(i,n)$	$V_0(i,n) = 0$	$V_0(i,n) = X(i,n)$
Value of project rights when rights expire	$V_m(i,N) = 0$	$V_m(i,N) = 0$	$V_m(i,N) = 0$

construction is not completed on or before date 8. All other aspects of the problem are unchanged.

8.2. **(Practice)** Suppose that there are three distinct stages of investment in Section 8.2, each taking one period to complete, and that the project rights are lost if construction is not completed on or before date 10. The associated stream of capital expenditure is J_1, J_2, J_3. All other aspects of the situation are unchanged.

   (a) Consider the case where the manager is able to delay each stage of investment as long as she chooses (although the project rights are still lost if construction is not completed on or before date 10).

      i. Draw the decision tree for this problem.

      ii. Derive the terminal conditions and the recursive equations needed to calculate the market value of the project rights.

      iii. Calculate the market value of the project rights at date 0 for the following parameter values: $X_0 = 390$, $U = 1.2$, $D = 1/U$, $K = 0.95$, $R_f = 1.10$, $J_1 = 25$, $J_2 = 110$, $J_3 = 121$.

   (b) Now suppose that the third stage must be completed immediately after the second stage.

      i. Modify the decision tree and recursive equations to reflect this change.

      ii. Repeat the numerical analysis for this case.

   (c) Finally, suppose that the second stage must be completed immediately after the first stage. The third stage can be delayed, as in part (a).

      i. Modify the decision tree and recursive equations to reflect this change.

      ii. Repeat the numerical analysis for this case.

   (d) Discuss these results.

8.3. **(Discussion)** The CEO of a large firm is considering two different ways of completing a project. The cash outflow associated with approach A has a lower present value than the corresponding cash flow stream for approach B. However, approach B has a steeper profile (that is, it tends to have its large cash flows relatively late in the construction process). Explain to the CEO why the difference in profiles means that he needs to consider more than just the present values of the two cash flow streams.

8.4. **(Application: Staged expansion of a business)** A firm currently operates one production facility, which generates net revenue of $X(i, n)$ at each node (i, n). The firm has the option to build up to two more identical facilities. Each one will cost I and will take one period to construct. Because of resource constraints within the firm, at most one facility can be constructed each period. No construction can begin from date 10 onwards. The risk-adjusted growth factor for the state variable equals K and the return on one-period risk-free bonds equals R_f, for some constants K and R_f. The state variable is equally likely to change by a constant factor of U or D each period.

(a) Draw the decision tree for the problem facing the firm's manager.

(b) Derive the terminal conditions and the recursive equations needed to calculate the market value of the firm.

(c) How does this situation compare with the one in Section 8.2?

(d) Calculate the market value of the firm at date 0, and identify an optimal expansion policy, for the following parameter values: $X_0 = 8$, $U = 1.25$, $D = 1/U$, $K = 0.94$, $R_f = 1.04$, $I = 100$.

(e) Should the firm expand more or less aggressively as it grows larger? Give an intuitive explanation.

8.5. **(Practice)** Reevaluate the numerical example in Section 8.3.3 for the following parameter values: $X_0 = 40$, $U = 1.18$, $D = 1/U$, $K = 0.99$, $R_f = 1.03$, $C_1 = 30$. Suppose that the mine contains three units of copper and that the extraction rights last until date 10.

8.6. **(Practice)** Suppose that extracting each unit of copper from the mine in Section 8.3 takes one period. No extraction can begin after date 9, but all other aspects of the situation are unchanged. Each extraction cost is incurred as soon as the firm begins extracting a unit of copper.

(a) Draw the decision tree for the problem facing the firm's manager.

(b) Derive the recursive equations needed to calculate the market value of the mine.

(c) Reevaluate the numerical example in Section 8.3.3 for the following parameter values: $X_0 = 15$, $U = 1.1$, $D = 1/U$, $K = 0.99$, $R_f = 1.05$, $C = 12$.

(d) Repeat all of the analysis for the case when it takes two periods to extract a unit of copper. (Suppose that extraction of a unit of copper cannot be interrupted, and that the firm can begin extracting one unit of copper while another one is in the middle of being extracted— that is, the firm can begin extracting one unit of copper each period.)

8.7. **(Discussion)** One method for valuing oil and gas resources is to use the product of the current net price (that is, the price less extraction cost) and the quantity of reserves.[9] Explain why this approach might give a poor estimate of the market value of those resources.

8.8. **(Application: Construction cost uncertainty)** A firm owns the right to build a new chemical manufacturing plant. Construction involves four stages, each of which takes one period to complete. The project rights are lost if

---

9. For example, the Federal Accounting Standards Advisory Board has proposed using this approach for Federal oil and gas resources (Federal Accounting Standards Advisory Board, 2007; Congressional Budget Office, 2007).

construction is not completed on or before date 8. The completed project will be worth A as soon as the final stage is completed, for some constant A. If the firm undertakes the next stage of the project at node (i, n) then it must pay $X(i, n)$ immediately. The risk-adjusted growth factor equals K and the return on one-period risk-free bonds equals R_f, for some constants K and R_f. The state variable is equally likely to change by a constant factor of U or D each period.

    (a) Draw the decision tree for the problem facing the firm's manager.

    (b) Derive the terminal conditions and the recursive equations needed to calculate the market value of the project rights.

    (c) How does this situation compare with the one in Section 8.3?

    (d) Calculate the market value of the project rights at date 0, and identify an optimal construction policy, for the following parameter values: $X_0 = 20$, $U = 1.25$, $D = 1/U$, $K = 1.01$, $R_f = 1.04$, $A = 104$.

8.9. **(Practice)** Suppose that the probability of successfully completing each stage of the R&D program in Section 8.4 can be different for different stages. Specifically, when there are m stages remaining, each attempt succeeds with probability q_m. All other aspects of the situation are unchanged.

    (a) Derive the recursive equations needed to calculate the market value of the development rights.

    (b) Reevaluate the numerical example in Section 8.4.3 for the case when $q_1 = 0.75$, $q_2 = 0.50$, $q_3 = 0.25$. That is, development becomes easier as each stage is completed.

    (c) Reevaluate the numerical example in Section 8.4.3 for the case when $q_1 = 0.25$, $q_2 = 0.50$, $q_3 = 0.75$. That is, development becomes more difficult as each stage is completed.

    (d) Discuss these results.

8.10. **(Practice)** Suppose that each attempt to complete the first stage of the R&D program in Section 8.4.3 costs $I_1 = 4$, whereas each attempt to complete the second and third stages costs $I_2 = I_3 = 15$. That is, the first exploratory stage is relatively inexpensive, while the subsequent implementation stages are very expensive. All other aspects of the situation are unchanged. Identify an optimal R&D policy for this problem.

8.11. **(Application: Learning by doing)** A firm has the right to attempt to develop a project at any time up to and including date 9. Only one successful development attempt is required to complete the project, and the mth development attempt will succeed with probability

$$q_m = \frac{1}{4}\left(1 - \frac{1}{2m}\right).$$

This "technical risk" is fully diversifiable and does not attract a risk premium. If the project is successfully developed at node (i, n) it will have a market value of $X(i, n)$ at that node. The risk-adjusted growth factor for the state variable equals the constant K and the return on one-period risk-free bonds is the constant R_f.

(a) Plot q_m as a function of m and use this graph to explain how the model specification captures the phenomenon of "learning by doing".

(b) Draw the decision tree for the problem facing the firm's manager. Identify and discuss the various project states.

(c) How does this situation compare with the one in Section 8.4?

(d) Derive the terminal conditions and the recursive equations needed to calculate the market value of the development rights.

(e) Calculate the market value of the development rights at date 0, and identify an optimal development policy, for the following parameter values: $X_0 = 55$, $U = 1.16$, $D = 1/U$, $K = 0.98$, $R_f = 1.04$, $I = 9$.

9

Über-compound Timing Options

Semiconductor production is extremely capital intensive, with the cost of building a new fabrication plant often measured in billions of dollars. The semiconductor industry is characterized by rapid growth in demand and high volatility. Rapid growth and technological change force firms to make frequent investments if they wish to remain competitive, but the volatility makes these investments very risky.

A firm building a fabrication plant must make many decisions. For example, when should it begin construction? Should it pay workers overtime in order to speed up construction? Should the firm build a larger facility than it will need for the foreseeable future, so that when the extra capacity is required it can be brought on stream quickly and cheaply? How should the firm respond if demand for the facility's output changes dramatically during construction? All of these decisions involve creating and destroying real options. Unlike the situations considered in Chapters 7 and 8, the firm must decide what to do as well as when to do it.

In March 1995 Micron Technology announced plans to build a semiconductor fabrication plant in Utah that would begin producing dynamic random access memory (DRAM) chips in August of the following year. The project was expected to cost $1.3 billion, comprising approximately $500 million to construct the buildings and $800 million for the equipment they would contain. Construction began in June 1995, with an accelerated construction schedule involving construction teams working extended shifts. Micron more than doubled the size of the planned plant in October 1995, with the project's total cost increasing to $2.5 billion, in part to build excess production capacity to be used if semiconductor demand continued to grow.

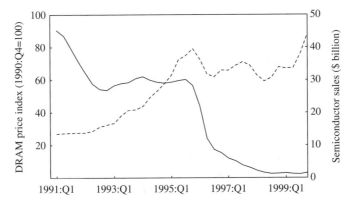

Figure 9.1. Semiconductor prices and sales

Note: The solid curve plots the DRAM price index constructed by Aizcorbe (2002), while the dashed curve shows quarterly worldwide semiconductor sales (in billions of dollars) reported by the Semiconductor Industry Association.

Micron's decision to rapidly build the facility reduced the value of its option to suspend or abandon construction prior to completion. However, the majority of the required expenditure related to installing equipment in the completed buildings, and Micron retained the option to avoid or delay this expenditure. Micron's decision to build excess capacity destroyed the option to wait and build the capacity only when demand had grown sufficiently, but it did allow the firm to exploit economies of scale in construction.

With the benefit of hindsight, the flexibility that Micron chose to forego would have been useful, because semiconductor prices plummeted at the end of 1995. The solid curve in Figure 9.1 plots an index of DRAM prices during the period 1991–2000 (Aizcorbe, 2002, Table A2), while the dashed curve shows quarterly worldwide semiconductor sales (in billions of dollars) reported by the Semiconductor Industry Association. Once prices began to fall, Micron could have carried on regardless and completed development of the plant, or it could have abandoned the project altogether.[1] Instead, by December 1995 Micron had announced that it would scale back the rate of construction, and in February the following year it announced that it would finish the complex's exterior shell, but delay purchasing and installing equipment until the semiconductor market strengthened.

Completing construction of the buildings provided Micron with a growth option: when conditions improved, Micron could resume development and begin

---

1. Different firms responded in different ways. For example, Samsung began construction of a fabrication plant in Texas in March 1996 and began producing DRAM chips there in September the following year.

production sooner and at lower cost than if it had to build a new plant from scratch. While waiting to exercise this growth option, Micron began to use one of the site's 12 buildings as a testing facility to support its operations elsewhere. After a ten-year wait and a change in output, investment resumed. In 2006, Micron and Intel formed IM Flash Technologies to produce NAND flash memory for digital cameras, MP3 players, and other consumer products. IM Flash began spending $1.2 billion to complete development of the facility that Micron began in 1995.

Micron's experience with its fabrication plant in Utah is an example of a situation where a decision maker has considerable freedom over how to achieve a particular goal. We introduce other examples of such problems in Section 9.1. The two examples that we consider in detail in this chapter are representative of this general class of situations. We analyze the problem of when and how to develop urban land in Section 9.2. Then, in Section 9.3, we return to the investment-timing problems of Sections 7.2 and 8.2 and allow the owner of the project rights to choose how (as well as when) to invest. We outline our approach to analyzing the general problem in Section 9.4.

9.1 EXAMPLES OF ÜBER-COMPOUND TIMING OPTIONS

As in the previous chapter, the situations considered here involve a series of actions that must be undertaken, possibly with some flexibility regarding when each action must occur. However, in this chapter there is more flexibility about the sequencing of the various actions. Perhaps the order can be changed. Perhaps some steps can be avoided altogether. Perhaps different pathways are possible.

9.1.1 Extending the Simple Timing Options of Chapter 7

The simplest situation of this type involves extending the problems discussed in Chapter 7. In those problems a project started out in one state and, at a time of the decision maker's choosing, changed into another state. Because there was only one of these "final states", the decision maker's only choice concerned when to make the change. Now we allow there to be multiple final states. There is still just one change allowed, but the decision maker can choose what that change will be, as well as when it will occur.

Urban Land Development The owner of a piece of vacant land has an option to construct an office building on the land. He chooses when to develop the land and how big to make the building. A larger building will offer more floor space and therefore have a higher sale price, but is disproportionately more expensive to construct. The optimal building size and development date depend on the strength of the market for office space. We discuss this problem in detail in Section 9.2.

Locating a New Factory A firm is considering investing in a new factory. Prospective demand is such that only one factory will be built, and there is some flexibility about when investment should occur. In addition, the firm is considering several different locations, which offer different combinations of land purchase costs, local and state taxes, and supporting infrastructure.

Building Flexibility into a Project A firm is considering building greater operating flexibility into a new factory. This flexibility will make construction more expensive, but it will make it easier to suspend production during future market downturns. If the manager delays investment until demand is very strong it may not be necessary to pay the extra construction costs needed to allow easier temporary suspensions in the future. On the other hand, the ability to build additional flexibility into the factory reduces the downside risk from delaying investment.

9.1.2 Extending the Compound Timing Options of Chapter 8

Just as we can extend the simple timing options of Chapter 7 by allowing the decision maker more choice about how to exercise the option, so we can extend the compound timing options of Chapter 8. The situations in the latter chapter involved a project that starts out in one state and moves through a specified sequence of states, with the order in which these changes occur being fixed. The decision maker's only choice concerned when to move from one state to the other. Now we give the decision maker much more flexibility about how to move between the various states.

Time to Build A firm has the option to develop a project. Development requires extensive construction, which has the potential to take several periods. However, the firm can speed up construction. This will involve greater capital expenditure, but has the advantage that the cash flows from the completed project will be received sooner. In contrast, slower construction gives the firm the option to abandon the project—and avoid some of the capital expenditure—if market conditions deteriorate. We discuss this problem in detail in Section 9.3.

Resource Extraction A firm owns the right to extract copper from a mine over a specified period of time. The state of the project can be described by the quantity of copper remaining in the mine, so that each time copper is extracted the project's state changes. In Section 8.3 the rate of extraction was fixed at one unit per period, so that the manager could change the state of the project by only one step per period. However, if variable extraction rates are possible, then the manager has the option to change the state by more than one step—by extracting at an accelerated rate—as long as copper remains in the mine.

R&D Programs A firm is attempting to develop a product, which will require successful completion of a series of steps. Each step requires expenditure on R&D and is not guaranteed to be successful. However, the firm has the option to increase R&D spending in return for a higher probability of successfully completing individual stages of the development program. This allows the firm to aggressively carry out development during periods when demand for the final product is strong, yet still continue some development at other times.

9.1.3 The General Über-compound Timing Option Problem

The best way to understand the typical problem considered in this chapter is to contrast it with the problems we met in the previous two chapters. In Chapter 7 we considered projects that begin in one state and, at a time of the decision maker's choosing, can be transformed into a particular second state. We expanded this family of problems in Chapter 8 by introducing an arbitrary number of states that the project would navigate in sequence. Most importantly, there was a well-defined order to the project-states, with the project having to pass through each state in a particular order. Thus, in both cases, the only choice available to the decision maker is the timing of the movements from one project-state to the next. In contrast, for the problems featuring in this chapter the decision maker can choose how to move between states as well as when to move. What distinguishes the problems in this chapter from those to be covered in Chapter 10 is that here the movement away from one state is irreversible. For example, the decision maker may be able to change the project from state 1 to either state 2 or 3, but once the move occurs the project cannot change back to state 1.

9.2 SOLVING THE LAND-DEVELOPMENT PROBLEM

9.2.1 Setting Up the Land-development Problem

The owner of a piece of vacant land has an option to construct an office building on the land.[2] For the sake of simplicity, we assume that construction takes one period and that the investment option expires if construction has not been completed on or before date 6. The owner can either construct a small building, costing I_s, or a large one, costing I_l, that is twice the size of the small one. All expenditure is incurred as soon as construction begins. We assume that larger buildings are disproportionately more expensive to construct, so that $I_l > 2I_s$. Once a building of one size is built it is not practicable to alter the size—that is, investment is irreversible.

We define the state variable $X(i, n)$ to be the market value of the land at node (i, n) when it includes a small office block. Since the large office block has twice the floor space of the small one, we suppose that the land is worth $2X(i, n)$ at node (i, n) when it includes a large office block. The land is worthless if construction of either sized building is not completed on or before date 6. The risk-adjusted growth factor associated with X equals the constant K. This means that the market value at node (i, n) of the right to a cash flow at date $n + 1$ that will equal $X(i, n + 1)$ if an up move occurs and $X(i + 1, n + 1)$ if a down move occurs is $KX(i, n)/R_f$, where R_f equals the return on one-period risk-free bonds.

9.2.2 Valuing the Land when the Decision Cannot be Delayed

In order to highlight the role that real options play in our subsequent results we start by considering this problem from the perspective of a land owner who must

---

2. The model in this section is a simplified version of the one in Titman (1985).

decide at date 0 what to build and when to build it. Investment might be delayed, but the decision is not. It is made at date 0.

If the land owner decides to build a small office block at date n, then he must pay I_s at date n. If he sells the office block immediately on completion then he will receive $X(\cdot, n+1)$ at date $n+1$. The market value at date 0 of the investment expenditure equals I_s/R_f^n. Because the risk-adjusted growth factor is constant, (4.10) implies that the market value at date 0 of the proceeds from selling the completed office block is

$$\left(\frac{K}{R_f}\right)^{n+1} X(0, 0).$$

The value of the land at date 0 is therefore equal to

$$\hat{V}_{s,n}(0, 0) = -\frac{I_s}{R_f^n} + \left(\frac{K}{R_f}\right)^{n+1} X(0, 0)$$

if the land owner decides to build a small office block at date n.

We can assess a policy of deciding to build a large office block at date n in the same way. The owner must pay I_l at date n and will receive $2X(\cdot, n+1)$ at date $n+1$. The market value of the land will equal

$$\hat{V}_{l,n}(0, 0) = -\frac{I_l}{R_f^n} + 2\left(\frac{K}{R_f}\right)^{n+1} X(0, 0).$$

If these are the only choices available to the land owner then he will choose the combination of investment date n and office-block size that maximizes the market value of the land at date 0.

9.2.3 Valuing the Land when the Decision Can be Delayed

Now we reconsider the problem, assuming that the land owner can delay the development decision. As usual, we begin by building the decision tree for this problem. At date 0, the land owner must construct a small office block on the land immediately, construct a large office block instead, or wait. These are represented by the actions labeled S ("small"), L ("large"), and W ("wait") in the decision tree shown in Figure 9.2.

If the land owner chooses to build an office block, then at date 1 he owns a piece of developed land and effectively receives a lump sum equal to its market value. Thus, if he chooses to invest at date 0 he will pay either I_s or I_l at date 0, receive a lump-sum cash flow of either $X(\cdot, 1)$ or $2X(\cdot, 1)$ at date 1, and then the decision tree terminates.

If, instead, the land owner chooses to wait at date 0 then he moves to date 1 in the decision tree, where he must choose from the same three actions: construct a small office block on the land immediately, construct a large office block instead, or wait. If he decides to invest (action S or L) then he will pay I_s or I_l at date 1, receive a lump-sum cash flow of $X(\cdot, 2)$ or $2X(\cdot, 2)$ at date 2, and then the decision

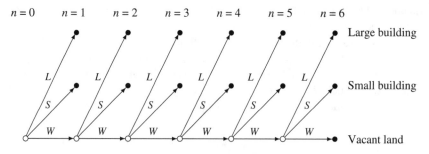

Figure 9.2. Decision tree for the land-development problem

tree terminates. If he decides to wait (action W) then he moves to date 2 in the decision tree and the situation repeats itself.

This process continues until date 6, when the development option has expired. The land owner cannot build an office block on the land, which must remain vacant.

This completes the construction of the decision tree shown in Figure 9.2. The remaining steps are to identify the binomial trees that are needed and to complete their construction. At any point in time the land will be in one of three possible states—vacant, with a small building, and with a large one. We let $V_v(i, n)$ denote the market value of vacant land at node (i, n), $V_s(i, n)$ denote its market value immediately after a small building is constructed, and $V_l(i, n)$ denote its market value immediately after a large building is constructed. Because of our choice of state variable, we have $V_s(i, n) = X(i, n)$ and $V_l(i, n) = 2X(i, n)$. Thus the only market value tree that we need to build is for vacant land.

Since construction takes one period and the development rights are lost if construction is not completed on or before date 6, it follows that

$$V_v(i, 6) = 0 \tag{9.1}$$

for all $i = 0, 1, \ldots, 6$. This is the terminal condition that we use to begin filling in the binomial tree for V_v.

Now we consider the problem facing the land owner at an arbitrary node (i, n), for any $n < 6$. He must choose one of three possible actions: constructing a small office block on the land immediately, constructing a large office block instead, or waiting. If he constructs a small office block on the land immediately then he pays I_s now and, upon selling the land at date $n + 1$, receives $V_s(i, n + 1) = X(i, n + 1)$ if the next move is up and $V_s(i + 1, n + 1) = X(i + 1, n + 1)$ if it is down. Since the market value at node (i, n) of the proceeds from the land sale is $KX(i, n)/R_f$, the payoff from building a small office block is

$$-I_s + \frac{KX(i, n)}{R_f}.$$

Similarly, if the land owner constructs a large office block on the land immediately then he pays I_l now and, upon selling the land at date $n + 1$, receives sales revenue that is worth $2KX(i, n)/R_f$ at node (i, n). The payoff from building a large office block is therefore

$$-I_l + \frac{2KX(i, n)}{R_f}.$$

Finally, if he waits then there is no cash flow at date n and the undeveloped land will be worth $V_v(i, n + 1)$ at date $n + 1$ if the next move is up and $V_v(i + 1, n + 1)$ if it is down, so that the payoff from waiting equals

$$\frac{\pi_u(i, n)V_v(i, n + 1) + \pi_d(i, n)V_v(i + 1, n + 1)}{R_f}.$$

The land owner will choose the action that maximizes the market value of the land, so that it is worth

$$V_v(i, n) = \max \left\{ -I_s + \frac{KX(i, n)}{R_f}, \; -I_l + \frac{2KX(i, n)}{R_f}, \right.$$
$$\left. \frac{\pi_u(i, n)V_v(i, n + 1) + \pi_d(i, n)V_v(i + 1, n + 1)}{R_f} \right\}. \tag{9.2}$$

We now have all the information we need to calculate the market value of the land and determine an optimal development policy. The following numerical example demonstrates the procedure.

9.2.4 A Numerical Example

In this example we analyze the real option to develop the piece of land described above. It costs $I_s = 100$ to build a small office block and $I_l = 250$ to build a large one. The land would currently sell for $X_0 = 125$ if it already had a small office block in place. Each period this market value is equally likely to grow by a factor of $U = 1.1500$ or $D = 1/U = 0.8696$, so that the market value of a small office block on the land is $X(i, n) = X_0 D^i U^{n-i}$ at node (i, n). The risk-adjusted growth factor is $K = 1.0000$, so that equation (3.8) implies that the risk-neutral probabilities of up and down moves are $\pi_u = 0.4651$ and $\pi_d = 0.5349$, respectively, throughout the tree. The one-period risk-free interest rate equals 2% per period, so that $R_f = 1.02$.

Our analysis of the situation when the land owner must decide at date 0 what to build and when to build it is summarized in Table 9.1. For the indicated investment date n, the second and third entries in each row report the market value of the undeveloped land at date 0 assuming that a small or a large office block is built at date n, respectively. For example, if the land owner decides to build a small office block on the land immediately, the land is worth

$$\hat{V}_{s,0}(0, 0) = -I_s + \left(\frac{K}{R_f} \right) X(0, 0) = -100.00 + \left(\frac{1.0000}{1.02} \right) 125.00 = 22.55.$$

Table 9.1. Analysis of the Option to Develop
Vacant Land when the Investment Decision
Must be Made Immediately

n	$\hat{V}_{s,n}(0,0)$	$\hat{V}_{l,n}(0,0)$
0	22.55	−4.90
1	22.11	−4.81
2	21.67	−4.71
3	21.25	−4.62
4	20.83	−4.53
5	20.42	−4.44

Because this is the highest market value in Table 9.1, if the decision has to be made at date 0 then the land owner should immediately begin construction of a small office block on the site.

Now we analyze the situation when the land owner can delay the development decision. The binomial tree for the state variable is shown in the top panel of Table 9.2. The tree for the market value of the undeveloped land, shown in the bottom panel, is constructed using backward induction in the usual way. We begin by using the terminal condition (9.1) to fill in the final column, and then use the recursive equation (9.2) to fill in the remaining columns, always working from right to left. The optimal action to take at each node is indicated by the shading of the cells in the bottom panel of Table 9.2: the land owner should immediately start constructing a small office block in the lightly-shaded cells and a large office block in the darkly-shaded cells, and wait in the remaining cells.

Initially it is optimal to wait, but any one of the three final outcomes (building small, building large, and leaving the land undeveloped) is possible—that is, it is possible to trace out a path to each of the two types of shaded cells or to unshaded cells in the final column of the tree. However, the bottom panel of Table 9.2 reveals that the set of possible outcomes quickly shrinks as time passes.

- If the first two moves are up then the land owner knows that ultimately the land will be developed. However, even at node $(0, 2)$ he cannot be certain whether he will end up building a small office block or a large one.
- If the first two moves are down then the land owner knows that he will not be building a large office block on the site because once he reaches node $(2, 2)$ he will end up either building a small office block or abandoning development altogether.

That is, if the market improves dramatically in the near future it is optimal to wait and build either a large office block if the market gets even stronger or a small office block if it does not. In contrast, if the market weakens significantly, then the land owner should wait and either abandon the site if the market gets even weaker or build a small office block if it does not.

Table 9.2. Analysis of the Option to Develop Vacant Land when the Investment Decision Can be Delayed

$X(i, n)$	0	1	2	3	4	5	6	
0	125.00	143.75	165.31	190.11	218.63	251.42	289.13	
1		108.70	125.00	143.75	165.31	190.11	218.63	
2			94.52	108.70	125.00	143.75	165.31	Step 1: Construct binomial
3				82.19	94.52	108.70	125.00←	tree for the state variable
4					71.47	82.19	94.52	
5						62.15	71.47	
6							54.04	

$V_v(i, n)$	0	1	2	3	4	5	6	
0	31.72	51.33	80.70	122.76	178.68	242.98	0.00	
1		15.85	27.71	47.14	77.44	122.76	0.00	Step 2: Fill in final column
2			6.12	11.85	22.55	40.93	0.00←	using equation (9.1)
3				1.36	2.99	6.56	0.00	
4					0.00	0.00	0.00	Step 3: Fill in remaining
5						0.00	0.00←	columns using
6							0.00	equation (9.2)

Thus, two quite different things can happen in the short run. However, the underlying rationale for waiting is similar in the two cases, which we see by considering the land owner's problem at nodes $(1, 4)$ and $(3, 4)$.

Consider the situation at node $(1, 4)$. It is optimal to wait and, after one period, build a large office block if the next move is up and a small one if the next move is down. Why does the land owner wait? If he built a small office block immediately his payoff would be

$$-I_s + \frac{KX(1, 4)}{R_f} = -100.00 + \frac{1.0000 \times 165.31}{1.02} = 62.07,$$

whereas if he built a large one his payoff would be

$$-I_l + \frac{2KX(1, 4)}{R_f} = -250.00 + \frac{2 \times 1.0000 \times 165.31}{1.02} = 74.14.$$

However, rather than build a large office block immediately, the land owner waits. From the bottom panel of Table 9.2, if the next move is up he will build a large office block and receive a payoff of $V_v(1, 5) = 122.76$, and if the next move is down he will build a small office block and receive a payoff of $V_v(2, 5) = 40.93$. That is, by waiting (rather than building immediately) he receives a payoff that is $122.76 - 74.14 = 48.62$ higher if an up move occurs and $74.14 - 40.93 = 33.21$ lower if a down move occurs. He fully exploits the up move by building a large office block, and is able to reduce the impact of a down move by building just a small office block. It is this asymmetry that leads the land owner to delay investing at node $(1, 4)$ and "roll the dice"—he will lose if the market weakens, but he will win much more if it strengthens.

Now consider the situation at node $(3, 4)$. It is optimal to wait and, after one period, build a small office block if the next move is up and abandon development altogether if the next move is down. If the land owner built a small office block immediately, instead of waiting, his payoff would be

$$-I_s + \frac{KX(3, 4)}{R_f} = -100.00 + \frac{1.0000 \times 94.52}{1.02} = -7.34,$$

while if he built a large one his payoff would be

$$-I_l + \frac{2KX(3, 4)}{R_f} = -250.00 + \frac{2 \times 1.0000 \times 94.52}{1.02} = -64.67.$$

However, rather than abandoning development immediately and receiving a payoff of zero, the land owner waits. From the bottom panel of Table 9.2, if the next move is up he will build a small office block and receive a payoff of $V_v(3, 5) = 6.56$, and if the next move is down he will abandon development and receive a payoff of zero. That is, by waiting (rather than abandoning immediately) he receives a payoff that is $6.56 - 0.00 = 6.56$ higher if an up move occurs and is unchanged if a down move occurs. He fully exploits the up move by building a small office block, and is able to eliminate the impact of a down move by abandoning development. Once more, it is this asymmetry that leads the land owner to delay investing at node $(3, 4)$.

There is much less asymmetry at node $(2, 4)$. Although it is optimal to build a small office block at that node and receive a payoff of 22.55, we can consider what the land owner would do at date 5 if he waited at date 4. From the bottom panel of Table 9.2, if he waits and the next move is up he will build a small office block and receive a payoff of $V_v(2, 5) = 40.93$, and if the next move is down he will also build a small office block, but this time the payoff is $V_v(3, 5) = 6.56$. That is, by waiting (rather than building a small office block immediately) he would receive a payoff that is $40.93 - 22.55 = 18.38$ higher if an up move occurs and is $22.55 - 6.56 = 15.99$ lower if a down move occurs. The asymmetry is much smaller than at the other two nodes. Indeed, the expected gain is not sufficient to compensate the owner for the risk associated with waiting and the delay in receiving the investment payoff, as can be seen by calculating the payoff from waiting at node $(2, 4)$, which equals

$$\frac{\pi_u(2,4)V_v(2,5)+\pi_d(2,4)V_v(3,5)}{R_f} = \frac{0.4651 \times 40.93+0.5349 \times 6.56}{1.02} = 22.11.$$

Because this is less than the payoff from building a small office block immediately, delay is not optimal.

The role of asymmetry in determining the optimal policy can be seen graphically in Figure 9.3, which plots the market value of the undeveloped land on the vertical axis and the market value of a small office building on the horizontal axis at different nodes (i, n). The two dashed lines show the payoffs from immediately

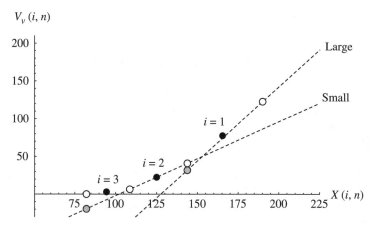

Figure 9.3. The market value of undeveloped land at date 4

constructing an office block on the land, with the steeper line corresponding to the large office block. The black dots correspond to the indicated nodes at date 4, while the white dots correspond to nodes at date 5. The gray dots show the outcomes of various suboptimal actions at date 5, which are explained below.

We begin by considering the case where $i = 1$. The black dot has coordinates $(X(1, 4), V_v(1, 4))$, so that it represents the land owner's situation at date 4. Because the black dot is centered above the line showing the investment payoff, waiting is better than constructing a large office block immediately. At date 5 the land owner will construct a large building if the next move is up (shown by the white dot to the right of the black dot) and a small one if it is down (shown by the white dot to the left). The gray dot below this one, which shows the payoff if the land owner were to construct a large building following a down move, illustrates the asymmetry that makes waiting valuable. The land owner's ability to substitute a small building for the large one (that is, to replace the gray dot with the white one) reduces the downside risk from waiting by enough to make waiting optimal.

Now consider the case where $i = 3$. This time the black dot has coordinates $(X(3, 4), V_v(3, 4))$, so that it also represents the land owner's situation at date 4, but this time when a small office block is less valuable. The black dot lies above both investment payoff lines, so that waiting is optimal. At date 5 the land owner will construct a small building if the next move is up (shown by the white dot to the right of the black dot) and leave the land undeveloped if it is down (shown by the white dot to the left). The gray dot below this one shows the payoff if the land owner were to construct a small building following a down move. This time it is the land owner's ability to substitute leaving the land undeveloped for constructing a small building that reduces the downside risk sufficiently for waiting to be optimal.

Finally, consider the case where $i = 2$. The black dot, with coordinates $(X(2, 4), V_v(2, 4))$, lies on the payoff line, indicating that immediate construction of a small office block is optimal. In this case, whether the next move is up (the white dot to the right) or down (the white dot to the left), the land owner would construct a small office block at date 5 if he did not invest at date 4. Thus, the land owner is not able to mitigate the downside risk associated with delaying construction by reducing the scale of the project as in the other two cases. Without this ability, waiting is not an optimal policy.

In a wide range of applications it can be very useful to plot the decision maker's payoff as a function of the state variable, as we have in Figure 9.3. It can be optimal to delay exercising the right to this payoff in regions where the payoff function is convex (that is, the slope of the curve increases as we move from left to right) because, as in the example in this section, this convexity introduces a favorable asymmetry into the payoff from waiting. That is, if the decision maker waits and the payoff increases then the gain will be large relative to the loss if he waits and the payoff falls.

The volatility in the state variable has the effect of smoothing out the "kinks" in the payoff function, as in Figure 9.3: the greater the volatility, the greater the extent of the smoothing that can be achieved by delaying investment. Indeed, for the example here, if the market value of a small office block is much more volatile then the intermediate region where immediate construction of a small office block is optimal can disappear. Figure 9.4 demonstrates this by redrawing Figure 9.3 for the case when the size of an up move is $U = 1.3000$ and that of a down move is $D = 1/1.3000 = 0.7692$. The black dots plot $(X(i, 4), V_v(i, 4))$ for the indicated values of i, while the white dots plot $(X(i, 5), V_v(i, 5))$. The greater volatility in the state variable has moved the central black dot upwards, so that it is now optimal to delay construction at node $(2, 4)$ rather than construct a small building immediately. The source of the increased value in waiting can be found in the gray dots: the left one shows that downside risk can be reduced by abandoning

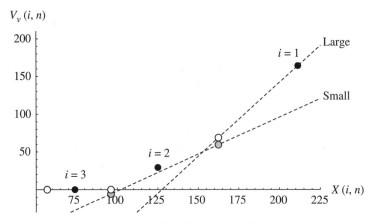

Figure 9.4. The market value of undeveloped land at date 4 when the state variable is more volatile

development if the next move is down, whereas the right one shows that upside risk can be increased by constructing a large building if the next move is up.

The impact of asymmetric risk that we have identified in this example is not unique to this situation. In fact, it plays a similar role in most, if not all, situations where real options are valuable. If we look closely at the examples throughout Chapters 6–11 we find similar asymmetric risks in every case.

9.3 SOLVING THE TIME-TO-BUILD PROBLEM

The situation we consider in this section is based on the investment timing problem analyzed in Sections 7.2 and 8.2. In Section 7.2 the investment program can be completed in one period, whereas in Section 8.2 it requires at least two periods, but completion of the project can be delayed (or even abandoned) after construction begins. However, in each of these examples, the construction technique was specified as part of the problem description. In this section we allow the owner to decide which construction technique to follow—and, most importantly, we allow her to use all available information when deciding what (as well as when) to build.

9.3.1 Setting Up the Time-to-build Problem

An individual owns the right to invest in a project, with this right being lost if construction is not completed on or before date 5. Investment involves two stages that must be undertaken before construction is complete and the project can be sold. As in the two earlier sections, the decision maker can still delay (and even abandon) completion of the project, but now she can also speed it up if she wishes. Specifically, she has the choice of how quickly to build the project.

- She can pay I and complete both stages of the project in one period.
- She can pay J_1 and complete the first stage in one period. Then, at some later date, she can pay J_2 and complete the second stage in one additional period. We assume that $I > J_2$, so that it will never be optimal to undertake fast construction of a half-completed project.

Construction costs are paid in advance and are sunk as soon as they are incurred—that is, each stage of investment is irreversible.

We set the state variable $X(i, n)$ equal to the market value of the completed project at node (i, n), as in Sections 7.2 and 8.2. We suppose that the risk-adjusted growth factor associated with X equals the constant K and that the return on one-period risk-free bonds equals the constant R_f.

One disadvantage of using the slow construction technique is that the project cannot be completed as quickly, delaying receipt of the proceeds from selling the completed project and (via the effect of discounting) reducing the present value. One advantage of this technique is that investment can be abandoned part way through (avoiding incurring the final instalment of J_2)—that is, by creating an abandonment option the slow construction technique offers greater flexibility.

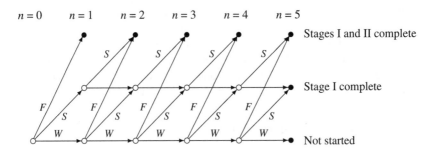

Figure 9.5. Decision tree for the time-to-build problem

There is another aspect to consider—the relative costs of the two techniques—but whether this favors one technique or the other depends on the relative sizes of I, J_1, and J_2.

9.3.2 Analyzing the Time-to-build Problem

We start by building the decision tree for this problem, and begin by considering the owner's problem at date 0. Since both construction stages are still to be undertaken, the owner can choose from one of three actions: build both stages of the construction program at once (that is, fast investment), undertake only the first stage (that is, slow investment), or wait. These are represented by the actions F (for "fast"), S (for "slow"), and W (for "wait") in the decision tree drawn in Figure 9.5. If she undertakes both stages of construction then there is a cash outflow of I at date 0 and after one period elapses the owner will be able to sell the completed project. In contrast, if the owner undertakes only the first stage then there is a cash outflow of J_1 at date 0 and after one period elapses the firm will have just one construction stage remaining. Finally, if she waits then there is zero cash flow at date 0 and when date 1 arrives the firm will still not have begun construction.

From date 1 onwards the firm will be in one of three states: both stages of the project will be completed, or Stage I alone will be completed, or construction will not have begun. We do not need to consider the owner's actions in the first case since then the investment program is complete, but we must consider the other two possibilities.

Suppose that only Stage I has been completed. Prior to date 5 the owner can either wait or she can undertake Stage II of the construction program. If she waits, then there is zero cash flow immediately and after one period elapses the firm will still have completed just one construction stage. In contrast, if she undertakes Stage II then the firm incurs capital expenditure of J_2 immediately and after one period elapses the owner will be able to sell the completed project. From date 5 onwards the owner can do nothing because the investment rights have expired.

In contrast, at any time prior to date 5, if construction has not begun, then the situation is the same as at date 0: the owner must undertake both stages of the construction program at once, undertake only the first stage, or wait. From date 5 onwards the owner can do nothing because the investment rights have expired.

This completes the construction of the decision tree shown in Figure 9.5. At any point in time the project will be in one of three possible states. We let $V_m(i, n)$ denote the market value of the project rights at node (i, n) when there are m stages of the investment program remaining to be completed; we need to consider $m = 0, 1, 2$. As in Section 8.2, $V_0(i, n) = X(i, n)$; that is, immediately after construction is completed, the project rights are worth whatever the owner would receive from selling the completed project. As a result, we need to build only two market-value trees, one for the project rights in the "Stage I complete" state ($m = 1$), and another for the project rights in the "not started" state ($m = 2$).

Since the project rights are lost if investment is not completed on or before date 5, it follows that

$$V_1(i, 5) = V_2(i, 5) = 0 \qquad (9.3)$$

for all $i = 0, 1, \ldots, 5$. These are the terminal conditions that we use to begin filling in the binomial trees for V_1 for V_2.

As in Section 8.2, we start at the end of the project investment process and work backwards in time. Thus, we begin by considering the case when the firm has already completed Stage I of the investment program. Consider the owner's situation at node (i, n). She must either wait or undertake Stage II of the construction program. If she waits, then there is zero cash flow now and after one period elapses the firm will still have just Stage II remaining: if an up move occurs the project rights will be worth $V_1(i, n + 1)$, while if a down move occurs they will be worth $V_1(i + 1, n + 1)$. The payoff from waiting therefore equals

$$\frac{\pi_u(i, n)V_1(i, n + 1) + \pi_d(i, n)V_1(i + 1, n + 1)}{R_f}.$$

In contrast, if the owner undertakes Stage II immediately, then there is a cash outflow of J_2 now and after one period elapses she will be able to sell the completed project: if an up move occurs she will be able to sell the completed project for $X(i, n + 1)$, while if a down move occurs the sale price will be $X(i + 1, n + 1)$. Using (4.10) shows that the market value at node (i, n) of the sales revenue equals $KX(i, n)/R_f$, so that the payoff from undertaking Stage II equals

$$-J_2 + \frac{KX(i, n)}{R_f}.$$

The owner will choose the action that maximizes the market value of the firm, so that the project rights are worth

$$V_1(i,n)=\max\left\{\frac{\pi_u(i,n)V_1(i,n+1)+\pi_d(i,n)V_1(i+1,n+1)}{R_f}, -J_2+\frac{KX(i,n)}{R_f}\right\}.$$
$$(9.4)$$

Now we turn to the remaining tree, for the case when the firm has not begun the first investment stage. Consider the owner's situation at node (i, n). She must wait or undertake Stage I or undertake both stages of the construction program. If she waits, then there is zero cash flow now and after one period elapses the firm will still not have begun construction: if an up move occurs the project rights will be worth $V_2(i, n+1)$, while if a down move occurs they will be worth $V_2(i+1, n+1)$. The corresponding payoff equals

$$\frac{\pi_u(i, n)V_2(i, n+1) + \pi_d(i, n)V_2(i+1, n+1)}{R_f}.$$

If the owner undertakes Stage I immediately, then there is a cash outflow of J_1 now and after one period elapses the firm will have just one construction stage to go: if an up move occurs the project rights will be worth $V_1(i, n+1)$, while if a down move occurs they will be worth $V_1(i+1, n+1)$. The payoff from undertaking Stage I is therefore

$$-J_1 + \frac{\pi_u(i, n)V_1(i, n+1) + \pi_d(i, n)V_1(i+1, n+1)}{R_f}.$$

Finally, if the owner undertakes both stages at once, then there is a cash outflow of I now and after one period elapses she will be able to sell the completed project. The market value at node (i, n) of the sales revenue equals $KX(i, n)/R_f$, so that the payoff from undertaking both stages at once equals

$$-I + \frac{KX(i, n)}{R_f}.$$

Because the owner chooses the action that maximizes the market value of the firm, the project rights are worth

$$V_2(i, n) = \max \left\{ \frac{\pi_u(i, n)V_2(i, n+1) + \pi_d(i, n)V_2(i+1, n+1)}{R_f}, \right.$$

$$-J_1 + \frac{\pi_u(i, n)V_1(i, n+1) + \pi_d(i, n)V_1(i+1, n+1)}{R_f},$$

$$\left. -I + \frac{KX(i, n)}{R_f} \right\}. \tag{9.5}$$

We now have all the information we need to calculate the market value of the project rights and determine an optimal investment policy. The following numerical example demonstrates the procedure.

9.3.3 A Numerical Example

We continue our analysis of the investment timing problem begun in Section 7.2 and continued in Section 8.2. If construction is not completed on or before date 5 then the option to invest in the project is lost forever. We suppose that if the completed project were available for sale immediately it would have market value $X_0 = 100$ and that each period this market value is equally likely to grow by a factor of either $U = 1.2500$ or $D = 1/U = 0.8000$. The resulting binomial tree for the market value of the completed project is shown in the top panel of

Table 9.3. Analysis of the Option to Invest in a Project when Construction Takes One or Two Periods and Can be Interrupted

$X(i, n)$	0	1	2	3	4	5
0	100.00	125.00	156.25	195.31	244.14	305.18
1		80.00	100.00	125.00	156.25	195.31
2			64.00	80.00	100.00	125.00
3				51.20	64.00	80.00
4					40.96	51.20
5						32.77

$V_1(i, n)$	0	1	2	3	4	5
0	5.75	23.14	49.93	83.41	125.26	0.00
1		1.15	5.17	23.14	49.93	0.00
2			0.08	0.36	1.71	0.00
3				0.00	0.00	0.00
4					0.00	0.00
5						0.00

$V_2(i, n)$	0	1	2	3	4	5
0	2.00	8.39	31.93	65.41	107.26	0.00
1		0.30	1.43	6.76	31.93	0.00
2			0.00	0.00	0.00	0.00
3				0.00	0.00	0.00
4					0.00	0.00
5						0.00

Table 9.3. The risk-adjusted growth factor is $K = 0.9000$ throughout the tree, so that equation (3.8) implies that the risk-neutral probabilities of up and down moves are $\pi_u = 0.2222$ and $\pi_d = 0.7778$, respectively, throughout the tree. The one-period risk-free interest rate equals 5%, so that $R_f = 1.05$.

Construction takes one or two periods. As in our earlier examples, construction in one period can be achieved at a cost of $I = 102$, while the slower construction method requires cash outlays of $J_1 = 6$ and $J_2 = 84$ in the first and second periods of construction. In Section 7.2.5 we assumed that the two-period construction program could not be interrupted, but this restriction was relaxed in Section 8.2. The market value of the project rights evolved according to the binomial trees shown in Tables 7.1, 7.2, and 8.1. In particular, the project rights are initially worth 1.88 if only the fast construction technique is available, 1.68 if only the uninterruptible slow technique is available, and 1.97 if only the interruptible slow technique is available.

Now we suppose that both the fast technique and the interruptible slow technique are available. Table 9.3 shows how the market value of the project rights evolves in this case. The middle panel describes $V_1(i, n)$, the market value of the project rights when just one stage remains to be completed, while the bottom panel describes $V_2(i, n)$, the market value of the project rights when construction has not yet begun. The lightly-shaded cells indicate nodes at which a single stage of the project is built, while the darkly-shaded cells show where it is optimal to build both stages at once.

The middle panels of Tables 8.1 and 9.3 show that once the first stage has been built the value of the project rights is the same whether or not the fast-construction option is available. This simply reflects the fact that once the first stage is built the option to build both stages at once has no value. However, comparing the bottom panels of these two tables shows that the fast-construction option increases the value of the project rights prior to the first stage being built. In fact, the market value of the project rights increases from 1.97 to 2.00. The origin of this increase in value can be found at node $(1, 4)$ in the bottom panel of Tables 8.1 and 9.3. In the first table the lack of a fast-construction option means that the project rights are worthless at this node, but in the second table it is still possible to complete the project by building both stages at once. This in turn alters the optimal behavior at node $(1, 3)$. In the first case it is optimal to build Stage I, but in the second case it is optimal to wait (and, if the next move is up, build both stages of the project at once at date 4): it is much more attractive to delay here, since the owner has one last chance to invest (at a cost) by using the fast technique at date 4.

9.4 SOLVING PROBLEMS INVOLVING ÜBER-COMPOUND TIMING OPTIONS

Recall that in the problems featured in this chapter the decision maker can choose how to move between states as well as when to move between them. The particular choices available to the decision maker will depend on the structure of the situation being analyzed. The only generic restriction on the movement between states is that any movement away from a state is irreversible.[3] This means that there is a natural ordering of project states. Some will be "final" states, meaning that if the project ever arrives in one of those states then the decision tree ends. Others can best be described as "intermediate" states, meaning that the decision maker is able to move the project from these states to other ones. For example, there are two final states in the land-development problem, corresponding to the land having a small or a large office building in place; there is one intermediate state, corresponding to the land being vacant. In contrast, in the investment timing problem there is one final state (in which the project's construction has been completed) and two intermediate ones (corresponding to one and two stages remaining to be built). The key feature of the general problem we consider is that once the project leaves one of the intermediate states it cannot return to that particular state. The fact that

---

3. In this section we only consider the case where each attempt to change the project state is guaranteed to be successful. The extension to handle uncertainty is straightforward.

the project-states have this structure means that we can fill in entire market-value trees in turn. (In Chapter 10 we see that construction of the trees is not quite so simple when moves between project-states can be reversed.)

We label the various project states by $m = 1, 2, \ldots, M$ and denote the (cum dividend) market value of the project at node (i, n) by $V_m(i, n)$ when it is in state m. For each intermediate project-state m we let J_m denote the collection of states that the project can switch to. For example, if $J_1 = \{1, 2, 4\}$ then the manager can switch the project from state 1 to any one of states 1, 2, and 4. If $J_2 = \{3\}$ then the only action available to the manager is to switch the project to state 3.[4]

For the particular problem we are studying, we need to be able to identify the market value of the project in each final state as a specific function of the state variable. For each intermediate project-state, we need to know the cash flow that will occur at node (i, n) if the manager switches the project from state m to any state j in the allowable set J_m. We denote this cash flow by $Y_{m,j}(i, n)$, so that the subscripts indicate (in order) the current state and the state after one period elapses.

The first step in analyzing this problem is to build the decision tree and use it to identify final and intermediate project-states and the allowable transitions between different project-states. Next we build a binomial tree for the state variable. Ultimately we need to complete trees for the market value of the project in each of the intermediate project-states, but we need to build these trees in a particular order.

We begin construction of the market value trees by identifying the "next-to-last" project-states, which are states that lead only to our so-called final states and to themselves. For example, in the time-to-build problem in Section 9.3, the only next-to-last state is the one when Stage I of the project has been completed. For each of these project-states we begin to construct its binomial tree by filling in the terminal nodes using the appropriate terminal condition. We then use backward induction to fill in the remaining entries.

Derivation of the recursive equation is straightforward. Suppose, for example, that the project is in state m at node (i, n), so that the manager must switch the project to one of the states in the set J_m.[5] If the manager chooses state j then the project generates a cash flow of $Y_{m,j}(i, n)$ immediately and, after one period, it will be worth $V_j(i, n + 1)$ if an up move occurs and $V_j(i + 1, n + 1)$ if a down move occurs. Note that, because we are at one of the "next-to-last" nodes, j will either be a final state (in which case $V_j(i, n + 1)$ and $V_j(i + 1, n + 1)$ are known functions of the state variable) or state m itself (in which case $V_j(i, n + 1)$ and $V_j(i + 1, n + 1)$ will have been calculated in the earlier stages of the backward

---

4. In some cases the actions available to the manager will vary with the date. For example, the precise contents of J_1 might be different on dates 1 and 2. We suppress this notation in the description here only to keep the notation as simple as possible. The extension to date-dependent choice sets is straightforward.

5. Note that this set may include the current project state, m, which would correspond to the "waiting" action we have met many times.

induction procedure). The market value of the project at node (i, n) therefore equals

$$Y_{m,j}(i, n) + \frac{\pi_u(i, n)V_j(i, n + 1) + \pi_d(i, n)V_j(i + 1, n + 1)}{R_f}$$

if the manager moves the project to state j. Since any state $j \in J_m$ can be chosen, and since the objective is to maximize the market value of the firm, the value of the project at node (i, n) in state m is

$$V_m(i,n) = \max_{j \in J_m} \left\{ Y_{m,j}(i,n) + \frac{\pi_u(i,n)V_j(i,n+1) + \pi_d(i,n)V_j(i+1,n+1)}{R_f} \right\}, \quad (9.6)$$

where $\max_{j \in J_m}$ indicates that we should evaluate the expression inside the brackets for each value of j in J_m and then take the maximum of these numbers as the value of $V_m(i, n)$.

Once we have filled in the binomial trees for all the "next-to-last" project-states, we move back to the previous set of states. These lead only to final states and "next-to-last" states. For example, in the time-to-build problem in Section 9.3, the only state in this category is the one when neither stage of the project has been completed. For each of these project-states we begin to construct its binomial tree by filling in the terminal nodes using the appropriate terminal condition and then use backward induction (together with (9.6)) to fill in the remaining entries. We continue like this, focusing on one set of project-states at a time, until we have worked our way back to the initial project-state.

By the time we have completed this procedure, we will have determined the current market value of the project together with an optimal policy for moving from one state to another.

The solution process can be summarized as follows:

1. Build the decision tree and use it to identify final and intermediate project-states and the allowable transitions between different project-states.
2. Build a tree for the state variable.
3. Calculate the market value of the project in each final state.
4. Build a tree for the market value of the project in each "next-to-last" state.
   (a) Start by using the appropriate terminal condition to fill in the final column of each of these trees.
   (b) Fill in the remaining nodes of the various trees, working from right to left, using the recursive formula in equation (9.6).
5. Repeat this procedure for the previous set of project-states.
6. Continue repeating this procedure for each cohort of project-states, until we have determined the current market value of the project.

Table 9.4 summarizes how the two situations considered in this chapter fit into this general scheme.

Table 9.4. Fitting the Examples into the General Approach

	Land Development Problem	Time-to-build Problem
State variable	Market value of land featuring a small office block	Market value of the completed project
Intermediate project states	1 = vacant	1 = not started 2 = first stage complete
Final project states	2 = small office block 3 = large office block	3 = both stages complete
Allowable transitions	$J_1 = \{1, 2, 3\}$	$J_1 = \{1, 2, 3\}$ $J_2 = \{2, 3\}$
Value of project in final states	$V_2(i, n) = X(i, n)$ $V_3(i, n) = 2X(i, n)$	$V_3(i, n) = X(i, n)$
Cash flows	$Y_{1,1}(i, n) = 0$ $Y_{1,2}(i, n) = -I_s$ $Y_{1,3}(i, n) = -I_l$	$Y_{1,1}(i, n) = 0$ $Y_{1,2}(i, n) = -J_1$ $Y_{1,3}(i, n) = -I$ $Y_{2,2}(i, n) = 0$ $Y_{2,3}(i, n) = -J_2$

9.5 PROBLEMS

9.1. **(Practice)** Suppose that the owner of the land in Section 9.2 receives rental income of J each period that it remains undeveloped (from car park rentals, for example). The development rights are lost if construction has not been completed on or before date 10, but all other aspects of the situation are unchanged.

    (a) Derive the recursive equation needed to calculate the market value of the undeveloped land.

    (b) Calculate the market value of the undeveloped land at date 0 for the following values of J: 0.00, 0.25, 0.50, 0.75, and 1.00. Use the following values for the other parameters: $X_0 = 18$, $U = 1.12$, $D = 1/U$, $K = 1.00$, $R_f = 1.03$, $I_s = 10$, $I_l = 30$.

    (c) What effect does the possibility of rental income from the undeveloped land have on the optimal development policy? Give an intuitive explanation for this behavior.

9.2. **(Practice)** Suppose that the large building in Section 9.2.4 takes two periods to construct. Construction cannot be interrupted once it has begun. All other aspects of the situation are unchanged.

    (a) Draw the decision tree for the problem facing the land owner.

    (b) Derive the terminal conditions and the recursive equation needed to calculate the market value of the undeveloped land.

    (c) Calculate the market value of the vacant land at date 0 and identify an optimal development policy. Give an intuitive explanation for the changes in the optimal development policy relative to the situation considered in Section 9.2.4.

9.3. (**Discussion**) Explain at an intuitive level why we still see blocks of vacant
land in urban areas that are experiencing booming property prices.

9.4. (**Application: Bringing a plant out of mothballs**) A firm owns a steel mill
that has been mothballed for some time. The mill can be reactivated, requiring
immediate expenditure of I and taking one period. A reactivated plant is worth
$X(i, n)$ at each node (i, n). Alternatively, it can be shut down permanently and
sold for scrap at any time, raising an immediate lump sum of J. The mill must
be shut down permanently at date 8 if it has not been reactivated by then.
The firm must pay C each period that it neither scraps nor reactivates the mill
in order to maintain the equipment. The risk-adjusted growth factor for the
state variable equals K and the return on one-period risk-free bonds equals
R_f, for some constants K and R_f. The state variable is equally likely to change
by a constant factor of U or D each period.

   (a) Draw the decision tree for the problem facing the firm's manager.
   (b) Derive the terminal conditions and the recursive equations needed to
       calculate the market value of the steel mill.
   (c) How does this situation compare with the one in Section 9.2?
   (d) Calculate the market value of the mothballed steel mill at date 0, and
       identify an optimal reactivation policy, for the following parameter
       values: $X_0 = 96, U = 1.21, D = 1/U, K = 0.99, R_f = 1.04, I = 80,$
       $J = 12, C = 1$.
   (e) What effect does changing the maintenance cost C have on the
       optimal reactivation policy? Give an intuitive explanation.

9.5. (**Practice**) Reevaluate the numerical example in Section 9.3.3 for the following
parameter values: $X_0 = 100, U = 1.15, D = 1/U, K = 0.99, R_f = 1.05, I =$
$83.5, J_1 = 30, J_2 = 50$. Suppose that the project rights are lost if construction
is not completed on or before date 8.

9.6. (**Practice**) Suppose that there are three distinct stages of investment in
Section 9.3 and that the project rights are lost if construction is not completed
on or before date 6. The firm can complete one stage in a single period at a
cost of I, or two stages in a single period at a cost of J. All other aspects of
the situation are unchanged.

   (a) Draw the decision tree for the problem facing the firm's manager.
   (b) Derive the recursive equations needed to calculate the market value
       of the project rights.
   (c) Calculate the market value of the project rights at date 0, and identify
       an optimal construction policy, for the following parameter values:
       $X_0 = 100, U = 1.18, D = 1/U, K = 0.99, R_f = 1.05, I = 30, J = 65$.
   (d) For this numerical example, what investment policy should the firm
       adopt if the first two moves are up? Give an intuitive explanation
       of how the firm's value would fall if it deviated from this policy at
       date 3.

9.7. (**Application: Resource extraction**) Consider the resource extraction problem
described in Section 8.3 and suppose that at any date when extraction is
allowed (and the mine contains two or more units of copper) the firm can

extract one unit of copper at a cost of C_1 or two units of copper at a total cost of C_2. The mine initially contains three units of copper and the extraction rights last until date 10. All other aspects of the situation are unchanged.

(a) Draw the decision tree for the problem facing the mine's manager.

(b) Derive the terminal conditions and recursive equations needed to calculate the market value of the mine.

(c) How does this situation compare with the one in Section 9.3?

(d) Calculate the market value of the mine at date 0, and identify an optimal extraction policy at the same date, for $C_2 = 61$ and $C_2 = 62$. Use the following values for the other parameters: $X_0 = 40$, $U = 1.18$, $D = 1/U$, $K = 0.99$, $R_f = 1.03$, $C_1 = 30$. Discuss the differences in the two cases. Give an intuitive explanation.

9.8. **(Application: R&D with variable intensity)** Suppose that the owner of the development rights in Section 7.4 is allowed to make two development attempts simultaneously. That is, at any node where development can be attempted, she can either pay I and succeed with probability q, or she can pay $2I$ and succeed with probability $2q - q^2$. Suppose that the development rights are lost if development is not completed on or before date 8. All other aspects of the problem are unchanged.

(a) Explain why a "double attempt" succeeds with probability $2q - q^2$ if the outcomes of the two attempts are statistically independent.

(b) Derive the terminal conditions and recursive equations needed to calculate the market value of the development rights.

(c) Calculate the market value of the development rights and an optimal development policy. Use the following parameter values: $X_0 = 10$, $U = 1.15$, $D = 1/U$, $K = 0.97$, $R_f = 1.05$, $I = 2$, $q = 0.3$. Discuss the results.

10

Switching Options

The US fertilizer industry has experienced some dramatic changes since the mid 1990s.[1] Input prices have climbed to historically high levels and become highly volatile. Output prices have also increased, but profit margins have generally fallen and become more volatile than in the past. Many fertilizer producers have suspended production, with many plants being mothballed or shut permanently. The reduced domestic supply has been offset by a substantial increase in imported fertilizer. This is evident in Figure 10.1, which plots annual production (the light gray bars) and net imports (that is, consumption less production; the dark gray bars) of ammonia—a major feedstock for producing nitrogen fertilizer—in the US. Domestic production has fallen from 85% of consumption in 1995 to 58% in 2006.

Natural gas is an important ingredient for producing ammonia, contributing 70–90% of the cost of production. Profitability of fertilizer production is therefore closely related to the spread between the prices of ammonia and natural gas. Figure 10.2 plots benchmark prices for fertilizers and wholesale natural gas: the US Gulf spot price for anhydrous ammonia (the solid curve, in dollars per ton) and the Henry Hub price for natural gas (the dashed curve, in dollars per million British thermal units (MMBtu)), respectively.[2] The graph shows that although the prices of ammonia and natural gas move together, the price spread is very volatile. It was extremely high for most of the mid-1990s. Although the ammonia price rose

---

1. Useful background on the US nitrogen fertilizer industry can be found in Huang (2007).
2. The scale for the natural gas price series reflects the amount (33.5 MMBtu) of natural gas that is typically required to produce each ton of anhydrous ammonia fertilizer.

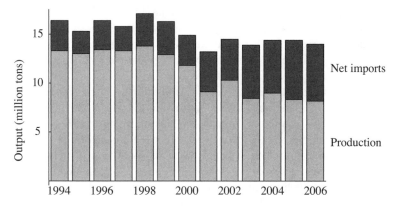

Figure 10.1. Annual ammonia consumption

Note: Annual US production (light gray bars) and net imports (that is, consumption less production; dark gray bars) of ammonia, as reported by the US Geological Survey.

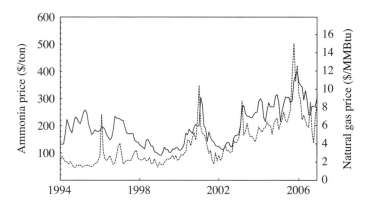

Figure 10.2. Prices of ammonia and natural gas

Note: The US Gulf spot price for anhydrous ammonia (solid curve, in dollars per ton) and the Henry Hub price for natural gas (dashed curve, in dollars per MMBtu).

when the natural gas price soared in 2000, the spread still narrowed dramatically (and even became negative). The spread widened again during 2003–2004, even though the natural gas price continued to rise. Apart from the period immediately after Hurricane Katrina in 2005, the price spread has continued to fluctuate around the 2003–2004 levels.

A fertilizer producer can choose from several courses of action when faced with a negative price spread. One is simply to carry on production and hope that the natural gas price falls sufficiently far relative to the fertilizer price that the business returns to profitability. Another approach is to temporarily suspend production and divert workers to activities such as plant maintenance, thus avoiding the cash outflows resulting from producing when fuel costs exceed the output price. However, at some point there will be no more maintenance or other productive work for displaced staff and a more permanent arrangement will need to be considered, such as mothballing the plant or shutting it down altogether.[3]

Mothballing the plant offers its owner the most flexibility, since production can then be resumed if market conditions improve in the future. However, ongoing expenditure will be required to maintain the plant in such a state that resumption is possible, and additional expenditure will still be required to bring the plant back up to operational status. There will also be the costs of laying off existing staff and then recruiting a new workforce if production is to be resumed in the future. Nevertheless, mothballing does at least create the option to resume operations in the future. In contrast, shutting the plant down altogether offers much less flexibility. It will require less expenditure in the short run (and it may even generate some cash inflow if plant and machinery can be salvaged), but any resumption of production will require a much more substantial investment in the future—perhaps even to the extent of building a brand new facility.

Getting the timing right is crucial to maximizing the market value of the firm. If mothballing occurs too soon, the manager may find that market conditions improve soon after the plant is taken out of production and a second set of costs will have to be incurred to get the plant operating again. The situation would be even worse if the manager had decided to shut the plant down. Of course, the firm may be losing money while the manager waits to mothball the plant, so waiting too long to stop production is also undesirable. The manager's problem is to decide when and how to stop production.[4] The optimal solution to this problem will depend on factors such as the volatility of natural gas and fertilizer prices, and the expenditure required to mothball a plant and to reactivate it.

Terra Industries' ammonia production facility in Donaldsonville, Louisiana, illustrates the choices available. There were originally two plants, previously owned by Mississippi Chemical, with a combined capacity of approximately one million tons per annum. Production at both plants had been suspended at times during the period of high gas prices, and one plant was permanently closed in March 2004. Production at the other plant stopped in December 2004, after Terra Industries bought Mississippi Chemical, which had filed for Chapter 11 bankruptcy reorganization the year before. This plant was mothballed in May 2005, since

---

3. Another response is to switch to an alternative feedstock. For example, in August 2004 Rentech Energy Midwest Corporation purchased an existing ammonia plant in Illinois, intending to convert it to use coal as the feedstock. The conversion time was estimated to be about three years, but the project was put on indefinite hold in December 2007, in part due to "stabilized natural gas prices and rising construction costs" ("Rentech Announces Plan for First Commercial Ultra-Clean Synthetic Fuels Plant That Will Lower Costs and Reduce Carbon Emissions", Rentech, Inc., 4 December 2007).

4. When market conditions improve, the manager will face the problem of when to reactivate a mothballed plant.

when the Donaldsonville site has been used solely as a storage and distribution terminal. However, in February 2008 Terra Industries announced that it planned to resume production at Donaldsonville: although US natural gas prices had not fallen, overseas prices had risen to the point that domestic production was favored.

The managers at Terra Industries had to decide when to stop production and how to stop it. They subsequently had to decide when to resume production. And if production does resume as scheduled, then at some future date they will once again have to decide when and how to stop production. The problem they face is just one example of a quite general class involving so-called switching options. We introduce this class of problems in Section 10.1 and analyze two representative examples in Sections 10.2 and 10.3. Finally, in Section 10.4 we describe the general technique for analyzing problems involving switching options.

10.1 EXAMPLES OF SWITCHING OPTIONS

10.1.1 The Option to Switch between Two States

In the simplest examples involving switching options, the project under consideration changes between two states. This means that the decision maker just has to choose when to switch from one state to the other. The key difference from the simple timing options considered in Chapter 7—which also involved just two states—is that we allow the decision maker to reverse past actions. That is, the project can move from one state to the other and then back again.

Many problems facing decision makers can be formulated in terms of switching options.

Temporarily Suspending Production A firm has the option to temporarily suspend production, possibly after incurring expenditure for purposes such as laying off staff. The firm can subsequently resume production, although this may involve additional expenditure. There are two states: operational and suspended. Each time the firm switches from one state to the other it destroys the option to wait and switch at a later date, but it creates the option to switch back again. We consider this problem in Section 10.2.

The Option to Switch Outputs A factory can produce two different products, but not simultaneously. It takes time and resources to set the factory up to manufacture each product line, so the manager would prefer a sustained period producing one output before switching to the alternative.

10.1.2 The Option to Switch between Multiple States

There is no reason to restrict attention to situations where a project switches between two possible states.[5] We can, in principle, have as many states as we wish.

---

5. Indeed, our two-state examples could naturally be generalized to multiple states. For example, there may be several different levels of capacity; a factory may be able to manufacture several different products.

Moreover, we can allow considerable flexibility about how the project moves from one state to another. For example, we can specify the sequence as part of the problem set-up, or we can allow the decision maker to choose how to move between the states (as well as when to move).

Expanding and Contracting Capacity A firm can switch between full, partial, and zero production. This generalizes the production-suspension problem by adding an intermediate project-state. The firm can expand output when demand is strong and reduce it when demand weakens.

Mothballing The manager of a firm who wishes to temporarily stop production has two choices. She can institute a temporary suspension, which will be expensive to maintain but has the advantage that production can be resumed relatively easily. Alternatively, she can mothball the plant, which has lower costs during the period when production has stopped but has the disadvantage that it is more expensive to resume production. Mothballing is ideally suited to situations when the manager anticipates that production will stop for a considerable period. There are three project states in this problem: operational, under temporary suspension, and mothballed. When the firm is operational, the manager can choose which of the other two states to move to next. We consider this problem in detail in Chapter 17.

Machinery Replacement A firm operates machinery that, due to factors such as increased maintenance costs or reduced efficiency as it ages, will need to be replaced in the future. The state of the project might be described by the age of the machinery or a measure of maintenance cost. As the machinery grows older the state of the project goes through a series of stages; when it is replaced, the state of the project reverts to being brand new, before starting through the cycle a second time. We analyze this situation in Section 10.3.

Inventory Management A firm operates a storage facility. The value of the facility derives from the firm's ability to buy a commodity when its price is low and sell it when the price is high. At a very simplistic level we might think of the facility being empty or full. The state of the project then switches from the first state to the second one each time the firm buys the commodity, and switches back again each time the firm sells the commodity. However, it is more realistic to think of there being a large number of different storage levels, in which case the state of the project moves from one storage level to the next as the firm buys more of the commodity, and then moves back again as the firm sells down its inventory.

The most important consequence of there being more than two project states is that there is a greater variety of possible transitions between project states to consider. With two states, the firm could only switch from one to the other and back again, but now other possibilities occur. Nevertheless, as we see in

Sections 10.3 and 10.4, the procedure for analyzing the problem is essentially the same.

10.1.3 The General Switching Option Problem

The various examples described above all fit into a very general framework. In this general setting a project starts in one state and, according to the policy adopted by the decision maker, moves through a series of states in the future. Not all changes will necessarily be able to be made in a single period, and some changes may not be allowed at all. In some cases there will be a set sequence of stages, as in the problems described in Chapter 8, so that the appropriate modeling techniques are almost identical to those used for compound timing options. However, in other cases there will be more than one order in which the project states can be traversed—the modeling techniques will then be similar to those in Chapter 9.

10.2 SOLVING THE PRODUCTION-SUSPENSION PROBLEM

The basis of the model featuring in this section is the production-suspension problem analyzed in Section 6.2. In that model the firm could suspend and resume production without incurring any additional expenditure. However, in reality there will often be some frictions that limit the ability of the firm to switch from one state to the other. In this section we modify the basic model structure of Section 6.2 by adding in such frictions.

10.2.1 Setting Up the Production-suspension Problem

A firm is currently producing one unit of output per period. Its only expenses are wages, and these cost W per unit of output produced. Production must cease permanently after date 5. However, prior to that date the firm can open and close its factory as many times as it chooses. There is no production when the factory is closed. At any date, immediately before producing output the firm can incur a fixed (and unrecoverable) cost of I_f and close the factory if it is currently open. Output and wage costs both fall to zero immediately. At any date, the firm can incur a fixed (and unrecoverable) cost of I_h and reopen the factory if it is currently closed. Output and wage costs both return to their usual values immediately. I_f and I_h represent the costs of firing and hiring workers, respectively. There are many possible explanations for I_f and I_h. For example, I_f might represent the cost of severance payments to workers laid off when the factory closes, while I_h might represent the costs of rebuilding a team of workers with specialist skills.

We suppose that the firm's output price is more volatile than wages, in which case it is sensible to define the state variable $X(i, n)$ to be the output price at node (i, n). The risk-adjusted growth factor for the output price equals the constant K and the return on one-period risk-free bonds equals the constant R_f. That is, the market value at node (i, n) of the right to a cash flow at date $n + 1$ that will equal $X(i, n + 1)$ if an up move occurs and $X(i + 1, n + 1)$ if a down move occurs equals $KX(i, n)/R_f$.

10.2.2 Analyzing the Production-suspension Problem

If the manager chose to keep the factory open for as long as possible, it would produce one unit of output per period from dates 0 to 5 inclusive. Thus the firm would generate a cash flow of $X(\cdot, n) - W$ at each node $(\cdot, n)$ for $n = 0, 1, \ldots, 5$. The simplest way to value this cash flow stream is to separate out the revenue from the wage cost and then value the two streams separately. We can repeat the calculations described in Section 6.2.2 to show that the factory is worth

$$\left(1 - \left(\frac{K}{R_f}\right)^6\right) \frac{R_f X(0, 0)}{R_f - K} - \left(1 - \left(\frac{1}{R_f}\right)^6\right) \frac{R_f W}{R_f - 1}$$

at date 0 if the manager decides never to suspend production.

If the output price falls in the future, it might be sensible to suspend production and only resume production once the output price returns to a sufficiently high level. Therefore any evaluation of the firm should allow the manager to operate the factory in a way that reflects movements in the firm's output price. We do exactly this in the remainder of this section.

The factory is open at date 0, so that the manager of the firm must initially do one of two things: close the factory immediately or wait. These are represented by the actions labeled C (for "close") and W (for "wait") in the decision tree shown in Figure 10.3. If she chooses to close the factory at date 0, then she incurs the "firing" expenditure immediately and at date 1 will have a factory that is closed. If, instead, she waits at date 0, she immediately pays wages and receives revenue from the factory's output; at date 1 the factory will still be open.

At date 1 the firm could be in either of two different situations depending on the actions taken by the manager at date 0. If the factory was closed at date 0 then the manager must either reopen the factory (labeled R) or wait. If she reopens the factory she immediately incurs the "hiring" expenditure and must pay wages, but receives revenue from selling the factory's output; at date 2 the factory will be open. In contrast, if the factory was kept open at date 0 then at date 1 the manager must either close the factory or wait. If she closes the factory she immediately incurs the firing expenditure and at date 2 the factory will be closed.

We continue like this, moving forward one date at a time. At dates 2–5 the firm will be in one of two states—open or closed—and the manager's available actions will be the same as at date 1. That is, she can close a factory that is open, or wait; she can reopen a factory that is closed, or wait. At date 6 the firm will also be

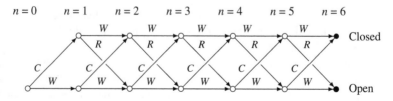

Figure 10.3. Decision tree for the production-suspension problem

in one of two states, but no further production is possible, so that the growth of the decision tree stops. This completes construction of the decision tree, which is shown in Figure 10.3.

The decision tree shows that at any date the factory will be in one of two states: open or closed. Therefore, we need to build two trees for the market value of the factory, one for each project-state. Let $V_o(i, n)$ denote the market value of the factory at node (i, n) if it is open when date n arrives, and let $V_c(i, n)$ denote its market value at the same node if it is closed when date n arrives.

From date 6 onwards the factory will be worthless in both states, since no production is possible after date 5. This gives us the terminal conditions

$$V_o(i, 6) = V_c(i, 6) = 0, \tag{10.1}$$

which hold for all $i = 0, 1, \ldots, 6$.

The next step is to consider the two project-states in turn, starting with the case when the factory is open. At any date prior to date 6 the manager of an open factory must either produce one unit of output or close the factory. If the manager decides to keep the factory open, then it generates a cash flow of $X(i, n) - W$ and after one period elapses the factory (which will still be open) will be worth $V_o(i, n + 1)$ if an up move occurs and $V_o(i + 1, n + 1)$ if a down move occurs. The payoff from this action is therefore

$$X(i, n) - W + \frac{\pi_u(i, n)V_o(i, n + 1) + \pi_d(i, n)V_o(i + 1, n + 1)}{R_f}.$$

Alternatively, if the manager decides to close the factory she must pay I_f immediately; after one period elapses the factory (which will be closed) will be worth $V_c(i, n + 1)$ if an up move occurs and $V_c(i + 1, n + 1)$ if a down move occurs. The payoff from this action is

$$-I_f + \frac{\pi_u(i, n)V_c(i, n + 1) + \pi_d(i, n)V_c(i + 1, n + 1)}{R_f}.$$

The manager chooses whichever action has the greater payoff, implying the recursive equation is

$$V_o(i, n) = \max \left\{ X(i, n) - W + \frac{\pi_u(i, n)V_o(i, n + 1) + \pi_d(i, n)V_o(i + 1, n + 1)}{R_f}, \right.$$

$$\tag{10.2}$$

$$\left. -I_f + \frac{\pi_u(i, n)V_c(i, n + 1) + \pi_d(i, n)V_c(i + 1, n + 1)}{R_f} \right\}$$

for dates $n = 5, \ldots, 1, 0$.

We also need to consider what happens if the factory is closed. At any date prior to date 6 the manager of a closed factory must either keep it closed or reopen the factory. If the manager decides to keep the factory closed, then it generates no cash flow at that date and after one period elapses (when the factory will still be closed) it will be worth $V_c(i, n+1)$ if an up move occurs and $V_c(i+1, n+1)$ if a down move occurs. The payoff from this action is therefore

$$\frac{\pi_u(i, n)V_c(i, n+1) + \pi_d(i, n)V_c(i+1, n+1)}{R_f}.$$

Alternatively, if the manager reopens the factory she must pay I_h immediately; the factory generates an immediate cash flow of $X(i, n) - W$ and after one period elapses it will be worth $V_o(i, n+1)$ if an up move occurs and $V_o(i+1, n+1)$ if a down move occurs. The payoff from this action is therefore

$$-I_h + X(i, n) - W + \frac{\pi_u(i, n)V_o(i, n+1) + \pi_d(i, n)V_o(i+1, n+1)}{R_f}.$$

Because the manager selects the action with the greater payoff, the recursive equation is

$$V_c(i, n) = \max \left\{ \frac{\pi_u(i, n)V_c(i, n+1) + \pi_d(i, n)V_c(i+1, n+1)}{R_f}, \right. \tag{10.3}$$

$$\left. -I_h + X(i, n) - W + \frac{\pi_u(i, n)V_o(i, n+1) + \pi_d(i, n)V_o(i+1, n+1)}{R_f} \right\}$$

for dates $n = 5, \ldots, 1, 0$.

We are now in a position to build the binomial trees that allow us to calculate the market value of the factory and determine an optimal operating policy. As usual, the first step is to build the binomial tree for the state variable, in this case the output price. Because there are two project-states, we need to build two trees of market values. In previous chapters, when we have had more than one tree to construct we have been able to build them in sequence. However, inspection of equations (10.2) and (10.3) shows that this will not be possible here. For instance, (10.2) shows that $V_o(i, n)$ depends on the next period's market value of the factory when it is closed, $V_c(\cdot, n+1)$. Similarly, (10.3) shows that $V_c(i, n)$ depends on the next period's market value of the factory when it is open, $V_o(\cdot, n+1)$. We cannot, for example, complete the tree for V_o and then complete the tree for V_c. Instead, it is necessary to fill in the two trees simultaneously.

The procedure is shown schematically in Table 10.1. We start by filling in the final column of each tree. Then (and only then) we fill in the second-to-last column of each tree, using equations (10.2) and (10.3) with $n = 5$. We continue working from right to left, using equations (10.2) and (10.3) to fill in a single column of both trees before moving back to the previous column. Eventually, we completely fill in both trees back to node $(0, 0)$. This technique is demonstrated in the next section.

10.2.3 A Numerical Example

The starting point for the numerical example analyzed in this section is the situation considered in Section 6.2. As in that example, we suppose that the

Table 10.1. The Procedure for Analyzing the Production-suspension Problem

Step 1: Use equations (10.1) to evaluate $V_o(i, 6)$ and $V_c(i, 6)$

$V_o(i, n)$	0	$\cdots$	5	6
0				$V_o(0, 6)$
1				$V_o(1, 6)$
2				$V_o(2, 6)$
3				$V_o(3, 6)$
4				$V_o(4, 6)$
5				$V_o(5, 6)$
6				$V_o(6, 6)$

$V_c(i, n)$	0	$\cdots$	5	6
0				$V_c(0, 6)$
1				$V_c(1, 6)$
2				$V_c(2, 6)$
3				$V_c(3, 6)$
4				$V_c(4, 6)$
5				$V_c(5, 6)$
6				$V_c(6, 6)$

Step 2: Use equations (10.2) and (10.3) with $n = 5$ to evaluate $V_o(i, 5)$ and $V_c(i, 5)$ respectively

$V_o(i, n)$	0	$\cdots$	5	6
0			$V_o(0, 5)$	$V_o(0, 6)$
1			$V_o(1, 5)$	$V_o(1, 6)$
2			$V_o(2, 5)$	$V_o(2, 6)$
3			$V_o(3, 5)$	$V_o(3, 6)$
4			$V_o(4, 5)$	$V_o(4, 6)$
5			$V_o(5, 5)$	$V_o(5, 6)$
6				$V_o(6, 6)$

$V_c(i, n)$	0	$\cdots$	5	6
0			$V_c(0, 5)$	$V_c(0, 6)$
1			$V_c(1, 5)$	$V_c(1, 6)$
2			$V_c(2, 5)$	$V_c(2, 6)$
3			$V_c(3, 5)$	$V_c(3, 6)$
4			$V_c(4, 5)$	$V_c(4, 6)$
5			$V_c(5, 5)$	$V_c(5, 6)$
6				$V_c(6, 6)$

Steps 3–6: $\cdots$

Step 7: Use equations (10.2) and (10.3) with $n = 0$ to evaluate $V_o(0, 0)$ and $V_c(0, 0)$ respectively

$V_o(i, n)$	0	$\cdots$	5	6
0	$V_o(0, 0)$	$\cdots$	$V_o(0, 5)$	$V_o(0, 6)$
1		$\cdots$	$V_o(1, 5)$	$V_o(1, 6)$
2		$\cdots$	$V_o(2, 5)$	$V_o(2, 6)$
3		$\cdots$	$V_o(3, 5)$	$V_o(3, 6)$
4			$V_o(4, 5)$	$V_o(4, 6)$
5			$V_o(5, 5)$	$V_o(5, 6)$
6				$V_o(6, 6)$

$V_c(i, n)$	0	$\cdots$	5	6
0	$V_c(0, 0)$	$\cdots$	$V_c(0, 5)$	$V_c(0, 6)$
1		$\cdots$	$V_c(1, 5)$	$V_c(1, 6)$
2		$\cdots$	$V_c(2, 5)$	$V_c(2, 6)$
3		$\cdots$	$V_c(3, 5)$	$V_c(3, 6)$
4			$V_c(4, 5)$	$V_c(4, 6)$
5			$V_c(5, 5)$	$V_c(5, 6)$
6				$V_c(6, 6)$

Table 10.2. Analysis of the Production-suspension Problem when there are No Switching Frictions

$X(i, n)$	0	1	2	3	4	5	6
0	10.00	12.50	15.63	19.53	24.41	30.52	38.15
1		8.00	10.00	12.50	15.63	19.53	24.41
2			6.40	8.00	10.00	12.50	15.63
3				5.12	6.40	8.00	10.00
4					4.10	5.12	6.40
5						3.28	4.10
6							2.62

$V_o(i, n)$	0	1	2	3	4	5	6
0	9.54	17.12	24.97	30.47	30.61	22.02	0.00
1		2.66	6.32	10.91	13.61	11.03	0.00
2			0.44	1.15	3.02	4.00	0.00
3				0.00	0.00	0.00	0.00
4					0.00	0.00	0.00
5						0.00	0.00
6							0.00

$V_c(i, n)$	0	1	2	3	4	5	6
0	9.54	17.12	24.97	30.47	30.61	22.02	0.00
1		2.66	6.32	10.91	13.61	11.03	0.00
2			0.44	1.15	3.02	4.00	0.00
3				0.00	0.00	0.00	0.00
4					0.00	0.00	0.00
5						0.00	0.00
6							0.00

current level of the output price is $X_0 = 10$ and that each period it is equally likely to grow by a factor of either $U = 1.2500$ or $D = 1/U = 0.8000$. The resulting binomial tree for the output price is shown in the top panel of Table 10.2. The risk-adjusted growth factor is $K = 0.9800$, so that equation (3.8) implies that the risk-neutral probabilities of up and down moves are $\pi_u = 0.4000$ and $\pi_d = 0.6000$, respectively, at every node. It costs $W = 8.5$ to produce each unit of output. The one-period risk-free interest rate equals 5%, so that $R_f = 1.05$.

This leaves the two parameters that determine the frictions embedded in the switching procedure. We consider two different combinations of values for these parameters, starting with the case where there are no frictions and then looking at a case where frictions are present. This allows us to demonstrate how the optimal operating policy changes when frictions are introduced.

Optimal Switching in the Absence of Frictions

We begin with the case where $I_f = 0$ and $I_h = 0$; that is, there are no frictions. The market value of the factory when it is open is shown in the middle panel of Table 10.2, while the market value when it is closed is shown in the bottom panel. The shaded cells indicate nodes at which it is optimal to exercise the firm's switching option. For example, the manager will close an open factory at node $(1, 1)$, while a closed factory will be reopened at node $(2, 4)$.

The switching regions in the tables are complements to each other. In other words, whenever it is optimal for an open factory to remain open (the unshaded cells in the middle panel) it is also optimal for a closed factory to reopen (the shaded cells in the bottom one). Likewise, whenever it is optimal for an open factory to close (the shaded cells in the middle panel) it is also optimal for a closed factory to remain closed (the unshaded cells in the bottom one). Thus, the optimal status of the factory at any point in time depends on the level of the output price at that time—and nothing else.

The two switching regions are determined by the sign of that period's net revenue—that is, on whether the output price is greater than or less than the wage cost.[6] One implication of this is that it is optimal for the firm to adopt a very aggressive operating policy—closing the factory as soon as the output price falls below the wage cost and reopening it as soon as the output price rises above this level.

Both of these results—the optimal status of the factory at each date depending only on the prevailing level of the output price, and the optimality of such an aggressive operating policy—change when there are frictions involved in the process of hiring and firing workers. Past levels of the output price influence the optimal status of the factory and it becomes optimal to adopt a more cautious operating policy.

The Impact of Switching Costs

Now we introduce a friction by supposing that the manager must make severance payments of 2 when she shuts the factory down, but incurs no additional expenditure each time the factory is reopened; that is, $I_f = 2$ and $I_h = 0$. The results for this case are given in Table 10.3. The procedure for constructing this table is exactly the same as that for constructing Table 10.2. All that changes is the level of the switching costs I_f and I_h. However, the two panels of the table reveal that the introduction of a friction alters the optimal operating policy in some significant ways.

---

6. This is exactly what happened in Section 6.2. In fact, the market value trees in Table 10.2 are identical to the one in Table 6.3. This is to be expected since, provided $I_f = I_h = 0$, the situation here is identical to that in Section 6.2.4.

Table 10.3. Analysis of the Production-suspension Problem when there Are Switching Frictions

$V_o(i, n)$	0	1	2	3	4	5	6
0	8.11	16.48	24.88	30.47	30.61	22.02	0.00
1		0.59	5.25	10.75	13.61	11.03	0.00
2			−1.60	−0.60	2.74	4.00	0.00
3				−2.00	−2.00	−0.50	0.00
4					−2.00	−2.00	0.00
5						−2.00	0.00
6							0.00

$V_c(i, n)$	0	1	2	3	4	5	6
0	8.11	16.48	24.88	30.47	30.61	22.02	0.00
1		2.23	5.25	10.75	13.61	11.03	0.00
2			0.40	1.04	2.74	4.00	0.00
3				0.00	0.00	0.00	0.00
4					0.00	0.00	0.00
5						0.00	0.00
6							0.00

The first point to note is that, unlike in Table 10.2, the two switching regions in Table 10.3 are not complements. Instead, they are separated by a region where it is optimal to leave an open factory open and a closed factory closed.[7] Consider, for example, node (2, 3). If the factory is open when we arrive at that node then the manager will keep it open at date 3, while if it is closed she will keep it closed. In this region the factory is more valuable closed than open, so—because no cash flow is generated by reopening a closed factory ($I_h = 0$)—the manager will choose not to reopen the factory. However, despite the factory being more valuable closed than open in this region, the manager will not close an open factory—the increase in market value is not sufficiently large to outweigh the expenditure required to close the factory ($I_f = 2$).

The existence of this "no-switching" region introduces some degree of inertia into the factory's optimal operating policy. For example, when we move from node (1, 1) to (2, 2), the output price falls from 8.00 to 6.40 and it is optimal to close the factory down. If we then move from node (2, 2) to (2, 3), so that the output price returns to its prior level of 8.00, it is still not optimal to reopen the factory. That is, the reduction in output price triggers the factory closure, but when

---

7. In Table 10.3 this region actually disappears at dates 2 and 4. However, this is a result of the relatively large step size we use in this numerical example. Problem 10.1 demonstrates what happens when the time step takes a smaller value.

the output price returns to its prior level the closure is not reversed.[8] In contrast, the operating policy was much more aggressive in the frictionless case—where if a price reduction triggered a factory closure then an immediate reversal of the price change triggered an immediate reopening of the factory.

The behavior described here can be explained by the costs associated with reversing a decision to close the factory (or, for that matter, to open it). For example, if the manager closes the factory at one date and then reopens it one period later she incurs total expenditure of $I_f + I_h$. She could have avoided this expenditure by keeping the factory open, receiving the net revenue from the factory's production at the first date instead. Even if the factory operates at a loss, it may be better to keep it open than to incur the fixed costs associated with a (possibly temporary) closure. Of course, if the closure is likely to last several periods then it may be worthwhile incurring these fixed costs. This is exactly the behavior revealed by Table 10.3: the manager closes the factory only when she can be confident that an early reopening will not be necessary (that is, she waits until the output price is below the wage cost by a considerable amount).

10.2.4 The Trade-off between Wages and Severance Pay

If the firm can reduce the level of severance pay then its shareholders benefit in two ways. First, holding the firm's hiring-and-firing policy constant, the reduced level of severance pay will reduce the market value of all future severance payments: the firm would still be firing the same number of workers at the same time; it would just be paying them less severance pay. However, there is a second, more subtle, effect. By reducing the cost of reversing the manager's decision to close the factory, lower levels of severance pay allow the manager to respond more aggressively to output price shocks. If the severance pay is removed altogether, she will close the factory rather than incur an operating loss. For example, comparison of Tables 10.2 and 10.3 shows that the manager would close the firm at node $(1, 1)$ rather than keeping it open and incurring an operating loss of $W - X(1, 1) = 8.50 - 8.00 = 0.50$, which is the optimal policy when $I_f = 2$. Similarly, she will reopen the factory to exploit any operating profit. If the severance pay is reduced but not eliminated, the manager will still tolerate some operating losses but will nevertheless be more aggressive in closing the factory than when $I_f = 2$.

Thus, firms are motivated to reduce the level of severance pay partly to reduce their expenses in the event that they shut down and partly to increase their operating flexibility (that is, to make it less expensive for them to exercise their real options). It will even be possible for a firm to increase the level of wages and still make the owners of the firm better off, provided that the level of severance pay is

---

8. This phenomenon, known as economic hysteresis, appears in many situations. Dixit (1992) provides an accessible introduction to the literature on this subject.

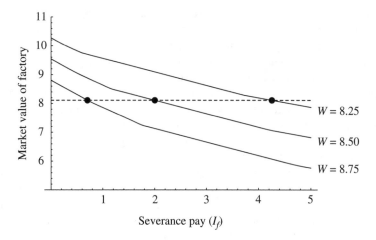

Figure 10.4. The effect of wages and severance pay on the market value of a factory

reduced sufficiently. The trade-off between the two payments can be examined using the analysis described in this section.

Figure 10.4 plots the market value of an open factory at node (0, 0) as a function of the level of severance pay I_f for the three indicated levels of the wage W. All other parameters are as specified in Section 10.2.3. As expected, the factory falls in value when the wage is increased and when severance pay is increased. The horizontal dashed line, which shows the market value of the factory in the baseline case where $I_f = 2$ and $W = 8.50$, can be used to illustrate the trade-off between wages and severance pay. For example, starting from the baseline case, suppose that the wage falls to 8.25. The graph shows that the factory is more valuable for any severance pay less than approximately 4.25. If, instead, the wage rises to 8.75, the critical level of severance pay is approximately 0.70.

10.3 SOLVING THE MACHINERY-REPLACEMENT PROBLEM

In this section we consider a problem that appears in almost all intermediate corporate finance texts—how often should a firm replace its machinery. These texts usually consider the problem using static DCF analysis, but we show how real options analysis allows for much more realistic managerial behavior. The particular real option involved is a switching option because each time machinery is replaced the firm switches back to having brand-new machinery. The replacement machinery ages, before it too is replaced and the firm once more switches back to having brand-new machinery.

One twist to the problem here is that, in order to isolate the switching option, we suppose that the firm is mandated to provide the output. For example, it could be a government agency producing the good, or perhaps the "firm" is actually a division of a larger firm, with the manager explicitly charged with minimizing costs. Regardless, with production (and therefore revenue) outside the manager's control, the only way to maximize the firm's market value is to minimize the market value of its flow of expenditure. This requires only a very minor change to our usual approach, but it is best to remember that in this section the manager is trying to minimize, not maximize, the market value that we calculate.

10.3.1 Setting Up the Machinery-replacement Problem

A firm must produce one unit of output per period from dates 0 to 5 inclusive. The firm currently operates machinery that has never been used before. As the machinery grows older it becomes less fuel-efficient. Specifically, the machinery uses a_1 units of fuel the first time it is used, a_2 units the second time, and a_3 units the third time, where a_1, a_2, and a_3 are constants satisfying $a_1 \leq a_2 \leq a_3$. The machinery cannot be used more than three times. At any date the firm can sell its existing machinery and replace it with brand-new (and therefore more fuel-efficient) machinery. The old machinery has a salvage value equal to S_1 if it has been used once, S_2 if it has been used twice, and S_3 if it has been used three times, where S_1, S_2, and S_3 are constants satisfying $S_1 \geq S_2 \geq S_3$. The proceeds from selling the machinery are received immediately after it is removed from service. The new machinery costs I and takes one period to install. The manager's problem is to decide when to replace the machinery.

The key source of uncertainty that the manager faces is the future fuel price: if fuel prices rise in the future, it will be especially expensive to operate old machinery, while if fuel prices are low it might be sensible to delay replacing the machinery, thereby delaying capital expenditure. Therefore, we define the state variable $X(i, n)$ to be the fuel price at node (i, n). We suppose that the risk-adjusted growth factor for the fuel price equals the constant K and that the return on one-period risk-free bonds equals the constant R_f.

10.3.2 Static DCF Analysis

The static DCF approach to the machinery-replacement problem is to choose the dates at which the machinery will be replaced—and then not to deviate from these plans no matter what happens to the fuel price in the future. The "optimal" dates are found by evaluating the market value of the expenditure stream for a selection of different policies and choosing the policy with the lowest cost (in market-value terms).[9] For the problem described above, the obvious contenders for a machinery-replacement policy are to replace the machinery each period, to replace it every second period, or to replace it every third period.

---

9. Most intermediate corporate finance textbooks that cover the machinery-replacement problem then go on to calculate the "equivalent annual cost" (EAC) of this market value, allowing us to compare EACs rather than the market value of the cash flow stream. The results, however, are the same. For an example, see pp. 340–341 of Grinblatt and Titman (2002).

Table 10.4. Static DCF Analysis of the Machinery-replacement Problem

	0	1	2	3	4	5
Replace Machinery after First Use						
Certainty equivalent						
Op. ex.	a_1X_0	a_1KX_0	$a_1K^2X_0$	$a_1K^3X_0$	$a_1K^4X_0$	$a_1K^5X_0$
Cap. ex.	I	I	I	I	I	0
Salvage	$-S_1$	$-S_1$	$-S_1$	$-S_1$	$-S_1$	$-S_1$
PV	$a_1X_0+I-S_1$	$\frac{a_1KX_0+I-S_1}{R_f}$	$\frac{a_1K^2X_0+I-S_1}{R_f^2}$	$\frac{a_1K^3X_0+I-S_1}{R_f^3}$	$\frac{a_1K^4X_0+I-S_1}{R_f^4}$	$\frac{a_1K^5X_0-S_1}{R_f^5}$
Replace Machinery after Second Use						
Certainty equivalent						
Op. ex.	a_1X_0	a_2KX_0	$a_1K^2X_0$	$a_2K^3X_0$	$a_1K^4X_0$	$a_2K^5X_0$
Cap. ex.	0	I	0	I	0	0
Salvage	0	$-S_2$	0	$-S_2$	0	$-S_2$
PV	a_1X_0	$\frac{a_2KX_0+I-S_2}{R_f}$	$\frac{a_1K^2X_0}{R_f^2}$	$\frac{a_2K^3X_0+I-S_2}{R_f^3}$	$\frac{a_1K^4X_0}{R_f^4}$	$\frac{a_2K^5X_0-S_2}{R_f^5}$
Replace Machinery after Third Use						
Certainty equivalent						
Op. ex.	a_1X_0	a_2KX_0	$a_3K^2X_0$	$a_1K^3X_0$	$a_2K^4X_0$	$a_3K^5X_0$
Cap. ex.	0	0	I	0	0	0
Salvage	0	0	$-S_3$	0	0	$-S_3$
PV	a_1X_0	$\frac{a_2KX_0}{R_f}$	$\frac{a_3K^2X_0+I-S_3}{R_f^2}$	$\frac{a_1K^3X_0}{R_f^3}$	$\frac{a_2K^4X_0}{R_f^4}$	$\frac{a_3K^5X_0-S_3}{R_f^5}$

This procedure is demonstrated in Table 10.4. Each panel summarizes the cash flow information for the indicated replacement policy. Within each panel, the first three rows report the certainty equivalents of a different cash flow stream. For example, the second panel describes the policy of replacing the machinery after it has been used twice. Thus, the firm will incur operating expenditure of $a_1X(0, 0)$ at date 0 when the machinery is used the first time, $a_2X(\cdot, 1)$ at date 1 when it is used the second time, $a_1X(\cdot, 2)$ at date 2 when the replacement machinery is used for the first time, and so on. The certainty equivalents of the first three cash flows, reported in Table 10.4, are a_1X_0, a_2KX_0, and $a_1K^2X_0$, respectively, where X_0 is the level of the fuel price at date 0. The other rows report the capital expenditure on new machinery and the proceeds from selling the old machinery. The fourth row of each panel gives the present value of the cash flows at each date: because the previous rows report the certainty equivalent cash flow in each case, we simply discount their sums, using the return on risk-free bonds.

The cost of adopting each policy can be calculated by adding up the present values in the fourth row of each panel. The best policy is the one with the lowest cost. Of course, this will only be the best policy out of the static DCF policies analyzed in Table 10.4. Policies that allow the manager to respond to falling fuel prices by delaying machinery replacement, for example, may have lower cost but they cannot be assessed using static DCF analysis. We need to use real options analysis to evaluate such policies.

10.3.3 Real Options Analysis

At date 0 the firm produces output using machinery that has not been used before. Immediately after production is complete the manager of the firm must either sell the firm's existing machinery and purchase new machinery to replace it, or wait. These options are represented by the actions labeled R (for "replace") and W (for "wait") in the decision tree shown in Figure 10.5. If the manager chooses to replace the firm's existing machinery, then at date 1 she faces exactly the same problem. That is, the firm will have to produce output using machinery that has not been used before and, immediately after production is complete, she must either sell the firm's existing machinery and purchase new machinery to replace it (action R), or she can wait (action W). If, instead, the manager chooses to wait at date 0, then at date 1 the firm will have to produce output using machinery that has already been used once before and, immediately after production is complete, either she must sell the firm's existing machinery and purchase new machinery to replace it (action R) or she can wait (action W). In both cases the manager must choose between replacing the firm's existing machinery with new machinery or waiting and, one period later, using machinery that is one period older (and hence has lower fuel-efficiency).

At date 2 the firm could be in any one of three different situations, depending on the actions taken by the manager at dates 0 and 1. If the machinery was replaced at date 1 then current production will use machinery that has not been used before and the manager must choose whether or not to replace it after production occurs. If the machinery was replaced at date 0 (but not replaced again at date 1) then current production will use machinery that has already been used once before and the manager must also choose whether or not to replace it. However, if the original machinery is still in place then the manager must replace it immediately after current production is completed—no further delay is possible.

This situation continues at dates 3 and 4, with the manager having the option to replace machinery that is one or two periods old, but being forced to replace machinery that is three periods old. Finally, at date 5 the firm produces the final remaining output using whatever machinery is available, after which that

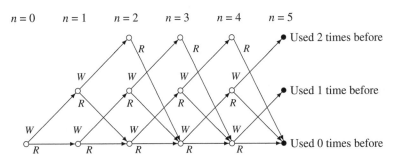

Figure 10.5. Decision tree for the machinery-replacement problem

machinery is sold. This completes construction of the decision tree shown in Figure 10.5.

The next step is to work systematically through the decision tree, starting by using it to identify the various market-value trees that we need to build. The three rows of nodes in the decision tree each correspond to a different project state, which is described by the age of the machinery. We therefore have to build binomial trees for the fuel price and for the market value of all future expenditure (net of salvage values) for each possible age of the firm's machinery—that is, four trees in total. Let $V_m(i, n)$ denote the market value at node (i, n) of all future expenditure, where m is the number of times the machinery has been used *before* date n.

At date 5 the firm produces one unit of output using the machinery it has in place and then sells the machinery for scrap. Suppose that the available machinery has been used m times before. Then production will require a_{m+1} units of fuel, so that the firm's operating expenditure equals $a_{m+1}X(i, 5)$. Since the firm receives S_{m+1} from selling the old machinery and does not need to buy replacement machinery, the total cash outflow is

$$V_m(i, 5) = a_{m+1}X(i, 5) - S_{m+1}. \qquad (10.4)$$

This is our terminal condition, which we use to begin constructing the trees for each V_m.

Now we consider a typical node (i, n) prior to date 5, so that the manager must ensure that machinery is available for future production. In the special case where $m = 2$, the machinery has reached the end of its productive life, forcing the manager to replace it as soon as it has produced the required unit of output. As a result, the firm's machinery will be brand new at date $n + 1$, when the market value of all future expenditure will equal $V_0(i, n + 1)$ if an up move occurs and $V_0(i + 1, n + 1)$ if a down move occurs. Since selling the old machinery raises S_3 and the new machinery costs I, the market value of all future expenditure at node (i, n) must equal

$$V_2(i, n) = a_3X(i, n) + I - S_3 + \frac{\pi_u(i, n)V_0(i, n + 1) + \pi_d(i, n)V_0(i + 1, n + 1)}{R_f}.$$
$$(10.5)$$

The remaining cases—that the machinery has been used at most once before—can be treated together because the actions available to the firm's manager at each node are identical in each case. The firm will have to produce that period's output using the existing machinery, regardless of what the manager decides about replacement. If the machinery has been used m times before, production will require a_{m+1} units of fuel, so that the firm's operating expenditure at date n equals $a_{m+1}X(i, n)$.

- If the manager decides not to replace the machinery then, at date $n + 1$, the machinery will have been used $m + 1$ times before, so that the market value of all future expenditure will equal $V_{m+1}(i, n + 1)$ if an up move occurs and $V_{m+1}(i + 1, n + 1)$ if a down move occurs. The payoff from not replacing the machinery is therefore

$$a_{m+1}X(i, n) + \frac{\pi_u(i, n)V_{m+1}(i, n + 1) + \pi_d(i, n)V_{m+1}(i + 1, n + 1)}{R_f}.$$

- In contrast, if she decides to replace the machinery then, at date $n + 1$, the machinery will be brand new, so that the market value of all future expenditure will equal $V_0(i, n + 1)$ if an up move occurs and $V_0(i + 1, n + 1)$ if a down move occurs. Since the firm receives S_{m+1} from selling the old machinery and pays I for its replacement, the payoff from replacing the machinery is

$$a_{m+1}X(i, n) + I - S_{m+1} + \frac{\pi_u(i, n)V_0(i, n + 1) + \pi_d(i, n)V_0(i + 1, n + 1)}{R_f}.$$

The manager wishes to *minimize* the market value of the firm's future expenditure, so she will choose whichever action has the *smaller* payoff. Thus,

$$V_m(i,n) = \min \left\{ a_{m+1}X(i,n) + \frac{\pi_u(i,n)V_{m+1}(i,n+1) + \pi_d(i,n)V_{m+1}(i+1,n+1)}{R_f}, \right.$$

$$\left. a_{m+1}X(i,n) + I - S_{m+1} + \frac{\pi_u(i,n)V_0(i,n+1) + \pi_d(i,n)V_0(i+1,n+1)}{R_f} \right\}.$$

$$(10.6)$$

This is the recursive equation that we use to fill in the trees for each V_m.

These equations completely determine the market value of all future expenditure by the firm, as well as the optimal machinery-replacement policy. We now demonstrate the entire procedure, using a numerical example.

10.3.4 A Numerical Example

We suppose that the current level of the fuel price is $X_0 = 10$ and that each period it is equally likely to grow by a factor of either $U = 1.2500$ or $D = 1/U = 0.8000$. The risk-adjusted growth factor is $K = 0.9800$, so that equation (3.8) implies that the risk-neutral probabilities of up and down moves are $\pi_u = 0.4000$ and $\pi_d = 0.6000$, respectively, throughout the tree. The one-period risk-free interest rate equals 5%, so that $R_f = 1.05$. The machinery costs $I = 50$ to purchase and install, and has salvage values of $S_1 = 12$, $S_2 = 5$, and $S_3 = 0$. The first time the machinery is used it requires $a_1 = 6$ units of fuel, but this figure climbs to $a_2 = 9$ and $a_3 = 10$ the second and third times it is used.

Table 10.5 summarizes the results of analyzing the machinery-replacement problem using static DCF analysis. It follows exactly the same format as Table 10.4. The top panel shows that always replacing the machinery immediately after its first use leads to relatively low operating expenditure and relatively high capital expenditure (which is only partly offset by the relatively high salvage values of the machinery). As the remaining panels illustrate, replacing the machinery less frequently raises operating expenditure and lowers capital expenditure. Overall, the best trade-off between the two—provided the manager uses static DCF

Table 10.5. Static DCF Analysis of the Machinery-replacement Problem

	0	1	2	3	4	5
Replace Machinery after First Use						
Certainty equivalent						
Op. ex.	60.00	58.80	57.62	56.47	55.34	54.24
Cap. ex.	50.00	50.00	50.00	50.00	50.00	0.00
Salvage	−12.00	−12.00	−12.00	−12.00	−12.00	−12.00
PV	98.00	92.19	86.73	81.61	76.79	33.09
Total	468.42					
Replace Machinery after Second Use						
Certainty equivalent						
Op. ex.	60.00	88.20	57.62	84.71	55.34	81.35
Cap. ex.	0.00	50.00	0.00	50.00	0.00	0.00
Salvage	0.00	−5.00	0.00	−5.00	0.00	−5.00
PV	60.00	126.86	52.27	112.05	45.53	59.82
Total	456.52					
Replace Machinery after Third Use						
Certainty equivalent						
Op. ex.	60.00	88.20	96.04	56.47	83.01	90.39
Cap. ex.	0.00	0.00	50.00	0.00	0.00	0.00
Salvage	0.00	0.00	0.00	0.00	0.00	0.00
PV	60.00	84.00	132.46	48.78	68.30	70.82
Total	464.36					

analysis—is obtained by always replacing machinery immediately after it has been used for a second time. The estimated cost of producing the required output is then 456.52.

Now we turn to real options analysis of the machinery-replacement problem. Our first task is to construct the binomial tree for the fuel price, which is shown in the top panel of Table 10.6. The remaining three panels of the table must be filled in simultaneously, using a similar technique to that described in Table 10.1. We begin by using the terminal condition (10.4) to fill in the final column of each panel. The next step is to use the recursive equation, with $n = 4$, to fill in the second-to-last column of each panel. We use (10.6) with $m = 0$ for the second panel, the same equation but with $m = 1$ for the third panel, and (10.5) for the bottom panel. We repeat this procedure for $n = 3, 2, 1, 0$, until all three binomial trees are completely filled in.

The shaded cells indicate nodes where it is optimal to replace the machinery. The location of these cells determines how we navigate through the various trees as the fuel price evolves. Since the machinery has not been used before date 0, we start at node (0, 0) of the second panel, where the market value of all current and future expenditure equals 451.25. Because this cell is unshaded, we do not replace the machinery at date 0 and will therefore be in the third panel—corresponding to

Table 10.6. Real Options Analysis of the Machinery-replacement Problem

$X(i, n)$	0	1	2	3	4	5
0	10.00	12.50	15.63	19.53	24.41	30.52
1		8.00	10.00	12.50	15.63	19.53
2			6.40	8.00	10.00	12.50
3				5.12	6.40	8.00
4					4.10	5.12
5						3.28

$V_0(i, n)$	0	1	2	3	4	5
0	451.25	454.18	436.34	391.95	309.77	171.11
1		316.00	306.18	271.73	207.82	105.19
2			210.98	183.46	139.24	63.00
3				118.33	87.40	36.00
4					54.22	18.72
5						7.66

$V_1(i, n)$	0	1	2	3	4	5
0	488.60	498.68	490.22	457.55	390.02	269.66
1		352.23	343.35	316.23	261.70	170.78
2			240.10	219.98	179.57	107.50
3				155.36	117.33	67.00
4					75.09	41.08
5						24.49

$V_2(i, n)$	0	1	2	3	4	5
0	503.60	516.18	510.84	482.08	419.43	305.18
1		367.20	358.35	333.73	282.32	195.31
2			251.50	232.98	194.57	125.00
3				165.48	138.41	80.00
4					102.47	51.20
5						32.77

machinery that has been used once before—at date 1. If the first move is up, the market value of the remaining expenditure equals 498.68 and, because this cell is shaded, the machinery is replaced—at date 2 we move back to the second panel of the table, corresponding to machinery that has not been used before. In contrast, if the first move is down, the market value of the remaining expenditure equals 352.23 and, because this cell is unshaded, the machinery is still not replaced—at date 2 we move down to the fourth panel of the table, corresponding to machinery that has been used twice before.

Table 10.6 shows that the manager should not replace the machinery at date 0, but if the next move in the fuel price is up, it will be optimal to replace the machinery at date 1; in contrast, if the first move is down, the machinery should be replaced at date 2 instead. Such flexibility is not allowed for in static DCF analysis, which explains why the market value of all future expenditure is 451.25 when real options analysis is used to choose the machinery-replacement policy and 456.52 when static DCF analysis is used.[10]

10.4 SOLVING PROBLEMS INVOLVING SWITCHING OPTIONS

We have examined two particular examples of switching options in this chapter. What distinguishes the switching-option problem from the other real options problems discussed in this book is that the project cycles through a set of distinct states, with some states occurring more than once. For example, in Section 10.2 a project alternated between being open and closed, while in Section 10.3 the age of a firm's machinery returned to zero each time the machinery was replaced. Many other arrangements are possible, depending on the number of distinct states and the ways in which the project can change from one state to another.

The general switching-option problem can be described as follows. There are M distinct project-states, which we label $m = 1, 2, \ldots, M$. For each project-state m we let J_m denote the collection of states that the project can switch to.[11] For example, if $J_1 = \{1, 2, 4\}$ then the manager can switch a project from state 1 to any one of states 1, 2, and 4. If $J_2 = \{3\}$ then the only action available to the manager is to switch the project to state 3.

We denote the (cum dividend) market value of the project at node (i, n) by $V_m(i, n)$ when it is in state m. For the particular problem we are studying we need to be able to identify the cash flow that will occur at node (i, n) if the manager of the project switches the project from state m to any state j in the allowable set J_m. We denote this cash flow by $Y_{m,j}(i, n)$, so that the subscripts indicate (in order) the current state and the state after one period elapses.

We begin by building the decision tree and using it to identify the set of project-states and the allowable transitions between different project-states. Once that is complete, we construct the binomial tree for the state variable. Ultimately we need to complete trees for the market value of the project in each of the M possible project-states. However, because of the ways in which the project can

---

10. At first glance, this might appear to contradict our claim in Section 2.3 that dynamic decision making leads to higher market values. The explanation is that here we are calculating the market value of expenditure. Provided that the firm's revenue is unaffected by its machinery-replacement policy, the lower market value of expenditure from using dynamic decision making results in a higher market value of the firm as a whole, consistent with our discussion in Section 2.3.

11. As in Section 9.4, we restrict attention to the case where each attempt to change the project's state is certain to succeed. Relaxing this restriction is straightforward.

cycle between states, we may not be able to fill these trees in one at a time. Instead, we may have to complete some of them simultaneously. We should start by using the appropriate terminal condition to fill in the terminal nodes of the various market-value trees, before using backward induction to fill in the remaining entries.

The recursive equation can be derived using techniques that will be familiar by now. Suppose the project is in state m at node (i, n), so that the manager must switch the project to one of the states in the set J_m. If state j is chosen then the project generates a cash flow of $Y_{m,j}(i, n)$ immediately and, after one period elapses, it will be worth $V_j(i, n + 1)$ if an up move occurs and $V_j(i + 1, n + 1)$ if a down move occurs. The payoff is therefore

$$Y_{m,j}(i, n) + \frac{\pi_u(i, n)V_j(i, n + 1) + \pi_d(i, n)V_j(i + 1, n + 1)}{R_f}.$$

Since the manager can choose to switch to any state $j \in J_m$, and since the objective is to maximize the market value of the firm, the value of the project at node (i, n) in state m is[12]

$$V_m(i, n) = \max_{j \in J_m} \left\{ Y_{m,j}(i, n) + \frac{\pi_u(i, n)V_j(i, n + 1) + \pi_d(i, n)V_j(i + 1, n + 1)}{R_f} \right\}.$$
$$(10.7)$$

By the time we have completed the backward induction procedure, we will have determined the current market value of the project together with an optimal policy for exercising the switching option.

The solution process can be summarized as follows:

1. Build the decision tree and use it to identify the set of project-states and the allowable transitions between different project-states.
2. Build a tree for the state variable.
3. Build a tree for the market value of the project in each possible state.
   (a) Start by using the appropriate terminal condition to fill in the final column of each of these trees.
   (b) Fill in the remaining nodes of the various trees, working from right to left, using the recursive formula in equation (10.7).

Table 10.7 summarizes how each of the situations considered in this chapter fits into this general scheme.

10.5 PROBLEMS

10.1. (**Practice**) Reevaluate the numerical example in Section 10.2.3 for the following parameter values: $X_0 = 2.70$, $U = 1.12$, $D = 1/U$, $K = 0.99$,

---

12. If something other than market value is used as the objective function, then it might be necessary to replace "max" with "min" in equation (10.7).

Table 10.7. Fitting the Examples into the General Approach

	Production-suspension Problem	Machinery-replacement Problem
State variable	Output price	Fuel price
Project states	$1 = $ open	$1 = $ brand new
	$2 = $ closed	$2 = $ used once
		$3 = $ used twice
Allowable transitions	$J_1 = \{1, 2\}$	$J_1 = \{1, 2\}$
	$J_2 = \{1, 2\}$	$J_2 = \{1, 3\}$
		$J_3 = \{1\}$
Cash flows	$Y_{1,1}(i, n) = X(i, n) - W$	$Y_{1,1}(i, n) = a_1 X(i, n) + I - S_1$
	$Y_{1,2}(i, n) = -I_f$	$Y_{1,2}(i, n) = a_1 X(i, n)$
	$Y_{2,1}(i, n) = -I_h + X(i, n) - W$	$Y_{2,1}(i, n) = a_2 X(i, n) + I - S_2$
	$Y_{2,2}(i, n) = 0$	$Y_{2,3}(i, n) = a_2 X(i, n)$
		$Y_{3,1}(i, n) = a_3 X(i, n) + I - S_3$

$R_f = 1.01$, $I_f = 2$, $I_h = 0$, $W = 2.10$. Production must cease permanently after date 20, but all other aspects of the model are unchanged.

    (a) Calculate the market value of the factory and an optimal operating policy.

    (b) Starting from node $(0, 0)$, how many successive down moves must occur before it is optimal to suspend production?

    (c) Starting from the node where suspension occurs in (b), how many successive up moves must occur before it is optimal to resume production?

    (d) Discuss the implications of this operating policy for how managers should respond to exogenous shocks.

10.2. **(Practice)** Suppose that the firm in Section 10.2 must pay C' on each date that production does not occur, up to and including date 20, after which production must cease permanently. All other aspects of the situation are unchanged.

    (a) Derive the recursive equations needed to calculate the market value of the factory.

    (b) Calculate the market value of the factory and an optimal operating policy for the following values of C': $0.00, 0.25, 0.50, 0.75$, and 1.00. Use the same values for the other parameters as in Problem 10.1.

    (c) What effect does the requirement to pay C' have on the region where it is optimal to keep an open factory open and a closed factory closed? Give an intuitive explanation for this behavior.

10.3. **(Practice)** Derive the recursive equations needed to calculate the market value of the factory in Section 10.2 if it takes one period to resume production. All other aspects of the situation are unchanged.

10.4. **(Extension: Resumption risk)** If production requires specialized staff, there is no guarantee that staff with the required skills will be able to be recruited at short notice. Suppose that each attempt to resume production in Section 10.2 is only successful with probability q. If resumption succeeds, then the firm produces one unit of output immediately. If it fails, then the manager can attempt to resume production in the future. This "resumption risk" is fully diversifiable. Production must cease permanently after date 6, but all other aspects of the model are unchanged.

   (a) Draw the decision tree for this problem.

   (b) Derive the terminal conditions and the recursive equations needed to calculate the market value of the factory.

   (c) Calculate the market value of the factory and an optimal investment policy for the following values of q: 0.00, 0.25, 0.50, 0.75, 1.00. Use the following parameter values: $X_0 = 8$, $U = 1.2$, $D = 1/U$, $K = 0.98$, $R_f = 1.04$, $I_f = 0$, $I_h = 0$, $W = 7$.

   (d) Does the manager become more or less reluctant to suspend production as resumption becomes more difficult? Explain this behavior in terms of the real options created and destroyed by suspending production.

10.5. **(Application: Mothballing a fertilizer manufacturing plant)** A firm is currently producing one unit of fertilizer per period at a constant cost of C per unit of output produced. The plant will be shut down permanently after date 20. Whenever the plant is open, the firm can mothball it or shut it down permanently. In each case, production stops immediately. Whenever the plant is in mothballs, the firm can reopen it (which takes one period) or shut it down permanently. The firm incurs expenditure of A at each date that it keeps the plant mothballed and I each time it reopens a mothballed plant. The firm's only other cash flows arise from selling fertilizer, for which the price at node (i, n) equals $X(i, n)$. The risk-adjusted growth factor for the state variable equals K and the return on one-period risk-free bonds equals R_f, for some constants K and R_f. The state variable is equally likely to change by a constant factor of U or D each period.

   (a) Construct the decision tree and use it to identify the various market-value trees that must be built.

   (b) Derive all required recursive equations and terminal conditions and specify the order in which the various trees must be filled in.

   (c) How does this situation compare with the one in Section 10.2?

   (d) Calculate the market value of the fertilizer manufacturing plant at date 0, and identify an optimal operating policy, for the following parameter values: $X_0 = 80$, $U = 1.12$, $D = 1/U$, $K = 0.99$, $R_f = 1.06$, $C = 70$, $A = 1$, $I = 40$.

   (e) Using different paths through the binomial tree as examples, discuss the various sequences of operating decisions that we might observe. For example, what factors should the plant's manager consider when deciding whether or not to mothball the plant? Use the language of real options to answer this question.

10.6. **(Practice)** In this problem we reevaluate the numerical example in Section 10.3.4 for the following parameter values: $X_0 = 10$, $U = 1.3$, $D = 1/U$, $K = 0.97$, $R_f = 1.04$, $I = 100$, $a_1 = a_2 = 5$, $a_3 = 10$, $S_1 = S_2 = S_3 = 0$. Suppose that the firm must produce output from dates 0 to 11 inclusive, but otherwise all other aspects of the situation are unchanged. How much can the firm save by using an optimal replacement policy rather than the best static DCF policy?

10.7. **(Practice)** Suppose that the machinery in Section 10.3 can be used up to four times. The firm must produce output from dates 0 to 11 inclusive, but otherwise all other aspects of the situation are unchanged.

    (a) Draw the decision tree for the problem facing the firm's manager.

    (b) Derive the recursive equations for this problem.

    (c) Solve this machinery-replacement problem for the situation where $a_4 = 12$, $S_4 = 0$, and all other parameters take the values in Problem 10.6. How much can the firm save by using an optimal replacement policy rather than the best static DCF policy?

10.8. **(Extension: Enhanced maintenance)** Suppose that the firm described in Section 10.3 has the option to pay additional maintenance costs that stop the machinery aging. Specifically, machinery that is three periods old can be kept in service for an additional period provided that the firm immediately pays a maintenance cost of M. The following period it is treated in exactly the same way as any machinery that is three periods old. In particular, this "lifetime-extension" option can be exercised as many times as the firm's manager wishes. In all other respects the situation is the same as that described in Section 10.3.

    (a) Draw the decision tree for the problem facing the firm's manager.

    (b) Derive the full set of terminal conditions and recursive equations.

    (c) Repeat all of the analysis for the case when the lifetime of a piece of machinery can be extended only once.

10.9. **(Application: Inventory management)** A firm produces one unit of grain per period at zero cost, from dates 0 to 9 inclusive. It costs the firm C to transport each unit of grain to market, where it sells for $X(i, n)$ at node (i, n). The firm owns a storage facility that is currently empty, but which has a capacity of three units. This gives the firm the option to store the grain it produces until the grain price is high. However, capacity constraints mean that the firm can transport at most two units of grain to market per period. The firm can dispose of grain only by selling it, and the storage facility must be empty after trading occurs at date 9. The risk-adjusted growth factor for the state variable equals K and the return on one-period risk-free bonds equals R_f. The state variable is equally likely to change by a constant factor of U or D each period.

    (a) Construct the decision tree and use it to identify the various market-value trees that must be built.

    (b) Derive all required recursive equations and terminal conditions and specify the order in which the various trees must be filled in.

(c) How does this situation compare with the one in Section 10.3?

(d) Calculate the market value of the firm and identify an optimal inventory-management policy for the following parameter values: $X_0 = 6$, $U = 1.2$, $D = 1/U$, $K = 1.01$, $R_f = 1.04$, $C = 5$.

(e) Using different paths through the binomial tree as examples, discuss the form of an optimal inventory-management policy. What factors should the firm's manager consider when deciding how much grain to transport to market? Use the language of real options to answer this question.

11

Learning Options

The costs associated with launching a new product do not stop once development of the product is complete. Building distribution infrastructure can be expensive and the cost of marketing can be substantial, especially for particularly innovative products for which no market currently exists. Much of this expenditure is irreversible. Testing a new product in a small set of markets prior to a full-scale launch allows a firm to acquire considerable information about the product's potential. If testing produces good news then the product can be launched on a much larger scale, and the main cost of the test marketing to the firm is that the payoff has been delayed for the duration of the testing.[1] However, if it produces bad news then the firm has avoided the incremental costs of a full-scale launch.

Whether or not the test-market approach is optimal in any given situation will depend on factors such as the potential information to be gained from test marketing, the delays introduced by test marketing, and the incremental expenditure associated with a full-scale launch. For example, if a product is especially innovative then the use of a test market is relatively attractive. However, if there is considerable heterogeneity across markets, the information gathered from test markets may reveal little about a product's full potential, making test marketing relatively unattractive.

The US market for light beer offers many examples of the various approaches firms adopt when launching new products. For example, Miller Brewing Company

---

1. There are other costs, such as raising the probability that a competitor mimics the new product sooner.

first introduced its lime and salt flavored light beer Miller Chill into markets in Arizona, Florida, New Mexico, San Diego, and Texas in March 2007.[2] After four weeks, Miller decided on a national rollout, which started in June that year. In contrast, when Anheuser-Busch launched Bud Light Lime in May 2008 it did so without putting the product into test markets first. One possible reason for the break from its tradition of always test-marketing its products is that successful launches of similar products by Anheuser-Busch (and, for that matter, Miller) reduced the uncertainty associated with the new product—the value of the learning option created by test marketing was sufficiently low that an immediate national rollout was optimal.

An important component of the value of the learning options associated with test markets is the ability to postpone or abandon a full-scale product launch. Miller exercised such an option in the case of its Miller Lite Brewers Collection. Three different light beers were tested in markets in Minneapolis, North Carolina, San Diego, and Baltimore from February 2008. In April Miller announced that the beers would be launched nationally, with the rollout complete by September. However, the rollout was postponed indefinitely in June 2008, while Miller continued test marketing.

In the models we have considered so far, we have implicitly assumed that the decision maker knows the precise level of key project parameters such as the investment expenditure in the investment timing models of Sections 7.2, 8.2, and 9.3, or the quantity of copper reserves in the resource extraction problem in Section 8.3. Our results would have been unaffected if there was some uncertainty surrounding these parameters, provided that the decision maker's beliefs regarding the parameters did not change over time. Clearly, the problems facing Miller and Anheuser-Busch do not fit into this mold—the whole point of test marketing is to learn more about key parameters that affect profitability. Therefore, in this chapter we allow for the possibility that the decision maker's beliefs change over time and that it is possible to influence how rapidly these changes occur.

A manager's ability to learn more about project parameters injects volatility into the value of a firm. Initially the value will be based on one distribution of possible parameter values. As new information arrives, this distribution changes, leading to changes in the firm's market value. For example, the value of a brewery prior to test marketing a new beer might be based on an expected market share of 20%. If test marketing reveals that the market share is likely to be 30% instead, then the value of the firm will rise. By definition, the precise content of the new information is unpredictable, so the resulting changes in the firm's value will be unpredictable as well. Thus, exercising a learning option introduces risk.

Real options embedded in a project can introduce asymmetry into the effect of any new information that is gathered. For example, a manager might accelerate investment if he receives good news about a project's profitability, while he might

---

2. Kesmodel (2007) describes the launch of Miller Chill.

be able to mitigate the effect of bad news by delaying investment or abandoning it altogether. As with market risk, he waits when the upside risk dominates the downside risk by enough to compensate for the delay in receiving the investment payoff. The crucial difference from the market risk case is that now the decision maker is actively generating the volatility in the payoff by going out and seeking more information.

Many of the situations we have met in Chapters 7–10 could be modified to incorporate learning options. Thus, in this chapter we do not add to the list of real options we have built up in recent chapters. Rather, we consider how learning options can be incorporated within the structures we have already developed. We introduce a variety of examples of learning options in Section 11.1 and then develop a way to model the learning process in Section 11.2. This is an important addition to our real options toolkit—once we have understood this material, it is reasonably straightforward (in principle at least) to add a learning component to the models introduced in previous chapters. We demonstrate this process by analyzing the staged roll-out of a new venture in Section 11.3 and the exploration and development of an oil field in Section 11.4. The general approach to analyzing learning options is summarized in Section 11.5.

11.1 EXAMPLES OF LEARNING OPTIONS

A typical example of a problem involving learning options arises if we modify the simple investment timing option of Section 7.2 by allowing the firm to gather information about the project while it waits. With this modification, the firm does not just wait until market conditions improve (which is the motivation for waiting in Chapter 7). Now it might use the waiting period to gather useful information about the eventual investment payoff. There are many such situations that arise when we introduce learning into our models.

Market Research A firm is considering launching a new product. Prior to investing in the facilities required to manufacture and market the product, the firm will conduct a program of market research. It might carry out its market research for a sustained period until it has a precise understanding of the demand for the product. However, if the early results of the market research are especially favorable and general market conditions are strong, then the firm might actually terminate the market research early and launch the product. This could be modeled as an extension of the investment timing problems in Sections 7.2, 8.2, and 9.3, with the firm having the option to gather information about the investment payoff while it waits to invest. Learning does not alter the realized payoff, only the manager's expected payoff.

Construction Cost Uncertainty A firm owns the right to complete construction of a project. The prices of crucial inputs vary over time, exposing the firm to market risk. In addition, the manager of the firm is uncertain about the length of time it will take to complete the project. However, as construction occurs the manager learns more about the construction time. If new information suggests that the project will take a long time (and considerable expenditure) to complete, the manager may abandon construction before the project is complete. This could be modeled as an extension of the sequential investment timing model discussed in Section 8.2.

R&D A firm is attempting to develop a new product. However, there is uncertainty surrounding the probability of success. At the beginning of the program, the manager believes that each development attempt will succeed with probability q_0. However, with each unsuccessful attempt she revises this probability downwards, first to q_1, then to q_2, and so on. Eventually either development succeeds or the program is abandoned. The manager must decide how many unsuccessful attempts to allow before abandoning the program. This is similar to the R&D problems analyzed in Sections 7.4 and 8.4, but now we add in the procedure for revising the manager's initial views regarding the program as more information becomes available.

Resource Extraction A firm owns the right to mine a piece of land for which the quality and quantity of reserves are uncertain. The firm will carry out a preliminary exploration stage during which its manager learns more about the reserves. At some point the firm will stop exploring and will either abandon the project or make the investment required to develop and then exploit the reserve. The timing of this decision will depend on both the information revealed during the exploration stage and the spot price of the resource to be extracted from the mine. We consider a similar problem in Section 11.4.

All of these examples fit within a fairly general structure. Some key characteristics of an investment opportunity, which will affect the payoff if and when investment actually occurs, are currently unknown. The manager can invest now and hope that those characteristics are favorable—that is, that the realized investment payoff is high. Alternatively, investment can be delayed while more information about the project characteristics is gathered. For example, the owner of the right to develop an oil field may drill some test wells as part of investigating the likely quantity of reserves. The motivation for doing so is that the firm might be able to avoid bad outcomes by discovering before investment that the realized investment payoff would be low.

   Before we look at two examples in detail we develop some new techniques that are needed to analyze problems involving learning options.

11.2 MODELING INFORMATION GATHERING

11.2.1 Generalizing our Concept of the "State of the Project"

In order to analyze these types of problems, we need to generalize how we think about the state of a project. Previously our description of a project's state reflected factors such as the stage of the project in its investment sequence, whether it was operating or idle, and so on. Now, however, the project state can also reflect the current information regarding some characteristic of the project that will affect its ultimate profitability. For example, the project might be an oil concession. Initially (especially in regions that have not been thoroughly explored) the decision maker may have little idea about just how much oil is in the ground. However, as more resources are devoted to investigating the area, the decision maker learns more about the oil reserves it contains. At any given date the description of the state of the oil field will reflect the available information about its quantity of reserves. The state of the project will change over time as the available information changes.

We start by identifying the possible values of the relevant project characteristics and attaching a probability to each one, given information that is available at date 0. For example, a potential oil field might be "large" or "small" with respective probabilities 0.25 and 0.75. These probabilities will change as time evolves and the decision maker gathers more information. For example, the probability that a potential oil field is large might rise to 0.40 (and the probability that it is small fall to 0.60) if initial investigations are encouraging; if they are discouraging, the respective probabilities might fall to 0.10 and rise to 0.90. The "engine room" of a model of learning options is the description of how the probability distribution that captures the decision maker's beliefs changes over time. We discuss this in more detail in Section 11.2.2.

The outcome of gathering information is uncertain. If it were not—that is, if a firm could perfectly predict what new information it is going to gather— then it would not need to gather the information in the first place. The ability to gather information therefore introduces an additional source of volatility (that is, in addition to market risk) into the payoff from waiting to invest. Provided that the project under consideration is not so large that market prices will change when the new information is revealed, the risk introduced by information gathering is diversifiable.[3] We can therefore treat the risk associated with information gathering in exactly the same way as we treated technical risk in Sections 7.4 and 8.4. In particular, the risk associated with information gathering will not attract a risk premium.

As we see in Sections 11.3 and 11.4, in order to estimate the value of gathering information about a project's characteristics we need to know the probability of receiving the different types of news ("good", "bad", and any other categories that we might wish to consider). We also need to know the information content of these news events. For example, we need to know exactly how good news affects the probability distribution of the various project characteristics. In Section 11.2.2 we see how these can be obtained and then, in Sections 11.3 and 11.4, we see how they can be used to analyze problems involving learning options.

---

3. Note, however, that the decision to exercise a learning option may well be triggered by market behavior. For example, we might explore a potential oil field only when the price of crude oil is high. Thus there will be an element of systematic risk, but this will come indirectly through market risk determining the timing of learning options being exercised, not from the outcome of the learning itself. The valuation approach we adopt makes this adjustment automatically.

11.2.2 Using Bayes' Theorem

We base our discussion in this section on an example in which a solitary project characteristic takes one of two values, which we call "large" and "small". For instance, if we are considering a firm that owns the right to develop an oil field then this characteristic might represent the quantity of reserves. The owner of the project rights has the option to acquire some information about this characteristic prior to investment. We suppose that the information will be either "good news" or "bad news", with good news indicating a relatively high probability, and bad news indicating a relatively low probability, that the project is large.

The simplest possibility, albeit an unrealistic one, is that all uncertainty is resolved at once. In this case, good news would indicate that the project is certain to be large, while bad news would indicate that it is certain to be small. Based on all information initially available (that is, before the news is received) the probability that the project is large equals the probability that the news will be good.

However, it is more realistic to assume that a single investigation does not completely determine the project characteristic. For example, as a firm carries out an exploration program it will gradually acquire more information about the quantity of oil reserves. In such circumstances we need to know several different probabilities in order to analyze the firm's learning option properly.

- Given all information currently available, what is the probability that the project is large and what is the probability that it is small? We denote these probabilities by $\Pr[L]$ and $\Pr[S]$ respectively.
- Given all information currently available, what is the probability that the firm will receive good news if it exercises its learning option and what is the probability that it will receive bad news? We denote these probabilities by $\Pr[G]$ and $\Pr[B]$ respectively.
- If the firm exercises its learning option and receives good news, what is the (revised) probability that the project is large and what is the probability that it is small? We denote these (conditional) probabilities by $\Pr[L|G]$ and $\Pr[S|G]$ respectively.
- If the firm receives bad news, what is the (revised) probability that the project is large and what is the probability that it is small? We denote these (conditional) probabilities by $\Pr[L|B]$ and $\Pr[S|B]$ respectively.

Because there are two possible values for the project characteristic and two possible outcomes from information gathering, there are four distinct outcomes that can occur: the project is large and the news is good; the project is large and the news is bad; the project is small and the news is good; and the project is small and the news is bad. As the next example demonstrates, if we know the probabilities of these four outcomes occurring, then we can completely determine all of the probabilities needed to analyze the firm's learning option.

Example 11.1. Suppose that the four outcomes occur with the probabilities shown in Table 11.1. For example, the project is large and the news is good with probability 0.20. We can read the probability of good news being

Table 11.1. A Complete Description of
the Outcomes of Information Gathering

	Large	Small	Sum
Good	0.20	0.30	0.50
Bad	0.05	0.45	0.50
Sum	0.25	0.75	1.00

received directly off the table. Since the project must be either large or small, it follows that the probability of the news being good equals

$$\Pr[G] = \Pr[G \text{ and } L] + \Pr[G \text{ and } S] = 0.20 + 0.30 = 0.50.$$

The probability of the news being bad must equal $\Pr[B] = 1 - \Pr[G] = 0.50$. We can also read the initial (that is, unconditional) probability distribution of the project's size directly off Table 11.1. Since the news must be either good or bad, it follows that the probability of the project being large equals

$$\Pr[L] = \Pr[L \text{ and } G] + \Pr[L \text{ and } B] = 0.20 + 0.05 = 0.25.$$

The probability of the project being small must equal $\Pr[S] = 1 - \Pr[L] = 0.75$.

The information contained in Table 11.1 also allows us to calculate the conditional probabilities. For example, suppose the firm exercises its learning option and receives good news. This can come about in two ways: the project is large and the news is good (which occurs with probability 0.20), or the project is small and the news is good (which occurs with probability 0.30). Therefore, conditional on receiving good news, the project is large with probability

$$\Pr[L|G] = \frac{\Pr[L \text{ and } G]}{\Pr[L \text{ and } G] + \Pr[S \text{ and } G]} = \frac{0.20}{0.20 + 0.30} = 0.40.$$

Similarly, conditional on receiving bad news, the project is large with probability

$$\Pr[L|B] = \frac{\Pr[L \text{ and } B]}{\Pr[L \text{ and } B] + \Pr[S \text{ and } B]} = \frac{0.05}{0.05 + 0.45} = 0.10.$$

That is, if good news is received, the likelihood of a large project rises from 25% to 40%. However, if bad news is received, the likelihood falls to 10%. ∎

We are not usually presented with all of the information contained in Table 11.1. Instead, we need to calculate some of the probabilities that we require. The simplest case is when we have estimates of the conditional probabilities and of the probabilities of good and bad news arriving. Then it is straightforward to estimate the current probabilities regarding the project characteristic.

Example 11.2. Suppose that we are equally likely to receive good and bad news, and that good news indicates the project is large with probability 0.40 while bad news indicates it is large with probability 0.10. Then the unconditional probability that the project is large (that is, the probability before the good or bad news arrives) must equal

$$Pr[L] = Pr[L|G]Pr[G] + Pr[L|B]Pr[B] = 0.40 \times 0.50 + 0.10 \times 0.50 = 0.25.$$

∎

However, often our most reliable estimate will be of the current (that is, unconditional) probability distribution of the project characteristics. Suppose, for instance, that we know the (unconditional) probability that the project is large, $Pr[L]$, the probability that a large project will result in good news, $Pr[G|L]$, and the probability that a small project will result in good news, $Pr[G|S]$.[4] Given these probabilities, we know that the project is small with probability

$$Pr[S] = 1 - Pr[L].$$

Since there are only two possible project sizes, large and small, good news occurs with probability

$$Pr[G] = Pr[G|L]Pr[L] + Pr[G|S]Pr[S]. \tag{11.1}$$

A result known as Bayes' theorem tells us that if good news occurs we should revise the probability that the project is large to

$$Pr[L|G] = \frac{Pr[G|L]Pr[L]}{Pr[G]}. \tag{11.2}$$

Similarly, if bad news occurs we should revise the probability that the project is large to

$$Pr[L|B] = \frac{Pr[B|L]Pr[L]}{Pr[B]}. \tag{11.3}$$

This gives us everything we need.

- Before we gather any information, the relevant probabilities of the project characteristics are $Pr[L]$ and $Pr[S]$.
- If we gather information, we get good news with probability $Pr[G]$ (given by equation (11.1)) and bad news with probability $Pr[B] = 1 - Pr[G]$.
  - Immediately after we get good news the relevant probabilities of the project characteristics become $Pr[L|G]$ (given by equation (11.2)) and $Pr[S|G] = 1 - Pr[L|G]$.

---

4. It is the possibility that large projects can generate bad news, and that small projects generate good news, that means information gathering only reduces—and does not eliminate—uncertainty. That is, even though the news is good the project may still be small.

- Immediately after we get bad news the relevant probabilities of the project characteristics become $\Pr[L|B]$ (given by equation (11.3)) and $\Pr[S|B] = 1 - \Pr[L|B]$.

The following example demonstrates the calculations.

Example 11.3. Suppose that 25% of oil fields of the type under consideration are large and the remaining 75% are small: $\Pr[L] = 0.25$ and $\Pr[S] = 0.75$. Further, suppose that a large oil field will generate good news 80% of the time, while a small field will generate good news 40% of the time, so that $\Pr[G|L] = 0.80$ and $\Pr[G|S] = 0.40$. Then good news must occur with probability

$$\Pr[G] = \Pr[G|L]\Pr[L] + \Pr[G|S]\Pr[S] = 0.80 \times 0.25 + 0.40 \times 0.75 = 0.50,$$

while bad news must occur with probability

$$\Pr[B] = 1 - \Pr[G] = 1 - 0.50 = 0.50.$$

Bayes' theorem tells us that if good news is received then the conditional probability that the field is large is

$$\Pr[L|G] = \frac{\Pr[G|L]\Pr[L]}{\Pr[G]} = \frac{0.80 \times 0.25}{0.50} = 0.40.$$

Similarly, if bad news is received then the conditional probability that the field is large is

$$\Pr[L|B] = \frac{\Pr[B|L]\Pr[L]}{\Pr[B]} = \frac{0.20 \times 0.25}{0.50} = 0.10.$$

That is, if good news is received, the likelihood of a large oil field rises from 25% to 40%. However, if bad news is received, the likelihood falls to 10%. ∎

When information can only be gathered gradually it will often be optimal to make more than one attempt to reduce uncertainty surrounding crucial project characteristics. For example, firms may drill more than one test well before they commit to developing an oil field. They will not necessarily abandon development rights just because the first piece of news is bad—the information gathered in second and subsequent rounds may be more encouraging than that gathered initially.

The probability of good news occurring and its effect on the conditional probabilities of the project being large need to be recalculated for each round of information gathering, even when the result of the second round is statistically independent of the first. The method is exactly the same as we described immediately prior to Example 11.3. All that changes is the set of inputs. The next example demonstrates the calculations required.

Example 11.4. We base our discussion on Example 11.3 and assume that the firm's owner carries out a second information-gathering exercise and that the results of this one are statistically independent of the first.

We begin with the case when the first information-gathering exercise has resulted in good news. Therefore, the revised probability that the oil reserve is large is 0.40 (so that the probability that it is small has fallen to 0.60). To determine the results of the second information-gathering exercise, we apply Bayes' theorem for a second time. Since we continue to suppose that $Pr[G|L] = 0.80$ and $Pr[G|S] = 0.40$, we get a second case of good news with probability

$$Pr[G] = Pr[G|L]Pr[L] + Pr[G|S]Pr[S] = 0.80 \times 0.40 + 0.40 \times 0.60 = 0.56,$$

while bad news must occur with probability

$$Pr[B] = 1 - Pr[G] = 1 - 0.56 = 0.44.$$

Bayes' theorem tells us that if good news is received then the conditional probability that the field will turn out to be large is

$$Pr[L|G] = \frac{Pr[G|L]Pr[L]}{Pr[G]} = \frac{0.80 \times 0.40}{0.56} = 0.57.$$

Similarly, if bad news is received then the conditional probability that the field will turn out to be large is

$$Pr[L|B] = \frac{Pr[B|L]Pr[L]}{Pr[B]} = \frac{0.20 \times 0.40}{0.44} = 0.18.$$

That is, if a second piece of good news is received, the likelihood of a large oil field rises from 40% to 57%. However, if bad news is received (to go with the earlier good news), the likelihood falls to 18%.

We can repeat these calculations for the case where the first piece of news about the oil field is bad. From above, the revised probability that the oil reserve is large is 0.10 (so that the probability that it is small has risen to 0.90). The second piece of news is good with probability

$$Pr[G] = Pr[G|L]Pr[L] + Pr[G|S]Pr[S] = 0.80 \times 0.10 + 0.40 \times 0.90 = 0.44,$$

while bad news occurs with probability

$$Pr[B] = 1 - Pr[G] = 1 - 0.44 = 0.56.$$

If good news is received then the conditional probability that the field will turn out to be large is

$$Pr[L|G] = \frac{Pr[G|L]Pr[L]}{Pr[G]} = \frac{0.80 \times 0.10}{0.44} = 0.18.$$

Similarly, if bad news is received then the conditional probability that the field will turn out to be large is

$$Pr[L|B] = \frac{Pr[B|L]Pr[L]}{Pr[B]} = \frac{0.20 \times 0.10}{0.56} = 0.036.$$

That is, if a second piece of bad news is received, the likelihood of a large oil field falls from 10% to 3.6%. However, if good news is received (to go with the earlier bad news), the likelihood rises to 18%.

To summarize, we began with the probability of a large reserve being 25%. If we get two pieces of good news, this probability increases to 57%, while getting two pieces of bad news drives it down to 3.6%. If the news is mixed (that is, one piece of good news and one piece of bad news) the probability falls to 18%.   ∎

The discussion in this section demonstrates how we can take some raw inputs and turn them into a model of the information-gathering process. The next two sections of this chapter apply these methods to two typical examples. In the first a firm considers how to launch a new venture with uncertain prospects, while the second considers the problem facing a firm that owns the right to develop an oil field containing uncertain reserves.

11.3 STAGING THE ROLL-OUT OF A NEW VENTURE

This section analyzes the problem of rolling out a new business venture when, as well as the usual market-wide risks that affect demand conditions, there is project-specific uncertainty about how successful the new venture will be.

11.3.1 Setting Up the Roll-out Problem

A firm owns the right to build up to five identical facilities at different locations. The firm has the option to start by developing a single facility (called "going local") and then expand to a nationwide operation by building at four additional sites. Alternatively, it can build all five facilities at once. Each facility costs I to build, which must be paid as soon as construction begins. Construction takes one period and the right to build each facility expires if construction is not completed on or before date 5. There is currently substantial uncertainty concerning how successful these facilities will be. If the venture is successful then each facility generates perpetual net revenue of $2X(i, n)$ per period, but if it is unsuccessful the net revenue is just $X(i, n)$ per period. Immediately after the first facility is built, the manager will learn whether the venture will be "successful" (with probability q) or "unsuccessful" (with probability $1 - q$).

The risk-adjusted growth factor associated with X equals the constant K. Thus, the market value at node (i, n) of a cash flow that will equal $X(i, n + 1)$ at date $n + 1$ if an up move occurs and $X(i + 1, n + 1)$ if a down move occurs is $KX(i, n)/R_f$, where R_f equals the constant return on a one-period risk-free bond.

11.3.2 Analyzing the Roll-out Problem

We start by building the decision tree, and begin by considering the manager's problem at date 0. Since no facilities have yet been built, the manager must go local, go national, or wait. These are represented by the actions L, N, and W in the decision tree drawn in Figure 11.1. If she goes local there is a cash outflow of I at date 0 and then one of two things will happen: the venture is successful (with probability q) or it is unsuccessful (with probability $1 - q$). If she goes

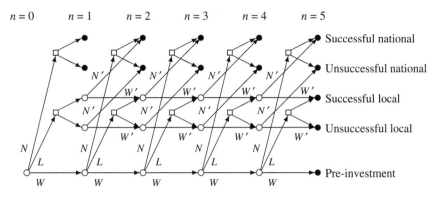

Figure 11.1. Decision tree for staging the roll-out of a new venture

national there is a cash outflow of $5I$ at date 0 and, again, either the venture is successful (with probability q) or it is unsuccessful (with probability $1 - q$). However, because there are no further investment decisions to take in this case, the decision tree ends. If she chooses to wait, there is no cash flow at date 0 and at date 1 there will still be no facilities built.

Thus, at date 1 we need to consider three different project-states: the initial state, with no facilities built; successful local expansion; and unsuccessful local expansion. In the first case the situation facing the firm's manager is exactly the same as at date 0. In the other two cases, the manager must either go national (labeled N' in Figure 11.1) or wait (labeled W'). If she chooses to go national, the firm pays $4I$ at date 1 and what happens next depends on the current state of the project. If the local expansion was successful then the national expansion will be successful as well, while if the local expansion was unsuccessful then the national expansion will be unsuccessful. Thus, there is no uncertainty about the result of going national if the firm first goes local. The more realistic situation, where even a successful local expansion might be unsuccessful nationally, can be analyzed using a model similar to the one in Section 11.4.

The situation at dates 2–4 is identical to that at date 1: we need to consider the same three project-states. Finally, at date 5 the right to expand is lost, so that the firm must remain in its then current state indefinitely. This completes the construction of the decision tree shown in Figure 11.1.

The decision tree identifies five possible project-states: pre-investment, successful local, unsuccessful local, successful national, and unsuccessful national. Since the market value of the project in each of the last two states can be written as an explicit function of the state variable, we need only to build binomial trees for the market value of the project in the first three states (together with a binomial tree for the state variable). We denote the market value of the development rights at node (i, n) by $V_{pi}(i, n)$ in the pre-investment state, by $V_{sl}(i, n)$ in the successful local state, and by $V_{ul}(i, n)$ in the unsuccessful local state.

Construction takes one period and the investment rights are lost if investment is not completed on or before date 5, so that

$$V_{pi}(i, 5) = 0 \tag{11.4}$$

for all $i = 0, 1, \ldots, 5$. If the firm has expanded locally prior to date 5 then it will continue to generate a perpetual cash flow from its local facility after date 5, so that (4.16) implies

$$V_{sl}(i, 5) = \frac{2R_f X(i, 5)}{R_f - K} \quad \text{and} \quad V_{ul}(i, 5) = \frac{R_f X(i, 5)}{R_f - K}. \tag{11.5}$$

These are the terminal conditions that we use to fill in the final column of each market-value tree. Now we turn to the recursive equations used to complete the three trees.

We begin by considering the problem facing the firm's manager at node (i, n) if going local has been successful. She must either wait or go national. If she waits, then the firm generates net revenue of $2X(i, n)$ immediately and will be worth $V_{sl}(i, n+1)$ at date $n+1$ if the next move is up and $V_{sl}(i+1, n+1)$ if it is down, implying a payoff of

$$2X(i, n) + \frac{\pi_u(i, n)V_{sl}(i, n+1) + \pi_d(i, n)V_{sl}(i+1, n+1)}{R_f}.$$

If the firm goes national instead, then the firm generates net revenue of $2X(i, n)$ immediately, spends $4I$ in building the four additional facilities, and generates a perpetual net revenue of $10X(\cdot, \cdot)$ from date $n + 1$ onwards. Since (4.16) implies that the claim to this perpetual net revenue stream is currently worth $10KX(i, n)/(R_f - K)$, the payoff from going national is

$$2X(i, n) - 4I + \frac{10KX(i, n)}{R_f - K}.$$

The manager will choose the action that maximizes the market value of the firm, so that the development rights are worth

$$V_{sl}(i, n) = \max \left\{ 2X(i, n) + \frac{\pi_u(i, n)V_{sl}(i, n+1) + \pi_d(i, n)V_{sl}(i+1, n+1)}{R_f}, \right.$$

$$\left. 2X(i, n) - 4I + \frac{10KX(i, n)}{R_f - K} \right\}. \tag{11.6}$$

The manager faces a similar problem if going local has been unsuccessful. Again, she must either wait or go national. If she waits, then the firm generates net revenue of $X(i, n)$ immediately and will be worth either $V_{ul}(i, n+1)$ or $V_{ul}(i+1, n+1)$ after one period elapses, so that the payoff equals

$$X(i, n) + \frac{\pi_u(i, n)V_{ul}(i, n+1) + \pi_d(i, n)V_{ul}(i+1, n+1)}{R_f}.$$

If she goes national, then the firm generates net revenue of $X(i, n)$ immediately, spends $4I$ in building the four additional sites, and generates a perpetual net revenue of $5X(\cdot, \cdot)$ from date $n + 1$ onwards. The corresponding payoff equals

$$X(i, n) - 4I + \frac{5KX(i, n)}{R_f - K}.$$

The manager chooses the action with the more valuable payoff, implying the recursive equation

$$V_{ul}(i, n) = \max \left\{ X(i, n) + \frac{\pi_u(i, n)V_{ul}(i, n + 1) + \pi_d(i, n)V_{ul}(i + 1, n + 1)}{R_f}, \right.$$

$$\left. X(i, n) - 4I + \frac{5KX(i, n)}{R_f - K} \right\}. \tag{11.7}$$

The situation facing the manager is only slightly more complicated when the project is in its initial state—that is, before any investment has taken place. She must do one of three things: wait, go local, or go national. If she waits, then the firm generates no cash flow immediately and will be worth either $V_{pi}(i, n + 1)$ or $V_{pi}(i + 1, n + 1)$ after one period elapses, depending on whether the next move is up or down. The payoff from waiting is therefore

$$\frac{\pi_u(i, n)V_{pi}(i, n + 1) + \pi_d(i, n)V_{pi}(i + 1, n + 1)}{R_f}.$$

If the firm goes national, then it spends $5I$ in building the five facilities. If the project is successful then it generates a perpetual net revenue of $10X(\cdot, \cdot)$ from date $n + 1$ onwards, but if it is unsuccessful this net revenue is just $5X(\cdot, \cdot)$. Because the risk associated with success or failure is diversifiable, this has the same market value as a perpetual cash flow of

$$q10X(\cdot, \cdot) + (1 - q)5X(\cdot, \cdot) = 5(1 + q)X(\cdot, \cdot).$$

The payoff from going national is therefore

$$-5I + 5(1 + q)\frac{KX(i, n)}{R_f - K}.$$

If the firm goes local, then it spends I in building the first facility. If an up move occurs then the firm will be worth either $V_{sl}(i, n + 1)$ or $V_{ul}(i, n + 1)$, depending on whether it is successful or not. Because the risk associated with success or failure is diversifiable, all we need to know about the market value of the development rights in the up state is its expected value. Since success occurs with probability q, this expected value is

$$qV_{sl}(i, n + 1) + (1 - q)V_{ul}(i, n + 1).$$

Similarly, if a down move occurs the expected market value of the development rights at date $n + 1$ equals

$$qV_{sl}(i + 1, n + 1) + (1 - q)V_{ul}(i + 1, n + 1).$$

The payoff from going local is therefore

$$-I + \frac{1}{R_f}\Big(\pi_u(i,n)(qV_{sl}(i,n+1)+(1-q)V_{ul}(i,n+1))$$

$$+\pi_d(i,n)(qV_{sl}(i+1,n+1)+(1-q)V_{ul}(i+1,n+1))\Big).$$

The manager chooses whichever action has the higher payoff, implying the recursive equation

$$V_{pi}(i,n)$$

$$=\max\Bigg\{\frac{\pi_u(i,n)V_{pi}(i,n+1)+\pi_d(i,n)V_{pi}(i+1,n+1)}{R_f}, -5I+5(1+q)\frac{KX(i,n)}{R_f-K},$$

$$-I+\frac{1}{R_f}\Big(\pi_u(i,n)(qV_{sl}(i,n+1)+(1-q)V_{ul}(i,n+1))$$

$$+\pi_d(i,n)(qV_{sl}(i+1,n+1)+(1-q)V_{ul}(i+1,n+1))\Big)\Bigg\}. \qquad (11.8)$$

We have now derived all of the equations needed to value the firm's development rights and obtain an optimal development policy. As usual, we begin by building the binomial tree for the state variable. We then construct the tree for the market value of the project rights if going local has been successful, using the terminal condition (11.5) and the recursive equation (11.6). The tree for the market value of the project rights if going local has been unsuccessful is constructed in the same way, but using the recursive equation (11.7) instead. Finally, we construct the tree for the market value of the project rights in their initial state, using the terminal condition (11.4) and the recursive equation (11.8). The following numerical example demonstrates the procedure.

11.3.3 A Numerical Example

In this section we suppose it costs $I = 155$ to build each facility and that the venture will be successful with probability $q = 0.4$. We further suppose that if an unsuccessful venture were currently in place then each facility would generate net revenue of $X_0 = 8$ and that each period this net revenue is equally likely to grow by a factor of either $U = 1.2500$ or $D = 1/U = 0.8000$. The resulting binomial tree for net revenue per (unsuccessful) facility is shown in the top panel of Table 11.2. The risk-adjusted growth factor is $K = 0.9900$, so that equation (3.8) implies that the risk-neutral probabilities of up and down moves are $\pi_u = 0.4222$ and $\pi_d = 0.5778$, respectively, at every node. The one-period risk-free interest rate equals 6%, so that $R_f = 1.06$.

As illustrated in Table 11.2, we begin by building the binomial tree for the state variable. We then fill in the tree for the market value of the project rights if going local has been successful, using equation (11.5) to fill in the final column and equation (11.6) to fill in the remaining ones. This procedure is repeated to fill in the tree for the market value of the project rights if going local has been

Table 11.2. Analysis of the Roll-out of a New Venture

$X(i, n)$	0	1	2	3	4	5	
0	8.00	10.00	12.50	15.63	19.53	24.41	
1		6.40	8.00	10.00	12.50	15.63	Step 1: Construct binomial
2			5.12	6.40	8.00	10.00 ←	tree for the state variable
3				4.10	5.12	6.40	
4					3.28	4.10	
5						2.62	

$V_{sl}(i, n)$	0	1	2	3	4	5	
0	527.43	814.29	1172.86	1621.07	2181.34	739.40	
1		332.07	527.43	814.29	1172.86	473.21 ←	Step 2a: Fill in final column using equation (11.5)
2			200.30	307.41	527.43	302.86	
3				124.05	155.06	193.83	Step 2b: Fill in remaining
4					99.24	124.05 ←	columns using
5						79.39	equation (11.6)

$V_{ul}(i, n)$	0	1	2	3	4	5	
0	146.83	208.38	313.33	500.54	780.67	369.70	
1		102.42	134.97	186.14	276.43	236.61 ←	Step 3a: Fill in final column using equation (11.5)
2			77.53	96.91	121.14	151.43	
3				62.03	77.53	96.91	Step 3b: Fill in remaining
4					49.62	62.03 ←	columns using
5						39.70	equation (11.7)

$V_{pi}(i, n)$	0	1	2	3	4	5	
0	133.55	265.89	462.50	771.87	1158.59	0.00	
1		50.70	117.94	252.55	462.50	0.00 ←	Step 4a: Fill in final column using equation (11.4)
2			6.83	17.15	17.00	0.00	
3				0.00	0.00	0.00	Step 4b: Fill in remaining
4					0.00	0.00 ←	columns using
5						0.00	equation (11.8)

unsuccessful: we use equation (11.5) to fill in the final column and equation (11.7) to fill in the remaining ones. Finally, we use equation (11.4) to fill in the final column of the tree for the market value of the project rights in their initial state, followed by repeated use of equation (11.8) to fill in the remaining columns.

The darkly-shaded cells in all three of these panels indicate the nodes where it is optimal to go national immediately, while the lightly-shaded cells in the bottom panel show where it is optimal to go local instead. As the table shows, if the first move is up then it is optimal to go local. If the venture is successful locally, then it is optimal to go national immediately, but the only way the firm will expand if the development is unsuccessful is if at least two of the next three moves in net revenue are up (that is, to nodes $(0, 3)$ or $(1, 4)$).

There are two reasons not to go national immediately. First, by initially going local the firm can avoid suffering the large loss caused by going national with an unsuccessful venture, while still being able to go national with a successful venture (albeit with the construction of four facilities delayed slightly). Second, by delaying even going local, the firm can wait and invest in more favorable market conditions. That is, it can exploit the asymmetry created by its option to invest at date 1 if market conditions improve and to delay further if they worsen.

The optimality or otherwise of initially delaying investment depends on many factors, an important one being the current level of net revenue that the venture would generate. To investigate the role of net revenue in the investment decision, Figure 11.2 plots the payoffs from going national immediately (the solid line), going local immediately (the dotted curve), and waiting (the dashed curve) as functions of the initial net revenue.[5] The two dots indicate where the optimal policies change. To the left of the first dot (where net revenue is approximately 8.39) it is optimal to wait, while to the right of the second dot (where net revenue is approximately 12.96) it is optimal to go national immediately. Between the two dots it is optimal to go local immediately.

Beyond a certain level (12.96 in this case), net revenue is so high that the firm is willing to risk going national with a venture that turns out to be unsuccessful.

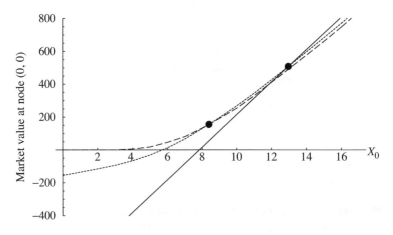

Figure 11.2. The effect of current net revenue on the market value of the option to roll out new facilities

---

5. This graph can be constructed by repeating the calculations above for a selection of different values of X_0, holding all other parameters constant at the values used in this section. For each value of X_0 we construct the equivalent of Table 11.2 and use it to evaluate the three payoffs.

It does not wait for a more favorable investment climate. It does not even delay going national in order to acquire information about its venture's prospects.

However, the firm will be more cautious for moderate levels of net revenue (between 8.39 and 12.96 in this case). While going national would still have a positive (expected) payoff, the opportunity to learn more about its venture by going local—and to avoid going national with an unsuccessful venture—is too valuable to pass up. The firm still invests immediately, but only in a local facility.

For lower levels of net revenue, the firm will not even invest in a local facility. It will wait for market conditions to improve instead. Notice that for levels of net revenue between approximately 5.71 and 7.83 the payoff from going local is positive even though the payoff from going national is negative. This reflects the fact that going local provides the firm with extremely valuable information about the venture's profitability at relatively low cost; the value of this learning option is included in the payoff from going local.

11.4 SOLVING THE OIL EXPLORATION PROBLEM

11.4.1 Setting Up the Oil Exploration Problem

A firm owns the right to develop and exploit an oil field. Development takes one period and costs I. Construction costs are paid in advance and are sunk as soon as they are incurred—that is, investment is irreversible. The rights to the project are lost if development is not completed on or before date 5. On the basis of all information available at date 0, the oil field is large with probability p_n and small with probability $1 - p_n$. (The "n" subscript indicates that this probability distribution is based on no new information.)

The firm has the option to drill a single test well at any time prior to developing the field. This requires expenditure of J, paid in advance, and takes one period to complete. Drilling a test well gives good news with probability q and bad news with probability $1 - q$. If good news is received the probability that the oil field is large rises to p_g, while if bad news is received the probability falls to p_b. The probabilities are related by $p_b < p_n < p_g$, so that good news really is good—that is, it makes a large oil field more likely—and bad news really is bad.

We suppose that a large developed oil field has a market value of $3X(i, n)$ at node (i, n), where $X(i, n)$ is the market value at node (i, n) of a small oil field that has just been developed. The risk-adjusted growth factor associated with X equals the constant K, while the return on one-period risk-free bonds equals the constant R_f.

11.4.2 Analyzing the Oil Exploration Problem

We start by building the decision tree, and begin by considering the manager's problem at date 0. He must gather information by drilling a test well, develop the field, or wait. These are represented by the actions G (for "gather"), D (for "develop"), and W (for "wait") in the decision tree drawn in Figure 11.3. If he drills a test well there is a cash outflow of J at date 0 and then either the test well

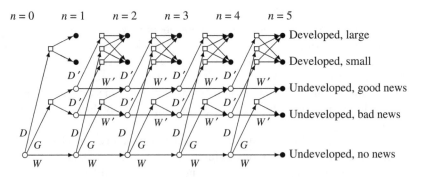

Figure 11.3. Decision tree for the option to develop an oil field

reveals good news (with probability q) or it reveals bad news (with probability $1 - q$). If he develops the field instead there is a cash outflow of I at date 0, at date 1 the field will be revealed to be either large (with probability p_n) or small (with probability $1 - p_n$), and then the decision tree ends. If he chooses to wait, there is no cash flow at date 0 and at date 1 the field will be undeveloped and without a test well.

Thus, at date 1 we need to consider three different project-states: the initial state; with a test well that has revealed good news; and with one that has revealed bad news. In the first case the situation facing the firm's manager is exactly the same as at date 0. In the other two cases, he must either develop the field (labeled D' in the decision tree) or wait (labeled W'). If he chooses to develop the field, the firm pays I at date 1, at date 2 the field will be revealed to be either large (with probability p_g if the test well's news was good and with probability p_b if it was bad) or small (with probability $1 - p_g$ or $1 - p_b$, depending on whether the test well delivered good or bad news), and then the decision tree ends

The situation at dates 2–4 is identical to that at date 1: we need to consider the same three different project-states. Finally, at date 5 the development rights are lost and the decision tree ends. This completes the construction of the decision tree shown in Figure 11.3.

The decision tree shows that there are five possible project-states.

- The oil field is undeveloped and there is no new information available. This is the project's initial state. The market value of the project at node (i, n) will equal $V_{un}(i, n)$ when it is in this state.
- The oil field is undeveloped and the test well has revealed good news; the market value is denoted by $V_{ug}(i, n)$.
- The oil field is undeveloped and the test well has revealed bad news; the market value is denoted by $V_{ub}(i, n)$.
- The oil field has just been developed and has been revealed to be large. If this occurs at node (i, n) its market value equals $V_{dl}(i, n) = 3X(i, n)$.
- The oil field has just been developed and has been revealed to be small. If this occurs at node (i, n) its market value equals $V_{ds}(i, n) = X(i, n)$.

Since the market value of the project in the last two states can be written as explicit functions of the state variable, we only need to build binomial trees for the market value of the project in the first three states.

Development of the oil field takes one period and the rights are lost if development is not completed on or before date 5. It follows that

$$V_{un}(i, 5) = V_{ug}(i, 5) = V_{ub}(i, 5) = 0 \qquad (11.9)$$

for all $i = 0, 1, \ldots, 5$, which comprise the terminal conditions that we use to fill in the final column of each market-value tree. Now we turn to the recursive equations used to complete the three trees.

We begin by considering the problem facing the firm's manager at node (i, n) if the oil field is undeveloped and the test well has revealed good news. He must choose one of two possible actions: develop the oil field immediately or wait. If he develops the oil field immediately then the firm pays I now and at date $n + 1$ receives a developed oil field that will be worth either $3X(i, n + 1)$ or $X(i, n + 1)$ if the next move is up and either $3X(i + 1, n + 1)$ or $X(i + 1, n + 1)$ if it is down. The first of each pair of values will occur if the field turns out to be large, which occurs with probability p_g; the second of each pair, corresponding to the case that the field turns out to be small, occurs with probability $1 - p_g$. Because the risk associated with the size of the oil field is diversifiable, all we need to know in order to calculate the market value is the expected payoff in each state. That is, this cash flow has the same market value at node (i, n) as one that pays

$$p_g 3X(i, n + 1) + (1 - p_g)X(i, n + 1) = (1 + 2p_g)X(i, n + 1)$$

if an up move occurs and

$$p_g 3X(i + 1, n + 1) + (1 - p_g)X(i + 1, n + 1) = (1 + 2p_g)X(i + 1, n + 1)$$

if a down move occurs. It follows that the payoff from developing the oil field equals

$$-I + (1 + 2p_g)\frac{KX(i, n)}{R_f}.$$

In contrast, if the manager waits then there is no cash flow at date n and the undeveloped oil field will be worth $V_{ug}(i, n + 1)$ at date $n + 1$ if the next move is up and $V_{ug}(i + 1, n + 1)$ if it is down, so that the payoff from waiting equals

$$\frac{\pi_u(i, n)V_{ug}(i, n + 1) + \pi_d(i, n)V_{ug}(i + 1, n + 1)}{R_f}.$$

The manager will choose the action that maximizes the market value of the firm, so that the development rights are worth

$$V_{ug}(i, n) = \max \left\{ -I + (1 + 2p_g)\frac{KX(i, n)}{R_f}, \right.$$

$$\left. \frac{\pi_u(i, n)V_{ug}(i, n + 1) + \pi_d(i, n)V_{ug}(i + 1, n + 1)}{R_f} \right\}. \qquad (11.10)$$

The situation facing the manager at node (i, n) if the oil field is undeveloped and the test well has revealed bad news is almost identical to the case when the test well revealed good news. All that changes is that the oil field will turn out to be large with the lower probability of p_b and that the value of the project rights if the manager waits will equal $V_{ub}(i, n + 1)$ at date $n + 1$ if the next move is up and $V_{ub}(i + 1, n + 1)$ if it is down. Therefore, the recursive equation in this case is just

$$V_{ub}(i, n) = \max \left\{ -I + (1 + 2p_b) \frac{KX(i, n)}{R_f}, \right.$$

$$\left. \frac{\pi_u(i, n)V_{ub}(i, n + 1) + \pi_d(i, n)V_{ub}(i + 1, n + 1)}{R_f} \right\}. \quad (11.11)$$

Finally, we turn to the recursive equation when the oil field is in its initial state—that is, the oil field is undeveloped and the test well has not been drilled. This situation is slightly more complicated because now the manager must choose one of three possible actions: drill a test well immediately, develop the oil field immediately, or wait. If the firm drills a test well then there is an immediate cash outflow of J. One period later the development rights will be worth either $V_{ug}(i, n + 1)$ or $V_{ub}(i, n + 1)$ if the next move is up and either $V_{ug}(i + 1, n + 1)$ or $V_{ub}(i + 1, n + 1)$ if it is down. The first of each pair of values will occur if the test well delivers good news, which occurs with probability q; the second of each pair, corresponding to the case that it delivers bad news, occurs with probability $1 - q$. Since the risk of receiving good or bad news is diversifiable, the payoff from drilling a test well equals

$$-J + \frac{1}{R_f} \left(\pi_u(i, n) \left(qV_{ug}(i, n + 1) + (1 - q)V_{ub}(i, n + 1) \right) \right.$$

$$\left. + \pi_d(i, n) \left(qV_{ug}(i + 1, n + 1) + (1 - q)V_{ub}(i + 1, n + 1) \right) \right).$$

If the firm develops the oil field immediately, then it pays I now and at date $n + 1$ receives a developed oil field that will be worth either $3X(i, n + 1)$ or $X(i, n + 1)$ if the next move is up and either $3X(i + 1, n + 1)$ or $X(i + 1, n + 1)$ if it is down. The first of each pair of values will occur if the field turns out to be large, which occurs with probability p_n; the second of each pair, corresponding to the case that the field turns out to be small, occurs with probability $1 - p_n$. Since the expected market value in the up state is

$$p_n 3X(i, n + 1) + (1 - p_n)X(i, n + 1) = (1 + 2p_n)X(i, n + 1)$$

and the expected market value in the down state is

$$p_n 3X(i + 1, n + 1) + (1 - p_n)X(i + 1, n + 1) = (1 + 2p_n)X(i + 1, n + 1),$$

the payoff from developing the oil field equals

$$-I + (1 + 2p_n) \frac{KX(i, n)}{R_f}.$$

If the manager waits, then there is no cash flow at date n and the undeveloped oil field will be worth $V_{un}(i, n + 1)$ at date $n + 1$ if the next move is up and $V_{un}(i + 1, n + 1)$ if it is down, so that the payoff from waiting equals

$$\frac{\pi_u(i, n)V_{un}(i, n + 1) + \pi_d(i, n)V_{un}(i + 1, n + 1)}{R_f}.$$

Since the manager chooses the action that maximizes the market value of the firm, the development rights are worth

$$V_{un}(i,n) = \max \left\{ -J + \frac{1}{R_f} \Big(\pi_u(i,n)\big(qV_{ug}(i,n+1)+(1-q)V_{ub}(i,n+1)\big) \right.$$
$$+\pi_d(i,n)\big(qV_{ug}(i+1,n+1)+(1-q)V_{ub}(i+1,n+1)\big)\Big),$$
$$-I+(1+2p_n)\frac{KX(i,n)}{R_f},$$
$$\left. \frac{\pi_u(i,n)V_{un}(i,n+1)+\pi_d(i,n)V_{un}(i+1,n+1)}{R_f} \right\}. \qquad (11.12)$$

The various binomial trees are constructed in much the same way as those in Section 11.3. We start with the tree for the state variable, and then build trees for the market value of the development rights if the oil field is undeveloped and the test well has revealed good news (using equation (11.10)) or bad news (using equation (11.11)). We then use the recursive equation (11.12) to build the tree for the market value of the project rights in their initial state. In each case, we begin by filling in the final column of the tree using the terminal condition (11.9). The procedure is demonstrated, using a numerical example, in the following section.

11.4.3 A Numerical Example

In this section we suppose that the current market value of a small developed oil field is $X_0 = 35$ and that each period this market value is equally likely to grow by a factor of $U = 1.1000$ or $D = 1/U = 0.9091$. The resulting binomial tree for the market value of a small developed oil field is shown in the top panel of Table 11.3. The risk-adjusted growth factor is $K = 0.9900$, so that equation (3.8) implies that the risk-neutral probabilities of up and down moves are $\pi_u = 0.4238$ and $\pi_d = 0.5762$, respectively, throughout the tree. The one-period risk-free interest rate equals 4%, so that $R_f = 1.04$.

Turning to the parameters that are unique to the particular oil field under consideration, we suppose that it costs $J = 2$ to drill a test well and $I = 50$ to develop the oil field. We use the learning process analyzed in the examples from Section 11.2. That is, good and bad news are equally likely; if good news is received then the likelihood of a large oil field rises from 25% to 40%, while if bad news is received then the probability falls to 10%. That is, we set

$$p_n = 0.25, \quad p_g = 0.40, \quad p_b = 0.10, \quad q = 0.50.$$

Table 11.3. Analysis of the Option to Develop an Oil Field

$X(i,n)$	0	1	2	3	4	5
0	35.00	38.50	42.35	46.59	51.24	56.37
1		31.82	35.00	38.50	42.35	46.59
2			28.93	31.82	35.00	38.50
3				26.30	28.93	31.82
4					23.91	26.30
5						21.73

$V_{ug}(i,n)$	0	1	2	3	4	5
0	9.97	15.97	22.57	29.82	37.80	0.00
1		5.08	9.97	15.97	22.57	0.00
2			1.84	4.52	9.97	0.00
3				0.00	0.00	0.00
4					0.00	0.00
5						0.00

$V_{ub}(i,n)$	0	1	2	3	4	5
0	0.24	0.58	1.42	3.48	8.54	0.00
1		0.00	0.00	0.00	0.00	0.00
2			0.00	0.00	0.00	0.00
3				0.00	0.00	0.00
4					0.00	0.00
5						0.00

$V_{un}(i,n)$	0	1	2	3	4	5
0	2.87	5.66	10.47	16.52	23.17	0.00
1		1.03	2.51	5.36	10.47	0.00
2			0.01	0.03	0.00	0.00
3				0.00	0.00	0.00
4					0.00	0.00
5						0.00

The bottom three panels of Table 11.3 show the market value of the development rights. The second panel, which reports the market value of the development rights if the test well has given good news, is constructed using equation (11.9) to fill in the final column and equation (11.10) to fill in the remaining ones. The third panel shows the market value of the development rights if the test well delivered bad news, and is constructed using the terminal condition (11.9) and the recursive equation (11.11). The bottom panel shows the market value of the development rights before a test well is drilled. Its entries are calculated using (11.9) and (11.12).

The darkly-shaded cells in all three of these panels indicate the nodes where it is optimal to develop the oil field, while the lightly-shaded cells in the bottom panel show where it is optimal to drill a test well. As the bottom panel shows, it is not optimal to do anything until date 2, and then the optimal action to take depends on market conditions. If the market value of developed oil fields is especially high (that is, at node $(0, 2)$) then it is optimal to develop the field without drilling a test well. In contrast, if the market value of a developed field is still equal to its initial value (that is, node $(1, 2)$) then it is optimal to drill a test well. Finally, if the market value of a developed field has fallen significantly then it is optimal to wait one more period and drill a test well at date 3 if the next move is up and let the development rights lapse if it is down.

Inspection of the second panel shows that if a test well is drilled at node $(1, 2)$ and the news is good then the field will be developed at date 3 with certainty—to see why, note that it is optimal to develop the field at both nodes $(1, 3)$ and $(2, 3)$. However, inspection of the third panel shows that if the news is bad the field will not be developed at all.

As this example shows, the outcome of the optimal development program depends on both future market conditions and information revealed about the characteristics of the oil field as a result of future exploration.

11.5 SOLVING PROBLEMS INVOLVING LEARNING OPTIONS

The two examples considered in Sections 11.3 and 11.4 are both particular instances of problems involving learning options. In this section we formulate a procedure for dealing with a reasonably general learning option problem of the type described at the beginning of this chapter. However, there are too many variations possible for us to easily describe an entirely general algorithm here. Therefore, we focus on a single round of information gathering. Provided we understand the solution to this problem, we should not have too much difficulty in solving problems involving more than one round of information gathering.

In the problem that we consider, a firm has the option to take a single action at a time of its choosing, but the payoff from doing so depends on an uncertain characteristic of a project. If it wishes, the firm can gather information about this characteristic once before it takes the action. The various possible categories of project characteristic are labeled $j = 1, 2, \ldots, J$. On the basis of all the information that is initially available (that is, before any additional information is gathered), the project characteristic is of type j with probability p_j. Information gathering has possible outcomes labeled $k = 1, 2, \ldots, K$, with outcome k occurring with probability q_k. If outcome k occurs then the probability that the project characteristic is of type j is revised to equal $p_{j,k}$. The risk associated with information gathering is fully diversifiable.

The market value of the project at node (i, n) is $V(i, n)$ if the firm has gathered no additional information and $V_k(i, n)$ if it has gathered information with outcome k. Before it gathers information, the project's net cash flow at node (i, n) equals $Y(i, n)$ if it waits and $G(i, n)$ if it gathers information. Its payoff if it acts and the project turns out to be of type j is $A_j(i, n)$. If the firm has already gathered information with outcome k then the project's net cash flow at node (i, n) equals $Y_k(i, n)$ while it waits; its payoff if it acts and the project turns out to be of type j is $A_{j,k}(i, n)$.

After building the decision tree and a binomial tree for the state variable, the next step is to build a tree for the market value of the project after information has been gathered, for each possible outcome of the learning process. We start with the terminal condition that is appropriate for the specific problem being analyzed, and then fill in the remainder of the tree using backward induction. Consider the case where the information gathering had outcome k. The manager must do one of two things at node (i, n): act or wait. If the manager acts, then the project generates a cash flow of $A_{j,k}(i, n)$ with probability $p_{j,k}$ for $j = 1, 2, \ldots, J$, so that the expected payoff equals

$$\sum_{j=1}^{J} p_{j,k} A_{j,k}(i, n).$$

If the manager waits, then the project generates a cash flow of $Y_k(i, n)$ and, after one period, it will be worth either $V_k(i, n + 1)$ or $V_k(i + 1, n + 1)$. This implies a payoff of

$$Y_k(i, n) + \frac{\pi_u(i, n) V_k(i, n + 1) + \pi_d(i, n) V_k(i + 1, n + 1)}{R_f}.$$

The manager will choose the action that maximizes the market value of the firm, so that the project is worth

$$V_k(i, n) = \max \left\{ \sum_{j=1}^{J} p_{j,k} A_{j,k}(i, n), \right.$$
$$\left. Y_k(i, n) + \frac{\pi_u(i, n) V_k(i, n + 1) + \pi_d(i, n) V_k(i + 1, n + 1)}{R_f} \right\}.$$
$$(11.13)$$

By the time we complete the backward induction procedure, we will have filled in the binomial tree for the market value of the firm when information gathering had outcome k. We do this for all possible values of k.

The final step is to build the market-value tree for the project prior to information gathering taking place. We start with the terminal condition that is appropriate for the specific problem being analyzed, and then fill in the remainder of the tree using backward induction. At an arbitrary node (i, n) the manager must act, gather information, or wait. If the manager acts, then the project has a payoff of $A_j(i, n)$ with probability p_j for $j = 1, 2, \ldots, J$, so that the expected payoff equals

$$\sum_{j=1}^{J} p_j A_j(i, n).$$

In contrast, if the manager gathers information, then the project generates a cash flow of $G(i, n)$ immediately. Since the outcome of gathering information will equal k with probability q_k, in which case the firm will be worth either $V_k(i, n + 1)$ or $V_k(i + 1, n + 1)$ after one period, the payoff from gathering information equals

$$G(i,n) + \frac{1}{R_f}\left(\pi_u(i,n)\left(\sum_{k=1}^{K} q_k V_k(i,n+1)\right) + \pi_d(i,n)\left(\sum_{k=1}^{K} q_k V_k(i+1,n+1)\right)\right).$$

Finally, if the manager waits, then the project generates a cash flow of $Y(i, n)$ and, after one period, it will be worth either $V(i, n + 1)$ or $V(i + 1, n + 1)$. The corresponding payoff equals

$$Y(i, n) + \frac{\pi_u(i, n)V(i, n + 1) + \pi_d(i, n)V(i + 1, n + 1)}{R_f}.$$

Since the manager will choose the action that maximizes the market value of the firm, we have

$$V(i, n) = \max\left\{\sum_{j=1}^{J} p_j A_j(i, n), G(i, n) + \frac{1}{R_f}\left(\pi_u(i, n)\left(\sum_{k=1}^{K} q_k V_k(i, n + 1)\right)\right.\right.$$

$$\left.\left. + \pi_d(i, n)\left(\sum_{k=1}^{K} q_k V_k(i + 1, n + 1)\right)\right), Y(i, n)\right.$$

$$\left. + \frac{\pi_u(i, n)V(i, n + 1) + \pi_d(i, n)V(i + 1, n + 1)}{R_f}\right\}. \qquad (11.14)$$

The backward induction procedure allows us to fill in the binomial tree for the market value of the project in its initial state and calculate its current market value, $V(0, 0)$.

The solution process can be summarized as follows:

1. Build the decision tree.
2. Build a tree for the state variable.
3. Build a tree for the market value of the project when information gathering has occurred with outcome k, for each possible value of k.
   (a) Start with the terminal condition.
   (b) Fill in the remainder of the tree, working from right to left, using the recursive formula in equation (11.13).
4. Build a tree for the market value of the project before any information has been gathered.
   (a) Start with the terminal condition.
   (b) Fill in the remainder of the tree, working from right to left, using the recursive formula in equation (11.14).

Table 11.4 summarizes how the two situations considered in this chapter fit into this general scheme.

Table 11.4. Fitting the Examples into the General Approach

	Rolling Out a New Venture	Developing an Oil Field
State variable	Net revenue of an unsuccessful facility	Market value of a small developed oil field
Project characteristics	1 = unsuccessful 2 = successful	1 = large 2 = small
Initial probability distribution	$p_1 = 1 - q$ $p_2 = q$	$p_1 = p_n$ $p_2 = 1 - p_n$
Results of gathering information	1 = unsuccessful 2 = successful	1 = good news 2 = bad news
Probability of results occurring	$q_1 = 1 - q$ $q_2 = q$	$q_1 = q$ $q_2 = 1 - q$
Revised probability distribution	$p_{1,1} = 1$ $p_{1,2} = 0$ $p_{2,1} = 0$ $p_{2,2} = 1$	$p_{1,1} = p_g$ $p_{1,2} = p_b$ $p_{2,1} = 1 - p_g$ $p_{2,2} = 1 - p_b$
Pre-learning cash flow if waiting	$Y(i, n) = 0$	$Y(i, n) = 0$
Pre-learning cash flow if gathering information	$G(i, n) = -I$	$G(i, n) = -J$
Pre-learning payoff from acting	$A_j(i, n) = -5I + \frac{5jKX(i,n)}{R_f - K}$	$A_j(i, n) = -I + \frac{(5-2j)KX(i,n)}{R_f}$
Post-learning cash flow if waiting	$Y_k(i, n) = kX(i, n)$	$Y_k(i, n) = 0$
Post-learning payoff from acting	$A_{j,k}(i, n) = kX(i, n) - 4I + \frac{5jKX(i,n)}{R_f - K}$	$A_{j,k}(i, n) = -I + \frac{(5-2j)KX(i,n)}{R_f}$

11.6 PROBLEMS

11.1. **(Practice)** Reevaluate the numerical example in Section 11.3.3 for the following parameter values: $X_0 = 12$, $U = 1.24$, $D = 1/U$, $K = 0.95$, $R_f = 1.04$, $I = 150$, $q = 0.4$. Suppose that the right to build each facility expires if construction is not completed on or before date 8, but all other aspects of the situation are unchanged. How much value can the firm add by investing locally first, rather than going national immediately?

11.2. **(Demonstration)** Suppose that going local in Section 11.3 involves building ψ facilities, while subsequently going national involves building the remaining $5 - \psi$ facilities. ψ does not need to be an integer. Reevaluate the numerical example in Section 11.3.3 for the following values of ψ: 0.0, 0.5, 1.0, ... , 4.5, 5.0. Keep all other aspects of the model unchanged. Calculate the market value of the development rights at date 0 for each value of ψ, as well as the optimal development decision at that date. Discuss the results.

11.3. **(Practice)** Suppose that constructing facilities in Section 11.3 takes two periods rather than one, that construction cannot be interrupted, and that construction costs are paid in advance. The firm cannot expand nationwide while it is in the middle of "going local". Information about the success of the venture is not revealed until construction of the first facility is complete. The right to build each facility expires if construction is not completed on or before date 8, but all other aspects of the situation are unchanged.

    (a) Draw the decision tree for the problem facing the firm's manager.

    (b) Derive the recursive equations needed to calculate the market value of the project rights.

    (c) Reevaluate the numerical example in Section 11.3.3 for the following parameter values: $X_0 = 6$, $U = 1.12$, $D = 1/U$, $K = 0.97$, $R_f = 1.02$, $I = 160$, $q = 0.4$.

    (d) Draw the decision tree and derive the recursive equations for the case when construction can be interrupted. Assume that investment involves two stages, each taking one period and each requiring expenditure of $I/2$ when that stage begins.

11.4. **(Practice)** Suppose that 30% of oil fields in a region are large, with the other 70% being small. Large fields generate good news 90% of the time, while small fields generate good news 60% of the time.

    (a) Calculate the probability that we receive good news. Use this to calculate the probability of a field being large, conditional on good news being received. Also calculate the probability of a field being large, conditional on bad news being received.

    (b) Using these probabilities, reevaluate the numerical example in Section 11.4.3 for the following parameter values: $X_0 = 50$, $U = 1.22$, $D = 1/U$, $K = 0.95$, $R_f = 1.05$, $I = 75$, $J = 1$. Suppose that the rights to the project are lost if development is not completed on or before date 10, but all other aspects of the situation are unchanged.

11.5. **(Demonstration)** Reevaluate the numerical example in Section 11.4.3 for the following values of J: 0.0, 0.5, 1.0, ... , 3.5, 4.0. Keep all other aspects of the model unchanged. Calculate the market value of the development rights at date 0 for each value of J, as well as the optimal development decision at that date. Discuss the results.

11.6. **(Practice)** Suppose that 20% of oil fields in a region are large, 30% are medium, and the other 50% are small. Large fields generate good news 90% of the time, medium ones generate good news 70% of the time, and small ones generate good news 40% of the time. Calculate the probability that a test well will produce good news. Use this to calculate the probability distribution of field size conditional on good news being received. Also calculate the probability distribution of field size conditional on bad news being received.

11.7. **(Application: R&D with an unknown probability of success)** Here we modify the R&D problems in Sections 7.4 and 8.4 by introducing uncertainty about the probability of success. With each unsuccessful attempt, the owner of the development rights revises her beliefs regarding the probability of success. She must decide how many unsuccessful attempts to allow before abandoning the program.

Suppose that there are two types of R&D projects: difficult and easy. Each attempt to develop a difficult project fails with probability $p_D = 1.0$, while each attempt to develop an easy project fails with probability $p_E = 0.4$. Projects are equally likely to be difficult or easy, so that the unconditional probability of the project being difficult is $a_D = 0.5$.

(a) Use Bayes' theorem to explain why the probability that the project is difficult, conditional on the first n development attempts all failing, is

$$\Pr[\text{difficult}|n \text{ failures}] = \frac{(p_D)^n a_D}{(p_D)^n a_D + (p_E)^n (1 - a_D)}.$$

Hint: For difficult projects, the first n attempts fail with probability $(p_D)^n$.

(b) Use this equation to calculate the sequence of conditional probabilities that the project is difficult. Calculate the corresponding sequence of probabilities that the next attempt will fail, and the sequence of success probabilities. Using these results, discuss how this example is the opposite of "learning by doing", at least as we used the term in Problem 8.11.

(c) Reevaluate the numerical example in Problem 8.11 using the sequence of probabilities in (b). Use the following parameter values: $X_0 = 32$, $U = 1.3$, $D = 1/U$, $K = 0.96$, $R_f = 1.05$, $I = 5$. The development rights are lost if development is not completed on or before date 6. Calculate the market value of the development rights and an optimal development policy.

(d) How long should development last if all moves in the state variable are up? How does the answer change if all moves in the state variable are down instead? Discuss these results.

(e) Discuss the benefit of making the first one or two development attempts when the probability of success is uncertain. Use the language of real options.

Part III

CALIBRATING THE MODEL

12

Calibration Using Spot and Futures Price Data

In many situations it is natural to adopt the spot price of a traded asset (often a commodity) as the state variable. For example, in the resource extraction problem of Section 8.3 the state variable was the price of copper, while in the machinery-replacement problem of Section 10.3 it was the price of fuel. Ready availability of spot price data also makes the spot price an attractive candidate for the state variable since such data can be used to estimate the parameters needed to build the tree (the size of up and down moves and the probabilities that they occur). Moreover, because the observed price of the traded asset reflects the market's attitude towards the risk of holding that asset in a portfolio, price data can also be used to estimate the risk-neutral probabilities.

In this chapter we make extensive use of spot, forward, and futures prices, so we begin by explaining exactly what these different prices represent. The spot price of a commodity is the price at which physical transactions occur. In contrast, forward and futures prices relate to transactions that will occur at a specified future date. Forward contracts are agreements between two parties to exchange an item for a specified price (the forward price) at a specified date (the delivery date). Futures contracts are similar, but they are traded on organized exchanges and are marked to market at the end of each trading day, when funds are transferred between the parties according to the amount by which the futures price has changed from the previous day.[1]

---

1. Throughout this book we assume that the risk-free interest rate is deterministic (meaning that, although the interest rate can change over time, it does so in an entirely predictable way—there

Table 12.1. Copper Futures Prices on 31 January 2004

Time until delivery	Cash	3 months	15 months	27 months
Price	1.129	1.120	1.067	1.026

Note: These are the cash and futures prices of Grade A copper (in dollars per pound) on the London Metal Exchange.

Observed spot prices can potentially be affected by liquidity problems, and may be contaminated by discounts and premia reflecting long-term relationships between the parties to a transaction. In contrast, because futures contracts are traded on exchanges, futures price data are readily available and liquidity problems will be less severe. Various proxies for the spot price have been suggested to mitigate some of these problems, such as using the shortest-term futures price available or extrapolating the two shortest-term futures prices back to calculate a hypothetical spot price.

We start our analysis in Section 12.1 by showing how to build a tree for the spot price using historical spot price data. Section 12.2 presents various approaches to estimating the risk-neutral probabilities that we need for our valuation formula, which vary according to their data requirements: we can use historical spot price data and a risk-adjustment model such as the CAPM; we can use historical data on spot and forward prices and estimate the relationship between the two prices; finally, we can use the term structure of futures prices at the time the analysis is being carried out. Section 12.3 offers some brief advice on how to choose from this menu of models and procedures.

We demonstrate the various techniques we meet by building a binomial tree for the spot price of copper.

Example 12.1. Our task is to build a binomial tree for the spot price of copper, extending from 31 January 2004 out 27 months, in which each time step represents three months. The London Metal Exchange (LME) is the main international market for copper, with its settlement prices widely used as reference prices for the valuation of copper-related activities. Contracts are traded and quoted in US dollars. We use monthly price data for the period from 31 January 1989 to 31 January 2004 from the LME. The cash price of Grade A copper, expressed in dollars per pound, will be our measure of the spot price. The solid curve in Figure 12.1 plots the spot price, while the dashed curve plots the three-month futures price. Table 12.1 reports closing futures prices on the LME on 31 January 2004. ∎

The techniques presented in this chapter are just a sample of those that can be used in practice. There are many alternatives, some of them involving sophisticated

---

is no uncertainty about future levels of the risk-free interest rate). One consequence of this assumption is that forward and futures prices are identical (Hull, 2008, Appendix to Chapter 5).

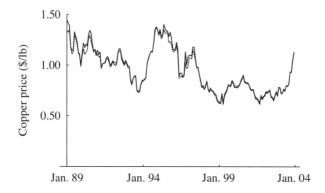

Figure 12.1. Spot and three-month futures prices of copper

Note: The cash price (solid curve) and three-month futures price (dashed curve) of Grade A copper (in dollars per pound) on the London Metal Exchange.

econometrics, and including them all would take us far beyond the intended scope of this book. The aim in this chapter is to present a selection of techniques that will allow us to deal with most situations we are likely to confront, and to get reasonable results.

12.1 CALIBRATING A TREE OF PRICES USING HISTORICAL DATA

In this section we show how to build a binomial tree for the price of an item. We present most of the construction in terms of the logarithm of the price. One motivation for this is that the volatility of a price will tend to be higher when the price is high than when it is low—and one way to achieve this is to build a model in which the logarithm of the price has constant volatility. Changes in the log price correspond to continuously compounded rates of return, so this assumption implies that rates of return have a constant standard deviation over time. The price will be more volatile when it is high than when it is low because the same rate of return is being applied to a higher base price.

We focus on two of the most popular processes for the log price: a random walk with drift and a first-order autoregressive process. They are widely applicable and capture a variety of realistic behavior. However, the realism of our models—and the accuracy of our results—will be improved if the time steps in our binomial trees are small. It is not at all realistic for the price of an item to take one of exactly two possible values one year from now, as would be the case if our binomial tree had annual steps. It is much better to have a large number of smaller steps. For example, if we break the year into 12 monthly steps then the price will take one of 13 values one year from now. If, instead, we use 52 weekly time steps then it has 53 possible values.

The time step in our model (which we denote by Δt_m) may be different from the time step in any data that we use to estimate the parameters of this model (which we denote by Δt_d). For example, we may wish to use daily data to calibrate a binomial tree with monthly time steps, or quarterly data to calibrate a tree with weekly time steps. Thus, we need to find a way of moving from one time step in the data to another one in the binomial tree. We do this via an intermediate step that "normalizes" the parameters of the assumed model for the price. That is, we take the estimates from our data and normalize them, then we take these normalized estimates and apply them to the appropriately sized tree.

12.1.1 A Price that Follows a Random Walk

A popular assumption when pricing financial derivatives is that the log price of the underlying asset follows a random walk with drift. That is, if p_j denotes the jth observation of the log price, then

$$p_{j+1} - p_j = \nu + u_{j+1}, \quad u_{j+1} \sim N(0, \phi^2), \tag{12.1}$$

where ν and ϕ are constants and u_{j+1} is a noise term.[2] In words, over each period the log price changes by an amount that is the sum of a constant (ν) and a random term that is normally distributed with mean equal to zero and standard deviation equal to another constant (ϕ). Problem 12.1 shows that the log price satisfies

$$p_j = p_0 + j\nu + u_1 + u_2 + \cdots + u_j, \tag{12.2}$$

which reveals two important properties. First, the log price is expected to grow by ν each step. Second, shocks to the log price are permanent. For example, if we increase u_1 by one unit then p_1 and p_2 (and indeed all future log prices) increase by one unit—the effect of the shock never dies out.[3]

Our approach to calibrating the price tree is to use historical price data to estimate the parameters ν and ϕ in (12.1), and then to use these parameters to build our binomial tree. However, as mentioned above, the frequency of our data often does not match the size of the time steps in the binomial tree that will be the basis of our real options analysis. We need a way to move between situations with different frequencies. For instance, as in Example 12.1, we may want to calibrate a tree with quarterly time steps using data with monthly observations. Fortunately, the theory of stochastic processes helps us out.

A stochastic process known as arithmetic Brownian motion with drift μ and volatility σ generalizes the process described by (12.1) to the situation where the log price is observed with an arbitrary frequency.[4] When viewed from date t, the change in p over the next Δt units of time is normally distributed with mean $\mu \Delta t$

---

2. In this chapter we follow the convention that P denotes the price while p denotes its natural logarithm. That is, $p = \log P$.

3. We see in Section 12.1.2 that shocks do gradually die out if the log price is mean reverting.

4. For an introduction to this and other stochastic processes, see Chapter 3 of Dixit and Pindyck (1994).

and variance $\sigma^2 \Delta t$, where μ and σ are constants. That is,

$$p_{t+\Delta t} - p_t \sim N(\mu \Delta t, \sigma^2 \Delta t).$$

The most distinctive feature of this process is that the variance of the change in the log price continues to grow as we look further and further into the future. While the expected value of the change equals μ per unit of time, there is no force keeping the log price close to this trend. Rather, the log price is free to wander far away from its expected path.

Under the process described by (12.1), changes in p are normally distributed with mean v and variance ϕ^2. Thus, the parameters v and ϕ in (12.1) are related to the drift and volatility of the arithmetic Brownian motion by the equations

$$v = \mu \Delta t \quad \text{and} \quad \phi^2 = \sigma^2 \Delta t.$$

These relationships are the key to our calibration technique, as we now demonstrate.

Step 1: Going from the Data to Normalized Estimates of the Parameters

Suppose that our data have one observation every Δt_d years and that changes in the log price have sample mean $\hat{v}$ and standard deviation $\hat{\phi}$. We can either estimate these directly, or we can regress the change in the log price on a constant as in equation (12.1). If the data-generating process for the log price is arithmetic Brownian motion with drift μ and volatility σ, then the population mean of changes in the log price is $\mu \Delta t_d$. Therefore, a sensible estimate of the drift parameter μ is the number $\hat{\mu}$ that makes the population mean equal the sample mean. That is, we choose $\hat{\mu}$ so that it satisfies

$$\hat{v} = \hat{\mu} \, \Delta t_d,$$

which implies that

$$\hat{\mu} = \frac{\hat{v}}{\Delta t_d}. \tag{12.3}$$

Likewise, the population variance of changes in the log price is $\sigma^2 \Delta t_d$. Therefore, a sensible estimate of the volatility parameter σ is the number $\hat{\sigma}$ that satisfies

$$\hat{\phi}^2 = \hat{\sigma}^2 \, \Delta t_d,$$

so that the population variance equals the sample variance. This implies that

$$\hat{\sigma} = \frac{\hat{\phi}}{\sqrt{\Delta t_d}}. \tag{12.4}$$

Our first step is therefore to estimate the mean and variance of changes in the log price from historical price data and use them, via equations (12.3) and (12.4), to estimate the normalized drift and volatility.

Step 2: Going from Normalized Estimates to the Tree for the Price

In the first step we took the estimates based on data with observations every Δt_d years and produced normalized estimates. Now we use these normalized estimates to fill out the binomial tree for the price, where each period will represent Δt_m years.

Our approach to specifying the level of the price at each node is straightforward. At node $(0, 0)$ we set the log price equal to the level it takes at the date the real options analysis is being carried out. In each subsequent period the log price either increases or decreases by $\hat\sigma\sqrt{\Delta t_m}$. This makes it quite easy to calculate the level of the log price at any node of the tree. For example, at node (i, n) there have been $n - i$ up moves and i down moves, so that the log price equals

$$\underbrace{\log P_0}_{\text{starting value}} + \underbrace{(n - i)(\hat\sigma\sqrt{\Delta t_m})}_{\text{effect of up moves}} + \underbrace{i(-\hat\sigma\sqrt{\Delta t_m})}_{\text{effect of down moves}}.$$

This simplifies to

$$x(i, n) = \log P_0 + (n - 2i)\hat\sigma\sqrt{\Delta t_m}, \tag{12.5}$$

where $x(i, n) = \log X(i, n)$. Taking exponentials of both sides of this equation shows that the level of the price at node (i, n) is

$$X(i, n) = e^{x(i,n)} = P_0 e^{(n-2i)\hat\sigma\sqrt{\Delta t_m}}. \tag{12.6}$$

This formula give us a closed-form expression for the price at any node of our binomial tree. We can use it to calculate the price at any given node, without going through the convoluted procedure of filling in the nodes from left to right by multiplying previous prices by up and down moves.

Nevertheless, it can still be useful to know the sizes of up and down moves. For example, they appear directly in several of the expressions for the risk-neutral probabilities, such as equations (3.3), (3.4), and (3.8). Since the price at node (i, n) is given by equation (12.6) and an up move takes the price to

$$X(i, n + 1) = P_0 e^{((n+1)-2i)\hat\sigma\sqrt{\Delta t_m}} = e^{\hat\sigma\sqrt{\Delta t_m}} X(i, n),$$

the size of an up move at this node must equal

$$U = \frac{X(i, n + 1)}{X(i, n)} = e^{\hat\sigma\sqrt{\Delta t_m}}. \tag{12.7}$$

Similarly, a down move takes the price to

$$X(i + 1, n + 1) = P_0 e^{((n+1)-2(i+1))\hat\sigma\sqrt{\Delta t_m}} = e^{-\hat\sigma\sqrt{\Delta t_m}} X(i, n),$$

so that the size of a down move equals

$$D = \frac{X(i + 1, n + 1)}{X(i, n)} = e^{-\hat\sigma\sqrt{\Delta t_m}}. \tag{12.8}$$

Notice that the sizes of up and down moves are constant throughout the tree.

Step 3: Calculating the Probabilities of Up and Down Moves

In order to completely describe the tree we must specify the probabilities of up and down moves at each node. Although our valuation formula uses only risk-neutral probabilities, it can still be useful to calculate the actual probabilities of up and down moves. For example, as we saw in Section 3.4.2, we need to know the actual probabilities if we wish to use the CAPM to estimate the risk-neutral probabilities.

We choose the probability of an up move at node (i, n) in such a way that the expected value of the change in the log price over the next period is equal to that implied by our normalized parameter estimates.[5] Specifically, we suppose that at node (i, n) the next move will be up with probability[6]

$$\theta_u(i, n) = \frac{1}{2} + \frac{\hat{\mu}\sqrt{\Delta t_m}}{2\hat{\sigma}}. \tag{12.9}$$

Notice that if $\hat{\mu}$ is positive (so that the log price is expected to increase over time) then up moves are more likely to occur than down moves. As we show in Appendix 12.A.1, the expected value of the change in the log price over the next period equals $\hat{\mu}\Delta t_m$. This is exactly the expected value when the log price follows arithmetic Brownian motion with drift $\hat{\mu}$.

We are also interested in the behavior of the variance of the change in the log price. As we show in Appendix 12.A.1, the variance of the change in the log price over the next period is equal to

$$\hat{\sigma}^2\Delta t_m - \hat{\mu}^2(\Delta t_m)^2.$$

Recall that the variance when the log price follows arithmetic Brownian motion with volatility $\hat{\sigma}$ equals $\hat{\sigma}^2\Delta t_m$, so that the variance in our binomial tree will not match that of the arithmetic Brownian motion precisely. However, as we demonstrate in Problem 12.4, the difference is small when Δt_m is small.[7]

To summarize, if we believe the log price follows a random walk then we can calibrate the binomial tree by working through four steps:

1. Estimate the mean and variance of changes in the log price from historical price data.
2. Estimate the normalized drift using (12.3) and the normalized volatility using (12.4).

---

5. Thus, even though the sizes of the up and down moves do not depend on the normalized drift parameter $\hat{\mu}$, we are still able to match that drift using our binomial tree.

6. Provided Δt_m is not too large, this probability will lie between 0 and 1. If $\theta_u(i, n)$ lies outside this interval then we should reduce the time step until the probability is positive and less than one. See Problem 12.3 for details.

7. The variance of the arithmetic Brownian motion is proportional to Δt_m, while the difference between the two variances is proportional to $(\Delta t_m)^2$. As $\Delta t_m \to 0$, the term involving $(\Delta t_m)^2$ goes to zero much faster than the term proportional to Δt_m. Thus, when Δt_m is small, the differences between the two variances will be insignificant.

Table 12.2. Manipulating Copper Spot Price Data

Date	j	P_j	$\log P_j$	$\Delta \log P_j$
Jan. 89	1	1.497	0.4034	n/a
Feb. 89	2	1.447	0.3697	−0.0337
Mar. 89	3	1.416	0.3476	−0.0221
Apr. 89	4	1.388	0.3276	−0.0200
$\vdots$	$\vdots$	$\vdots$	$\vdots$	$\vdots$
Oct. 03	178	0.933	−0.0693	0.1368
Nov. 03	179	0.941	−0.0613	0.0080
Dec. 03	180	1.053	0.0514	0.1128
Jan. 04	181	1.129	0.1213	0.0699
			Mean	−0.001567
			Std dev.	0.06390

3. Fill in the binomial tree for the price using (12.6).
4. Estimate the probability of an up move at each node using (12.9).

We can apply this technique to the data set introduced in Example 12.1.

Example 12.2. Table 12.2 shows the beginning and end of our data set and
the steps that are required to estimate a random walk process for the copper
price. The raw prices are shown in the third column of the table, and the
corresponding log prices are shown in the fourth column. The final column
shows the changes in the log prices during each month in our sample period.
As the table reports, the average "log difference" is $\hat{v} = -0.001567$, while
the standard deviation is $\hat{\phi} = 0.06390$. Since the data are monthly, we have
$\Delta t_d = 1/12$, implying that the normalized estimates of the drift and volatility
parameters equal

$$\hat{\mu} = \frac{\hat{v}}{\Delta t_d} = \frac{-0.001567}{1/12} = -0.01880$$

and

$$\hat{\sigma} = \frac{\hat{\phi}}{\sqrt{\Delta t_d}} = \frac{0.06390}{\sqrt{1/12}} = 0.2213$$

respectively.

We now have all the information we need to build a binomial tree for
the spot price. Date 0 in the tree is to correspond to 31 January 2004, so
Table 12.2 indicates that the initial price is $X(0, 0) = 1.129$. Each step in
the tree is to represent three months. Therefore $\Delta t_m = 1/4$, so that the sizes
of up and down moves are

$$U = e^{\hat{\sigma}\sqrt{\Delta t_m}} = e^{0.2213\sqrt{1/4}} = 1.1170$$

Table 12.3. A Random Walk for the Copper Price

$X(i, n)$	0	1	2	3	4	5	6	7	8	9
0	1.129	1.261	1.409	1.574	1.758	1.963	2.193	2.450	2.737	3.057
1		1.011	1.129	1.261	1.409	1.574	1.758	1.963	2.193	2.450
2			0.905	1.011	1.129	1.261	1.409	1.574	1.758	1.963
3				0.810	0.905	1.011	1.129	1.261	1.409	1.574
4					0.725	0.810	0.905	1.011	1.129	1.261
5						0.649	0.725	0.810	0.905	1.011
6							0.581	0.649	0.725	0.810
7								0.520	0.581	0.649
8									0.466	0.520
9										0.417

and

$$D = e^{-\hat{\sigma}\sqrt{\Delta t_m}} = e^{-0.2213\sqrt{1/4}} = 0.8952$$

respectively. The resulting binomial tree for the spot price of copper is shown in Table 12.3. The probability of an up move equals

$$\theta_u(i, n) = \frac{1}{2} + \frac{\hat{\mu}\sqrt{\Delta t_m}}{2\hat{\sigma}} = \frac{1}{2} + \frac{-0.01880\sqrt{1/4}}{2 \times 0.2213} = 0.4788$$

at every node in the tree.   ■

12.1.2 A Price that is Mean Reverting

The random walk process that we have just considered is not the only possible process that prices can follow. Indeed, there are strong arguments that the prices of commodities should not follow a random walk. A sudden increase in a commodity spot price will typically be met with an increase in supply and consequent price reductions as the price moves back towards the commodity's long-run marginal cost of production. Similarly, a sudden fall in price will see a reduction in supply as some firms shut down unprofitable production facilities and others exit the industry altogether, triggering future price increases. The ability to draw down inventories in response to a positive price shock (and to raise them in response to a negative one) also affects the dynamics of commodity spot prices.[8] While factors such as adjustment costs, barriers to entry and exit, and other real-world complications dampen the impact of these responses to sudden price changes, they will not eliminate them. As a result, shocks to commodity spot prices are unlikely to be permanent, in contrast to shocks to a price that follows a random

---

8. Pindyck (2001) has a very useful discussion of the economics underlying commodity price behavior, including the role played by storage.

walk. Processes with such transitory shocks are said to be mean reverting. In this section we see how to calibrate a spot price tree to one popular mean-reverting process.

We suppose that the log price follows a first-order autoregressive process (usually referred to as an AR(1) process). That is, if p_j denotes the jth observation of the log price, then

$$p_{j+1} - p_j = \alpha_0 + \alpha_1 p_j + u_{j+1}, \quad u_{j+1} \sim N(0, \phi^2), \tag{12.10}$$

for some constants α_0, α_1, and ϕ, where α_1 is negative. This process exhibits mean reversion. For example, suppose that p_j is so large that $\alpha_0 + \alpha_1 p_j$ is negative (this is why it is important that $\alpha_1 < 0$). Then the expected value of $p_{j+1} - p_j$ is also negative, meaning that the log price is expected to fall in the short term. Similarly, if p_j is so small that $\alpha_0 + \alpha_1 p_j$ is positive then the log price is expected to rise. In either case, the log price is being pulled back to a long-run level where $\alpha_0 + \alpha_1 p_j$ equals zero (and where p_j equals $\alpha_0/(-\alpha_1)$). As a result, if the log price follows an AR(1) process, sudden shocks to the price do not last—the price is gradually pulled back towards its long-run level.

Problem 12.5 shows that the log price satisfies

$$p_j = (1 + \alpha_1)^j p_0 + \left(1 - (1 + \alpha_1)^j\right) \left(\frac{\alpha_0}{-\alpha_1}\right) + (1 + \alpha_1)^{j-1} u_1$$

$$+ (1 + \alpha_1)^{j-2} u_2 + \cdots + (1 + \alpha_1)^1 u_{j-1} + (1 + \alpha_1)^0 u_j. \tag{12.11}$$

Three things stand out. First, p_j is the sum of a series of noise terms and a weighted average of the initial log price p_0 and some number $\alpha_0/(-\alpha_1)$. Second, because $(1 + \alpha_1)^j$ tends to zero as j grows very large (because $1 + \alpha_1 < 1$), the weight shifts towards $\alpha_0/(-\alpha_1)$ as we look further into the future. Thus $\alpha_0/(-\alpha_1)$ is the long-run level of the log price. Third, shocks to the log price are transitory. For example, if we increase u_1 by one unit then p_1 increases by one unit, while p_2 increases by just $1 + \alpha_1 < 1$ units, p_3 increases by the even smaller amount $(1 + \alpha_1)^2$, and so on. While the higher value of u_1 affects all future prices, the effect dies out as we look further into the future.

As in the previous section, we calibrate the price tree by using historical price data to estimate the parameters α_0, α_1, and ϕ in (12.10), converting them so that they are expressed in normalized terms, and then using the normalized parameters to build our binomial tree. Once again the theory of stochastic processes helps us to move between situations with different time steps.

The so-called Ornstein–Uhlenbeck process with rate of mean reversion a, long-run level b, and volatility σ generalizes the AR(1) process to the situation where the log price is observed with arbitrary frequency. When viewed from date t, the change in the log price over the next Δt units of time is normally distributed with a mean of $(1 - e^{-a\Delta t})(b - p_t)$ and a variance of $\sigma^2(1 - e^{-2a\Delta t})/2a$, where a, b, and σ are constants. That is,

$$p_{t+\Delta t} - p_t \sim N\left((1 - e^{-a\Delta t})(b - p_t), \frac{\sigma^2}{2a}(1 - e^{-2a\Delta t})\right). \tag{12.12}$$

If $p_t > b$ then the expected change in the log price is negative, while if $p_t < b$ then the expected change is positive. That is, the log price trends back towards b, indicating that b is the long-run level. If a is large (so that $1 - e^{-a\Delta t}$ is close to one) then the expected value of $p_{t+\Delta t} - p_t$ is close to $b - p_t$, making the expected value of $p_{t+\Delta t}$ close to b. That is, large values of a indicate that the log price is strongly mean reverting.[9]

There are two other points regarding the process in (12.12) worth making. First, the variance of $p_{t+\Delta t} - p_t$ can be shown to be a decreasing function of the parameter a. (See Problem 12.7 for a demonstration.) This means that, holding σ constant, the variance of changes in the log price is relatively low when the forces of mean reversion are strong. The intuition for this result gets at the very essence of mean reversion: sudden shocks to the log price do not last, as mean reversion pulls the price back towards its long-run level; when mean reversion is strong, the price gets little opportunity to stray far from its long-run level.

Second, when Δt is very large, both $e^{-a\Delta t}$ and $e^{-2a\Delta t}$ are close to zero. Equation (12.12) then tells us that $p_{t+\Delta t} - p_t$ is normally distributed with mean $b - p_t$ and variance $\sigma^2/2a$. Equivalently, $p_{t+\Delta t}$ is normally distributed with mean b and variance $\sigma^2/2a$. That is, as we look further and further into the future, the distribution of the log price converges to a well-defined distribution. As a result, the distribution of the log price 50 years from now is almost identical to the distribution 100 years from now. This is perhaps the key difference between a mean-reverting process and a random walk: the variance of the random walk continues to grow as we look further into the future, while that of a mean-reverting process levels off.

Under the process described by (12.10), changes in p are normally distributed with mean $\alpha_0 + \alpha_1 p_j$ and variance ϕ^2. Thus, the parameters α_0, α_1, and ϕ in (12.10) are related to the Ornstein–Uhlenbeck parameters by the equations

$$\alpha_0 = (1 - e^{-a\Delta t})b, \quad \alpha_1 = -(1 - e^{-a\Delta t}), \quad \phi^2 = \frac{\sigma^2}{2a}(1 - e^{-2a\Delta t}).$$

Step 1: Going from the Data to Normalized Estimates of the Parameters

We begin the calibration procedure by fitting the AR(1) model described by (12.10) to our data, which we assume have one observation every Δt_d years. That is, our first step is to regress the change in the log price on a constant and the lagged log price. If the data-generating process for the log price is the Ornstein–Uhlenbeck process described by (12.12), then the true values of α_0, α_1, and ϕ are

$$\alpha_0 = (1 - e^{-a\Delta t_d})b, \quad \alpha_1 = -(1 - e^{-a\Delta t_d}), \quad \phi^2 = \frac{\sigma^2}{2a}(1 - e^{-2a\Delta t_d}).$$

---

9. As we show in Problem 12.6, the expected value of $p_{t+\Delta t}$ is half-way between the current value (p_t) and the long-run level (b) after $\Delta t = (\log 2)/a$ units of time. For this reason, $(\log 2)/a$ is said to equal the half-life of the log price.

If the regression gives us estimates $\hat{\alpha}_0$, $\hat{\alpha}_1$, and $\hat{\phi}$, then sensible estimates of the parameters a, b, and σ are the numbers $\hat{a}$, $\hat{b}$, and $\hat{\sigma}$ that satisfy

$$\hat{\alpha}_0 = (1 - e^{-\hat{a}\Delta t_d})\hat{b}, \quad \hat{\alpha}_1 = -(1 - e^{-\hat{a}\Delta t_d}), \quad \hat{\phi}^2 = \frac{\hat{\sigma}^2}{2\hat{a}}(1 - e^{-2\hat{a}\Delta t_d}).$$

Solving these equations for $\hat{a}$, $\hat{b}$, and $\hat{\sigma}$ shows that our normalized parameter estimates are

$$\hat{a} = \frac{-\log(1 + \hat{\alpha}_1)}{\Delta t_d}, \quad \hat{b} = \frac{-\hat{\alpha}_0}{\hat{\alpha}_1}, \quad \hat{\sigma} = \hat{\phi}\left(\frac{2\log(1 + \hat{\alpha}_1)}{\hat{\alpha}_1(2 + \hat{\alpha}_1)\Delta t_d}\right)^{1/2}. \quad (12.13)$$

Thus, once we have run the regression in equation (12.10) we substitute the parameter estimates into (12.13) to obtain the normalized parameter estimates.

Step 2: Going from Normalized Estimates to the Tree for the Price

Now we use these normalized estimates to fill out the binomial tree for the price, using exactly the same method as for the random walk.[10] (We will shortly see how mean reversion is captured by the calculation of the probabilities of up moves.) If each period in our binomial tree represents Δt_m years, then the tree for the log price starts at $x(0, 0) = \log P_0$ and each period the log price increases or decreases by $\hat{\sigma}\sqrt{\Delta t_m}$ depending on whether an up or a down move occurs. Therefore, as in equation (12.5), the log price at node (i, n) equals

$$x(i, n) = \log P_0 + (n - 2i)\hat{\sigma}\sqrt{\Delta t_m}.$$

Taking exponentials of both sides of this equation shows that the level of the price at node (i, n) is

$$X(i, n) = e^{x(i,n)} = P_0 e^{(n-2i)\hat{\sigma}\sqrt{\Delta t_m}}. \quad (12.14)$$

As in the case of a random walk, the sizes of up and down moves are

$$U = e^{\hat{\sigma}\sqrt{\Delta t_m}} \quad \text{and} \quad D = e^{-\hat{\sigma}\sqrt{\Delta t_m}}.$$

Step 3: Calculating the Probabilities of Up and Down Moves

Just as we did for the random walk, here we choose the probabilities of up and down moves in such a way that the expected value of the change in the log price over the next period is equal to the value that is implied by our normalized parameter estimates. As we show in Appendix 12.A.1, if the probability of an up move at node (i, n) equals

$$\theta_u(i, n) = \frac{1}{2} + \frac{(1 - e^{-\hat{a}\Delta t_m})(\hat{b} - x(i, n))}{2\hat{\sigma}\sqrt{\Delta t_m}} \quad (12.15)$$

---

10. Our binomial tree for the mean-reverting process is drawn from Nelson and Ramaswamy (1990), where alternative processes for the state variable are also considered.

then the expected change in the log price is

$$(1 - e^{-\hat{a}\Delta t_m})(\hat{b} - x(i, n)),$$

which is the same as the expected value for the Ornstein–Uhlenbeck process. We also show in Appendix 12.A.1 that the variance of the change in the log price is approximately equal to

$$\hat{\sigma}^2 \Delta t_m - \hat{a}^2(\hat{b} - x(i, n))^2(\Delta t_m)^2.$$

Although this is not the same as the variance for the Ornstein–Uhlenbeck process, the difference rapidly disappears as the step size Δt_m tends to zero.

The mean-reverting nature of the spot price is reflected in the formula for the probability of an up move. From equation (12.15), if the log price is currently higher than its long-run level (that is, $x(i, n) > b$) then an up move is less likely than a down move (that is, $\theta_u(i, n) < \frac{1}{2}$). As the log price grows larger, a down move becomes even more likely. Conversely, if the log price is currently lower than its long-run level then an up move is more likely than a down move; as the log price becomes smaller, an up move becomes even more likely. Thus, we see that the log price is drawn back towards its long-run level by our choice of probability structure.

However, there are complications. If $x(i, n)$ is sufficiently large then $\theta_u(i, n)$ will be negative, which is incompatible with $\theta_u(i, n)$ being a probability. Similarly, if $x(i, n)$ is sufficiently small then $\theta_u(i, n)$ will be greater than one. Again, this is incompatible with $\theta_u(i, n)$ being a probability. Our solution to this is to reset $\theta_u(i, n)$ to zero if the expression in equation (12.15) is negative and to reset it to one if the expression in equation (12.15) is greater than one. In other words, we set the probability of an up move at node (i, n) equal to[11]

$$\theta_u(i, n) = \begin{cases} 0 & \text{if } \frac{1}{2} + \frac{(1-e^{-\hat{a}\Delta t_m})(\hat{b}-\log X(i,n))}{2\hat{\sigma}\sqrt{\Delta t_m}} \le 0, \\ \frac{1}{2} + \frac{(1-e^{-\hat{a}\Delta t_m})(\hat{b}-\log X(i,n))}{2\hat{\sigma}\sqrt{\Delta t_m}} & \text{if } 0 < \frac{1}{2} + \frac{(1-e^{-\hat{a}\Delta t_m})(\hat{b}-\log X(i,n))}{2\hat{\sigma}\sqrt{\Delta t_m}} < 1, \\ 1 & \text{if } \frac{1}{2} + \frac{(1-e^{-\hat{a}\Delta t_m})(\hat{b}-\log X(i,n))}{2\hat{\sigma}\sqrt{\Delta t_m}} \ge 1. \end{cases}$$

(12.16)

Thus, there will be some nodes of the tree where the next move is certain to be down. These are nodes where $\theta_u(i, n) = 0$, which correspond to values of i and n where

$$\frac{1}{2} + \frac{(1 - e^{-\hat{a}\Delta t_m})(\hat{b} - \log X(i, n))}{2\hat{\sigma}\sqrt{\Delta t_m}} \le 0.$$

---

11. A simple way to implement this formula in practice is to set the probability of an up move equal to $\min\{1, \max\{0, \theta_u(i, n)\}\}$, where $\theta_u(i, n)$ is the expression in equation (12.15). If $\theta_u(i, n)$ is negative then $\min\{1, \max\{0, \theta_u(i, n)\}\} = \min\{1, 0\} = 0$ resets it to zero; if it is greater than one then $\min\{1, \max\{0, \theta_u(i, n)\}\} = \min\{1, \theta_u(i, n)\} = 1$ resets it to one. This avoids the use of complicated if/then statements.

It is straightforward to show that this condition is equivalent to

$$\log X(i, n) \geq \hat{b} + \frac{\hat{\sigma}\sqrt{\Delta t_m}}{1 - e^{-\hat{a}\Delta t_m}} \approx \hat{b} + \frac{\hat{\sigma}}{\hat{a}\sqrt{\Delta t_m}}.$$

That is, if the price ever becomes too large, the next move is certain to be down. Similarly, there will be some nodes of the tree where the next move has to be up. These are nodes where $\theta_u(i, n) = 1$, which correspond to values of i and n where

$$\frac{1}{2} + \frac{(1 - e^{-\hat{a}\Delta t_m})(\hat{b} - \log X(i, n))}{2\hat{\sigma}\sqrt{\Delta t_m}} \geq 1.$$

It is straightforward to show that this condition is equivalent to

$$\log X(i, n) \leq \hat{b} - \frac{\hat{\sigma}\sqrt{\Delta t_m}}{1 - e^{-\hat{a}\Delta t_m}} \approx \hat{b} - \frac{\hat{\sigma}}{\hat{a}\sqrt{\Delta t_m}}.$$

That is, if the price ever becomes too small, the next move is certain to be up.

The binomial tree corresponding to a mean-reverting price is therefore truncated at high and low values of the spot price. Figure 12.2 shows one such binomial tree. It has the usual form, but now some nodes have only one arrow leaving them, indicating that the next move is known with certainty in these cases. This leads to some nodes (represented by the empty circles) being unreachable from node $(0, 0)$. For example, since $\theta_u(0, 3) = 0$, if the first three moves are up then the fourth move must be down, making it impossible to reach node $(0, 4)$. This also makes node $(0, 5)$ inaccessible, since the only way for the first five moves to be up is if the first four moves are up, and that cannot happen. Thus, once one node in the top part of the tree cannot be reached, all nodes that can *only* be reached from that node cannot be reached.[12] The spot price tree drawn in Figure 12.2 also has $\theta_u(2, 2) = 1$. That is, if the first two moves are down then the third move must be up. In other words it is impossible to reach node $(3, 3)$ since the first three moves cannot all be down. But this also makes node $(4, 4)$ inaccessible, since the only way for the first four moves to be down is if the first three moves are down.

It might seem that this truncation of the tree would drastically complicate our calculations—no longer can we just start at the terminal nodes and work backwards through the tree, applying the risk-neutral pricing formula as we go. However, as we see in the next section, it actually is this simple. The key is to make sure that we specify probabilities at all nodes, even the unreachable ones. This additional information corresponds to the dotted arrows in Figure 12.2, which show the moves from unreachable nodes. They are not important for understanding the dynamics of the spot price—the price will never arrive at those nodes, so we do not need to know where the price would go next—but we will see that keeping them in the tree makes the backward induction procedure straightforward.

---

12. Some nodes that can be reached from an unreachable node can also be reached from other nodes and so are not themselves unreachable. Node $(1, 5)$ is one such example, since the move from node $(1, 4)$ is possible even though the move from node $(0, 4)$ is not.

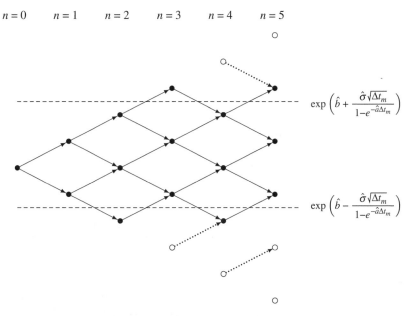

Figure 12.2. A truncated binomial tree for the state variable

To summarize, the technique for calibrating the binomial tree for a mean-reverting price can be reduced to four straightforward steps:

1. Estimate the AR(1) model in (12.10) using historical log price data.
2. Estimate the normalized Ornstein–Uhlenbeck parameters using (12.13).
3. Fill in the binomial tree for the price using (12.14).
4. Estimate the probability of an up move at each node using (12.16).

This procedure is demonstrated in the following example, which calibrates a mean-reverting process for the copper spot price.

Example 12.3. It is straightforward to apply the technique just described to the data set introduced in Example 12.1. Estimating the AR(1) model using the ordinary least-squares method results in the relationship

$$p_{j+1} - p_j = \underset{(0.004893)}{-0.004761} - \underset{(0.02055)}{0.04858 p_j} + u_{j+1}, \quad \text{Var}[u_{j+1}] = 0.003981,$$

where the numbers in brackets indicate the standard errors of the associated parameter estimates.[13] It follows that the parameters we need in order to

---

13. The standard deviation of the error term will be reported as the "standard error of the regression" or the "root mean square error" in many software packages.

evaluate the equations in (12.13) are

$$\hat{\alpha}_0 = -0.004761, \quad \hat{\alpha}_1 = -0.04858, \quad \hat{\phi} = \sqrt{0.003981} = 0.06309.$$

Since the data are monthly, we have $\Delta t_d = 1/12$. Substituting these parameters into the equations in (12.13) shows that the normalized estimates of the required parameters are

$$\hat{a} = \frac{-\log(1 + \hat{\alpha}_1)}{\Delta t_d} = \frac{-\log(1 - 0.04858)}{1/12} = 0.5977,$$

$$\hat{b} = \frac{-\hat{\alpha}_0}{\hat{\alpha}_1} = \frac{0.004761}{-0.04858} = -0.09799,$$

and

$$\hat{\sigma} = \hat{\phi} \left(\frac{2 \log(1 + \hat{\alpha}_1)}{\hat{\alpha}_1 (2 + \hat{\alpha}_1) \Delta t_d} \right)^{1/2} = 0.06309 \left(\frac{2 \log(1 - 0.04858)}{-0.04858 \times (2 - 0.04858) \times \frac{1}{12}} \right)^{1/2}$$

$$= 0.2240.$$

This gives us all the information we need to build a binomial tree for the spot price. As in Example 12.2, date 0 in the tree is to correspond to 31 January 2004, so the initial price is $X(0, 0) = 1.129$. Similarly, each step in the tree represents three months, so that $\Delta t_m = 1/4$. The sizes of up and down moves are

$$U = e^{\hat{\sigma}\sqrt{\Delta t_m}} = e^{0.2240\sqrt{1/4}} = 1.1185$$

and

$$D = e^{-\hat{\sigma}\sqrt{\Delta t_m}} = e^{-0.2240\sqrt{1/4}} = 0.8940$$

respectively. The resulting binomial tree for the spot price of copper is shown in the top panel of Table 12.4.

The next move is certain to be down whenever

$$\log X(i, n) \geq \hat{b} + \frac{\hat{\sigma}\sqrt{\Delta t_m}}{1 - e^{-\hat{a}\Delta t_m}} = -0.09799 + \frac{0.2240\sqrt{1/4}}{1 - e^{-0.5977 \times (1/4)}} = 0.7091,$$

which occurs whenever

$$X(i, n) \geq e^{0.7091} = 2.032.$$

Similarly, the next move is certain to be up whenever

$$\log X(i, n) \leq \hat{b} - \frac{\hat{\sigma}\sqrt{\Delta t_m}}{1 - e^{-\hat{a}\Delta t_m}} = -0.09799 - \frac{0.2240\sqrt{1/4}}{1 - e^{-0.5977 \times (1/4)}} = -0.9051,$$

which occurs whenever

$$X(i, n) \leq e^{-0.9051} = 0.4045.$$

Between these two bounds there will be positive probabilities attached to both up and down moves. The precise probabilities can be seen in the bottom

Table 12.4. A Mean-reverting Process for the Copper Price

$X(i, n)$	0	1	2	3	4	5	6	7	8	9
0	1.129	1.263	1.412	1.580	1.767	1.977	2.211	2.473	2.766	3.094
1		1.009	1.129	1.263	1.412	1.580	1.767	1.977	2.211	2.473
2			0.902	1.009	1.129	1.263	1.412	1.580	1.767	1.977
3				0.807	0.902	1.009	1.129	1.263	1.412	1.580
4					0.721	0.807	0.902	1.009	1.129	1.263
5						0.645	0.721	0.807	0.902	1.009
6							0.577	0.645	0.721	0.807
7								0.515	0.577	0.645
8									0.461	0.515
9										0.412

$\theta_u(i, n)$	0	1	2	3	4	5	6	7	8	9
0	0.3641	0.2947	0.2253	0.1560	0.0866	0.0172	0.0000	0.0000	0.0000	0.0000
1		0.4335	0.3641	0.2947	0.2253	0.1560	0.0866	0.0172	0.0000	0.0000
2			0.5029	0.4335	0.3641	0.2947	0.2253	0.1560	0.0866	0.0172
3				0.5723	0.5029	0.4335	0.3641	0.2947	0.2253	0.1560
4					0.6417	0.5723	0.5029	0.4335	0.3641	0.2947
5						0.7111	0.6417	0.5723	0.5029	0.4335
6							0.7805	0.7111	0.6417	0.5723
7								0.8499	0.7805	0.7111
8									0.9193	0.8499
9										0.9887

panel of Table 12.4. A down move is much more likely than an up move where the spot price is high, while up moves become much more likely in those parts where the spot price is low. Thus, our binomial tree captures the mean reversion evident in the historical data.

Although we have filled in the entire binomial tree, the nodes indicated by the shaded cells in each panel of Table 12.4 cannot possibly be reached. For example, node $(0, 7)$ cannot be reached because if the spot price reaches node $(0, 6)$ then it is certain to move to node $(1, 7)$. ∎

The spot prices appearing in the binomial trees constructed in Examples 12.2 and 12.3 are almost identical. For example, $X(0, 6)$ equals 2.193 in the first case and 2.211 in the second. The similarities can be traced back to the normalized volatilities: $\hat{\sigma} = 0.2213$ for the random walk and $\hat{\sigma} = 0.2240$ for the mean-reverting process. While the prices in the trees are similar, the probabilities of up moves are quite different. For example, $\theta_u(0, 6)$ equals 0.4788 in Example 12.2 and zero in Example 12.3. However, the fundamental valuation formula that we derived in Chapter 3 uses the risk-neutral probabilities, not the actual probabilities. Thus it might seem that the choice between a random walk and a mean-reverting process will not make much difference to the market values that we calculate.

However, in Section 12.2 we see that mean reversion can affect the risk-neutral probabilities that we calculate. Thus, our choice of process—random walk or mean reverting—is an important one.[14] We discuss this issue in Section 12.3.

12.2 CALIBRATING RISK-NEUTRAL PROBABILITIES

Once we have built a tree for the state variable, the next step is to estimate the risk-neutral probabilities of up and down moves at each node of the tree. Recall from equation (3.2) that the risk-neutral probability of an up move is

$$\pi_u = \frac{ZR_f - X_d}{X_u - X_d},$$ (12.17)

where Z is the current price of the spanning asset (that is, an asset that will be worth X_u if an up move occurs and X_d if a down move occurs). In practice the risk-neutral probabilities may not be constant across the binomial tree. This poses no difficulties in principle, and few in practice. We just need to be very careful that we calculate the risk-neutral probabilities appropriate for each node of the tree. We calculate the risk-neutral probability of an up move at node (i, n) of the tree according to

$$\pi_u(i, n) = \frac{Z(i, n)R_f - X(i + 1, n + 1)}{X(i, n + 1) - X(i + 1, n + 1)},$$

which is just the expression in (12.17) with X_d replaced by $X(i + 1, n + 1)$, X_u replaced by $X(i, n + 1)$, and Z replaced by $Z(i, n)$. The risk-neutral probability of a down move at node (i, n) is then equal to

$$\pi_d(i, n) = 1 - \pi_u(i, n)$$

and the risk-neutral pricing formula is

$$V(i, n) = Y(i, n) + \frac{\pi_u(i, n)V(i, n + 1) + \pi_d(i, n)V(i + 1, n + 1)}{R_f},$$ (12.18)

where $Y(i, n)$ is the cash flow at node (i, n) and $V(\cdot, \cdot)$ is the market value of the asset at the indicated node.

In this section we develop some techniques for estimating the risk-neutral probabilities. However, first we must see how to deal with one complication that can arise when we allow the price to be mean reverting: the actual probability of an up move can equal zero or one at some nodes of the tree. At such nodes there is actually no risk associated with movements in the state variable—and this must be reflected in the risk-neutral pricing formula. For example, if an up move occurs with certainty then the current market value of a cash flow is equal to the

---

14. There are many possible processes to choose from in addition to our random walk and mean-reverting ones. Nelson and Ramaswamy (1990) explain how to build binomial trees to represent many of these possibilities.

value it will take in the up state discounted back to the present using the risk-free interest rate. This is exactly the value resulting from application of equation (12.18) provided that the risk-neutral probability of an up move equals one. Similarly, if a down move occurs with certainty then the current market value of a cash flow is equal to the value it will take in the down state discounted back to the present using the risk-free interest rate. Again, this is exactly the value resulting from application of equation (12.18), but now the risk-neutral probability of an up move must equal zero. Thus, the formula for the risk-neutral probability of an up move must equal[15]

$$
\pi_u(i, n) = \begin{cases} 0 & \text{if } \theta_u(i, n) = 0, \\ \frac{Z(i,n)R_f - X(i+1,n+1)}{X(i,n+1) - X(i+1,n+1)} & \text{if } 0 < \theta_u(i, n) < 1, \\ 1 & \text{if } \theta_u(i, n) = 1. \end{cases} \tag{12.19}
$$

Using equation (12.19) allows us to follow our standard valuation approach. We fill in the final column of the table representing the binomial tree for a cash flow's market value and, working from right to left, use the risk-neutral pricing formula to fill in each remaining element of the table. This greatly simplifies the structure of the spreadsheets we use.[16]

12.2.1 Using the CAPM

Our first approach to estimating risk-neutral probabilities uses the same historical price data used to build the price tree and invokes the CAPM. Recall from Section 3.4 that if the CAPM holds then the market value of the spanning asset equals $Z = KX/R_f$, where

$$
K = E[\tilde{R}_x] - (E[\tilde{R}_m] - R_f)\beta_x, \tag{12.20}
$$

$\tilde{R}_x = \tilde{X}/X$, $\tilde{R}_m$ is the one-period return on the market portfolio, and

$$
\beta_x = \frac{\text{Cov}[\tilde{R}_x, \tilde{R}_m]}{\text{Var}[\tilde{R}_m]}
$$

is the usual CAPM beta applied to the proportional change in the state variable. From equation (3.10), the risk-neutral probability of an up move at node (i, n) is equal to

$$
\pi_u(i, n) = \theta_u(i, n) - \frac{(E[\tilde{R}_m] - R_f)\beta_x}{U - D}.
$$

---

15. If the time step is large, $\pi_u(i, n)$ might still be less than zero or greater than one. However, the problem will disappear if we make the step size sufficiently small.

16. It does, however, result in many unnecessary calculations. Appendix 12.A.2 shows how ignoring the inaccessible parts of the tree can greatly speed up the calculations.

Since we already have estimates of U, D, and $\theta_u(i, n)$, the only additional information we need in order to estimate $\pi_u(i, n)$ is the market risk premium $E[\tilde{R}_m] - R_f$ and the price beta β_x.

The task of estimating the market risk premium is not unique to real options analysis. Indeed, estimating the market risk premium is a controversial issue and saying much about it here would take us beyond the scope of the book. However, because the market risk premium is not project specific (or even application specific) and there are many competing estimates available, it is not difficult to find an estimate of $E[\tilde{R}_m] - R_f$. This just leaves us with the problem of estimating the price beta.

The approach that we follow is quite straightforward. We take the residuals from the regression used to estimate σ—that is, (12.1) in the case of a random walk and (12.10) in the case of the mean-reverting process—and regress them on a constant and the contemporaneous returns on a proxy for the market portfolio. That is, we estimate

$$\hat{u}_j = \gamma_0 + \gamma_1 r_{m,j} + v_j, \tag{12.21}$$

where $r_{m,j}$ is the return on the market portfolio proxy. The estimated slope coefficient ($\hat{\gamma}_1$) is our estimate of beta.

In order to implement this procedure we need a proxy for the market portfolio. It is common to use a broadly based stock index, such as the Standard and Poor's S&P 500 index of large publicly held companies trading on the New York Stock Exchange and NASDAQ, and we use the S&P 500 index in the examples below.[17] In order to be consistent with the dependent variable in (12.21), the market return should be continuously compounded. The simplest means of calculating the returns—which need to include dividends as well as capital gains—is to take differences in the logarithm of a so-called total return index, which is calculated assuming that all dividends and other distributions are immediately reinvested.

The case where the log price follows a random walk is the simplest to consider and is demonstrated in the following example.

Example 12.4. When we regress the residuals from (12.1) on a constant and the realized return on the S&P 500 index we obtain

$$\hat{u}_j = \underset{(0.004822)}{-0.003835} + \underset{(0.1102)}{0.2436 r_{m,j}} + v_j.$$

Thus our beta estimate for the copper spot price is $\beta_x = 0.2436$. In their survey of Chief Financial Officers carried out in December 2003—just before date 0 in our binomial tree—Graham and Harvey (2007) found a median market risk premium of 3.6% per annum. Given that each step in

---

17. However, the question of what constitutes a sensible choice of market portfolio when dealing with commodity (futures) prices has caused some debate. For instance, Marcus (1984) suggests that the proxy for the market portfolio should attach a weight of approximately 90% to a share price index and 10% to an index of commodity prices.

our binomial tree represents three months, we use $E[\tilde{R}_m] - R_f = 0.0360 \times (3/12) = 0.0090$ as our estimate of the market risk premium. Since the expected growth factor is

$$E[\tilde{R}_x] = \theta_u U + (1 - \theta_u)D = 0.4788 \times 1.1170 + 0.5212 \times 0.8952 = 1.0014,$$

the risk-adjusted growth factor equals

$$K = E[\tilde{R}_x] - (E[\tilde{R}_m] - R_f)\beta_x = 1.0014 - 0.0090 \times 0.2436 = 0.9992$$

at each node. We can either calculate the risk-neutral probability of an up move directly, using

$$\pi_u = \theta_u - \frac{(E[\tilde{R}_m] - R_f)\beta_x}{U - D} = 0.4788 - \frac{0.0090 \times 0.2436}{1.1170 - 0.8952} = 0.4689,$$

or indirectly, using

$$\pi_u = \frac{K - D}{U - D} = \frac{0.9992 - 0.8952}{1.1170 - 0.8952} = 0.4689.$$

We get the same value in each case. ∎

The technique is similar if the log price follows an AR(1) process. All that changes is that we must allow for the fact that the actual probability of an up move is not constant across the tree.

Example 12.5. When we regress the residuals from (12.10) on a constant and the realized return on the S&P 500 index we obtain

$$\hat{u}_j = \underset{(0.004731)}{-0.002504} + \underset{(0.1081)}{0.2689 r_{m,j}} + v_j.$$

Thus our beta estimate for the copper spot price is $\beta_x = 0.2689$. We continue to use $E[\tilde{R}_m] - R_f = 0.0090$ as our estimate of the market risk premium, so that the constant to be subtracted from the actual probability of an up move equals

$$\frac{(E[\tilde{R}_m] - R_f)\beta_x}{U - D} = \frac{0.0090 \times 0.2689}{1.1185 - 0.8940} = 0.0108.$$

This leads to the risk-neutral probabilities of up moves shown in Table 12.5. The shaded cells indicate nodes where $\theta_u(i, n) = 0$, and where we must therefore set $\pi_u(i, n)$ equal to zero. ∎

The calculations in this example involve an implicit assumption that the price beta does not depend on the length of the interval over which returns are measured. This assumption allows us to take the beta estimated from the data, which relates to a holding period of Δt_d, and apply it to a different holding period, the time step in the binomial tree with length Δt_m. However, we have already seen that when the log price follows an AR(1) process, the variance of the change in the log price depends on the length of time over which the change is measured—recall that shocks to the log price tend to be short-lived as the forces of mean reversion pull

Table 12.5. Risk-neutral Probabilities Derived from the CAPM for a Mean-reverting Copper Price

$\pi_u(i, n)$	0	1	2	3	4	5	6	7	8	9
0	0.3534	0.2840	0.2146	0.1452	0.0758	0.0064	0.0000	0.0000	0.0000	0.0000
1		0.4227	0.3534	0.2840	0.2146	0.1452	0.0758	0.0064	0.0000	0.0000
2			0.4921	0.4227	0.3534	0.2840	0.2146	0.1452	0.0758	0.0064
3				0.5615	0.4921	0.4227	0.3534	0.2840	0.2146	0.1452
4					0.6309	0.5615	0.4921	0.4227	0.3534	0.2840
5						0.7003	0.6309	0.5615	0.4921	0.4227
6							0.7697	0.7003	0.6309	0.5615
7								0.8391	0.7697	0.7003
8									0.9085	0.8391
9										0.9779

the log price back towards its long-run level. As we see in Appendix 12.A.3, if it is the correlation between changes in the log price and the market return (rather than beta) that is the same for different holding periods, then we need to make a simple adjustment to the slope coefficient in (12.21). Specifically, the beta that we should use to calculate K is

$$\beta_x = \hat{\gamma}_1 \sqrt{\frac{\Delta t_d}{\Delta t_m} \cdot \frac{1 - e^{-2\hat{a}\Delta t_m}}{1 - e^{-2\hat{a}\Delta t_d}}},$$

where $\hat{\gamma}_1$ is the estimated slope coefficient in (12.21) and $\hat{a}$ is given in (12.13).

In our example, we have $\hat{a} = 0.5977$. With $\Delta t_d = 1/12$ and $\Delta t_m = 1/4$, we get $\beta_x = 0.95\hat{\gamma}_1$, so that the adjustment is very small (especially given the magnitude of our beta estimate). However, if our binomial tree had annual time steps the multiplier would fall to 0.78, so the adjustment is not always trivial.

12.2.2 Matching the Relationship between Spot and Futures Prices

The validity of using the CAPM as described in Section 12.2.1 relies on two key assumptions. First, it requires that the CAPM correctly compensates investors for bearing risk. Unfortunately, there is a large literature that suggests that in fact the CAPM does a poor job of capturing the rewards for bearing risk.[18] Second, it requires that the historical data provide a reliable indication of future behavior. We cannot necessarily rely on this being true. Even if both of these assumptions hold, estimates of beta and the market risk premium can be very imprecise. For these reasons, it is desirable to have alternative means of estimating the

---

18. See, for example, Fama and French (2004).

risk-neutral probabilities. This section introduces an approach that, while it still uses historical data, does not rely on the CAPM.

The approach we follow is to estimate the relationship between the spot price and the one-period-ahead futures price at any point in time. This relationship can be estimated using historical spot and futures price data.[19] As we saw in Section 3.3, the risk-neutral probabilities at node (i, n) can be written as

$$\pi_u(i, n) = \frac{F(i, n) - X(i + 1, n + 1)}{X(i, n + 1) - X(i + 1, n + 1)} \quad (12.22)$$

and

$$\pi_d(i, n) = \frac{X(i, n + 1) - F(i, n)}{X(i, n + 1) - X(i + 1, n + 1)},$$

where $F(i, n)$ is the period-ahead futures price at node (i, n). If data on the period-ahead futures price are available, we might estimate the relationship between spot and futures prices to obtain a function f that maps the spot price at any given date into the period-ahead futures price at that date; that is, we look for a function f such that $F(i, n) = f(X(i, n))$ to a reasonable approximation. Thus, the estimated risk-neutral probability of an up move at node (i, n) equals

$$\pi_u(i, n) = \frac{f(X(i, n)) - X(i + 1, n + 1)}{X(i, n + 1) - X(i + 1, n + 1)}.$$

The term of the futures contract must match the time step in our binomial tree—there is no point in matching the relationship between spot and month-ahead futures prices if each step in the binomial tree represents one week. The precise futures price data that we require are often unavailable.[20] One approach is to take the futures prices we do observe and interpolate between the adjacent contracts to estimate the hypothetical futures price with the delivery date we are seeking. For instance, suppose that we observe futures prices for delivery n_1 and n_2 years from now, but each time step in the binomial tree represents Δt_m years, where $n_1 < \Delta t_m < n_2$. Figure 12.3 illustrates the approach we follow. The two observed futures prices, $\hat{F}_{n_1}$ and $\hat{F}_{n_2}$, are represented by gray dots in the graph. We estimate the futures price for delivery Δt_m years from now to be the number $\hat{F}_{\Delta t_m}$ such that the point $(\Delta t_m, \log \hat{F}_{\Delta t_m})$ lies on the line joining the points $(n_1, \log \hat{F}_{n_1})$ and $(n_2, \log \hat{F}_{n_2})$. This implies that

$$\frac{\log \hat{F}_{\Delta t_m} - \log \hat{F}_{n_1}}{\Delta t_m - n_1} = \frac{\log \hat{F}_{n_2} - \log \hat{F}_{n_1}}{n_2 - n_1},$$

19. As Problem 12.13 demonstrates, the approach described in this section is equivalent to writing the convenience yield from holding the commodity as a deterministic function of the spot price.

20. This problem does not arise in the extended example we are considering in this chapter, since we have data on three-month futures prices and wish to build a tree with quarterly time steps.

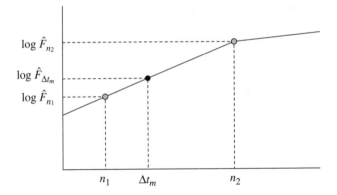

Figure 12.3. Extracting information from observed futures prices

which we can rearrange to show that

$$\log \hat{F}_{\Delta t_m} = \left(\frac{n_2 - \Delta t_m}{n_2 - n_1} \right) \log \hat{F}_{n_1} + \left(\frac{\Delta t_m - n_1}{n_2 - n_1} \right) \log \hat{F}_{n_2}. \qquad (12.23)$$

Example 12.6. Table 12.1 reports that the spot and three-month copper futures prices were $1.129 and $1.120 on 31 January 2004. The implied one-month futures price has logarithm

$$\log \hat{F}_{\Delta t_m} = \left(\frac{\frac{3}{12} - \frac{1}{12}}{\frac{3}{12} - 0} \right) \log 1.129 + \left(\frac{\frac{1}{12} - 0}{\frac{3}{12} - 0} \right) \log 1.120 = 0.1188,$$

which implies that the one-month futures price is $\hat{F}_{\Delta t_m} = \exp(0.1188) = 1.126$ dollars per pound. ∎

One other point needs to be remembered when estimating the relationship between the spot and futures prices. The difference between the futures price and the spot price reflects the level of the convenience yield between the current date and the futures contract's delivery date. This makes it important to use data with the time between observations being at least as great as the time until delivery of the futures contract. If we used higher frequency data, we would expect there to be serial correlation in the residuals in our regression. For instance, if we used monthly data and three-month futures contracts, a shock to the convenience yield in one month would affect the futures price for three consecutive observations. If, instead, we used quarterly data, that shock will affect only a single observation.

We illustrate our approach by estimating the risk-neutral probabilities for the copper spot price trees discussed in the earlier examples in this chapter.

Example 12.7. We need to estimate the relationship between the period-ahead futures price and the spot price. Since each step in our binomial tree represents three months, we use the three-month futures price. In order to

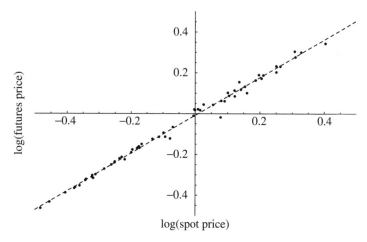

Figure 12.4. Relationship between spot and futures copper prices

match the data frequency with the length of the futures contract, we restrict our data set to quarterly observations of the spot and futures prices.

Figure 12.4 shows the scatter plot of the log futures price against the log spot price, using three-monthly observations spanning the period from 31 January 1989 to 31 January 2004, suggesting an approximately linear relationship. To estimate this relationship we regress the log futures price on a constant and the log spot price, obtaining

$$\log F = \underset{(0.002412)}{-0.008749} + \underset{(0.0103)}{0.9263} \log X + w, \qquad (12.24)$$

where w is the error term. The fact that the slope coefficient is less than one indicates that shocks to the spot price are not fully passed on to the futures price. For instance, if the spot price increases by 1% then the futures price increases by approximately 0.93%. Thus, even though the price for immediate delivery of the commodity has increased by 1%, the price for future delivery of the same commodity has increased by less than 1%. This is what we would anticipate seeing with a mean-reverting spot price, since the increase in the spot price is then expected to be offset in the future as the force of mean reversion pulls the spot price back towards its long-run level. This anticipated movement restricts the increase in the futures price.

Taking the exponential of each side of the estimated relationship in (12.24) implies that

$$F = e^{-0.008749+0.9263 \log X} = e^{-0.008749} e^{\log X^{0.9263}} = 0.9913 X^{0.9263}.$$

It follows that provided the actual probability of an up move at node (i, n) is strictly greater than 0 and strictly less than 1, the risk-neutral probability

Table 12.6. Risk-neutral Probabilities for the Copper Price that are Consistent with the Spot–futures Relationship

$\pi_u(i, n)$	0	1	2	3	4	5	6	7	8	9
0	0.3939	0.3579	0.3222	0.2868	0.2517	0.2168	0.0000	0.0000	0.0000	0.0000
1		0.4302	0.3939	0.3579	0.3222	0.2868	0.2517	0.2168	0.0000	0.0000
2			0.4668	0.4302	0.3939	0.3579	0.3222	0.2868	0.2517	0.2168
3				0.5037	0.4668	0.4302	0.3939	0.3579	0.3222	0.2868
4					0.5409	0.5037	0.4668	0.4302	0.3939	0.3579
5						0.5784	0.5409	0.5037	0.4668	0.4302
6							0.6163	0.5784	0.5409	0.5037
7								0.6544	0.6163	0.5784
8									0.6929	0.6544
9										0.7316

of an up move there equals

$$\pi_u(i, n) = \frac{0.9913X(i, n)^{0.9263} - X(i+1, n+1)}{X(i, n+1) - X(i+1, n+1)} = \frac{0.9913X(i, n)^{-0.0737} - D}{U - D}.$$

If the actual probability of an up move is equal to zero then the risk-neutral probability will be zero as well. Similarly, if the actual probability of an up move is equal to one then the risk-neutral probability equals one as well.

The risk-neutral probabilities are shown in Table 12.6, assuming that the spot price follows the (mean-reverting) process described by Table 12.4. A down move is much more likely than an up move in those parts of the table where the spot price is high, while up moves becomes much more likely in those parts where the spot price is low. The shaded cells show where the actual probability of an up move equals zero, and where the risk-neutral probability is accordingly set equal to zero. ∎

12.2.3 Matching the Current Term Structure of Futures Prices

Section 12.2.2 showed how to estimate the risk-neutral probabilities in order to match the historical relationship between the spot price and the period-ahead futures price. In this section we show how we can instead match the current futures prices for a whole range of delivery dates.[21]

The key to this technique is to allow the one-period-ahead futures price that appears in the expressions for the risk-neutral probabilities to take different values at different nodes according to

$$F(i, n) = K_n X(i, n),$$

---

21. Amin et al. (1995) introduced this technique, using a model formulated in continuous time.

for some constants $K_0, K_1, K_2, \ldots$. Thus the ratio of the futures price to the spot price depends on the date but not on the number of down moves. In Appendix 12.A.4 we show that this special structure implies that the futures price for delivery at date n equals

$$F_n(0, 0) = K_{n-1} \cdots K_1 K_0 X(0, 0)$$

at node $(0, 0)$. This gives us just enough freedom to choose the numbers $K_0, K_1, K_2, \ldots$ so that the model's implied futures prices match those that we currently observe in the futures market.

Suppose that the term structure of futures prices is currently described by the numbers $\hat{F}_0, \hat{F}_1, \hat{F}_2, \ldots$. Specifically, the spot price is currently observed to equal $\hat{F}_0$, the futures price for delivery at date 1 is currently observed to equal $\hat{F}_1$, and so on. If we set

$$X(0, 0) = \hat{F}_0$$

then our binomial tree for the spot price starts at the level currently observed in the spot market. If we set

$$K_0 = \frac{\hat{F}_1}{\hat{F}_0}$$

then the model's implied one-period-ahead futures price equals

$$F_1(0, 0) = K_0 X(0, 0) = \frac{\hat{F}_1}{\hat{F}_0} \cdot \hat{F}_0 = \hat{F}_1,$$

which is the level that we currently observe in the futures market. Similarly, if we set

$$K_1 = \frac{\hat{F}_2}{\hat{F}_1}$$

then the model's implied two-period-ahead futures price equals

$$F_2(0, 0) = K_1 K_0 X(0, 0) = \frac{\hat{F}_2}{\hat{F}_1} \cdot \frac{\hat{F}_1}{\hat{F}_0} \cdot \hat{F}_0 = \hat{F}_2,$$

which is also the level that we currently observe in the futures market.

In general, we use the formula

$$K_m = \frac{\hat{F}_{m+1}}{\hat{F}_m}.$$

The m-period-ahead futures price that is implied by our calibrated process for the spot price is then

$$F_m(0, 0) = K_{m-1} \cdots K_2 K_1 K_0 X(0, 0) = \hat{F}_m.$$

This means that we can use the observed term structure of futures prices to calculate the K_m terms (and therefore ensure that the spot price tree is consistent with observed futures prices).

This approach leads to very simple expressions for the risk-neutral probabilities. For instance, the risk-neutral probability of an up move occurring at node (i, n) equals

$$\pi_u(i, n) = \frac{F(i, n) - X(i + 1, n + 1)}{X(i, n + 1) - X(i + 1, n + 1)}$$

$$= \frac{K_n X(i, n) - DX(i, n)}{UX(i, n) - DX(i, n)}$$

$$= \frac{K_n - D}{U - D}.$$

The risk-neutral probability of a down move occurring at node (i, n) is therefore equal to

$$\pi_d(i, n) = 1 - \pi_u(i, n) = \frac{U - K_n}{U - D}.$$

(Notice that the risk-neutral probabilities depend on the date n, but not on the number of down moves i.) We can go one step further and substitute in the expressions for U and D, to get

$$\pi_u(i, n) = \frac{\frac{\hat{F}_{n+1}}{\hat{F}_n} - e^{-\hat{\sigma}\sqrt{\Delta t_m}}}{e^{\hat{\sigma}\sqrt{\Delta t_m}} - e^{-\hat{\sigma}\sqrt{\Delta t_m}}}.$$

This shows that, under this approach, the risk-neutral probabilities are calibrated using a combination of historical spot price data (to calculate $\hat{\sigma}$) and current futures price data (to calculate $\hat{F}_{n+1}/\hat{F}_n$).

We can use this approach to estimate the risk-neutral probabilities for our copper spot price tree.

Example 12.8. Because we only observe a subset of the required futures prices, we begin by estimating the remaining ones by interpolating the term structure. The calculations are summarized in the top two rows of Table 12.7. The top row gives the logarithms of the observed futures prices. The shaded cells correspond to the cash, three-month, 15-month, and 27-month prices that we observe. We linearly interpolate between these points to fill in the remainder of the row, using equation (12.23). For example, we can use the three-month and 15-month log futures prices to estimate the six-month log futures price, obtaining

$$\log \hat{F}_2 = \left(\frac{n_2 - \Delta t_m}{n_2 - n_1}\right) \log \hat{F}_{n_1} + \left(\frac{\Delta t_m - n_1}{n_2 - n_1}\right) \log \hat{F}_{n_2}$$

$$= \left(\frac{\frac{15}{12} - \frac{6}{12}}{\frac{15}{12} - \frac{3}{12}}\right) \log 1.120 + \left(\frac{\frac{6}{12} - \frac{3}{12}}{\frac{15}{12} - \frac{3}{12}}\right) \log 1.067$$

$$= 0.1014.$$

Table 12.7. Matching the Current Term Structure of Futures Prices

n	0	1	2	3	4	5	6	7	8	9
$\log \hat{F}_n$	0.1213	0.1137	0.1014	0.0892	0.0769	0.0647	0.0551	0.0454	0.0358	0.0261
$\hat{F}_n$	1.129	1.120	1.107	1.093	1.080	1.067	1.057	1.046	1.036	1.026
K_n	0.9924	0.9878	0.9878	0.9878	0.9878	0.9904	0.9904	0.9904	0.9904	–
$\pi_u(\cdot, n)$	0.4379	0.4175	0.4175	0.4175	0.4175	0.4291	0.4291	0.4291	0.4291	–

The second row of the table gives the futures prices themselves, which we obtain by taking exponentials of the first row. For example,

$$\hat{F}_2 = e^{\log \hat{F}_2} = e^{0.1014} = 1.107.$$

Once we have constructed the term structure of futures prices, calculation of the risk-neutral probabilities is straightforward. The third row of Table 12.7 shows the risk-adjusted growth factors, which vary over time. Because K_n depends on $\hat{F}_{n+1}$, these extend out only as far as date 8, as do the risk-neutral probabilities. Fortunately, this does not cause us any problems as we never need to know the risk-neutral probabilities at terminal nodes. The bottom row of the table gives the risk-neutral probabilities of up moves, which also vary over time, using the volatility estimate from Example 12.2. ■

One potential disadvantage of this approach is that the risk-neutral probabilities do not depend on the level of the spot price. That is, the risk-neutral probability of an up move at node (i, n) depends on the date n, but not the number of down moves i. Thus, even if the actual process for the spot price is mean reverting, using this calibration approach effectively imposes the random walk model on the risk-neutral process for the spot price. However, the approach does offer one important advantage: matching the current term structure of futures prices makes it consistent with static DCF analysis, which would (or should) use these futures prices to value future cash flows. If we build the spot price tree the way that is being described here, then the market value of an optionless project should equal the static DCF value. This might make it easier to communicate the results of real options analysis to decision makers who are more comfortable with static DCF analysis.

12.3 DECIDING WHICH APPROACH TO USE

Several different approaches to calibrating the tree for a spot price have been presented in this chapter: the spot price may follow a random walk or it may be mean reverting, and we have seen three different methods for calculating risk-neutral probabilities. How should we decide which combination to use?

The economics of price determination will often lead us to choose between the random walk and mean-reverting processes. For example, we should expect commodity prices to be mean reverting due to the entry that occurs during periods of high prices and the exit that occurs during periods of low prices. Entry will lead to downward pressure on price, exit to upward pressure. Ultimately, however, the choice between a random walk and mean reversion may be an empirical issue.

The regression for the random walk with drift, (12.1), is actually a special case of the regression for the AR(1) process, (12.10). That is, if we set the coefficient α_1 in (12.10) equal to zero, we obtain (12.1). Therefore, a sensible approach to deciding which process to use is to begin by estimating the AR(1) process. If the spot price actually follows a random walk then we should find that $\hat{\alpha}_1$ is close to zero. (Due to sampling error it may even be slightly positive.) We can then estimate (12.1) and work through the three steps for building a tree when the log price follows a random walk with drift. If we find that $\hat{\alpha}_1$ is significantly negative then we proceed to build a tree for the case of a mean-reverting spot price.[22]

Once we have chosen the process for the spot price, we are left with the problem of estimating the risk-neutral probabilities. Here, unfortunately, the choice is less clear cut. Given its poor empirical performance, it is probably best to use the CAPM only as a last resort. However, in some circumstances we have no choice but to use the CAPM—such as when forward or futures prices are not available. When they are available, we have a choice: match the historical relationship between spot and futures prices, or match the current term structure of futures prices. If the spot price is mean reverting, then the first approach will usually be better because, as Example 12.7 shows, the mean reversion may also be evident in the risk-neutral probabilities. However, while it will match the historical relationship between the spot price and the one-period futures price, it is unlikely to exactly match the current term structure of all futures prices. If matching this is important for a particular problem and the first approach gives a very poor fit to the term structure, then it might be worth adopting the second approach.

12.4 PROBLEMS

12.1. (**Demonstration**) Suppose that the logarithm of a price evolves according to the random walk with drift described by (12.1).
    (a) Use (12.1) with $j = 0$ to write p_1 in terms of p_0.
    (b) Use (12.1) with $j = 1$ to write p_2 in terms of p_1.
    (c) Combine these answers to write p_2 in terms of p_0.
    (d) Repeat this procedure to write p_3, p_4, and p_5 in terms of p_0.
    (e) Discuss the results.

12.2. (**Practice**) Suppose that the logarithm of the gold price follows a random walk and that the quarterly change in the logarithm of the gold price has

---

22. If we want to formally test the null hypothesis that $\alpha_1 = 0$, we cannot use the t-distribution to calculate critical values. Instead, we must use a Dickey–Fuller test or one of several similar tests designed specifically for random walk behavior.

mean 0.005 and standard deviation 0.102. The price of gold is currently $600/oz.

   (a) Build a binomial tree for the price of gold that has 12 monthly time steps.
   (b) For each of the drift and volatility in turn, double the parameter, recalculate the tree, and discuss the effect on the behavior of the gold price.

12.3. **(Practice)** Suppose that the logarithm of a firm's output price follows arithmetic Brownian motion with estimated drift of $\hat{\mu} = 0.1$ and estimated volatility of $\hat{\sigma} = 0.08$. Use (12.9) to calculate the probability of an up move when each period represents 1, 0.5, and 0.25 years. Discuss the results.

12.4. **(Demonstration)** Suppose that the log price follows arithmetic Brownian motion with drift $\mu = 0.04$ and volatility $\sigma = 0.18$. For $\Delta t_m = 0.20, 0.19, 0.18, \ldots, 0.01$, calculate the ratio of the variance of changes in the log price in our binomial tree and the variance of changes in the log price when it follows the arithmetic Brownian motion. Discuss the results.

12.5. **(Demonstration)** Repeat Problem 12.1, but this time suppose that the logarithm of the price evolves according to the AR(1) process described by (12.10).

12.6. **(Demonstration)** Suppose that the logarithm of the price of an item follows the Ornstein–Uhlenbeck process described by (12.12). Show that, when viewed from date t, the expected value of $p_{t+\Delta t}$ is half-way between the current value (p_t) and the long-run level (b) after $\Delta t = (\log 2)/a$ units of time.

12.7. **(Demonstration)** Suppose that the logarithm of the price of an item follows the Ornstein–Uhlenbeck process described by (12.12) with $b = 0.5$ and $\sigma = 0.27$. Calculate the standard deviation of the monthly change in the logarithm of the price for $a = 0.5, 1.0, 1.5, 2.0$. Discuss the results.

12.8. **(Practice)** Suppose that the logarithm of a commodity price follows an Ornstein–Uhlenbeck process with estimated normalized parameters $\hat{a} = 3.4$, $\hat{b} = 0.3$, and $\hat{\sigma} = 0.28$. The commodity price is currently $1.65.

   (a) Build a binomial tree for the commodity price with 13 weekly time steps.
   (b) Calculate the actual probability of an up move at each node.
   (c) For each parameter $\hat{a}$, $\hat{b}$, and $\hat{\sigma}$ in turn, double the parameter, recalculate the tree, and discuss the effect on the behavior of the commodity price.

12.9. **(Practice)** Suppose that we obtain

$$p_{j+1} - p_j = \underset{(0.002105)}{-0.005422} - \underset{(0.0568)}{0.1215 p_j} + u_{j+1}, \quad \text{Var}[u_{j+1}] = 0.02756,$$

when we regress the change in the logarithm of a commodity price on a constant and the lagged log price. The data are quarterly. Build a binomial tree for the price with 6 monthly time steps, assuming that the price is currently $1.21. Calculate the actual probability of an up move at each node.

12.10. (**Practice**) Suppose that the state variable follows the process described in Problem 12.8. Calculate the levels of the state variable at which the binomial tree is truncated for the cases that each period represents one month, one week, and one day. Discuss the results.

12.11. (**Practice**) Suppose that when we regress the residuals from the model in Problem 12.9 on a constant and the return on a proxy for the market portfolio we obtain

$$\hat{u}_j = \underset{(0.02842)}{-0.01205} + \underset{(0.382)}{1.274} r_{m,j} + v_j.$$

Using the CAPM, with a market risk premium of 1% per month, calculate the risk-neutral probability of an up move at each node in the tree in Problem 12.9.

12.12. (**Practice**) Suppose that the spot price of a commodity is currently $140, the two-month futures price is $150, and the five-month futures price is $145.
   (a) Assuming that the normalized volatility is $\hat{\sigma} = 0.18$, build a tree for the spot price with five monthly time steps.
   (b) Use linear interpolation of the log futures prices to estimate the one-month, three-month, and four-month futures prices.
   (c) Calculate risk-neutral probabilities in such a way that the model matches the current term structure of futures prices.

12.13. (**Demonstration**) In Section 3.2, we saw that when the state variable is the price of a commodity we can write $Z = X - C$, where C is the convenience yield from holding that commodity. Show that the approach in Section 12.2.2 is equivalent to writing the convenience yield as an explicit function of the spot price. Derive this function for the situation considered in Example 12.7.

12.14. (**Extension**) Suppose that the one-period-ahead futures price at node (i, n) equals $F_{n+1}(i, n) = a + bX(i, n)$, for some constants a and b.
   (a) Show that, provided the risk-neutral probability of an up move equals the expression in equation (12.22), the two-period-ahead futures price at node (i, n) equals

$$F_{n+2}(i, n) = a(1 + b) + b^2 X(i, n).$$

   (b) Show that the three-period-ahead futures price at node (i, n) equals

$$F_{n+3}(i, n) = a(1 + b + b^2) + b^3 X(i, n).$$

   (c) Explain why continuing this pattern will show that the m-period-ahead futures price at node (i, n) equals

$$F_{n+m}(i, n) = \frac{a(1 - b^m)}{1 - b} + b^m X(i, n).$$

(d) Suppose that we have estimated that the state variable and the m-period-ahead futures price are related by

$$F = \hat{\alpha}_0 + \hat{\alpha}_1 X + w,$$

where $\hat{\alpha}_0$ and $\hat{\alpha}_1$ are estimated parameters and w is a noise term. What values of a and b are consistent with this relationship? (We use this approach to estimate the risk-neutral probabilities in Chapter 17.)

12.A APPENDIX

12.A.1 Mean and Variance of Changes in the Log Price

A Price that Follows a Random Walk

Suppose that the probability of an up move at node (i, n) equals

$$\theta_u(i, n) = \frac{1}{2} + \frac{\hat{\mu}\sqrt{\Delta t_m}}{2\hat{\sigma}}.$$

Then the expected change in the log price is

$$\begin{aligned}
E_{(i,n)}[x(\cdot, n+1) - x(i, n)] &= \theta_u(i, n)\hat{\sigma}\sqrt{\Delta t_m} + (1 - \theta_u(i, n))(-\hat{\sigma}\sqrt{\Delta t_m}) \\
&= (2\theta_u(i, n) - 1)\hat{\sigma}\sqrt{\Delta t_m} \\
&= \hat{\mu}\Delta t_m,
\end{aligned}$$

where $E_{(i,n)}$ indicates that we take the expectation at node (i, n). We also have

$$\begin{aligned}
E_{(i,n)}[(x(\cdot, n+1) - x(i, n))^2] &= \theta_u(i, n)(\hat{\sigma}\sqrt{\Delta t_m})^2 + (1 - \theta_u(i, n))(-\hat{\sigma}\sqrt{\Delta t_m})^2 \\
&= \hat{\sigma}^2\Delta t_m,
\end{aligned}$$

which implies that the variance of the change at node (i, n) is

$$\begin{aligned}
\text{Var}_{(i,n)}[x(\cdot, n+1) - x(i, n)] &= E_{(i,n)}[(x(\cdot, n+1) - x(i, n))^2] \\
&\quad - \left(E_{(i,n)}[x(\cdot, n+1) - x(i, n)]\right)^2 \\
&= \hat{\sigma}^2\Delta t_m - (\hat{\mu}\Delta t_m)^2.
\end{aligned}$$

A Price that is Mean Reverting

Suppose that the probability of an up move at node (i, n) equals

$$\theta_u(i, n) = \frac{1}{2} + \frac{(1 - e^{-\hat{a}\Delta t_m})(\hat{b} - x(i, n))}{2\hat{\sigma}\sqrt{\Delta t_m}}.$$

Then the expected change in the log price is

$$E_{(i,n)}[x(\cdot, n+1) - x(i, n)] = \theta_u(i, n)\hat\sigma\sqrt{\Delta t_m} + (1 - \theta_u(i, n))(-\hat\sigma\sqrt{\Delta t_m})$$
$$= (2\theta_u(i, n) - 1)\hat\sigma\sqrt{\Delta t_m}$$
$$= (1 - e^{-\hat a \Delta t_m})(\hat b - x(i, n)).$$

We also have

$$E_{(i,n)}[(x(\cdot, n+1) - x(i, n))^2] = \theta_u(i, n)(\hat\sigma\sqrt{\Delta t_m})^2 + (1 - \theta_u(i, n))(-\hat\sigma\sqrt{\Delta t_m})^2$$
$$= \hat\sigma^2 \Delta t_m,$$

which implies that the variance of the change at node (i, n) is

$$\mathrm{Var}_{(i,n)}[x(\cdot, n+1) - x(i, n)] = E_{(i,n)}[(x(\cdot, n+1) - x(i, n))^2]$$
$$- \left(E_{(i,n)}[x(\cdot, n+1) - x(i, n)]\right)^2$$
$$= \hat\sigma^2 \Delta t_m - (1 - e^{-\hat a \Delta t_m})^2(\hat b - x(i, n))^2.$$

For small values of Δt_m the term $1 - e^{-\hat a \Delta t_m}$ is approximately equal to $\hat a \Delta t_m$, so that

$$\mathrm{Var}_{(i,n)}[x(\cdot, n+1) - x(i, n)] \approx \hat\sigma^2 \Delta t_m - \hat a^2(\hat b - x(i, n))^2(\Delta t_m)^2.$$

12.A.2 Truncating the Binomial Tree

When modeling a mean-reverting state variable it is simplest to calculate probabilities and market values at each node of the binomial tree, including those nodes that are unreachable. However, this simplicity comes at the cost of a large number of unnecessary calculations. In this appendix we show how to identify the nodes of the tree where probabilities and market values do not need to be calculated.

Inspection of Figure 12.2 shows that the largest value of the state variable that we need to consider corresponds to the first point at which an uninterrupted series of up moves takes us above

$$\exp\left(\hat b + \frac{\hat\sigma\sqrt{\Delta t_m}}{1 - e^{-\hat a \Delta t_m}}\right).$$

This corresponds to the smallest integer n such that

$$X_0 \exp\left(n\hat\sigma\sqrt{\Delta t_m}\right) \geq \exp\left(\hat b + \frac{\hat\sigma\sqrt{\Delta t_m}}{1 - e^{-\hat a \Delta t_m}}\right),$$

which is the smallest integer n such that

$$n \geq \frac{1}{1 - e^{-\hat a \Delta t_m}} + \frac{\hat b - \log X_0}{\hat\sigma\sqrt{\Delta t_m}}.$$

We denote this by

$$\bar{n} = \text{Ceiling}\left[\frac{1}{1 - e^{-\hat{a}\Delta t_m}} + \frac{\hat{b} - \log X_0}{\hat{\sigma}\sqrt{\Delta t_m}}\right].$$

Similarly, the smallest value of the state variable that we need to consider corresponds to the first point at which an uninterrupted series of down moves takes us below

$$\exp\left(\hat{b} - \frac{\hat{\sigma}\sqrt{\Delta t_m}}{1 - e^{-\hat{a}\Delta t_m}}\right).$$

This corresponds to the smallest integer n such that

$$X_0 \exp\left(-n\hat{\sigma}\sqrt{\Delta t_m}\right) \le \exp\left(\hat{b} - \frac{\hat{\sigma}\sqrt{\Delta t_m}}{1 - e^{-\hat{a}\Delta t_m}}\right),$$

which is the smallest integer n such that

$$n \ge \frac{1}{1 - e^{-\hat{a}\Delta t_m}} - \frac{\hat{b} - \log X_0}{\hat{\sigma}\sqrt{\Delta t_m}}.$$

We denote this by

$$\underline{n} = \text{Ceiling}\left[\frac{1}{1 - e^{-\hat{a}\Delta t_m}} - \frac{\hat{b} - \log X_0}{\hat{\sigma}\sqrt{\Delta t_m}}\right].$$

Therefore, we only need to consider nodes (i, n) for which the net number of up moves, which equals $(n - i) - i = n - 2i$, is less than or equal to $\bar{n}$ and the net number of down moves, $2i - n$, is less than or equal to $\underline{n}$. That is, we only consider nodes for which

$$-\underline{n} \le n - 2i \le \bar{n}.$$

Equivalently, at date n we only consider nodes for which

$$\frac{n - \bar{n}}{2} \le i \le \frac{n + \underline{n}}{2}.$$

12.A.3 Estimating Beta when the Spot Price is Mean Reverting

Suppose that the log spot price follows the AR(1) process described in Section 12.1.2 and that the logarithm of the total return index follows the random walk described in Section 12.1.1. Then the residuals in (12.10) have variance

$$\frac{\hat{\sigma}^2}{2\hat{a}}(1 - e^{-2\hat{a}\Delta t_d}).$$

The rate of return on the market portfolio will have variance $\hat{\sigma}_m^2 \Delta t_d$, where $\hat{\sigma}_m$ is the normalized volatility of the total return index. It follows that the estimated slope coefficient in (12.21) will equal

$$\hat{\gamma}_1 = \frac{\hat{\rho}\sqrt{\frac{\hat{\sigma}^2}{2\hat{a}}(1 - e^{-2\hat{a}\Delta t_d})}}{\hat{\sigma}_m\sqrt{\Delta t_d}},$$

where $\hat{\rho}$ is the correlation between changes in the log price and the market return. Replacing Δt_d with Δt_m everywhere shows that the beta that we need for our binomial tree equals

$$\hat{\beta}_x = \frac{\hat{\rho}\sqrt{\frac{\hat{\sigma}^2}{2\hat{a}}(1 - e^{-2\hat{a}\Delta t_m})}}{\hat{\sigma}_m\sqrt{\Delta t_m}}.$$

Eliminating $\hat{\rho}$ between the two equations gives

$$\frac{\hat{\beta}_x}{\hat{\gamma}_1} = \frac{\frac{\hat{\rho}\sqrt{\frac{\hat{\sigma}^2}{2\hat{a}}(1-e^{-2\hat{a}\Delta t_m})}}{\hat{\sigma}_m\sqrt{\Delta t_m}}}{\frac{\hat{\rho}\sqrt{\frac{\hat{\sigma}^2}{2\hat{a}}(1-e^{-2\hat{a}\Delta t_d})}}{\hat{\sigma}_m\sqrt{\Delta t_d}}} = \sqrt{\frac{\Delta t_d}{\Delta t_m} \cdot \frac{1 - e^{-2\hat{a}\Delta t_m}}{1 - e^{-2\hat{a}\Delta t_d}}},$$

as required.

12.A.4 Matching the Current Term Structure of Futures Prices

We begin by deriving the recursive equation that determines the behavior of futures prices. Suppose that we enter into a long futures position at node (i, n) for delivery at some future date m. At date $n + 1$ we receive a payoff from marking to market equal to $F_m(i, n + 1) - F_m(i, n)$ if an up move occurs and to $F_m(i + 1, n + 1) - F_m(i, n)$ if a down move occurs. Since the market value of the futures position is zero at node (i, n), the futures price must satisfy

$$0 = \frac{\pi_u(i, n)(F_m(i, n + 1) - F_m(i, n)) + \pi_d(i, n)(F_m(i + 1, n + 1) - F_m(i, n))}{R_f},$$

which implies that

$$F_m(i, n) = \pi_u(i, n)F_m(i, n + 1) + \pi_d(i, n)F_m(i + 1, n + 1).$$

That is, the futures price at date n equals the expected value of the futures price at date $n + 1$, provided the expected value is calculated using the risk-neutral probabilities.

Now we consider the situation described in Section 12.2.3. Suppose that the one-period-ahead futures price at node (i, n) equals

$$F_{n+1}(i, n) = K_n X(i, n)$$

for a series of constants $K_0, K_1, K_2, \ldots$, so that the risk-neutral probabilities of up and down moves at node (i, n) equal

$$\pi_u(i, n) = \frac{K_n X(i, n) - X(i + 1, n + 1)}{X(i, n + 1) - X(i + 1, n + 1)}$$

and

$$\pi_d(i, n) = \frac{X(i, n + 1) - K_n X(i, n)}{X(i, n + 1) - X(i + 1, n + 1)}$$

respectively. It can be shown that the futures price for delivery at an arbitrary date n equals

$$F_n(0, 0) = K_0 K_1 \cdots K_{n-1} X(0, 0)$$

at node $(0, 0)$. We do not prove the general result. Instead, we demonstrate that it holds for $n = 1, 2, 3$.

By definition, the futures price for delivery at date 1 equals

$$F_1(0, 0) = K_0 X(0, 0),$$

so that the result clearly holds when $n = 1$. The other two cases can be confirmed using the recursive equation for futures prices, as we now show.

Consider the contract for delivery at date 2. At node $(0, 1)$ the futures price equals $F_2(0, 1) = K_1 X(0, 1)$, while at node $(1, 1)$ it equals $F_2(1, 1) = K_1 X(1, 1)$. Therefore, at node $(0, 0)$ the futures price for delivery at date 2 equals

$$
\begin{aligned}
F_2(0,0) &= \pi_u(0,0)F_2(0,1) + \pi_d(0,0)F_2(1,1) \\
&= \left(\frac{K_0 X(0,0) - X(1,1)}{X(0,1) - X(1,1)} \right) K_1 X(0,1) + \left(\frac{X(0,1) - K_0 X(0,0)}{X(0,1) - X(1,1)} \right) K_1 X(1,1) \\
&= K_1 K_0 X(0,0),
\end{aligned}
$$

as required.

Now consider the example of a futures contract for delivery at date 3. At node $(i, 2)$, the futures price equals $F_3(i, 2) = K_2 X(i, 2)$, so that at node $(i, 1)$ it equals

$$
\begin{aligned}
F_3(i,1) &= \pi_u(i,1)F_3(i,2) + \pi_d(i,1)F_3(i+1,2) \\
&= \left(\frac{K_1 X(i,1) - X(i+1,2)}{X(i,2) - X(i+1,2)} \right) K_2 X(i,2) + \left(\frac{X(i,2) - K_1 X(i,1)}{X(i,2) - X(i+1,2)} \right) K_2 X(i+1,2) \\
&= K_2 K_1 X(i,1).
\end{aligned}
$$

At node $(0, 0)$, the futures price for delivery at date 3 therefore equals

$$
\begin{aligned}
F_3(0,0) &= \pi_u(0,0)F_3(0,1) + \pi_d(0,0)F_3(1,1) \\
&= \left(\frac{K_0 X(0,0) - X(1,1)}{X(0,1) - X(1,1)} \right) K_2 K_1 X(0,1) + \left(\frac{X(0,1) - K_0 X(0,0)}{X(0,1) - X(1,1)} \right) K_2 K_1 X(1,1) \\
&= K_2 K_1 K_0 X(0,0),
\end{aligned}
$$

as required.

13

Calibration Using Option Price Data

This chapter shows how to calibrate the tree for the state variable using current market prices of options and other derivative securities with payoffs that are sensitive to the level of the state variable. Thus, rather than relying on historical data on the state variable as in Chapter 12—and hoping that historical behavior gives an accurate guide to future behavior—we are able to use current market data exclusively. Because option prices are typically sensitive to the level of volatility of the underlying asset's price, current option prices have the potential to yield useful information about the future volatility of the state variable. And it is future volatility, not the historical volatility that we estimate using historical data, that is relevant for current decision making.

While the "forward-looking" calibration technique developed in this chapter is very powerful (and we will see that it is quite straightforward to implement), it has one limitation—it can only be used to calibrate the trees as far out as the expiry date of the options being used. Most commodity options traded on organized exchanges are in fact options on commodity futures contracts.[1] While futures options are traded with distant expiry dates relative to other exchange-traded options, the time until expiry will still be short relative to many real options applications. For example, crude oil futures options with expiry dates up to 33 months in the future are traded on the New York Mercantile Exchange (NYMEX), but 33 months may well be too short for many situations we face.

---

1. Useful background on options markets can be found in Chapter 8 of Hull (2008). Chapter 14 of the same source discusses futures options.

Nevertheless, when the required data are available, the techniques developed in this chapter offer an extremely effective means of calibrating the tree for the state variable.

The procedure is quite straightforward. In principle, we begin by building a binomial tree for the futures price and then build a binomial tree for the price of the option contract. Once these trees have been built we use the model's predicted option prices to assess the accuracy of the first tree. If the predicted option price differs from the current market price then we go back and adjust the parameters determining the futures price tree and start all over again, continuing to repeat the process until the predicted price of the option matches the one we observe in financial markets. We then build a tree for the state variable that is consistent with the futures price tree.[2]

Throughout this chapter we use the following example to demonstrate the various calibration methods. It is typical of the situations we meet in practice.

Example 13.1. We aim to build a tree for the spot price of crude oil as at 17 April 2008 and extending out as far as the middle of November 2008. On 17 April the spot price of West Texas Intermediate (WTI) crude oil was \$114.86 per barrel. We use light, sweet crude oil futures prices from NYMEX as well as the prices of options on the December 2008 futures contract. The American-style options expire on 17 November, while their European-style counterparts expire on 20 November; trading in the futures contracts themselves terminates on 20 November and deliveries can occur at any time in December 2008. Thus the options expire after 214 and 217 days respectively, while the futures contract has a delivery date between 227 and 258 days. If we let each time step in our binomial tree represent half a month, the options expire at date 14 and the underlying futures contract has delivery at date 15.[3]

We use the observed prices of the call options listed in Table 13.1 and the term structure of observed futures prices reported in Table 13.2, and estimate the log futures prices for even-numbered delivery dates by taking the average of the adjacent log futures prices.[4] For example, the log futures price for delivery at date 8 will be set equal to

$$\log \hat{F}_8 = \frac{\log \hat{F}_7 + \log \hat{F}_9}{2} = \frac{4.729 + 4.723}{2} = 4.726.$$

The corresponding futures price is $\hat{F}_8 = 112.82$ dollars per barrel.

---

2. The procedure is more sophisticated than this in practice. For example, we use numerical optimization routines to find the best parameters for building the futures price tree. Nevertheless, this stylized description gives a good indication of the procedure we follow.

3. That is, we assume that delivery occurs at the beginning of December.

4. This is the same interpolation procedure that we used to derive equation (12.23).

Table 13.1. Crude Oil Futures Option
Prices on 17 April 2008

Strike	Settlement Price	
	Euro.	Amer.
80	31.36	31.59
90	23.01	23.14
100	15.85	15.92
110	10.35	10.39
120	6.64	6.67
130	4.38	4.39

Note: NYMEX settlement prices on 17 April 2008
for call options on the light, sweet crude oil futures
contract for delivery in December 2008.

Table 13.2. The Term Structure of Crude Oil Futures Prices on 17 April 2008

n	0	1	3	5	7	9	11	13	15
Delivery month	Spot	May	Jun.	Jul.	Aug.	Sep.	Oct.	Nov.	Dec.
$\hat{F}_n$	114.86	114.86	114.45	113.82	113.14	112.50	111.93	111.40	110.89
$\log \hat{F}_n$	4.744	4.744	4.740	4.735	4.729	4.723	4.718	4.713	4.709

Note: NYMEX settlement prices (in dollars per barrel) on 17 April 2008 for the light, sweet crude oil futures
contract.

The interest rates on six month and one year Treasury Bills were 1.58%
and 1.77%, respectively, on 17 April 2008. Since our tree is to extend out
over a seven-month period, we set the risk-free interest rate equal to the
appropriate weighted average:

$$r_f = r_{6m} + \frac{1}{6}(r_{1y} - r_{6m}) = 0.0158 + \frac{1}{6}(0.0177 - 0.0158) = 0.0161.$$

The calculation of these yields is based on semi-annual interest payments,
so that the implied return on a one-year risk-free bond is

$$\left(1 + \frac{0.0161}{2}\right)^2 = 1.01618.$$

This implies a return on one-period risk-free bonds equal to

$$R_f = (1.01618)^{1/24} = 1.00067,$$

which we assume is constant throughout the tree.   ∎

In this chapter we see how to build a tree for the spot price of crude oil that is
consistent with the data in Example 13.1, all of which is "forward looking". That
is, we do not need to rely on historical data at all. We present the discussion in

this chapter in terms of options (expiring at some date M) on futures contracts (for delivery at some later date N), so that the options' underlying asset is a futures contract. However, our approach will usually apply to options on other underlying assets as well. When it does not, we highlight the restrictions.

We begin in Section 13.1 by seeing how to build a futures price tree that is consistent with the price of a single observed option on that futures contract. Sections 13.2 and 13.3 show how to build a futures price tree that is consistent with a whole set of observed option prices. Finally, in Section 13.4 we see how to build trees for the state variable that are consistent with the futures price trees constructed in Sections 13.1–13.3.

13.1 IMPLIED VOLATILITY

Before we describe the first method it is useful to reflect on the approach, described in Chapter 12, using historical data. Recall that we estimate the (normalized) volatility, $\hat{\sigma}$, from historical data and then use it to calculate the sizes of up and down moves via $U = \exp(\hat{\sigma}\sqrt{\Delta t_m})$ and $D = \exp(-\hat{\sigma}\sqrt{\Delta t_m})$. We then use these to construct the binomial tree by starting with the current level of the state variable and filling in the tree from left to right, multiplying the state variable by U or D as appropriate. The final step is to estimate the risk-neutral probability using either the historical behavior of the spot (and possibly futures) price or the current term structure of futures prices. The key parameter, the volatility estimate, is obtained by using only the historical behavior of the spot price.

The approach that we describe in this section uses only currently observed option prices to get our estimates of U (equivalently $\hat{\sigma}$) and the risk-neutral probabilities. Essentially, we look for a value of U that gives a binomial tree that generates theoretical option prices that are as close as possible to those currently observed in liquid option markets.

Consistent with the trees we have built so far, we build our tree in such a way that the size of an up move is the same at every node of the tree and that the sizes of up and down moves are related by $D = 1/U$.[5] We start the tree at the currently observed level of the futures price for delivery at date N, $\hat{F}_N$, and then apply the series of up and down moves. Thus, the futures price at node (i, n) for delivery at date N equals

$$F_N(i, n) = \hat{F}_N U^{n-i} D^i = \hat{F}_N U^{n-2i}. \tag{13.1}$$

As we show in Appendix 13.A.1, when options are written on a futures contract the risk-neutral probability of an up move at node (i, n) equals

$$\pi_u(i, n) = \frac{F_N(i, n) - DF_N(i, n)}{UF_N(i, n) - DF_N(i, n)} = \frac{1 - 1/U}{U - 1/U} = \frac{1}{1 + U}. \tag{13.2}$$

---

5. We relax both of these restrictive assumptions somewhat in the next two sections, where we allow the size of an up move to take different values at different nodes.

This result will be extremely useful, because it means that all we need to know in order to completely specify the behavior of the futures price (that is, the trees of prices and risk-neutral probabilities) are the currently observed futures price for delivery at date N and the size of an up move. Equation (13.1) gives the level of the futures price at all nodes of the tree, while equation (13.2) gives the risk-neutral probability of an up move throughout the tree.

We begin by constructing the tree for the futures price for an arbitrary value of $U > 1$, extending it out as far as the options' expiry date. Next, we build a tree for the price of the futures options. As usual, we start with the column corresponding to the options' expiry date and then fill in the tree using the appropriate recursive equations, working from right to left. The specific terminal conditions and recursive equations will depend on the nature of the options.[6]

- American and European futures call options have the terminal condition

$$C^A(i, M) = C^E(i, M) = \max\{F_N(i, M) - S, 0\}, \qquad (13.3)$$

  where M is the expiry date and S is the strike price. However, the two options have different recursive equations. Since European options cannot be exercised prior to their expiry date, their recursive equation is

$$C^E(i, n) = \frac{\pi_u(i, n)C^E(i, n + 1) + \pi_d(i, n)C^E(i + 1, n + 1)}{R_f}. \qquad (13.4)$$

  The possibility of early exercise means that American call options use the recursive equation

$$C^A(i, n) = \max\left\{F_N(i, n) - S, \frac{\pi_u(i, n)C^A(i, n+1) + \pi_d(i, n)C^A(i+1, n+1)}{R_f}\right\}. \qquad (13.5)$$

- Similarly, the terminal condition for American and European futures put options is

$$P^A(i, M) = P^E(i, M) = \max\{S - F_N(i, M), 0\}. \qquad (13.6)$$

  The appropriate recursive equations are

$$P^E(i, n) = \frac{\pi_u(i, n)P^E(i, n + 1) + \pi_d(i, n)P^E(i + 1, n + 1)}{R_f} \qquad (13.7)$$

---

6. The approach described in this section can, in principle, be used with any type of derivative security. We would need to modify the tree of derivative prices to reflect the characteristics of the derivatives being used, but otherwise the procedure is exactly the same as the one we describe here.

for European futures put options and

$$P^A(i,n) = \max\left\{ S - F_N(i,n), \frac{\pi_u(i,n)P^A(i,n+1) + \pi_d(i,n)P^A(i+1,n+1)}{R_f} \right\}$$

(13.8)

for their American counterparts.

Now, for any value of U we can use the option-price tree to calculate our model's predicted market value for an individual futures option. In principle we could reevaluate this tree using different values of U until we found one for which the calculated price matched its observed counterpart. In practice we use the numerical routines in whichever software package we are using to build the price trees to find U such that the predicted option price equals the observed one.

The entire procedure is demonstrated in the following example.

Example 13.2. We begin by building the required trees with an arbitrary value of U. For now, we set $U = 1.05$, but once we have completed building all required trees we will go back and choose the value of U so that the model's option price matches the observed market price. With this value of U, we build the tree for the futures price out as far as the options' expiry date, using

$$F_{15}(i, n) = \hat{F}_{15} U^{n-2i} = 110.89 \times 1.05^{n-2i}.$$

Part of this tree is shown in the top panel of Table 13.3.

The next step is to build the tree for the option prices. We consider the at-the-money options in detail. They expire at date $M = 14$, have strike prices of \$110, and have current market prices of \$10.35 and \$10.39 for the European and American options respectively. The price tree for the European option is shown in the middle panel of Table 13.3. We start by using (13.3) to fill in the column corresponding to the option's expiry date, and then fill in the remainder of the tree from right to left, using (13.4). The tree for the American option, shown in the bottom panel of Table 13.3, is constructed in much the same way. The terminal condition, (13.3), is the same, but the recursive equation is now (13.5).

For this particular value of U, the option prices are \$8.35 and \$8.37, considerably lower than the observed prices of \$10.35 and \$10.39. We need to find U such that $C^E(0, 0) = 10.35$ if we wish to match the European option's market price, or $C^A(0, 0) = 10.39$ if we wish to match the American option's price instead. It turns out that for the American option this yields an up move equal to $\hat{U} = 1.06334$. Table 13.4 repeats the relevant calculations of Table 13.3 for this value of U. Notice that the futures price still matches the value we observe in the futures market, but now the theoretical option price also equals its observed market counterpart. ∎

Table 13.3. Valuing Futures Options when $U = 1.05$

$F_{15}(i, n)$	0	1	2	...	12	13	14
0	110.89	116.43	122.26	...	199.14	209.10	219.55
1		105.61	110.89	...	180.63	189.66	199.14
2			100.58	...	163.84	172.03	180.63
⋮					⋮	⋮	⋮
12					61.75	64.84	68.08
13						58.81	61.75
14							56.01

$C^E(i, n)$	0	1	2	...	12	13	14
0	8.35	11.40	15.22	...	89.02	99.03	109.55
1		5.46	7.77	...	70.53	79.61	89.14
2			3.27	...	53.76	61.99	70.63
⋮					⋮	⋮	⋮
12					0.00	0.00	0.00
13						0.00	0.00
14							0.00

$C^A(i, n)$	0	1	2	...	12	13	14
0	8.37	11.43	15.27	...	89.14	99.10	109.55
1		5.47	7.78	...	70.63	79.66	89.14
2			3.27	...	53.84	62.03	70.63
⋮					⋮	⋮	⋮
12					0.00	0.00	0.00
13						0.00	0.00
14							0.00

Although we are most interested in the binomial tree for the futures price and the associated risk-neutral probabilities, it can be useful to calculate the corresponding level of volatility, known as the option's implied volatility. Recall from Section 12.1.1 that when we used historical price data to build the tree of prices we set the size of an up move equal to

$$U = e^{\hat{\sigma}\sqrt{\Delta t_m}}.$$

Solving this equation for $\hat{\sigma}$ shows that the level of volatility implied by our calibrated value of U is

$$\hat{\sigma} = \frac{\log \hat{U}}{\sqrt{\Delta t_m}}.$$

Table 13.4. Valuing a Futures Option when $U = 1.06334$

$F_{15}(i, n)$	0	1	2	...	12	13	14
0	110.89	117.91	125.38	...	231.72	246.39	262.00
1		104.28	110.89	...	204.93	217.91	231.72
2			98.07	...	181.25	192.73	204.93
⋮					⋮	⋮	⋮
12					53.07	56.43	60.00
13						49.91	53.07
14							46.93

$C^A(i, n)$	0	1	2	...	12	13	14
0	10.39	14.30	19.26	...	121.72	136.39	152.00
1		6.73	9.65	...	94.93	107.91	121.72
2			3.98	...	71.25	82.73	94.93
⋮					⋮	⋮	⋮
12					0.00	0.00	0.00
13						0.00	0.00
14							0.00

Table 13.5. Volatility Implied by the Prices of Options on the December 2008 Crude Oil Futures Contract on 17 April 2008

Strike Price	European			American		
	Price	$\hat{U}$	$\hat{\sigma}$	Price	$\hat{U}$	$\hat{\sigma}$
80	31.36	1.06326	0.3005	31.59	1.06498	0.3084
90	23.01	1.06353	0.3017	23.14	1.06408	0.3043
100	15.85	1.06297	0.2992	15.92	1.06320	0.3002
110	10.35	1.06325	0.3004	10.39	1.06334	0.3009
120	6.64	1.06294	0.2990	6.67	1.06305	0.2995
130	4.38	1.06638	0.3149	4.39	1.06642	0.3151

For instance, the level of volatility implied by the calculations in Table 13.4 is

$$\hat{\sigma} = \frac{\log 1.06334}{\sqrt{1/24}} = 0.3009.$$

Example 13.3. The previous example estimated the size of an up move implied by the observed price of an American futures call option with a strike price of $110. If we repeat the calculations there for the other options in our sample, we obtain the up moves and implied volatilities reported in Table 13.5. ∎

The whole process can be summarized by the following four steps.

1. For an arbitrary value of U, use equation (13.1) to build a binomial tree for the futures price for delivery at date N.
2. Use equation (13.2) to calculate the risk-neutral probability of an up move at each node.
3. Build a tree for the price of the futures option. Fill in the tree starting with the column corresponding to the terminal nodes, then working from right to left, filling in the remaining columns using the appropriate recursive equation.
4. Find a value of $U > 1$ that sets the model's option price equal to the current observed market price.

It will often be the case that options on the same underlying asset and with the same expiry date, but with different strike prices, will have different implied volatilities. This indicates that a single binomial tree for the underlying cannot explain all observed option prices. For example, Table 13.5 shows that we need $\hat{\sigma} = 0.3004$ to correctly value a European call with a strike price of \$110, but we need $\hat{\sigma} = 0.3149$ to correctly value one with a strike price of \$130.[7] One response, which we introduce in Section 13.2, is to allow the size of up moves to vary throughout the binomial tree. A less sophisticated response maintains the assumption that U is constant and instead tries to find a single value of U such that all option prices are close to those observed in financial markets. One approach is simply to use some sort of weighted average of the individual implied volatilities.[8] Another is to find the value of U that minimizes the sum of the squared pricing errors for all options in our sample.[9] Yet another alternative, which places greater significance on the prices of options that are heavily traded, is to minimize a weighted sum of squared pricing errors, where a greater weight is attached to those options with large trading volumes. These are no more difficult than the first procedure, although more calculations are involved. In particular, there will be multiple option-price trees rather than the single tree used before. While this increases the amount of work required, it does not increase the complexity.

The main problem with the approaches that we have just described is that they force the risk-neutral probabilities to be constant throughout the binomial tree. For commodity prices, especially, we need more flexibility. In the remainder of this chapter we show how we can extend these methods to allow the risk-neutral probability of an up move to vary across the tree by allowing some more freedom with respect to the sizes of up and down moves.

---

7. Many markets have quite distinctive relationships between options' strike prices and their implied volatilities, known as volatility smiles.

8. Mayhew (1995) surveys the literature on implied volatility and discusses several different weighting schemes that can be used to calculate a single measure of volatility from several different observed option prices.

9. The procedure is demonstrated in Problem 13.3.

13.2 IMPLIED BINOMIAL TREES: EUROPEAN OPTIONS

In this section we see how to construct a binomial tree for the futures price that begins at the observed level $\hat{F}_N$ and generates European futures option prices equal to those observed in financial markets for a set of options simultaneously. We use a two-step procedure. First, in Section 13.2.1, we calculate the risk-neutral probability of ending up at each of the terminal nodes. Second, in Section 13.2.2, we use this information to build the futures price tree.[10]

However, before we can implement this method, we need to specify the level of the futures price at each of the tree's terminal nodes. The usual approach is to take the implied volatility from an at-the-money futures call option and, assuming for the time being that it is constant throughout the tree, use it to calculate the terminal values of the futures price. Thus, if $\hat{\sigma}$ is our implied volatility estimate, then the futures price at each terminal node (i, M) is set equal to

$$F_N(i, M) = \hat{F}_N e^{(M-2i)\hat{\sigma}\sqrt{\Delta t_m}}. \tag{13.9}$$

13.2.1 Estimating the Risk-neutral Probability of Reaching Each Terminal Node

What makes the method we are going to develop so powerful is the simple relationship between the price of a European option at node $(0, 0)$ and the risk-neutral probabilities of ending up at the various terminal nodes of the binomial tree for the futures price. For our purposes, the most important features of these options are that they generate cash flow only on their expiry date and that we know how this cash flow relates to the state variable. Specifically, if the options expire at date M then their cash flow at node (i, M) equals

$$\max\{F_N(i, M) - S, 0\}$$

in the case of a European call option with strike price S, and

$$\max\{S - F_N(i, M), 0\}$$

in the case of a European put option with the same strike price. Our discussion in Section 4.2.1 shows that the market value of a European call option at node $(0, 0)$ is

$$C^E(0, 0) = \frac{1}{(R_f)^M} \sum_{i=0}^{M} a_i \max\{F_N(i, M) - S, 0\},$$

where a_i is the risk-neutral probability of ending up at node (i, M). That is, we calculate the expected payoff (using the risk-neutral probabilities) and discount

---

10. Jackwerth (1999) surveys the literature on implied binomial trees and related techniques. Arnold et al. (2006) describe how to build an implied binomial tree in a spreadsheet.

it back to date 0 using the risk-free interest rate. Similarly, the market value of a European put option is

$$P^E(0,0) = \frac{1}{(R_f)^M} \sum_{i=0}^{M} a_i \max\{S - F_N(i,M), 0\}$$

at node $(0,0)$. In both cases, the market value of the option is a linear function of the probabilities $\{a_0, a_1, \ldots, a_M\}$.

In very general terms, our approach is to find a set $\{a_0, a_1, \ldots, a_M\}$ of risk-neutral probabilities for the terminal nodes that has two properties:

- The model generates call and put option prices that match those we currently observe in the markets.
- The probability distribution is "sensible". There are many different definitions of "sensible" that we could use here. We require that the probability distribution is "as close as possible" to the one corresponding to our initial implied volatility estimate $\hat{\sigma}$, in a sense that we explain shortly.

To achieve this, we need to specify two things: an objective function for our problem, and the constraints.

The starting point for our objective function is the implied volatility estimate that we used in (13.9). Since the corresponding up move is $\hat{U} = e^{\hat{\sigma}\sqrt{\Delta t_m}}$, the associated risk-neutral probability of an up move is

$$\hat{\pi}_u = \frac{1}{1+\hat{U}}.$$

From equation (4.8), the corresponding probability of arriving at node (i, M) equals

$$\Pr{}^*[\text{arrive at node } (i, M)] = \frac{M!}{i!(M-i)!} \hat{\pi}_u^{M-i} (1 - \hat{\pi}_u)^i,$$

which we denote by $\hat{a}_i$. We choose the probabilities $\{a_0, a_1, \ldots, a_M\}$ in order to minimize the sum of squared differences between our probabilities and those corresponding to the initial implied volatility estimate.[11] That is, we seek to minimize

$$\sum_{i=0}^{M} (a_i - \hat{a}_i)^2. \tag{13.10}$$

The next step is to specify the constraints that we impose on our choice of probabilities. First, because they are probabilities, they must all be nonnegative and they must sum to one. In fact, as we will see in Section 13.2.2, we have to

---

11. Jackwerth and Rubinstein (1996) consider the performance of different objective functions.

divide by these probabilities later on, so we actually require them to be strictly positive. Thus, our first set of constraints is

$$a_i \geq t \text{ for all } i \quad \text{and} \quad \sum_{i=0}^{M} a_i = 1, \tag{13.11}$$

where t is a small positive number that we can specify. (We set $t = 10^{-6}$ in the examples below.) Second, we want our tree to generate a futures price at node $(0, 0)$ that matches the one we observe in financial markets. Therefore, we impose the requirement that

$$\sum_{i=0}^{M} a_i F_N(i, M) = \hat{F}_N, \tag{13.12}$$

where $\hat{F}_N$ is the observed futures price for delivery at date N.[12] Finally, we require that our tree generates prices for the options in our sample that equal observed prices. This gives our final constraints,

$$\frac{1}{(R_f)^M} \sum_{i=0}^{M} a_i \max\{F_N(i, M) - S, 0\} = \hat{C}_S^E \tag{13.13}$$

and

$$\frac{1}{(R_f)^M} \sum_{i=0}^{M} a_i \max\{S - F_N(i, M), 0\} = \hat{P}_S^E, \tag{13.14}$$

where $\hat{C}_S^E$ and $\hat{P}_S^E$ are the observed European call and put option prices, respectively, for options with a strike price of S. We have one of these constraints for each option in our sample.

Therefore, our task is to find numbers $\{a_0, a_1, \ldots, a_M\}$ that minimize the function in (13.10) and satisfy all of the constraints in (13.11)–(13.14). We denote our solution by $\{a_0^*, a_1^*, \ldots, a_M^*\}$. The objective function is a quadratic function of the choice variables, while all of the constraints are linear functions of these variables.[13] Thus we have to solve a so-called quadratic programming problem. It is relatively straightforward to solve numerically.

Example 13.4. We apply this method to the European options described in Example 13.1, using $\hat{U} = 1.06334$, so that the initial implied volatility

---

12. The discussion in Appendix 13.A.1 can be extended to show that the futures price at date 0 equals the expected value of the futures price (for the same delivery date) at date M, provided that the expectation is calculated using the risk-neutral probabilities.

13. It is the linearity of the constraints that makes this method so powerful, and this linearity arises because we are using European options. As we explain in Section 13.3, if we attempted to match the observed prices of American options then we would have nonlinear constraints, which would make this a much more difficult constrained optimization problem to solve.

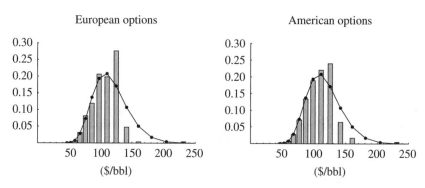

Figure 13.1. Terminal nodal probabilities implied by the prices of options on the December 2008 crude oil futures contract on 17 April 2008

estimate is $\hat{\sigma} = 0.3009$. The corresponding risk-neutral probability of an up move occurring is $\hat{\pi}_u = 0.4847$. The solutions for the nodal probabilities (the a_i^*s) are shown by the bar chart in the left-hand graph in Figure 13.1, while the curve shows the $\hat{a}_i$s. Relative to the baseline case, there is a much smaller probability of the futures price climbing higher than approximately $140. However, there is a much higher probability of a terminal value of approximately $125.   ∎

Now that we have calculated the risk-neutral probabilities of arriving at each of the terminal nodes in our futures price tree, the next step is to fill in the rest of the tree.

13.2.2 Filling in the Remainder of the Futures Price Tree

Rubinstein (1994) developed a scheme that uses the prices at the terminal nodes and the risk-neutral probabilities of ending up at each of these nodes to build the entire tree. This comes at the price of imposing some additional structure on the tree. The assumption we make is that all of the various paths ending at any particular terminal node occur with the same probability. For example, there are M different paths to node $(1, M)$—one has the single down move occurring first, another has it occurring second, and so on, up until the last path which has the sole down move occurring last. We assume that all of these paths are equally likely. Since the total probability of ending up at node $(1, M)$ equals a_1^*, each one of these paths must occur with probability a_1^*/M.

When implementing this scheme we need to keep track of the so-called nodal probabilities $\psi(i, n)$, which give the (risk-neutral) probability of passing through node (i, n). We already know that $\psi(i, M) = a_i^*$ for each $i = 0, 1, \ldots, M$. We also know the values of each $F_N(i, M)$. Now we need to calculate $\psi(\cdot, n)$ and $F_N(\cdot, n)$ for all values of $n < M$. The procedure is quite straightforward, and involves filling

Table 13.6. Building an Implied Binomial Tree

$\psi(i, n)$	0	1	2	3	
0	1	$\psi(0, 1)$	$\psi(0, 2)$	$\psi(0, 3)$ ←	Step 1a: Fill in final column
1		$\psi(1, 1)$	$\psi(1, 2)$	$\psi(1, 3)$	using $\psi(i, M) = a_i^*$
2			$\psi(2, 2)$	$\psi(2, 3)$ ←	Step 1b: Fill in remaining
3				$\psi(3, 3)$	columns using (13.15)

$\pi_u(i, n)$	0	1	2	3	
0	$\pi_u(0, 0)$	$\pi_u(0, 1)$	$\pi_u(0, 2)$	–	
1		$\pi_u(1, 1)$	$\pi_u(1, 2)$	–	← Step 2: Fill in using (13.16)
2			$\pi_u(2, 2)$	–	
3				–	

$F_N(i, n)$	0	1	2	3	
0	$\hat{F}_N$	$F_N(0, 1)$	$F_N(0, 2)$	$F_N(0, 3)$ ←	Step 3a: Fill in final column
1		$F_N(1, 1)$	$F_N(1, 2)$	$F_N(1, 3)$	using (13.9)
2			$F_N(2, 2)$	$F_N(2, 3)$ ←	Step 3b: Fill in remaining
3				$F_N(3, 3)$	columns using (13.17)

in the remainder of the trees for ψ, π_u, and F_N working from right to left in the familiar way.[14] We construct the three trees in turn.

1. Calculate the nodal probability at each node at each date n using

$$\psi(i, n) = \left(\tfrac{n+1-i}{n+1}\right) \psi(i, n + 1) + \left(\tfrac{i+1}{n+1}\right) \psi(i + 1, n + 1). \qquad (13.15)$$

2. Calculate the risk-neutral probability of an up move at each node at each date n using

$$\pi_u(i, n) = \frac{\left(\tfrac{n+1-i}{n+1}\right) \psi(i, n + 1)}{\psi(i, n)}. \qquad (13.16)$$

3. Calculate the futures price at each node at each date n using

$$F_N(i, n) = \pi_u(i, n)F_N(i, n + 1) + (1 - \pi_u(i, n))F_N(i + 1, n + 1). \qquad (13.17)$$

Table 13.6 summarizes the construction of the implied binomial tree, using the case of a tree that extends out as far as date 3. We begin by filling in the tree for the nodal probabilities, using the outputs of the quadratic programming problem to fill in the final column and (13.15) to complete the rest of the table, working from right to left, one column at a time. The next step is to construct the tree of

---

14. A derivation of the key equations, (13.15)–(13.17), is included in Appendix 13.A.2.

Table 13.7. Implied Binomial Tree Using European Options

$\psi(i, n)$	0	1	2	...	12	13	14
0	1.0000	0.4813	0.2338	...	0.0262	0.0259	0.0256
1		0.5187	0.4950	...	0.0036	0.0039	0.0042
2			0.2711	...	0.0002	0.0000	0.0000
⋮					⋮	⋮	⋮
12					0.0001	0.0008	0.0059
13						0.0000	0.0000
14							0.0000

$\pi_u(i, n)$	0	1	2	...	12	13	14
0	0.4813	0.4858	0.5042	...	0.9885	0.9884	n/a
1		0.4772	0.4683	...	1.0000	1.0000	n/a
2			0.4853	...	0.0057	0.8000	n/a
⋮					⋮	⋮	⋮
12					0.9838	0.9989	n/a
13						0.0667	n/a
14							n/a

$F_{15}(i, n)$	0	1	2	...	12	13	14
0	110.89	119.94	133.06	...	261.30	261.65	262.00
1		102.49	107.55	...	231.71	231.72	231.72
2			97.88	...	160.55	200.20	204.93
⋮					⋮	⋮	⋮
12					59.79	60.00	60.00
13						47.34	53.07
14							46.93

risk-neutral probabilities, using (13.16). Because of the form of this equation, we can calculate the entries in the table in any order. Finally, we construct the tree for the futures price. We start with the final column, using (13.9) together with our initial implied volatility estimate, before completing the remainder of the table using (13.17).

Example 13.5. When we apply this method to the terminal nodal probabilities calculated in Example 13.4, we obtain the trees that are shown in Table 13.7. The top panel shows how the nodal probabilities evolve throughout the tree. For example, the risk-neutral probability of arriving at node $(0, 2)$ is 0.2338, while the other two possible nodes at that date, $(1, 2)$ and $(2, 2)$, occur with respective probabilities 0.4950 and 0.2711. The middle panel shows the risk-neutral probability of an up move at each node in the tree, while the bottom panel shows the evolution of the futures price corresponding to delivery at date 15. Notice that although the levels of the futures price at the initial and terminal nodes match those in Table 13.4, the behavior is quite different in the intermediate nodes.   ∎

We have now completed construction of a binomial tree for the futures price. As we will see in Section 13.4, it is straightforward to build the corresponding tree for the state variable, which is what we are ultimately interested in. However, first we see how to modify the construction in this section so that it can handle American futures options.

13.3 IMPLIED BINOMIAL TREES: AMERICAN OPTIONS

The approach described in the previous section will not work when applied to American options because the possibility of early exercise means that their market value at date 0 depends on the distribution of the futures price at all dates up to and including the options' expiry date, not just the distribution on the expiry date. We have seen in Section 13.2.2 that the futures price at these intermediate nodes can be derived from the a_i^*s, but the dependence is nonlinear.[15] Thus, even if we wrote the futures price at each intermediate node as a function of the terminal nodal probabilities, the constraints in our constrained optimization problem would no longer be linear functions of the choice variables. This greatly complicates finding a solution. Therefore, we adopt a slightly different approach in this section that preserves the linearity of the constraints. As a result, we still have to solve a quadratic programming problem.

In very general terms, our approach is to use the observed prices of American options to tell us something about the European option prices that the model has to generate. That is, as in the previous section we use our model to calculate the prices of European options, but now we use data on American options. We are able to do this because of the theoretical relationships between the prices of American and European futures options, as we now explain.[16]

Because American options possess all of the features of European options with the same expiry date and strike price—but have the added feature that they can be exercised early—European options cannot be worth more than analogous American ones. Therefore, our terminal nodal probabilities $\{a_0, a_1, \ldots, a_M\}$

---

15. To see why, note from (13.17) that the futures prices are functions of the risk-neutral probabilities. By (13.16), the latter are nonlinear functions of the nodal probabilities.

16. Although the discussion in this chapter has centered on futures options, most of the material can be applied to other derivatives (and other underlying variables). However, the relationships between the prices of American and European options that we use in this section require that we are dealing with options on futures prices. The general technique will be applicable in other situations, but appropriate relationships that we use to bound the prices of American options will need to be found (or derived) for each particular situation.

must satisfy

$$\frac{1}{(R_f)^M} \sum_{i=0}^{M} a_i \max\{F_N(i, M) - S, 0\} \leq \hat{C}_S^A \qquad (13.18)$$

and

$$\frac{1}{(R_f)^M} \sum_{i=0}^{M} a_i \max\{S - F_N(i, M), 0\} \leq \hat{P}_S^A, \qquad (13.19)$$

where $\hat{C}_S^A$ and $\hat{P}_S^A$ are the observed American call and put option prices, respectively, for options with a strike price of S. We have one of these constraints for each option in our sample.

The inequalities in (13.18) and (13.19) apply to American options on any underlying variable. However, our second set of inequalities apply specifically to options on futures contracts. Chaudhury and Wei (1994) proved that if we use the risk-free interest rate to compound the current price of a European futures option forward to its expiry date then we obtain an upper bound on the price of the corresponding American futures option.[17] This motivates our second set of constraints,

$$\sum_{i=0}^{M} a_i \max\{F_N(i, M) - S, 0\} \geq \hat{C}_S^A \qquad (13.20)$$

and

$$\sum_{i=0}^{M} a_i \max\{S - F_N(i, M), 0\} \geq \hat{P}_S^A. \qquad (13.21)$$

For example, the left-hand side of (13.20) is the compounded price of a European call option with a strike price of S, which must be at least as great as the observed price of an American futures option with the same strike price and expiry date.[18]

Therefore, our task is to find numbers $\{a_0, a_1, \ldots, a_M\}$ that minimize the function in (13.10) and satisfy the earlier constraints in (13.11)–(13.12), as well as the new ones in (13.18)–(13.21). The new constraints are still linear functions of the choice variables, so we still just need to solve a quadratic programming problem. The next example shows the results of applying this procedure to our ongoing example involving crude oil futures options.

---

17. Melick and Thomas (1997) used these bounds to infer the (risk-neutral) distribution of the underlying asset's price.

18. The constraints in (13.18) and (13.20) impose upper and lower bounds on $\sum_{i=0}^{M} a_i \max\{F_N(i, M) - S, 0\}$ of $(R_f)^M \hat{C}_S^A$ and $\hat{C}_S^A$ respectively. The ratio of these two bounds, which equals the return on an M-period risk-free bond, will reflect the level of the risk-free interest rate and the time until the options expire. If interest rates are not too high then the bounds will be reasonably close, given the expiry dates for typical American futures options.

Example 13.6. We apply this method to the American options described in Example 13.1, using $\hat{\sigma} = 0.3009$ as our initial implied volatility estimate as in Example 13.4. The solutions for the nodal probabilities are shown by the bar chart in the right-hand graph in Figure 13.1. As was the case when we used European options, there is a smaller probability of the futures price climbing higher than approximately $140 and a higher probability of a terminal value of approximately $125 relative to the baseline case. However, the change is not as extreme as we found with European options. ∎

Once we have found the terminal probabilities $\{a_0^*, a_1^*, \ldots, a_M^*\}$, we can fill in the entire tree for the futures price using the same technique as in Section 13.2.2.

Example 13.7. When we apply this method to the terminal nodal probabilities calculated in Example 13.6, we obtain the trees that are shown in Table 13.8. The format is exactly the same as in Table 13.7, with the top panel showing the nodal probabilities, the middle panel showing the risk-neutral probabilities of up moves, and the bottom panel showing the evolution of the futures price. The initial and terminal futures prices are the same as in the previous table, but the intermediate values are slightly different, reflecting the different nodal probabilities at the terminal nodes. ∎

We can now construct a binomial tree for the futures price, using observed prices of either European or American futures options. Our final task in this chapter is to use the futures-price tree to build the tree for the state variable.

13.4 FROM A FUTURES-PRICE TREE TO A STATE-VARIABLE TREE

We set the state variable at node (i, n) equal to

$$X(i, n) = \frac{\hat{F}_n}{\hat{F}_N} F_N(i, n), \tag{13.22}$$

where $\hat{F}_n$ is the current observed futures price for delivery at date n. This tree for the state variable has two desirable properties.[19] First, it is consistent with the tree for the futures price for delivery at date N—that is, if we construct the futures price tree starting from the state variable tree, we obtain a futures price of $F_N(i, n)$ at each node (i, n). Second, at node $(0, 0)$ the futures price for an arbitrary delivery date $n \leq N$ equals $\hat{F}_n$, consistent with the values currently observed in the futures market.

Thus, we can use equation (13.22) to construct the binomial tree for the state variable from the futures price trees we constructed in the earlier sections. Not only will the state-variable tree be consistent with the option prices used to construct

---

19. We prove that these properties hold in Appendix 13.A.3.

Table 13.8. Implied Binomial Tree Using American Options

$\psi(i, n)$	0	1	2	...	12	13	14
0	1.0000	0.4817	0.2343	...	0.0211	0.0207	0.0204
1		0.5183	0.4949	...	0.0040	0.0043	0.0046
2			0.2708	...	0.0011	0.0000	0.0000
⋮					⋮	⋮	⋮
12					0.0022	0.0031	0.0076
13						0.0020	0.0022
14							0.0018

$\pi_u(i, n)$	0	1	2	...	12	13	14
0	0.4817	0.4863	0.5006	...	0.9843	0.9841	n/a
1		0.4775	0.4727	...	1.0000	1.0000	n/a
2			0.4818	...	0.0009	0.8000	n/a
⋮					⋮	⋮	⋮
12					0.1068	0.3485	n/a
13						0.0779	n/a
14							n/a

$F_{15}(i, n)$	0	1	2	...	12	13	14
0	110.89	119.65	131.57	...	261.05	261.52	262.00
1		102.75	108.37	...	231.71	231.72	231.72
2			97.61	...	160.33	200.20	204.93
⋮					⋮	⋮	⋮
12					48.27	55.48	60.00
13						47.41	53.07
14							46.93

the futures-price tree, but it will also be consistent with the current term structure of futures prices.

Example 13.8. In this example we construct the spot price tree that is derived from the futures price tree that we built in Example 13.7. The values at each node can be completed in any order. For instance, at node $(0, 0)$ the spot price equals

$$X(0, 0) = \frac{\hat{F}_0}{\hat{F}_{15}} F_{15}(0, 0) = \frac{114.86 \times 110.89}{110.89} = 114.86,$$

which (by construction) is the level of the spot price currently observed in the spot market. The calculations at other nodes are just as simple.

Table 13.9. Spot Price Tree Implied by American Futures Options

$X(i, n)$	0	1	2	...	12	13	14
0	114.86	123.93	136.04	...	262.88	262.72	262.60
1		106.43	112.04	...	233.33	232.78	232.25
2			100.93	...	161.45	201.12	205.40
⋮					⋮	⋮	⋮
12					48.61	55.74	60.14
13						47.63	53.19
14							47.04

For example,

$$X(1, 2) = \frac{\hat{F}_2}{\hat{F}_{15}} F_{15}(1, 2) = \frac{114.65 \times 108.37}{110.89} = 112.04.$$

The resulting spot price tree is shown in Table 13.9. ∎

The whole process described in this chapter is straightforward. The required inputs are the current term structure of futures prices (interpolated, if necessary, so that we have a futures price for each date in our proposed binomial tree) and a collection of option prices, either European or American. We begin by calculating the implied volatility for each of these options. If all options have a similar implied volatility then we can use the common value to build our tree for the state variable. If not, then we can use the option prices to formulate a quadratic programming problem that, when solved, gives us the risk-neutral probability of arriving at each terminal node of our binomial tree. We then fill in the complete tree for the futures price, before finally constructing the state-variable tree.

13.5 PROBLEMS

13.1. (**Practice**) A futures call option has a strike price of $140 and expires at date 6. The underlying futures price is currently $148, the option is European, and the option price is $13.10. The return on one-period risk-free bonds is $R_f = 1.005$ and each period represents one month.
   (a) Calculate the theoretical price of the option if the size of an up move in the futures price is $U = 1.04, 1.05, \ldots, 1.08$.
   (b) Calculate the implied volatility for this option.
   (c) What is the implied volatility if the option is actually American?

13.2. (**Practice**) Repeat Problem 13.1 for a put option with a strike price of $150 and a market value of $9.80.

13.3. (**Extension**) Three futures call options, all expiring at date 8 and having respective strike prices of $11.50, $12.00, and $12.50, are currently trading for $0.70, $0.41, and $0.23. The options are European and the underlying

futures price is currently $11.98. The return on one-period risk-free bonds is $R_f = 1.0025$ and each period represents one week.
  (a) Calculate the implied volatility for each call option.
  (b) Find the level of the volatility parameter that minimizes the sum of squared differences between the observed option prices and their theoretical counterparts.

13.4. (**Practice**) Three futures call options, written on the same futures contract, all expire at date 6. Their strike prices are $110, $120, and $130, and their current market values are $13.20, $7.30, and $4.10 respectively. All options are European, the underlying futures price is currently $120, and the return on one-period risk-free bonds is $R_f = 1.01$.
  (a) Calculate $F_N(i, 6)$ for each $i = 0, 1, \ldots, 6$, assuming that the size of an up move in the underlying futures price is $\hat{U} = 1.07$.
  (b) Calculate the risk-neutral probability of arriving at node $(i, 6)$ for each $i = 0, 1, \ldots, 6$, assuming that the size of an up move in the underlying futures price is $\hat{U} = 1.07$. That is, calculate the $\hat{a}_i$s.
  (c) Find numbers $\{a_0, a_1, \ldots, a_6\}$ that minimize the function in (13.10) and satisfy all of the constraints in (13.11)–(13.14).

13.5. (**Practice**) Repeat Problem 13.4 for the case when all options are American. Use the appropriate constraints in part (c).

13.6. (**Practice**) Suppose that the spot price of a commodity is currently $2.30 and that the futures prices for delivery at dates 2 and 4 are $2.28 and $2.24 respectively. The current price of a futures call option with a strike price of $2.30 and expiring at date 3 is $0.10. The option is American and is written on the futures contract for delivery at date 4. The return on a one-period risk-free bond is $R_f = 1.01$ and each period represents three months.
  (a) Calculate the implied volatility of the futures price for delivery at date 4.
  (b) Estimate the current futures prices for delivery at dates 1 and 3.
  (c) Build a tree for the spot price that is consistent with current observed futures and option prices.

13.A APPENDIX

13.A.1 Risk-neutral Probabilities when the State Variable is a Futures Price

Suppose that we are currently at node (i, n) and that we hold a portfolio comprising A one-period risk-free bonds and B long futures positions. This portfolio generates a cash flow of

$$AR_f + B(F_N(i, n+1) - F_N(i, n))$$

in the up state and

$$AR_f + B(F_N(i+1, n+1) - F_N(i, n))$$

in the down state. In each case the first component is the payoff from the bond and the second is the payoff from marking-to-market the futures position. We choose A and B in order to replicate the cash flow of $Y(i, n + 1)$ in the up state and $Y(i + 1, n + 1)$ in the down state. That is, we choose A and B such that

$$AR_f + B(F_N(i, n + 1) - F_N(i, n)) = Y(i, n + 1),$$

$$AR_f + B(F_N(i + 1, n + 1) - F_N(i, n)) = Y(i + 1, n + 1).$$

Solving these two equations for A and B shows that

$$A = \frac{\pi_u(i, n)Y(i, n + 1) + \pi_d(i, n)Y(i + 1, n + 1)}{R_f}$$

and

$$B = \frac{Y(i, n + 1) - Y(i + 1, n + 1)}{F_N(i, n + 1) - F_N(i + 1, n + 1)},$$

where

$$\pi_u(i, n) = \frac{F_N(i, n) - F_N(i + 1, n + 1)}{F_N(i, n + 1) - F_N(i + 1, n + 1)}$$

and

$$\pi_d(i, n) = \frac{F_N(i, n + 1) - F_N(i, n)}{F_N(i, n + 1) - F_N(i + 1, n + 1)}.$$

Since the market value of each futures position is zero, the replicating portfolio costs A to construct. The law of one price implies that the cash flow's market value at node (i, n) equals A, which takes the same form as our risk-neutral valuation formula in equation (3.1) but with a different expression for the risk-neutral probabilities.

We can rearrange the equation for $\pi_u(i, n)$ to obtain

$$F_N(i, n) = \pi_u(i, n)F_N(i, n + 1) + (1 - \pi_u(i, n))F_N(i + 1, n + 1).$$

That is, the futures price at node (i, n) equals the expected value of the futures price at date $n + 1$, provided the expected value is calculated using the risk-neutral probabilities.

13.A.2 Rubinstein's Implied Binomial Tree

Rubinstein (1994) assumes that all paths that reach a particular node occur with the same probability. Since there are $n!/((n - i)!i!)$ different paths to node (i, n), each such path must occur with probability

$$\psi(i, n) \bigg/ \frac{n!}{(n - i)! i!} = \frac{(n - i)! i! \psi(i, n)}{n!}.$$

Similarly, each path to node $(i, n + 1)$ must occur with probability

$$\frac{(n + 1 - i)! i! \psi(i, n + 1)}{(n + 1)!}$$

and each path to node $(i + 1, n + 1)$ must occur with probability

$$\frac{(n - i)!\,(i + 1)!\,\psi(i + 1, n + 1)}{(n + 1)!}.$$

Consider an arbitrary path that reaches node (i, n). It will go on to either node $(i, n + 1)$ or $(i + 1, n + 1)$. Therefore, the probability of reaching node (i, n) by any particular path must equal the sum of the probabilities of reaching nodes $(i, n + 1)$ and $(i + 1, n + 1)$ via the same path. That is,

$$\frac{(n - i)!\,i!\,\psi(i, n)}{n!} = \frac{(n + 1 - i)!\,i!\,\psi(i, n + 1)}{(n + 1)!} + \frac{(n - i)!\,(i + 1)!\,\psi(i + 1, n + 1)}{(n + 1)!}.$$

Multiplying both sides of this equation by $n!/((n - i)!i!)$ gives equation (13.15).

Since the path involving a final up move occurs with probability

$$\frac{(n + 1 - i)!\,i!\,\psi(i, n + 1)}{(n + 1)!},$$

while one involving a final down move occurs with probability

$$\frac{(n - i)!\,(i + 1)!\,\psi(i + 1, n + 1)}{(n + 1)!},$$

the probability of an up move at node (i, n) must equal

$$\pi_u(i, n) = \frac{\frac{(n+1-i)!\,i!\,\psi(i,n+1)}{(n+1)!}}{\frac{(n+1-i)!\,i!\,\psi(i,n+1)}{(n+1)!} + \frac{(n-i)!\,(i+1)!\,\psi(i+1,n+1)}{(n+1)!}}.$$

This simplifies to equation (13.16), as required.

Equation (13.17) is derived in Appendix 13.A.1.

13.A.3 Properties of the State-variable Tree

We already know that the risk-neutral probability of an up move at node (i, n) that is implied by the tree of futures prices equals

$$\pi_u(i, n) = \frac{F_N(i, n) - F_N(i + 1, n + 1)}{F_N(i, n + 1) - F_N(i + 1, n + 1)}.$$

All that is required for the state-variable tree and the futures-price tree to be consistent is that they use the same risk-neutral probabilities. Solving (13.22) for $F_N(i, n)$ shows that

$$F_N(i, n) = \frac{\hat{F}_N}{\hat{F}_n} X(i, n).$$

If we use this equation to replace all the futures prices in the formula for $\pi_u(i, n)$ with values of the state variable, we obtain

$$\pi_u(i, n) = \frac{\frac{\hat{F}_N}{\hat{F}_n} X(i, n) - \frac{\hat{F}_N}{\hat{F}_{n+1}} X(i + 1, n + 1)}{\frac{\hat{F}_N}{\hat{F}_{n+1}} X(i, n + 1) - \frac{\hat{F}_N}{\hat{F}_{n+1}} X(i + 1, n + 1)}.$$

This reduces to

$$\pi_u(i, n) = \frac{K_n X(i, n) - X(i+1, n+1)}{X(i, n+1) - X(i+1, n+1)},$$

where

$$K_n = \frac{\hat{F}_{n+1}}{\hat{F}_n}$$

is exactly the same expression for the risk-adjusted growth factor that we used in Section 12.2.3. Therefore, the two trees are consistent provided that we use this value for K_n.

The analysis in Section 12.2.3 confirms the second property of the state-variable tree. There we demonstrated that the tree of state variables with K_n given above generates futures prices at node $(0, 0)$ that are equal to those observed in futures markets. Thus, our state-variable tree must also be consistent with the observed term structure of futures prices.

14

Calibrating Trees of Alternative State Variables

The previous two chapters have considered situations where the state variable is the price of a traded asset or commodity. We were able to exploit two key features. First, there is usually plenty of historical data to use to calibrate our models. Second, observed prices incorporate market-determined adjustments for risk, so that we do not always need to impose theoretical risk-adjustment models on the data.

In this chapter we consider the calibration problem when the state variable is not the price of a traded asset. It may, for example, be some measure of demand for a product, the difference between two prices (such as the spread between a firm's output and input prices), or the net revenue generated by a project. Another possibility, which has its own set of calibration techniques, is that the state variable is the market value of a recently completed project. In some cases it will be possible to use the techniques developed in Chapters 12 and 13 to calibrate trees of these variables, but in many cases it will not be. Therefore, in this chapter, we present some techniques for building binomial trees for state variables that are not the prices of traded assets.

The simplest possibility to consider is when the state variable must always be positive, percentage rates of change are believed to have constant volatility, and historical data are available. Then we can use the methods of Chapter 12 even though the state variable is not the price of a traded asset. We can calibrate the binomial tree using the methods of Section 12.1, starting by taking logarithms of the state variable and then modeling either a random walk or a mean-reverting process, depending on whether we believe shocks to the state variable are permanent (in which case we could use the random walk model of Section 12.1.1) or transitory (in which case we could use the mean-reverting model in Section 12.1.2). The risk-neutral probabilities can be estimated using the CAPM as described in Section 12.2.1. If futures or options on the state variable are traded, then we can use the techniques discussed in Sections 12.2.2 and 12.2.3 and Chapter 13.[1]

In this chapter we consider two situations in which this approach is not possible. In the first case, discussed in Section 14.1, it is not appropriate to model the logarithm of the state variable. The most obvious reason might be that the state variable can take negative values. In the second case, which is discussed in Section 14.2, the state variable is the market value of a project that has just been completed. The problem here is that the state variable cannot be observed directly. We conclude this chapter (and this part of the book) in Section 14.3 by briefly discussing the issues that we need to address when choosing a state variable to use as part of a real-options analysis of a problem.

Throughout this chapter we use the following example of investment in the agricultural chemical industry to illustrate the various calibration procedures.

Example 14.1. A firm has the option to reopen a mothballed nitrogen fertilizer manufacturing plant in the Corn Belt region of the US. The facility will cost $100 million to reopen and will be able to produce approximately one million tons of ammonia and urea ammonium nitrate solution annually. The option to reopen the plant is being evaluated at the end of January 2006 and will expire one year later.

The investment payoff depends on the market value of an operational nitrogen fertilizer plant which, in turn, depends on such factors as the price of natural gas (a key input in the production process) and the prices of the plant's main outputs, ammonia and urea ammonium nitrate solution.   ■

14.1 NON-PRICE STATE VARIABLES

If the state variable is always greater than zero and we believe that it is more volatile when its level is high than when it is low, we could model the logarithm of the state variable in exactly the same way that we analyzed prices in Sections 12.1 and 12.2. However, it will not always be appropriate to assume that the state variable must be positive. One such situation arises in the case of the fertilizer manufacturing plant introduced in Example 14.1.

Example 14.2. A fertilizer production plant uses approximately 33.5 MMBtu (million British thermal units) of natural gas to produce each ton of

---

1. Some non-price state variables are actually the basis for option contracts and other financial derivatives traded on exchanges. For example, it is possible to buy and sell options on crude oil stocks, price spreads, and weather conditions in various cities.

anhydrous ammonia fertilizer. A real-options analysis of the decision to reopen such a plant might therefore use

$$P = A - 33.5G$$

as the state variable, where A is the spot price of ammonia and G is the spot price of natural gas. We construct data on the price spread P using the US Gulf spot price for anhydrous ammonia (in dollars per ton) and the Henry Hub price for natural gas (in dollars per MMBtu). These are widely regarded as benchmark prices for fertilizers and wholesale natural gas in the US.[2] Our data are monthly and span the period from February 1996 to January 2006. Figure 14.1 plots the price spread over our sample period. Notice that the spread is negative at times during this period, which prevents us from using the approach described in Section 12.1.   ∎

In the case of the ammonia–natural gas price spread, the state variable becomes negative whenever the input price exceeds the output price. The procedure described in Section 12.1 is clearly not appropriate for such situations: for a start, we cannot take the logarithm of any negative values of the state variable. In this section we see how to calibrate a tree for state variables such as the ammonia–natural gas price spread, and how to estimate the risk-neutral probabilities.

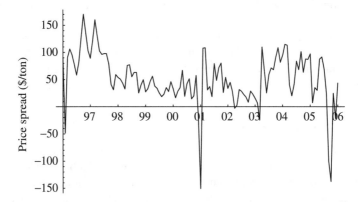

Figure 14.1. Spread between the prices of ammonia and natural gas

Note: The price spread is constructed using the US Gulf spot price for anhydrous ammonia (in dollars per ton) and the Henry Hub price for natural gas (in dollars per MMBtu), assuming that production of each ton of anhydrous ammonia requires 33.5 MMBtu of natural gas.

---

2. Useful background on the US nitrogen fertilizer industry can be found in Huang (2007).

14.1.1 Calibrating the Tree for the State Variable

We follow exactly the same procedure as in Section 12.1, but applied to the state variable rather than its logarithm. All that changes is that we do not take logarithms of our historical observations of the state variable. That is, we fit the regression (either (12.1) or (12.10)) using the state variable (rather than its logarithm) as p_j, then proceed in the usual way, normalizing the parameters and building the binomial tree using

$$X(i, n) = X_0 + (n - 2i)\hat{\sigma}\sqrt{\Delta t_m}. \tag{14.1}$$

Estimated volatility $\hat{\sigma}$ is given by (12.4) if the state variable follows a random walk and in (12.13) if it is mean reverting.

Equation (14.1) provides the simplest way to fill in the tree for the state variable because it provides a straightforward expression for the state variable at each node. However, it is interesting to see how the levels of the state variable at different nodes compare. For example,

$$X(i, n + 1) = X_0 + ((n + 1) - 2i)\hat{\sigma}\sqrt{\Delta t_m} = X(i, n) + \hat{\sigma}\sqrt{\Delta t_m}. \tag{14.2}$$

That is, each up move involves *adding*

$$U = \hat{\sigma}\sqrt{\Delta t_m}$$

to the current level of the state variable. Similarly,

$$X(i + 1, n + 1) = X(i, n) - \hat{\sigma}\sqrt{\Delta t_m}, \tag{14.3}$$

so that each down move involves adding

$$D = -\hat{\sigma}\sqrt{\Delta t_m}.$$

Thus, rather than up and down moves being multiplicative as in Section 12.1, they are now additive.

The probability of an up move is given by (12.9) or (12.16)—depending on whether the state variable follows a random walk or is mean reverting—but is applied to the level of the state variable, rather than its logarithm. In the first case, the probability of an up move at node (i, n) is

$$\theta_u(i, n) = \frac{1}{2} + \frac{\hat{\mu}\sqrt{\Delta t_m}}{2\hat{\sigma}},$$

while in the second case it equals

$$\theta_u(i, n) = \begin{cases} 0 & \text{if } \frac{1}{2} + \frac{(1-e^{-\hat{a}\Delta t_m})(\hat{b}-X(i,n))}{2\hat{\sigma}\sqrt{\Delta t_m}} \leq 0, \\ \frac{1}{2} + \frac{(1-e^{-\hat{a}\Delta t_m})(\hat{b}-X(i,n))}{2\hat{\sigma}\sqrt{\Delta t_m}} & \text{if } 0 < \frac{1}{2} + \frac{(1-e^{-\hat{a}\Delta t_m})(\hat{b}-X(i,n))}{2\hat{\sigma}\sqrt{\Delta t_m}} < 1, \\ 1 & \text{if } \frac{1}{2} + \frac{(1-e^{-\hat{a}\Delta t_m})(\hat{b}-X(i,n))}{2\hat{\sigma}\sqrt{\Delta t_m}} \geq 1. \end{cases} \tag{14.4}$$

Thus, the calibration process is exactly as in Section 12.1, except that we apply it to the state variable rather than the logarithm of the state variable. We illustrate the procedure in the following example.

Example 14.3. Estimating the AR(1) model for the price spread using the ordinary least-squares method results in the estimated relationship

$$P_{j+1} - P_j = \underset{(5.62)}{25.60} - \underset{(0.0796)}{0.5030}P_j + u_{j+1}, \quad \text{Var}[u_{j+1}] = 1756, \quad (14.5)$$

where the numbers in brackets indicate the standard errors of the associated parameter estimates. It follows that the parameters we need in order to evaluate the equations in (12.13) are

$$\hat{\alpha}_0 = 25.60, \quad \hat{\alpha}_1 = -0.5030, \quad \hat{\phi} = \sqrt{1756} = 41.90.$$

Since the data are monthly, we have $\Delta t_d = 1/12$. Substituting these parameters into (12.13) shows that the normalized estimates of the parameters are

$$\hat{a} = \frac{-\log(1 + \hat{\alpha}_1)}{\Delta t_d} = \frac{-\log(1 - 0.5030)}{1/12} = 8.390,$$

$$\hat{b} = \frac{-\hat{\alpha}_0}{\hat{\alpha}_1} = \frac{-25.60}{-0.5030} = 50.90,$$

and

$$\hat{\sigma} = \hat{\phi}\left(\frac{2\log(1 + \hat{\alpha}_1)}{\hat{\alpha}_1(2 + \hat{\alpha}_1)\Delta t_d}\right)^{1/2} = 41.90\left(\frac{2\log(1 - 0.5030)}{-0.5030 \times (2 - 0.5030) \times (1/12)}\right)^{1/2}$$

$$= 197.8.$$

This gives us all the information we need to build a binomial tree for the price spread. Date 0 in the tree corresponds to the end of January 2006, when the price spread was $X_0 = 43.76$. Each step in the tree represents half a month, so that $\Delta t_m = 1/24$, and we extend the tree three months into the future.[3] The sizes of up and down moves are

$$U = \hat{\sigma}\sqrt{\Delta t_m} = 197.8\sqrt{1/24} = 40.38$$

and

$$D = -\hat{\sigma}\sqrt{\Delta t_m} = -197.8\sqrt{1/24} = -40.38$$

respectively. The resulting binomial tree for the price spread is shown in the top panel of Table 14.1.

---

3. If we were using the price spread to analyze the problem described in Example 14.1 then we would need to extend the tree much further into the future—past the one-year lifetime of the option and well into the life of the fertilizer plant once it has been reopened. Thus, the tree we present here is built only to illustrate the calibration procedure.

Table 14.1. A Mean-reverting Process for the Ammonia–Natural Gas Price Spread

$X(i, n)$	0	1	2	3	4	5	6
0	43.76	84.14	124.52	164.89	205.27	245.65	286.03
1		3.38	43.76	84.14	124.52	164.89	205.27
2			−37.00	3.38	43.76	84.14	124.52
3				−77.37	−37.00	3.38	43.76
4					−117.75	−77.37	−37.00
5						−158.13	−117.75
6							−198.51

$\theta_u(i, n)$	0	1	2	3	4	5	6
0	0.5261	0.3786	0.2311	0.0836	0.0000	0.0000	0.0000
1		0.6736	0.5261	0.3786	0.2311	0.0836	0.0000
2			0.8211	0.6736	0.5261	0.3786	0.2311
3				0.9686	0.8211	0.6736	0.5261
4					1.0000	0.9686	0.8211
5						1.0000	1.0000
6							1.0000

The next move is certain to be down whenever

$$X(i, n) \geq \hat{b} + \frac{\hat{\sigma}\sqrt{\Delta t_m}}{1 - e^{-\hat{a}\Delta t_m}} = 50.90 + \frac{197.8\sqrt{1/24}}{1 - e^{-8.390 \times (1/24)}} = 187.77.$$

It is certain to be up whenever

$$X(i, n) \leq \hat{b} - \frac{\hat{\sigma}\sqrt{\Delta t_m}}{1 - e^{-\hat{a}\Delta t_m}} = 50.90 - \frac{197.8\sqrt{1/24}}{1 - e^{-8.390 \times (1/24)}} = -85.97.$$

There will be positive probabilities attached to both up and down moves between these two bounds. The precise probabilities, calculated using (14.4), are given in the bottom panel of Table 14.1. Reflecting the mean reversion evident in the historical data, a down move is much more likely than an up move in those parts of the table where the price spread is high, whereas up moves become much more likely in those parts where the price spread is low. Some nodes cannot be reached at all. These nodes are represented by the shaded cells in the table. For example, since the next move is certain to be up at node $(4, 4)$, we cannot possibly reach node $(5, 5)$. ∎

14.1.2 Calibrating Risk-neutral Probabilities

From equation (3.7), the CAPM implies that the risk-neutral probability of an up move equals

$$\pi_u(i, n) = \theta_u(i, n) - \frac{(E[\tilde{R}_m] - R_f)\beta_X}{X(i, n + 1) - X(i + 1, n + 1)}$$

at node (i, n), where

$$\beta_X = \frac{\text{Cov}[\tilde{X}, \tilde{R}_m]}{\text{Var}[\tilde{R}_m]}$$

is the CAPM beta applied to the level of the state variable.[4] The additive nature of up and down moves, as described in equations (14.2) and (14.3), allows us to write

$$\pi_u(i, n) = \theta_u(i, n) - \frac{(E[\tilde{R}_m] - R_f)\beta_X}{U - D}.$$

The calibration process is illustrated in the following example, which estimates the risk-neutral probabilities for the price-spread tree in Table 14.1.

Example 14.4. As in Example 12.4, we use the S&P 500 total return index as our proxy for the market portfolio. When we regress the residuals from (14.5) on a constant and the realized return on the S&P 500 index we obtain

$$\hat{u}_j = -0.6358 + 87.84 r_{m,j} + v_j.$$
$$\quad\quad (3.8611) \quad\quad (87.37)$$

Since the state variable is mean reverting, we apply the adjustment described in Appendix 12.A.3 to convert our β_X estimate from the monthly frequency of our data to the twice-monthly frequency of our binomial tree. The resulting estimate of β_X equals

$$\beta_X = 87.84\sqrt{\frac{\Delta t_d}{\Delta t_m} \cdot \frac{1 - e^{-2\hat{a}\Delta t_m}}{1 - e^{-2\hat{a}\Delta t_d}}} = 87.84\sqrt{\frac{1/12}{1/24} \cdot \frac{1 - e^{-2\times 8.390\times(1/24)}}{1 - e^{-2\times 8.390\times(1/12)}}} = 101.53.$$

In their survey of Chief Financial Officers carried out in November 2005, Graham and Harvey (2007) found a median market risk premium of 2.5% per annum. Given that each step in our binomial tree represents half a month, we use $E[\tilde{R}_m] - R_f = 0.025 \times (1/24) = 0.001042$ as our estimate of the market risk premium. The risk-neutral probabilities of up moves can therefore be found by subtracting

$$\frac{(E[\tilde{R}_m] - R_f)\beta_X}{U - D} = \frac{0.001042 \times 101.53}{40.38 - (-40.38)} = 0.0013$$

from the actual probabilities in the bottom panel of Table 14.1. ∎

---

4. There are four exceptions. When $\theta_u(i, n)$ equals zero or one we set $\pi_u(i, n)$ equal to zero or one respectively, so that the certain cash flow is discounted at the risk-free interest rate. Otherwise, when subtracting $(E[\tilde{R}_m] - R_f)\beta_X/(X(i, n + 1) - X(i + 1, n + 1))$ would make $\pi_u(i, n)$ negative, we set the risk-neutral probability of an up move equal to zero; when it would make $\pi_u(i, n)$ greater than one, we set the risk-neutral probability of an up move equal to one.

At this stage we have all we need to implement our valuation model. However, it can be useful to interpret our measure of systematic risk, β_X, in terms of the more familiar return-beta of the CAPM. For example, when beta is calculated using rates of return as in Section 12.2.1, we can say that an asset with $\beta = 1$ has the same amount of systematic risk as the market portfolio, and that an asset with $\beta = 0.5$ has half as much risk. Clearly, the ammonia–natural gas price spread does not have more than a hundred times the risk of the market portfolio! Therefore, we conclude this section by seeing how to interpret β_X in terms of the traditional RADR formulation of the CAPM.

The approach we follow is to calculate the market value at date 0 of a cash flow of $X(\cdot, n)$ to be received at date n, for a range of values of n, and then to infer from these market values the corresponding RADRs. We work through the details for the case where $n = 1$ here, and leave consideration of other cases to Problem 14.2.

The expected value of the cash flow to be received at date 1 is

$$E[X(\cdot, 1)] = \theta_u(0, 0)X(0, 1) + (1 - \theta_u(0, 0))X(1, 1),$$

while the market value of this cash flow at date 0 is

$$V_1(0, 0) = \frac{\pi_u(0, 0)X(0, 1) + (1 - \pi_u(0, 0))X(1, 1)}{R_f}.$$

The *annualized* RADR implied by this market value, which we denote by ρ_1, satisfies

$$V_1(0, 0) = \frac{E[X(\cdot, 1)]}{(1 + \rho_1)^{\Delta t_m}},$$

where Δt_m is the length of each time step in the binomial tree. That is,

$$\rho_1 = \left(\frac{E[X(\cdot, 1)]}{V_1(0, 0)}\right)^{1/\Delta t_m} - 1.$$

Example 14.5. For the example considered throughout this section, the expected value of the state variable after one period is

$$E[X(\cdot, 1)] = \theta_u(0, 0)X(0, 1) + (1 - \theta_u(0, 0))X(1, 1)$$

$$= 0.5261 \times 84.14 + (1 - 0.5261) \times 3.38$$

$$= 45.87.$$

In order to estimate the market value of an asset that pays $X(\cdot, 1)$ at date 1 we need an estimate of R_f. We are ultimately interested in building a binomial tree that spans three months, so we use the yield on three-month US Treasury Bills at the end of January 2006, which was 4.47%. Because the calculation of this yield assumes semi-annual compounding, the implied return on a one-year risk-free bond is

$$\left(1 + \frac{0.0447}{2}\right)^2 = 1.04520.$$

This implies a return on one-period risk-free bonds equal to $R_f = (1.04520)^{1/24} = 1.001844$. Since the risk-neutral probability of an up move at node $(0, 0)$ is

$$\pi_u(0, 0) = \theta_u(0, 0) - 0.0013 = 0.5248,$$

the estimated market value of the asset is

$$V_1(0, 0) = \frac{0.5248 \times 84.14 + (1 - 0.5248) \times 3.38}{1.001844} = 45.68.$$

It follows that the (annualized) one-period RADR for price-spread risk is

$$\rho_1 = \left(\frac{E[X(\cdot, 1)]}{V_1(0, 0)}\right)^{1/\Delta t_m} - 1 = \left(\frac{45.87}{45.68}\right)^{24} - 1 = 0.1047,$$

or 10.47% per annum.

When we repeat this procedure for all values of $n = 1, 2, \ldots, 24$ we obtain the RADRs plotted as the solid curve in Figure 14.2. The RADR is high for short-term price-spread risk, but converges to a long-run level of approximately 4.65% per annum. The dashed curves in the graph show the term structure of RADRs for three other values of the current price spread. The middle curve shows what happens when $X_0 = \hat{b} = 50.90$, which is the long-run level of the price spread. The bottom curve corresponds to $X_0 = \hat{b} + \hat{\sigma}/\sqrt{2\hat{a}} = 99.19$, which is one standard deviation above the long-run level, while the top curve corresponds to $X_0 = \hat{b} - \hat{\sigma}/\sqrt{2\hat{a}} = 2.61$.[5]

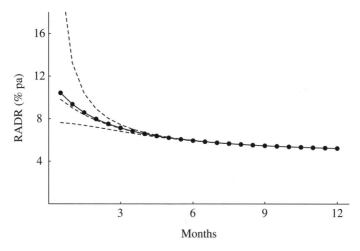

Figure 14.2. The term structure of price-spread risk

---

5. The discussion in Section 12.1.2 shows that the long-run distribution of the spread has mean b and variance $\sigma^2/2a$.

In all cases the RADR falls to the same long-run level as the cash flow occurs further in the future, but the short-term price risk is a decreasing function of the current level of the price spread.[6]

The cause of this behavior can be found in the fact that the size of the shock to the price spread is independent of the level of the spread. This property, which is a consequence of our assumption that the spread follows an AR(1) process, means that the covariance between the shock to the price spread and the return on the market portfolio is also independent of the level of the spread. As a result, we subtract the same (dollar) risk premium from the expected value of the state variable after one period, regardless of the current spread. The proportional effect will be relatively small when the expected value is large (which will be the case when the current level of the price spread is high), implying a relatively low RADR. For distant cash flows, the expected value of the cash flow is not especially sensitive to the current spread, so that the proportional effect of subtracting a constant dollar risk premium from the expected value will be similar for all levels of the current spread.   ■

In principle, the techniques we apply to the price spread in Examples 14.2–14.5 can be applied to any state variable for which we have historical data. Now we consider some especially useful techniques that we can use when the state variable is the market value of a recently completed project.

14.2 MARKET VALUES AS STATE VARIABLES

In this section we consider some of the issues that arise when we make the state variable the market value of a recently completed project. We made exactly this choice in the investment timing problem analyzed in Sections 7.2, 8.2, and 9.3, as well as the land development problem in Section 9.2. In all of these examples the risk associated with fluctuations in the market value of the completed project is an important source of risk confronting the owner of the project rights. The market value of the completed project was thus an obvious choice for the state variable.[7] Using this state variable keeps the model relatively simple. For example, it would be much more difficult to analyze the investment timing problem if

---

6. However, the RADR is only sensitive to the current level of the price spread for horizons so short that discounting plays a minor role. Thus, the discount factor $(1 + \rho_n)^{-n\Delta t_m}$ will be quite insensitive to the current level of the price spread for all values of n. This is demonstrated in Problem 14.2.

7. There will be situations in which the market value of the completed project is *not* a sensible choice of state variable. In some cases it may not even make sense to think of a "completed project". (Consider, for example, the option to temporarily suspend production in Sections 6.2 and 10.2, or the resource extraction problem in Section 8.3.) In other cases, it may not be possible to express relevant cash flows in terms of the market value of any single "project" (as in the machinery-replacement problem of Section 10.3).

the state variable had been demand for the completed project's output. It would be more difficult still if we attempted to incorporate the individual sources of risk—revenues, operating costs, and so on—explicitly in the valuation model.

The information needed to build a tree for the state variable here is the same as for any other choice of state variable: we need to know its current value, the sizes of up and down moves throughout the tree, the probabilities of up moves occurring, and the risk-neutral probabilities.

14.2.1 Using Comparison Firms

At first glance it appears that this state variable is the price of a traded asset. Indeed, at any particular node the state variable is the price of a newly-built project—which, even if it is not actually being traded at present, can in principle be traded in the future. However, in this case the "underlying asset" is different at different dates. For example, $X(0, 0)$ is the price of a project if it is completed at node $(0, 0)$, while $X(0, 1)$ is the price of a (necessarily different) project if it is completed at node $(0, 1)$. Thus, the state variable represented in the binomial tree is not the price of a single traded asset.

Recall from Chapter 3 that our approach to estimating the market value of an asset is to build a replicating portfolio made up of just enough units of the risk-free bond and a spanning asset so that the portfolio generates the same cash flow as the asset being valued. The risk-neutral probability of an up move at node (i, n) equals

$$\pi_u(i, n) = \frac{Z(i, n)R_f - X(i+1, n+1)}{X(i, n+1) - X(i+1, n+1)},$$

where $Z(i, n)$ is the market value at node (i, n) of an asset that pays $X(i, n+1)$ after one period if the next move is up and $X(i+1, n+1)$ if it is down. We cannot use the "newly-built project" as the spanning asset because if the project is newly built when we set up our replicating portfolio it will not be newly built one period later. What we do instead is use a portfolio containing ongoing firms—which are traded (or tradable) assets—to replicate the payoff of the spanning asset.

We need to identify ongoing firms that are similar to the project under investigation. These so-called comparison firms must be undertaking just enough capital expenditure to maintain their current condition: that is, their assets are not deteriorating, but neither are the firms being transformed by new investment. The market values of such firms then serve as a reasonable proxy for the market value of a newly-built project. In some circumstances we can use historical data on the firms' market value to calibrate the tree for the state variable and to estimate the risk-neutral probabilities. We describe two such situations here.

First, consider a generic comparison firm. Suppose that it is worth $X(i, n)$ at node (i, n) and that its free cash flow at that node equals $C(i, n)$. This is the difference between the cash flow from operations and cash investment. If we purchased the firm at date n we would have to pay $X(i, n)$. We would immediately receive the cash flow from the firm's operations and then incur just enough expenditure to maintain the firm in its current state; that is, we would receive cash flow equal to $C(i, n)$. The net expenditure at date n would therefore equal $X(i, n) - C(i, n)$. After one period elapses the firm would be worth $X(i, n + 1)$ if an up move occurs and $X(i + 1, n + 1)$ if a down move occurs. The law of one price implies that

$$Z(i, n) = X(i, n) - C(i, n),$$

so that the risk-neutral probability of an up move equals

$$\pi_u(i, n) = \frac{(X(i, n) - C(i, n))R_f - X(i + 1, n + 1)}{X(i, n + 1) - X(i + 1, n + 1)} \tag{14.6}$$

for this problem.

The second case arises in the context of resource extraction problems, for which it is often sensible to let $X(i, n)$ equal the market value of one unit of the resource at node (i, n). Consider a firm that owns 100 units of the resource, which it is currently depleting at the constant rate δ. For simplicity, we assume that the firm has no outstanding debt and has issued 100 shares. The firm generates a net cash flow of $C(i, n)$ per share at node (i, n), where—because each share currently amounts to ownership of one unit of the resource—the share price is $X(i, n)$. If we acquired $e^{\delta \Delta t}$ of the firm's shares then we would have to spend $e^{\delta \Delta t} X(i, n)$ at date n, but we would receive cash flow of $e^{\delta \Delta t} C(i, n)$ immediately, implying net expenditure of $e^{\delta \Delta t}(X(i, n) - C(i, n))$. In return, we would own $e^{\delta \Delta t}$ units of the resource at date n and therefore just one unit at date $n + 1$, with market value $X(\cdot, n + 1)$. This is exactly the payoff of the spanning asset, so that the law of one price implies

$$Z(i, n) = e^{\delta \Delta t}(X(i, n) - C(i, n)).$$

The risk-neutral probability of an up move therefore equals

$$\pi_u(i, n) = \frac{e^{\delta \Delta t}(X(i, n) - C(i, n))R_f - X(i + 1, n + 1)}{X(i, n + 1) - X(i + 1, n + 1)}$$

at node (i, n).

With both of these possibilities, the challenge of estimating the required parameters remains. While using the market value of the completed project as the state variable offers the possibility of using market prices as described here, it will not always be easy to do so. We generally need to be quite creative in the data we choose and to make sure that our comparison firms really are comparable. Even firms that are apparently within the same industry will often differ substantially from the completed project that underlies our real-option problem. For example, one way in which errors can be introduced is if the comparison firm contains embedded growth options not present in the project under investigation.[8]

---

8. However, one advantage of using comparison firms is that we can reasonably assume that their market value incorporates the value of any real options that are embedded in the completed project: this will be the case if the firms are managed optimally and financial markets are efficient.

For example, using a pharmaceutical firm as a comparison firm for a completed R&D project is not generally appropriate as the pharmaceutical firm's share price reflects its own R&D programs. Similarly, if we are analyzing the option to explore and develop an oil reserve, only firms whose main assets are proven developed reserves provide suitable comparisons for the completed project (that is, for a developed oil reserve).

The next example describes a firm that provides a reasonable comparison for the project introduced in Example 14.1.

> **Example 14.6.** Terra Nitrogen Company L.P. owns and operates a nitrogen fertilizer manufacturing facility in Oklahoma, as well as terminal operations in Nebraska and Illinois. The facility's principal outputs, ammonia and urea ammonium nitrate solution, are sold to customers in the Central and Southern Plains and Cornbelt regions of the US. The facility can produce 1.1 million tons of ammonia and 2.3 million tons of urea ammonium nitrate solution annually. Terra Industries Inc. holds 75% of the outstanding units of TNCLP, and the remaining 25% are traded on the New York Stock Exchange. TNCLP's structure requires it to pay all free cash flow in dividends.
>
> At the end of December 2005, TNCLP had almost no debt, 18.69 million shares outstanding with a closing price of $24.55, and cash (and cash equivalents) worth $34.0 million. In 2005, TNCLP had free cash flow of $14.8 million. ∎

14.2.2 Enterprise Value versus Equity Value

Recall that we are trying to model the behavior of the market value of a particular asset using data on a firm that owns a similar asset (and little else). We cannot just consider the market value of the comparison firm's equity, because some of the cash flow generated by the asset is paid to the firm's bondholders. Thus, the starting point of our analysis is the sum of the market value of the firm's equity and the market value of its debt. However, part of this sum will derive from the comparison firm's cash holding: since we are interested only in the behavior of the market value of a particular asset, we need to strip out the effect of cash holdings from our analysis. We do this by decomposing the value of the firm into

$$\text{debt} + \text{equity} = \text{enterprise} + \text{cash}, \qquad (14.7)$$

where "enterprise" measures the market value of the firm's non-cash assets. Thus, we focus our attention on the comparison firm's enterprise value, which equals the sum of the market value of the firm's outstanding shares, debt, minority interest and preferred shares, minus its total cash and cash equivalents. Where data on the market value of a firm's debt are unavailable or unreliable, and that firm's debt has relatively low risk, we often use the book value of the firm's debt as a proxy for its market value.

Once we have estimated a comparison firm's enterprise value we need to translate this into an estimate of the market value of a newly-built project of the type appearing in our real-options problem. The following example demonstrates one way to perform this translation.

Example 14.7. The situation considered in Example 14.1 involves a nitrogen fertilizer plant that will be able to produce a total of one million tons of ammonia and urea ammonium nitrate solution each year. The TNCLP plant in Example 14.6 can produce 1.1 million tons of ammonia and 2.3 million tons of urea ammonium nitrate solution each year. At the end of December 2005 TNCLP had a market capitalization of \$458.8 million, implying an enterprise value of \$424.8 million. Thus, one estimate of the market value of a newly-built plant is

$$\frac{1}{1.1 + 2.3} \times 424.8 = 124.95$$

million dollars.[9,10]   ■

In practice we may not wish to use the comparison firms to estimate the current level of the state variable as in Example 14.7, deciding that project-specific factors would make the resulting estimate unreliable. However, comparison firms may still provide useful information regarding the volatility of the project's market value, even if they do not provide much information about the level of its market value. Obtaining such volatility estimates is our next task.

14.2.3 Estimating Volatility

We are interested in the volatility of the comparison firm's enterprise value. Referring back to equation (14.7), and noting that cash holdings and the market value of debt will be relatively stable, we see that the change in enterprise value over any given period will approximately equal the change in equity value. However, depending on the relative amounts of the firm's cash and debt, the volatility of the enterprise value will be greater than or less than the volatility of its equity value. For example, a firm with little cash and substantial debt will have an enterprise value much larger than its equity value. Thus, the proportional change in enterprise value over any period will be smaller than the proportional change in equity value—the absolute changes are approximately equal, but the base values are different.

We estimate the volatility of the comparison firm's enterprise value by first measuring the volatility of its equity value and then "de-levering" our estimate.

---

9. This is likely to overestimate the market value of a newly-built plant, given that TNCLP owns terminal facilities as well as its manufacturing plant in Oklahoma.

10. The calculation here does not allow for any economies of scale in plant operation. Where this is believed to be an issue and data are available on a selection of plants of differing sizes, we could regress enterprise value on plant size in order to estimate the market value of a newly-built project.

As we shall see, the de-levering procedure is straightforward. It is analogous to the procedure for converting equity betas into asset betas that should be familiar to anyone who has estimated the cost of capital as part of a capital budgeting exercise.[11] As with any use of comparison firms, the results will be only as good as the choice of comparison firms—and finding firms that are a good match for the project under consideration will not always be easy. Ultimately, we have to trade off the good and the bad. The "good" in this case is that we are usually able to estimate the comparison firm's equity volatility very accurately; the "bad" is that the equity volatility of this firm may not be a good estimate of the enterprise volatility of the project we are analyzing. As with all calibration exercises, the decision whether or not to use the approach described in this section depends on the analyst's judgment of this trade off.

Let N_j denote the enterprise value of the comparison firm at observation j; that is, $N_j = D_j + E_j - A_j$, where D_j is the market value of the comparison firm's debt, E_j is the market value of its equity, and A_j is its holding of cash and cash equivalents. In this section we assume that log N_j follows a random walk with drift. We are interested in estimating the normalized drift and volatility of the process for the log enterprise value. One possibility would be to do so directly: gather time series data on the enterprise value, take logarithms, take differences, and normalize the mean and standard deviation of the change in the logarithm of the enterprise value. That is, we implement the process described in Section 12.1.1, but apply it to the enterprise value rather than the price of an item. However, while it should not be too difficult to gather data on the market value of the firm's equity with a sufficiently high frequency for our estimates to be meaningful, finding data on the value of debt will be much more difficult. We therefore need a method for estimating the volatility of the log enterprise value that does not rely on having access to high-frequency debt value data.

As we show in Appendix 14.A, provided the market value of the firm's debt is relatively stable over time, the change in the logarithm of the enterprise value can be written

$$\Delta \log N_j \approx \frac{\Delta \log E_j}{1 + \frac{D_j - A_j}{E_j}}.$$

In all-equity firms that hold no cash, the change in log enterprise value will be equal to the change in log equity value. However, as leverage increases, shocks will be borne disproportionately by the equity value, with the value of debt being relatively stable. Just as financial leverage can increase a firm's systematic risk (as measured by its equity beta), so it amplifies total risk (as measured by the firm's equity return volatility). Thus, we estimate the mean and standard deviation of equity

---

11. See, for example, pp. 377–391 of Grinblatt and Titman (2002).

returns and scale them back by dividing both by one plus the (net) debt:equity ratio to obtain estimates of the mean and standard deviation of changes in the log enterprise value.[12]

We now demonstrate the estimation procedure in the context of the situation considered in Example 14.1.

Example 14.8. If we use ten years of weekly share price data on TNCLP, ending at 31 January 2006, we find that the average weekly change in the log share price equals -0.00009911, while the standard deviation equals 0.07953. The firm has no outstanding debt, but we do need to make an adjustment for its cash holding. Using the most recent values of debt, equity, and cash, we see that this adjustment amounts to dividing the mean and standard deviation by

$$1 + \frac{\text{debt} - \text{cash}}{\text{equity}} = 1 + \frac{0 - 34}{458.8} = 0.9259.$$

Our estimates for the mean and standard deviation of the weekly change in log enterprise value are therefore

$$\hat{v} = \frac{-0.00009911}{0.9259} = -0.0001070$$

and

$$\hat{\phi} = \frac{0.07953}{0.9259} = 0.08589$$

respectively. The normalized values are

$$\hat{\mu} = \frac{\hat{v}}{\Delta t_d} = \frac{-0.0001070}{1/52} = -0.005566$$

and

$$\hat{\sigma} = \frac{\hat{\phi}}{\sqrt{\Delta t_d}} = \frac{0.08589}{\sqrt{1/52}} = 0.6194.$$

Recall that our estimate of the current market value of a completed project is $X_0 = 124.95$. We build a binomial tree comprising four quarterly steps, so that $\Delta t_m = 1/4$ and up and down moves are

$$U = e^{\hat{\sigma} \sqrt{\Delta t_m}} = e^{0.6194 \times \sqrt{1/4}} = 1.3630$$

---

12. Strictly speaking, because of time variation in the debt:equity ratio we should scale the change in log equity value *before* we calculate the mean and standard deviation. However, given that we usually have access to higher frequency data on share prices than on debt values, it may be necessary to use some long-run average of the debt:equity ratio, in which case either we can take the mean and standard deviation of the scaled change in log equity values, or we can scale the mean and standard deviation of the (unscaled) change in log equity values.

Table 14.2. The Real Option to Invest in a Fertilizer Manufacturing Facility

$X(i, n)$	0	1	2	3	4
0	124.95	170.31	232.14	316.41	431.27
1		91.67	124.95	170.31	232.14
2			67.26	91.67	124.95
3				49.35	67.26
4					36.20

$V(i, n)$	0	1	2	3	4
0	42.08	76.03	132.14	216.41	331.27
1		17.59	35.67	70.31	132.14
2			4.45	10.54	24.95
3				0.00	0.00
4					0.00

and

$$D = e^{-\hat{\sigma}\sqrt{\Delta t_m}} = e^{-0.6194 \times \sqrt{1/4}} = 0.7337.$$

Up moves occur with probability

$$\theta_u = \frac{1}{2} + \frac{\hat{\mu}\sqrt{\Delta t_m}}{2\hat{\sigma}} = \frac{1}{2} + \frac{-0.005566 \times \sqrt{1/4}}{2 \times 0.6194} = 0.4978.$$

The top panel of Table 14.2 shows how the state variable evolves in this case. ∎

We used historical share price data in this example, but in principle any estimate of equity return volatility can be used. For example, if equity options are traded on the comparison firm's stock then we could use the level of volatility that is implied by current option prices.

One approach that we should *not* adopt is to use the estimated volatility of an underlying factor as our estimate of the volatility of the market value of a project. For example, we should not use the volatility of the spot price of crude oil to estimate the volatility of the market value of a developed oil reserve. Features such as operating leverage mean that a project's market value may have a quite different volatility from the underlying factors that determine that market value. Unless we can estimate the relative volatilities, we cannot use the factor-volatility directly.[13]

---

13. Davis (1998) derives the theoretical relationship between the volatility of a project's market value and that of its output price in various situations. Even in the relatively simple cases he

14.2.4 Estimating Risk-neutral Probabilities

The only problem remaining is to estimate the risk-neutral probabilities. From equation (14.6), the risk-neutral probability of an up move equals

$$\pi_u = \frac{(1 - C/X)R_f - D}{U - D},$$

where C is an estimate of the comparison firm's free cash flow and X is its enterprise value. This approach is demonstrated in the following example.

Example 14.9. The one-year risk-free rate (the yield on a one-year Treasury Bill) was 4.58% per annum at the end of January 2006. As we explained in Example 14.5, because this yield is based on semi-annual compounding, the implied return on a one-year risk-free bond is

$$\left(1 + \frac{0.0458}{2}\right)^2 = 1.04632.$$

This implies a return on one-period risk-free bonds equal to $R_f = (1.04632)^{1/4}$ = 1.01139. Since TNCLP's free cash flow was \$14.8 million in 2005 (or \$3.7 million per quarter) and the enterprise value was \$424.8 million at the end of 2005, we set

$$\frac{C}{X} = \frac{3.7}{424.8} = 0.008709.$$

The risk-neutral probability of an up move therefore equals

$$\pi_u = \frac{(1 - C/X)R_f - D}{U - D} = \frac{(1 - 0.008709) \times 1.01139 - 0.7337}{1.3630 - 0.7337} = 0.4273$$

at each node.

Assuming the plant can be reopened instantaneously, at date 4 the owner either invests in the project, paying $I = 100$ and immediately receiving a completed project worth $X(i, 4)$, or allows the investment option to die. Thus, the project rights are worth $V(i, 4) = \max\{X(i, 4) - I, 0\}$ at each node $(i, 4)$. At each earlier date n, the owner can either invest or wait, so that

$$V(i, n) = \max\left\{X(i, n) - I, \frac{\pi_u(i, n)V(i, n + 1) + \pi_d(i, n)V(i + 1, n + 1)}{R_f}\right\}.$$

The terminal condition and recursive equation allow us to fill in the tree for the market value of the project rights, which is shown in the bottom

---

considers, the ratio of the two volatilities can vary over time, making estimation of market-value volatility from output-price volatility extremely difficult. Because of the complications involved, this process is best avoided in practice.

panel of Table 14.2. Shaded cells indicate nodes where investment is optimal. The optimal policy is therefore to delay investment for at least six months. ∎

14.3 THE CHOICE OF STATE VARIABLE

In this chapter we have developed techniques for calibrating trees for state variables that are not the prices of traded assets. When we use non-price state variables we are more likely to have to rely on theoretical models such as the CAPM and on comparison firms that may not make for especially good comparisons. So why use such state variables? Why not use some underlying commodity price, for example?

As long as financial markets are reasonably efficient they will generally do a better job of estimating the value of assets than we can. This, after all, is the rationale for the valuation approach that we developed in Chapter 3. Therefore we should try to keep our models as close to the data as possible. For example, if we are analyzing an option to develop an oil reserve, then we might use the market value of developed reserves as the state variable. By doing so, we would be using the information that market prices reveal about the value of developed reserves and concentrating our efforts on analyzing the option to convert undeveloped reserves into developed ones. We could, if we wished, take the price of crude oil as the state variable and then try to model the market value of developed reserves in terms of the spot price (perhaps using the methods in Section 8.3). However, this approach presumes that our analysis can uncover some component of value in this particular developed reserve that the market is unaware of. If the reserve we are analyzing is special in some way, then this might be an entirely reasonable approach. But if it is not, then we need to ask ourselves what we can uncover that the market cannot. All we might achieve by attempting to model the reserve in terms of a more fundamental variable, such as the price of crude oil, is to introduce substantial error into our calculations. If we are really interested in the option to develop undeveloped reserves, then perhaps the prospect of introducing such errors is not worthwhile. We should, in short, trust the market to accurately value developed reserves.

However, the choice is not always clear cut. If we model the situation down as far as input and output prices, we should be able to calibrate the tree for the state variable relatively accurately: there should be ample data available, and we might be able to use futures and option prices to estimate the market adjustment for risk. Because we cannot possibly incorporate all the features of the decision maker's situation in our model, in doing so we introduce the possibility of substantial model error. In contrast, if we adopt the market value of the newly-completed project as the state variable, much of this model risk disappears. This comes at the expense of substantial estimation error, because even though we may be able to estimate the behavior of the market value of a comparison firm accurately, this comparison firm might not be especially relevant for a problem. Thus, estimation error will be especially high if there are few truly comparable comparison firms for us to use.

Ultimately we must trade off estimation error and model error when choosing a state variable.

14.4 PROBLEMS

14.1. **(Practice)** Consider the calibration of the ammonia–natural gas price spread in Section 14.1.

(a) Using the values of $\hat{a}$, $\hat{b}$, and $\hat{\sigma}$ in Example 14.3, build a tree for the price spread with 13 weekly periods (that is, $\Delta t_m = 1/52$).

(b) For each parameter $\hat{a}$, $\hat{b}$, and $\hat{\sigma}$ in turn, double the parameter, recalculate the tree, and discuss the effect on the behavior of the price spread.

14.2. **(Practice)** This problem extends the material on RADRs in Section 14.1.2.

(a) Extend the analysis in Example 14.5 by building binomial trees to calculate the expected value and market value at date 0 of a cash flow of $X(\cdot, 2)$ to be received at date 2. (See Problem 4.15 for more on calculating the expected value.) Calculate the annualized RADR implied by these calculations.

(b) Repeat these calculations for a cash flow of $X(\cdot, 3)$ to be received at date 3, and then again for a cash flow of $X(\cdot, 4)$ to be received at date 4.

(c) Calculate the discount factor $(1 + \rho_n)^{-n\Delta t_m}$ for $n = 1, 2, 3, 4$, using the three values of X_0 in Figure 14.2. Discuss the results.

14.3. **(Practice)** The state variable for a problem equals the market value of a brand-new oil refinery with a capacity of 100,000 barrels per day. We have selected a comparison firm that owns refineries with a total capacity of 320,000 barrels per day and that had free cash flow of $453 million in the last year. The firm has debt with a book value of $627 million, cash and cash equivalents of $139 million, and 57 million shares on issue. The share price is currently $35.93. Based on monthly data, the change in the log of the share price (adjusted to reflect dividend payments) has a mean of 0.012 and a standard deviation of 0.135. Suppose that the risk-free interest rate equals 2% per annum (with annual compounding).

Use this information to build a binomial tree for the state variable spanning 13 weekly periods (so that $\Delta t_m = 1/52$) and estimate the risk-neutral probability of an up move.

14.A APPENDIX: CALCULATING ENTERPRISE RETURNS

Provided x is small, we can write $\log(x + 1) \approx x$. Therefore

$$\Delta \log N_j \equiv \log N_{j+1} - \log N_j = \log\left(\frac{N_{j+1}}{N_j}\right) = \log\left(\frac{\Delta N_j}{N_j} + 1\right) \approx \frac{\Delta N_j}{N_j}.$$

Since $N_j = D_j + E_j - A_j$, we can write

$$\frac{\Delta N_j}{N_j} = \frac{\Delta D_j + \Delta E_j - \Delta A_j}{D_j + E_j - A_j} \approx \frac{\Delta E_j}{D_j + E_j - A_j},$$

provided the change in debt value (net of cash and cash equivalents) is small relative to the change in equity value. Therefore

$$\Delta \log N_j \approx \frac{\Delta E_j}{D_j + E_j - A_j} = \frac{\Delta E_j / E_j}{(D_j + E_j - A_j)/E_j} \approx \frac{\Delta \log E_j}{1 + \frac{D_j - A_j}{E_j}}.$$

Part IV

PUTTING THE PIECES TOGETHER

15

Forestry Management and Valuation

At the beginning of 2008 the owner of a 35-year-old Douglas-fir forest in the Pacific Northwest wishes to know when to harvest his forest and how much it is currently worth. The owner estimates that ongoing forest management costs are $6 per acre per year and that regenerating the land after harvest and replanting trees will cost $350 per acre.[1] It will cost approximately $175 to harvest each thousand board feet (Mbf) of timber and transport it to a mill.[2] The forest currently contains 10 Mbf of merchantable timber per acre; this is expected to increase to 20 Mbf by the time the trees are 50 years old.

The harvest decision is complicated by the fact that timber prices are highly volatile. For example, the average mill price (which we define shortly) for a typical grade of Douglas-fir log fell from $1024/Mbf in 1979 to $440/Mbf in 1984, before climbing back to $1207/Mbf in 1993. In the final quarter of 2007 the average mill price for this log grade was $470/Mbf. The fact that Douglas-fir trees are typically harvested when they are 50–70 years old gives the forest owner considerable freedom to wait and harvest the trees when the price of timber is high.

Consider the problem facing the forest owner when the timber price is high relative to its long-run average. He can harvest the forest immediately or he can wait. Because the forest continues to grow while the owner waits, if the price stays high (or rises further) then he will receive an even higher payoff if he harvests later;

---

1. In this chapter all prices are expressed in December 2007 dollars.
2. One board foot represents a solid piece of wood that measures 12 inches by 12 inches by 1 inch. It is the standard unit of measurement of logs and lumber in the Pacific Northwest.

if the price falls then he can simply delay the harvest even longer, waiting for the price to increase again. The forest owner must therefore solve an optimal timing problem.[3] It is slightly more complicated than the simple timing problems featured in Chapter 7 because as soon as the forest is harvested the land is replanted in trees that will themselves be available for harvest many years in the future. Thus, the forest harvest problem is an example of the switching option problem considered in Chapter 10.

15.1 SETTING UP THE MODEL

Our first task is to choose a state variable that reflects the risks confronting the forest owner and can be calibrated reasonably accurately. We choose a timber price, but there are several such prices to choose from, one for each stage of the timber-processing sequence.

The stumpage price is the price at which a forest owner can sell the right to harvest timber. It is the price of timber while it is still standing, so that the purchaser is responsible for harvesting and transporting the timber. It would therefore seem to be an ideal state variable for this problem. However, stumpage prices vary across different forests, depending on the quality of the trees, the ease with which the forest can be harvested (for example, stumpage prices will be relatively low for forests on steep land), and the cost of transporting the harvested logs to be milled. This makes it difficult to get reliable data for a particular site. The data that are usually reported are average prices observed in a particular region over a particular period of time.[4]

Once the trees have been cut down, the logs are transported to a mill for processing, where they are often stored in a holding pond. A log's mill price (also known as the pond price) is what it is worth in the mill's pond. Since transporting a log from the forest to the mill is expensive, the mill price will be more than the stumpage price by an amount that reflects the cost of cutting a tree down, some preliminary processing, and transporting it to the mill. As is the case for stumpage prices, we usually have to rely on period-average price data when calibrating a binomial tree of mill prices. However, because the prices will be mill-specific (rather than forest-specific), it is rather easier to estimate the process for the mill

---

3. The problem of when to harvest a forest has an important place in the history of finance theory: Faustmann (1849) used static DCF analysis to derive the optimal time between harvests on land that would be replanted immediately after each harvest. Many papers using real options analysis have appeared in recent years. For example, Thomson (1992) shows how to determine an optimal harvest policy when changes in timber prices are described by a binomial tree representation of a random walk. Insley and Rollins (2005) consider a mean-reverting timber price, but in a model that is much more mathematically demanding than the one presented in this chapter.

4. For example, the U.S. Department of Agriculture reports the annual average stumpage price for Douglas-fir sawtimber sold from national forests in western Washington and western Oregon (Skog and Risbrudt, 1982; Howard, 2007).

price at a given mill than it is to estimate the process for the stumpage price at a particular forest.

At the end of the harvesting process, the trees will have been converted into timber of a readily measured quality and quantity, the value of which is given by the lumber price. Its homogeneous nature means that there are much better data on the lumber price than on stumpage and mill prices. Indeed, the Chicago Mercantile Exchange has traded lumber futures contracts since 1969 and options on these contracts since 1987. The futures contracts require delivery of lumber from mills in Oregon, Washington, Idaho, Wyoming, Montana, Nevada, California, British Columbia, or Alberta.

Our only means of estimating the risk-neutral probabilities when using stumpage or mill prices as the state variable is to fit the CAPM to historical price data.[5] This approach would also be possible with lumber prices, but in that case alternative techniques would also be possible due to the availability of futures and options contracts on lumber. For example, we could use the historical relationship between futures and spot prices, or build the binomial tree implied by current option prices.

We have to choose between using the stumpage price (which is the price most relevant to the forest owner, but for which the data are relatively poor), the mill price, and the lumber price (which is only indirectly relevant to the forest owner, but for which very good data are available). Thus, we face a trade-off between relevance and data quality. In this chapter we opt for the compromise offered by mill prices.[6] That is, we let $X(i, n)$ denote the mill price (in dollars per Mbf) at note (i, n).

Now we turn to the remaining features of our model. The forest owner incurs a cash flow of C dollars per acre per period, representing the ongoing costs of maintaining a growing forest. Harvesting the forest is instantaneous and costs H dollars per Mbf of marketable timber (inclusive of transportation costs). The forest contains $Q(t)$ Mbf of marketable timber per acre if it is harvested when the trees are t years old, where Q is a deterministic function of age. As soon as the harvest is complete, the owner must pay G dollars per acre to regenerate the land and plant new trees.

There is no natural date at which the harvest option expires in our problem.[7] In effect, the forest owner can delay the harvest indefinitely, but we need to impose

---

5. Whether or not the CAPM adequately captures the reward for bearing mill-price or stumpage-price risk is an open question. For example, the mill owner will operate in markets that are much less liquid than the financial markets in which the CAPM is typically applied. The CAPM does not contain compensation for bearing liquidity risk.

6. In practical applications we might test the sensitivity of our results to this choice of data set by, for example, repeating the analysis using stumpage price data.

7. However, a natural terminal date might arise when the owner of the trees leases the land from another party. Then the lease arrangements will often specify that harvest must occur before a certain date.

some terminal date N so that we have somewhere to begin the backward induction process. Therefore we assume that the forest must be harvested on or before date N, for some number N that we make sufficiently large that the optimal policy and the value of the forest are unaffected by changes in N. When we value the forest, we choose N to correspond to a period of 150 years.

We assume that the revenue from harvesting the forest is taxed as income (not capital gains) and that all expenditure (both ongoing maintenance costs and harvest costs, as well as regeneration costs) is tax-deductible as soon as it is incurred. The tax rate T reflects federal, state, and local taxes. The return on one-period risk-free bonds is R_f.

15.2 THE SOLUTION PROCEDURE

The harvest payoff has two components. The first is the net cash flow from cutting the trees, transporting them to a mill, and selling them. The second is the value of the bare land that remains after the harvest, which equals the market value of the net cash flows from future harvests (less forest maintenance and regeneration costs). It follows that the market value of bare land is an endogenous quantity—it depends on the harvest policy adopted by the forest owner. Thus, we need to calculate the optimal harvest policy and the market value of bare land simultaneously.

We assume that the mill price is mean reverting, which implies that the market value of bare land does not depend on current timber prices: whether the current price is high or low has no effect on the distribution of the timber price decades from now when the trees to be planted on bare land will be harvested. Thus, for the time being we set the market value of bare land equal to B dollars per acre for some constant B. We see how to calculate B shortly, but for now we just treat it as a constant.

The first step in analyzing this problem is to construct the associated decision tree. At date 0, the forest owner must either harvest the trees or wait. These are represented by the actions labeled H and W in the decision tree shown in Figure 15.1. If he harvests then the forest owner receives the associated payoff (including the value of bare land) and the decision tree ends.[8] If, instead, he chooses to wait at date 0, then we move to date 1 in the decision tree, where the forest owner must choose from the same two actions. This process continues until the terminal date N, when the forest must be harvested.

The decision tree identifies two relevant project-states: before and after harvest. However, because we will be able to write the harvest payoff at each node as a function of the state variable there, we need to calculate only the market value

---

8. Strictly speaking, the decision tree actually continues at this point, with the land being replanted in trees that will be harvested at some future date. However, we collapse all forest rotations beyond the current one into the constant B, allowing us to terminate the decision tree as in Figure 15.1.

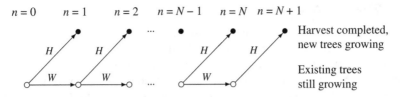

Figure 15.1. Decision tree for forestry valuation

of the forest in the before-harvest state. We let $V(i, n)$ denote the (cum dividend) market value of one acre of the forest. For reasons that will become clear shortly, we consider a forest of an arbitrary age. Specifically, we assume that the trees are m periods old at date 0. It follows that if the forest is harvested at date n then it will yield $Q((m + n)\Delta t_m)$ Mbf of marketable timber per acre, where Δt_m is the length of each time period in our binomial tree.

Consider the situation facing the forest owner at node (i, n). If he harvests the forest then he must pay harvest costs of $HQ((m + n)\Delta t_m)$ immediately, he receives revenue of $X(i, n)Q((m + n)\Delta t_m)$ immediately from selling the harvested trees, and he is left owning bare land that is worth B per acre. Since he must pay tax of

$$T(X(i, n) - H)Q((m + n)\Delta t_m)$$

it follows that the harvest payoff equals

$$(1 - T)(X(i, n) - H)Q((m + n)\Delta t_m) + B.$$

In contrast, if the forest owner decides to wait then he must pay maintenance costs of C per acre, less tax of TC per acre; after one period each acre of the forest will be worth either $V(i, n + 1)$ or $V(i + 1, n + 1)$, depending on whether an up or a down move occurs. The payoff from waiting is therefore

$$-(1 - T)C + \frac{\pi_u(i, n)V(i, n + 1) + \pi_d(i, n)V(i + 1, n + 1)}{R_f}.$$

Since the forest owner seeks to maximize the market value of the forest, the market value at node (i, n) must equal

$$V(i, n) = \max \left\{ (1 - T)(X(i, n) - H)Q((m + n)\Delta t_m) + B, \right.$$
$$\left. -(1 - T)C + \frac{\pi_u(i, n)V(i, n + 1) + \pi_d(i, n)V(i + 1, n + 1)}{R_f} \right\}$$

$$(15.1)$$

for all $n = N - 1, \ldots, 1, 0$. Since harvesting is compulsory at date N, the terminal condition is

$$V(i, N) = (1 - T)(X(i, N) - H)Q((m + N)\Delta t_m) + B. \qquad (15.2)$$

This terminal condition, together with the recursive equation, completely determines the market value of the forest, as well as the optimal harvest policy.

15.3 DATA AND CALIBRATION

We use quarterly average mill prices for Douglas-fir sawtimber delivered to mills in northwest Oregon, which are reported by the Oregon Department of Forestry from 1977 onwards. These prices are converted into December 2007 dollars per Mbf using the Consumer Price Index for all urban consumers.[9] The resulting time series is shown in Figure 15.2. The four curves correspond to different lumber grades, the top three to logs suitable for construction lumber and the bottom one to logs suitable for the production of wood chips. We use the best of the timber grades (called "Number 2 sawmill" by the Oregon Department of Forestry) as the proxy for our state variable. Our data span the period from the beginning of 1977 to the end of 2007.

There are strong arguments that mill prices should be mean reverting. For instance, a sudden increase in mill prices would be expected to trigger increased harvest activity and consequent price reductions as prices respond to the increased supply of timber. Similarly, a sudden fall in prices will see a reduction in supply as forest owners delay harvests, leading to price increases. This is our motivation for using the mean-reverting process introduced in Section 12.1.2 to model the behavior of the mill price.

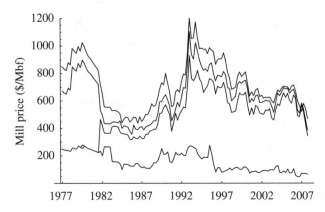

Figure 15.2. Prices for Douglas-fir sawtimber

Note: Quarterly average mill prices for Douglas-fir sawtimber delivered to mills in northwest Oregon, reported by the Oregon Department of Forestry, converted into December 2007 dollars per Mbf using the Consumer Price Index for all urban consumers.

9. That is, we divide each nominal price by the contemporaneous level of the CPI and then multiply the result by the level of the CPI in the final quarter of 2007. We use the CPI to deflate prices because it is the intertemporal consumption trade-off that interests the investors who ultimately determine the market values we are estimating.

We apply the method of Section 12.1.2 to these price data.[10] Estimating the AR(1) model for the logarithm of the mill price using the ordinary least-squares method results in the estimated relationship

$$p_{j+1} - p_j = \underset{(0.1697)}{0.2092} - \underset{(0.02586)}{0.03263 p_j} + u_{j+1}, \quad \mathrm{Var}[u_{j+1}] = 0.005088, \quad (15.3)$$

where the numbers in brackets indicate the standard errors of the associated parameter estimates. The parameters we need in order to evaluate the equations in (12.13) are

$$\hat{\alpha}_0 = 0.2092, \quad \hat{\alpha}_1 = -0.03263, \quad \hat{\phi} = \sqrt{0.005088} = 0.07133.$$

Since the data are quarterly, we have $\Delta t_d = 1/4$. Substituting these parameters into the equations in (12.13) shows that the normalized estimates of the required parameters are

$$\hat{a} = 0.1327, \quad \hat{b} = 6.411, \quad \hat{\sigma} = 0.1450.$$

This gives us all the information we need to build a binomial tree for the mill price. Our starting point is the most recent mill price of \$470/Mbf.[11] We use monthly time steps, so that $\Delta t_m = 1/12$ and the sizes of up and down moves are

$$U = e^{\hat{\sigma}\sqrt{\Delta t_m}} = e^{0.1450\sqrt{1/12}} = 1.0427$$

and

$$D = e^{-\hat{\sigma}\sqrt{\Delta t_m}} = e^{-0.1450\sqrt{1/12}} = 0.9590$$

respectively. Using equation (12.16), the probability of an up move at node (i, n) equals

$$\theta_u(i, n) = \frac{1}{2} + \frac{(1 - e^{-\hat{a}\Delta t_m})(\hat{b} - \log X(i, n))}{2\hat{\sigma}\sqrt{\Delta t_m}} = 1.3422 - 0.1314 \log X(i, n)$$

if this number lies between 0 and 1, equals 0 if it is negative, and equals 1 otherwise.

Before we estimate the CAPM we need to consider an issue that arises when using period-average data. When specifying the regression used to estimate beta we need to make an assumption regarding the period over which mill price changes are measured. We treat the prices as applying to the end of the indicated quarter, so that the change in the reported price between quarters j and $j + 1$ corresponds to a return over quarter $j + 1$. Accordingly, we regress the AR(1)-regression residual $\hat{u}_{j+1}$ on a

---

10. The method in Section 12.1.2 is designed for use with prices that are observed at regular intervals, rather than the average of prices observed at irregular dates during these intervals. However, since we do not have access to timber price data of the first type, we are forced to apply the method to our average-price data.

11. The mean reversion in timber prices, combined with the length of time the forest owner has to wait before harvesting the trees, means that our results are not sensitive to the choice of X_0.

constant and the return on a proxy for the market portfolio over quarter $j + 1$.[12] We use the S&P 500 total return index as our proxy for the market portfolio and obtain

$$\hat{u}_j = \underset{(0.006575)}{-0.002138} + \underset{(0.0835)}{0.1131 r_{m,j}} + v_j.$$

After allowing for mean reversion via the adjustment in Appendix 12.A.3, our beta estimate for the mill price is $\beta_x = 0.1144$.

In their survey of Chief Financial Officers carried out in November 2006, Graham and Harvey (2007) found a median market risk premium of 3.4% per annum. Each step in our binomial tree will represent one month, so we use $E[\tilde{R}_m] - R_f = 0.034 \times (1/12) = 0.002833$ as our estimate of the market risk premium. From equation (3.10), the risk-neutral probability of an up move equals

$$\pi_u(i, n) = \theta_u(i, n) - \frac{(E[\tilde{R}_m] - R_f)\beta_x}{U - D} = \theta_u(i, n) - 0.003869$$

at node (i, n).[13]

At the end of 2007, the yield on 20-year Treasury inflation-protected securities (TIPS) was approximately 2%.[14] Since interest on TIPS is paid semi-annually, the implied return on a one-year risk-free bond is

$$\left(1 + \frac{0.02}{2}\right)^2 = 1.0201.$$

It follows that the return on a one-period risk-free bond is $R_f = (1.0201)^{\Delta t_m}$. With monthly time steps we have $R_f = (1.0201)^{1/12} = 1.001660$.

Each period the forest owner pays C to maintain the growing forest. Since there are $1/\Delta t_m$ such payments each year, equation (4.13) shows that the market value of the annual maintenance expenditure (measured at the start of each year) equals

$$C + \left(1 - \left(\frac{1}{R_f}\right)^{1/\Delta t_m - 1}\right)\frac{C}{R_f - 1} = \left(1 - \left(\frac{1}{R_f}\right)^{1/\Delta t_m}\right)\frac{R_f C}{R_f - 1}.$$

---

12. If we assumed that the reported prices applied to the beginning of the indicated quarter, then we would have to interpret the change in the reported price between quarters j and $j + 1$ as the return over quarter j. For the data used here we obtain almost exactly the same beta estimate if we use this approach. Some of the difficulties in estimating beta when timber prices are period-averaged are discussed by Washburn and Binkley (1990).

13. There are three exceptions. When $\theta_u(i, n)$ equals 0 or 1 we set $\pi_u(i, n)$ equal to 0 or 1 respectively. Otherwise, when subtracting $(E[\tilde{R}_m] - R_f)\beta_x/(U - D)$ would make $\pi_u(i, n)$ negative, we set the risk-neutral probability of an up move equal to zero.

14. Since these are real rates of return, yields on TIPS would seem to provide ideal estimates of the real risk-free interest rate. However, the market for TIPS is not as liquid as that for many other Treasury securities, so our estimate of the risk-free interest rate might be biased upwards by the presence of a liquidity premium in TIPS yields. In practical applications we might carry out a sensitivity analysis on the level of the risk-free interest rate to assess the effect such a premium might be having on our results.

Assuming that the annual maintenance costs of $6/acre are paid at the start of each year, we can achieve expenditure with the same present value by choosing C such that

$$6 = \left(1 - \left(\frac{1}{R_f}\right)^{1/\Delta t_m}\right) \frac{R_f C}{R_f - 1} \quad \Leftrightarrow \quad C = 6 \left(\frac{1 - \left(\frac{1}{R_f}\right)}{1 - \left(\frac{1}{R_f}\right)^{1/\Delta t_m}}\right).$$

With monthly time steps, we obtain $C = 0.5046$. Harvest costs are $H = 175$ and regeneration costs are $G = 350$.

A common approach when analyzing optimal harvest policies is to suppose that the volume of merchantable timber in Mbf per acre, $Q(t)$, and the age of the trees, t, are related by

$$\log Q(t) = a_0 - \frac{a_1}{t},$$

for some constants a_0 and a_1.[15] Although more accurate estimates of a_0 and a_1 could be obtained using actual yield tables for the particular forest being valued, we simply choose the values that are implied by the current and projected sizes of the forest that we are analyzing. Since each acre of the 35-year-old forest currently contains 10 Mbf of merchantable timber and is expected to contain 20 Mbf when the trees are 50 years old, we choose a_0 and a_1 such that $Q(35) = 10$ and $Q(50) = 20$. These conditions imply that

$$\log 10 = a_0 - \frac{a_1}{35} \quad \text{and} \quad \log 20 = a_0 - \frac{a_1}{50}.$$

Solving this system of equations gives $a_0 = 4.613$ and $a_1 = 80.87$.

Finally, we assume that the tax rate is $T = 0.4$, reflecting federal, state, and local taxes.

15.4 RESULTS

Estimating the Market Value of Bare Land

Our first task is to estimate the value of bare land.[16] The simplest way to do this uses an iterative procedure to calculate the market value of an acre of land that contains trees that have just been planted at date 0 (so that $m = 0$). We begin by supposing that bare land has zero value when these trees are eventually harvested. That is, we use equations (15.1) and (15.2) to build the tree for the market value of the forest in the special case where $m = 0$ (so that the trees have just been planted) and $B = 0$ (so that bare land has zero value when the trees are harvested).

---

15. See, for example, Brazee and Mendelsohn (1988) and Thomson (1992).

16. Recall that the land is replanted in trees immediately after each harvest, so that the land is only bare temporarily. Its value reflects the cash flows from all future forestry operations.

Table 15.1. Iterative Procedure for
Valuing Bare Land

Iteration	B	$V(0,0)$	B'
0	0	2962	2752
1	2752	3684	3474
2	3474	3895	3685
3	3685	3959	3749
4	3749	3978	3768
5	3768	3984	3774
6	3774	3986	3776
7	3776	3987	3777
8	3777	3987	3777
9	3777	3987	3777
10	3777	3987	3777

The resulting market value of the forest at date 0 is $V(0,0) = 2962$. Since this land contains newly-planted trees, this suggests that the market value of bare land at date 0 should equal

$$B' = V(0,0) - (1-T)G = 2962 - (1-0.4)350 = 2752.$$

That is, the market values of bare land and newly-planted land differ by the post-tax regeneration costs. Our new estimate of the market value of bare land is therefore $B = 2752$. We now recalculate the binomial tree for $V(i, n)$ using this value for B. This time we find that $V(0,0) = 3684$, implying a bare-land value of $B' = 3474$. We can continue like this, updating B each time we calculate the binomial tree until the bare-land values converge to one another. The results are reported in Table 15.1, which shows the sequence of bare-land values for the first ten iterations. This table shows that if bare land is worth \$3777/acre when the current forest is eventually harvested then bare land will also be worth \$3777/acre now. Thus, given the characteristics of this particular forest and the behavior of mill prices, the market value of bare land equals \$3777/acre if the forest owner follows a value-maximizing harvest policy. In our subsequent analysis of this problem we set $B = 3777$.

Valuing the Trees Currently on the Land

We now have all the information we need to analyze the 35-year-old forest on the land. One approach would be to rebuild the binomial tree for a forest that is 35 years old at date 0. However, it is much easier to use the table that we constructed when calculating B and just look ahead to the column corresponding to date 420 (when newly-planted trees will be the same age as the ones in the forest we are studying). For example, after 210 up moves and 210 down moves the mill price is still equal to $X(210, 420) = 470$. The forest is worth

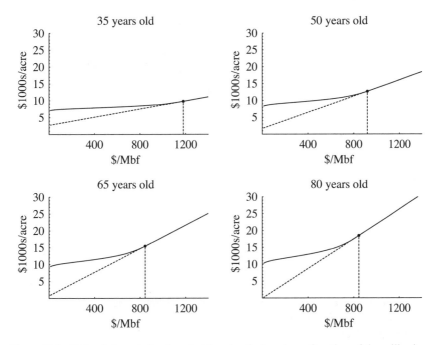

Figure 15.3. Estimated market value of a Douglas-fir forest as a function of the mill price for various forest ages (thousands of dollars per acre)

$V(210, 420) = 7943$ at this node. Thus, we estimate that—provided the forest owner follows a value-maximizing harvest policy—his 35-year-old forest is currently worth $7943 per acre.

It is just as easy to estimate the market value of the forest for different levels of the mill price and different ages. For example, the top left-hand graph in Figure 15.3 considers the case of a 35-year-old forest. The solid curve plots the market value of the forest as a function of the mill price, while the upward-sloping dashed line plots the payoff from harvesting the forest immediately.[17] To the right of the dot the two curves coincide, indicating that immediate harvest would be optimal in this case. However, to the left of the dot it is optimal for the forest owner to delay harvesting. In this case the harvest threshold, which is the mill price corresponding to the dot where the two curves join, is approximately $1180/Mbf. The other graphs in Figure 15.3 reproduce this analysis for various forest ages. As the forest grows older the harvest payoff increases due to the greater quantity of merchantable

---

17. The curve can be drawn by constructing a scatter plot, with $X(\cdot, 420)$ on the horizontal axis and $V(\cdot, 420)$ on the vertical axis. The line can be drawn the same way, with the payoff from harvesting replacing $V(\cdot, 420)$ at each node.

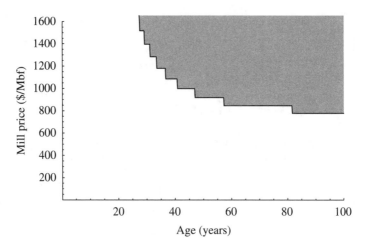

Figure 15.4. Harvest threshold for a Douglas-fir forest

timber on the land, and the harvest threshold falls (that is, the dot showing where the two curves separate shifts left).

We can calculate the harvest threshold for all possible ages of the forest. It is drawn as a function of the forest's age in Figure 15.4. If the combination of forest age and mill price corresponding to node (i, n) lies in the shaded region then it is optimal to harvest the forest at that node. For very young forests the threshold is so high that they will always be left to grow. However, as the forest's age increases the price threshold falls. For trees between 60 and 80 years of age, the threshold is approximately \$844/Mbf; for ages of 80–100 years, it is \$777/Mbf.

The discussion following equation (12.12) shows that as we look far into the future the logarithm of the mill price is normally distributed with mean b and variance $\sigma^2/2a$. Thus the price threshold of \$844 corresponds to a point that is

$$\frac{\log 844 - \hat{b}}{\sqrt{\hat{\sigma}^2/2\hat{a}}} = 1.16$$

standard deviations above the mean of the logarithm of the mill price. Seen in the context of the long-run distribution of the mill price, the optimal harvest threshold is not especially high.

The Value of Flexibility

Static DCF analysis is sometimes used to determine harvest policies. This approach involves specifying the harvest date and then following that harvest policy indefinitely—regardless of what might happen to timber prices in the meantime. It is interesting to compare the market value of the forest considered in this chapter when such inflexible harvest policies are followed.

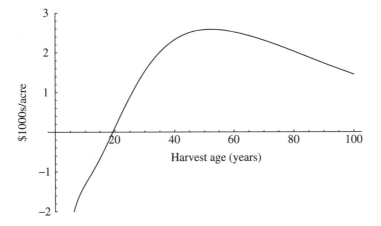

Figure 15.5. The market value of bare land when harvest times are fixed in advance

It is straightforward to modify our solution approach for the situation when the harvest date is fixed in advance. Suppose, for example, that the owner of a newly planted forest has decided to harvest the trees as soon as they are M periods old. The terminal condition is still given by equation (15.2), but now it applies at date M instead of date N. At all earlier dates the forest owner must wait, so that the recursive equation becomes

$$V(i, n) = -(1 - T)C + \frac{\pi_u(i, n)V(i, n + 1) + \pi_d(i, n)V(i + 1, n + 1)}{R_f}.$$

With these changes, we follow our usual procedure. In particular, we find the market value of bare land using the same recursive procedure that we described at the beginning of this section. All that changes is the recursive equation used to calculate B' for each value of B.

The results of this procedure are shown in Figure 15.5. It plots the market value of bare land (in thousands of dollars per acre) as a function of the age at which the forest will be harvested and replanted. The highest market value, \$2586/acre, is achieved by harvesting the forest every 52 years. This needs to be contrasted with the market value of bare land when a value-maximizing flexible policy is followed, which we found to be \$3777/acre. Thus, flexibility adds approximately 46% to the value of bare land.

The Effect of Different Sized Binomial Trees

When using the modeling techniques developed in this book to analyze real-world problems we need to be aware that the market values and optimal policies that they generate potentially depend on the dimensions of our binomial tree. That is, if we were to change the step size Δt_m or the number of periods N or both—but keep all other aspects of our model unchanged—we might find that our estimated

Table 15.2. The Effect of Binomial-tree Size on the Market Value of Bare Land

Δt_m	Years until Harvest Must Occur ($N \Delta t_m$)						
	50	75	100	125	150	175	200
1	3031	3625	3766	3793	3797	3798	3798
1/2	3022	3616	3755	3782	3787	3787	3787
1/3	3019	3612	3751	3778	3783	3784	3784
1/4	3017	3611	3750	3776	3781	3782	3782
1/6	3016	3609	3748	3774	3779	3780	3780
1/8	3015	3608	3747	3774	3778	3779	3779
1/12	3014	3607	3746	3773	3777	3778	3778

market values change. This is a consequence of the fact that our binomial tree is approximating a more general type of process, known as an Itô process, in which time evolves continuously. As Δt_m becomes very small the differences between our approximation and the underlying Itô process disappear, so that in principle we just need to build our binomial trees with a very large number of very small time steps. However, if we make the time steps too small then solving the model will be computationally demanding. The best way to check that our time step is sufficiently small for our results to be reliable is to repeat our calculations for a selection of different values of the two key parameters, Δt_m and N. Reducing our time step should not alter the results significantly.

Table 15.2 shows the market value of bare land for different combinations of the binomial tree's dimensions. Each row corresponds to a different step size (Δt_m), while each column corresponds to a different age at which the forest owner is compelled to harvest the trees (which equals $N \Delta t_m$). Bare land becomes more valuable as we move across each row, which is to be expected given that as we do so we are increasing the forest owner's harvest-timing flexibility. Greater flexibility cannot reduce the market value of the forest, and it can increase it. However, as the table shows, beyond approximately 150 years additional flexibility has negligible value. The table also shows that the market value of bare land is converging to approximately \$3777/acre as the time steps become very small. Thus, our decision to use monthly time steps appears to be sensible.

15.5 PROBLEMS

15.1. **(Practice)** Implement the model described in Section 15.2 using 300 periods, each representing six months.

15.2. **(Practice)** This problem examines the effect of mill price volatility on the market value of a forest and shows how this relationship can be used to estimate an implied volatility for the mill price.

    (a) Estimate the market value of bare land for several different levels of the volatility of the mill price.

(b) Give an intuitive explanation for the relationship between σ and B.

(c) Suppose that bare land in the same region as the forest being valued sells for $4100 per acre. Use this information to calculate an implied volatility measure and use this to estimate the market value of the 35-year-old forest. Discuss the advantages and disadvantages of this market value estimate relative to the one calculated in Section 15.4.

15.3. **(Practice)** Suppose that the harvest takes one period to complete. All harvest-related cash flows are generated exactly one period after the harvest decision is made; once the decision is made, the harvest cannot be interrupted.

(a) Derive the terminal conditions and recursive equations for this problem.

(b) Estimate the market value of bare land, using the calibration in Section 15.3.

(c) How has increasing the harvest lead time to one period affected the forest's market value? Give an intuitive explanation.

15.4. **(Practice)** Repeat Problem 15.3, but this time for the situation when there is a two-period harvest lead time. All harvest-related cash flows are generated exactly two periods after the harvest decision is made; once the decision is made, the harvest cannot be interrupted.

16

Developing a Gas Field

An all-equity firm owns the right to develop and exploit a natural gas field in the South Central United States. The field has already been explored and is believed to contain 100 billion cubic feet (Bcf) of recoverable gas. The lease agreement that gives the firm these development rights requires the firm to relinquish them if development is not completed within ten years. The firm's manager expects that it will take four years of continuous development and $60 million of expenditure per year to develop the field. However, she is conscious of possible cost overruns, estimating that the development time has a standard deviation of one year. Our task is to derive an optimal development policy and value the firm's development rights as at the beginning of 2008.[1]

Developing a gas field is an expensive and lengthy process. The existing exploratory wells must be completed by installing the well casings that strengthen the sides of the well holes, the equipment that is needed underground to extract gas, and the wellheads used to control gas extraction. In addition, it is necessary

---

1. McCormack and Sick (2001) give useful background on the development of oil and gas reserves. Smit (1997) analyzes offshore oil concessions in the Netherlands using a model in which the logarithm of the state variable, the spot price of crude oil, follows a random walk on a binomial tree. He models all stages of the investment process from exploration to exploitation. Paddock et al. (1988) wrote an important early paper using real options theory to analyze offshore leases in the Gulf of Mexico. Their model is formulated in continuous time, so that the analysis is less accessible to practitioners than the approach we follow in this chapter.

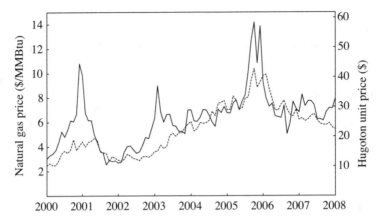

Figure 16.1. Natural gas and related prices

Note: Spot price of natural gas at the Henry Hub (solid curve) and Hugoton Royalty Trust share price (dashed curve), converted into December 2007 dollars using the Consumer Price Index for all urban consumers.

to build the network of gathering pipelines needed to transport the natural gas to a processing plant.

The manager faces a difficult decision. She needs to make a series of large irreversible investments, which (provided they are completed on time) will only generate a payoff several years after investment begins. The final payoff is risky because the market value of a developed gas field will reflect, to some extent, prevailing natural gas prices—and they can be highly volatile. For instance, the solid curve in Figure 16.1 plots the spot price of natural gas at the Henry Hub (expressed in December 2007 dollars per million British thermal units), which is widely regarded as the benchmark price for the North American natural gas market.[2]

The manager needs to decide when to begin developing the field and, once development is underway, whether to continue. This flexibility, combined with the volatility in gas prices, might give her a strong incentive to delay beginning development. If developed fields increase in value while she waits, the manager can aggressively pursue development of the field in the future and the only cost will be a delay in receiving the first gas extracted from the field. However, if the value of developed fields falls, then the manager can simply surrender the lease. This ability to mitigate the effect of bad news introduces an asymmetry into the payoff from waiting that, as we have seen in previous chapters, can make delaying development optimal.

---

2. The dashed curve shows the share price of a comparison firm, which will be introduced in Section 16.3.

With ten-year development rights and an expected development time of four years, it might seem that the manager has considerable timing flexibility. However, her problem is complicated because the uncertainty surrounding the actual development time required means that she does not know exactly how much timing flexibility she has. If the manager waits too long before beginning development, she may find that she runs out of time to develop the field and must relinquish the rights with development only partly completed. On the other hand, if she does not wait and development is easier than expected, but the developed field's value falls in the meantime, the manager may (with the benefit of hindsight) wish that development had been delayed. These are some of the possibilities that the firm's manager must consider.

16.1 SETTING UP THE MODEL

Our first task is to choose a state variable that captures the risks that are most relevant when considering how to develop a gas field. It must also be able to be calibrated, so we may need to trade off relevance and data availability.

One approach would be to take the spot price of natural gas as the state variable. It would be relatively easy to calibrate a tree for the spot price—spot price data are available, and we could use available futures price data to match either the historical relationship between spot and futures prices or the current term structure of futures prices. However, in order to derive an optimal development policy we need to know the market value of the field once it has been developed. If we used the gas spot price as the state variable, then we would need to calculate the market value of the developed field for all possible spot prices. Since the relationship between this market value and the spot price of gas depends on the firm's extraction policy, we would need to model the extraction stage in detail in order to calculate the market value of the developed field. As well as complicating our analysis, this would mean that our derived optimal development policy would be reliant on the accuracy of our modeling of the extraction stage.

We avoid these difficulties by making the state variable $X(i, n)$ equal to the market value at node (i, n) of the gas field if it is developed and ready to enter production at date n. The market value of reserves about to enter production already incorporates the benefits from following an optimal extraction policy, so we do not need to model the extraction stage in detail. In fact, the firm's problem effectively ends as soon as development is completed. Moreover, as we see in Section 16.3, we can estimate the process for the market value of developed reserves using comparison firms.

The state variable determines how market risk affects the firm, but in this problem there is a second source of risk: development-cost uncertainty.[3] We model

---

3. Cost overruns can be substantial. For example, in July 2005 Shell announced that the anticipated cost of developing the Sakhalin II oil and gas field had increased from $9–11 billion to $20 billion.

development-time uncertainty using the R&D model in Section 8.4. That is, we split development of the field into M distinct stages, all of which must be successfully completed in order to develop the gas field. The firm has the option to attempt to complete the latest stage at each node. Each attempt requires irrecoverable expenditure of I, takes one period, and succeeds with probability q.[4] Development-cost risk is diversifiable.

The firm has the option to develop the gas field on or before date N. It loses the development rights after this date if development is incomplete, without receiving any compensation for its past capital expenditure. We assume that all capital expenditure is tax deductible as soon as it is incurred, with the firm facing a tax rate of T. The risk-neutral probability of an up move (which we assume is constant) equals π_u, and the return on a one-period risk-free bond equals R_f. This completes the specification of the model.

16.2 THE SOLUTION PROCEDURE

The decision tree for the manager's problem, which is shown in Figure 16.2, is constructed in the same way as the decision tree for the R&D problem in Section 8.4. At date 0 all M stages remain to be completed and the manager must either attempt to complete the first stage (action A) or wait (action W). A development attempt will either succeed (with probability q) and at date 1 there

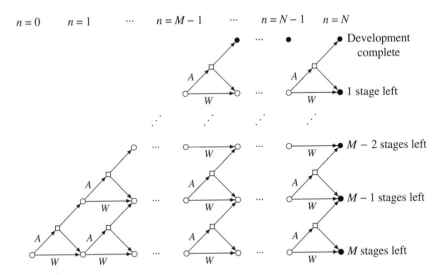

Figure 16.2. Decision tree for gas-reserve development

---

4. In Appendix 16.A we derive the distribution of the time required to develop the field, including its mean and variance.

will be just $M - 1$ stages remaining to be developed, or it will fail (with probability $1 - q$) and the project will still have M stages remaining at date 1. If she chooses to wait, there will still be M stages remaining to be developed.

The project will be in one of two states at date 1: either there will be M stages remaining to be completed or there will be $M - 1$ stages. In the first case, the situation facing the manager of the firm is exactly the same as at date 0. In the second case, the manager must either attempt to develop the second stage of the project or wait. If she chooses a development attempt, either the attempt succeeds and at date 2 there will be just $M - 2$ stages remaining to be developed, or the attempt fails and the project will still have $M - 1$ stages remaining at date 2. If she chooses to wait, at date 2 there will still be $M - 1$ stages remaining to be developed.

We continue like this, building the decision tree out as far as date $N - 1$. From date $M - 1$ onwards we need to consider the possibility that the firm has just one development stage remaining. When this happens the treatment of a development attempt is slightly different. Now, if the firm's manager chooses a development attempt, one of two things will happen: the attempt succeeds and at the next date the gas field is developed and ready to begin production, and the decision tree terminates; or the attempt fails and the project still has one stage remaining after one period. Finally, at date N the relinquishment requirement means that the development rights are lost: the firm's rights are worthless and the decision tree terminates.

We let $V_m(i, n)$ denote the market value of the development rights at node (i, n) when there are m stages still to complete, for $m = 0, 1, \ldots, M$. There are two types of terminal conditions, corresponding to when development ends and to the relinquishment date. As soon as the field has been successfully developed, the project rights are worth the current level of the state variable, so that

$$V_0(i, n) = X(i, n) \qquad (16.1)$$

at all nodes (i, n). If there are still $m > 0$ stages remaining when the firm must relinquish its rights, then the development rights are worthless, so that

$$V_m(i, N) = 0 \qquad (16.2)$$

for all $i = 0, 1, \ldots, N$. This completes the set of terminal conditions.

We now turn to the recursive equation that applies at each earlier date, when there are $m > 0$ stages remaining to be completed. At node (i, n) the manager of the firm must either wait or attempt to complete the current stage. If she decides to wait then there is no cash flow at date n, but at date $n + 1$ the development rights (still with m stages remaining) will be worth $V_m(i, n + 1)$ if an up move occurs and $V_m(i + 1, n + 1)$ if a down move occurs. The payoff from waiting is therefore[5]

$$\frac{\pi_u V_m(i, n+1) + \pi_d V_m(i+1, n+1)}{R_f}.$$

Suppose, instead, that the manager attempts development. If an up move occurs, then either the attempt succeeds, so that the development rights are worth $V_{m-1}(i, n+1)$, or it fails and they are worth $V_m(i, n+1)$. The risk associated with success or failure is diversifiable, so all we need to know about the market value of the development rights in the up state is its expected value, which equals

$$qV_{m-1}(i, n+1) + (1-q)V_m(i, n+1).$$

Similarly, if a down move occurs, the expected market value of the development rights at date $n+1$ equals

$$qV_{m-1}(i+1, n+1) + (1-q)V_m(i+1, n+1).$$

The payoff from attempting development is therefore equal to[6]

$$-(1-T)I + \frac{1}{R_f}\left(\pi_u\left(qV_{m-1}(i, n+1) + (1-q)V_m(i, n+1)\right)\right.$$

$$\left. + \pi_d\left(qV_{m-1}(i+1, n+1) + (1-q)V_m(i+1, n+1)\right)\right).$$

Since the manager of the firm will take whichever action has the higher payoff, the market value of the development rights at node (i, n) equals

$$V_m(i,n) = \max\left\{ \frac{\pi_u V_m(i, n+1) + \pi_d V_m(i+1, n+1)}{R_f}, \right.$$

$$-(1-T)I + \frac{1}{R_f}\left(\pi_u\left(qV_{m-1}(i, n+1) + (1-q)V_m(i, n+1)\right)\right.$$

$$\left.\left. + \pi_d\left(qV_{m-1}(i+1, n+1) + (1-q)V_m(i+1, n+1)\right)\right)\right\}. \quad (16.3)$$

This recursive equation, together with the terminal conditions, completely determines the market value of the development rights, as well as the optimal development policy.

---

5. We calibrate the model in such a way that the risk-neutral probabilities are constant throughout the tree, so we write π_u rather than $\pi_u(i, n)$ in the valuation formula.

6. Recall that all development expenditure is tax deductible as soon as it is incurred.

16.3 DATA AND CALIBRATION

The state variable is the market value of the gas field as soon as it is ready to enter production. We use the market value of developed reserves already in production to calibrate the tree for the state variable, using data from a comparison firm.

Exploration and production firms might seem to be ideal candidates for comparison firms. Their shares are traded in highly liquid markets and they own producing gas reserves. Unfortunately, they also often have extensive exploration activities, so that their share prices will reflect the value of the exploration and development options embedded in their portfolios of energy assets. These options would distort estimates of both the level and the volatility of the market value of reserves in production.

Energy royalty trusts do not have these problems.[7] These trusts are entitled to a fixed proportion of the net proceeds from oil and gas produced at their underlying properties. The trusts are not subject to corporate tax provided that they are managed passively. In particular, no new properties can be added to a trust once it has been set up. The royalties paid out by the trusts decline over time as their reserves dwindle, until the trusts are eventually dissolved. Thus, the share prices of energy trusts reflect the value of specific reserves; they are not contaminated by exploration or development expenditure, beyond the ongoing development expenditure required to maintain production from a gas field that is being depleted.

Many of these trusts own royalty interests in fields that produce both oil and gas, but some receive royalties from fields that produce only relatively small amounts of oil (or none at all). In this chapter we focus on one such trust: Hugoton Royalty Trust, which receives 80% of the net proceeds from the sale of oil and gas produced by specific fields in Kansas, Oklahoma, and Wyoming.[8] Units in the trust have been traded on the New York Stock Exchange since April 1999, so that we have more than eight years of available data. The unit price (expressed in December 2007 dollars) is shown by the dashed curve in Figure 16.1.

There are three parameters we need to estimate in order to specify our underlying valuation model: the current level of the state variable, its volatility, and the risk-neutral probability of an up move. We use our comparison firm to estimate each one.

We start by calculating the market value of developed reserves that is implied by the Hugoton share price, which was $22.43 at the end of 2007. Since there were 40 million shares outstanding, no debt, and $5.214 million in cash and cash equivalents, the entity value at the end of 2007 was $891.986 million. At that time, the underlying properties were assessed as having 352.732 Bcf of

---

7. Tarquinio (2004) provides a useful introduction to royalty trusts.

8. In practice we might use several comparison firms to reduce the possibility that our calibration is contaminated by some aspect of a particular firm.

developed reserves.[9] Since Hugoton is entitled to 80% of the net revenue generated by these properties, its entity value relates to just $0.8 \times 352.732 = 282.186$ Bcf of developed reserves. The implied market value of developed gas reserves is therefore

$$\frac{891.986}{282.186} = 3.161$$

dollars per thousand cubic feet (Mcf) of gas. However, Hugoton is not subject to corporate tax, so that this figure is the market value of the pre-tax net revenue from extracting gas from the reserve. Assuming a tax rate of $T = 0.4$ (to allow for federal, state, and local taxes), our estimate of the market value of developed gas reserves is $0.6 \times 3.161 = 1.897$ dollars per Mcf. Since the field we are analyzing contains 100 Bcf, our estimate for the initial level of the state variable is $189.7 million.

Our next task is to estimate the volatility of changes in the state variable. Assuming that the quantity of reserves declines at a predictable rate—which is an approximation, but a reasonable one—we can use the volatility of royalty trust share prices as our estimate of the volatility of the market value of developed reserves.[10] We use share price and dividend data from December 1999 to December 2007, converting all prices into December 2007 dollars using the Consumer Price Index for all urban consumers, and fitting the random walk model described in Section 12.1.1. The monthly change in the log share price has mean 0.008260 and standard deviation 0.08722. We use the approach described in Section 14.2.3 to convert these into approximate means and standard deviations in the monthly change in the log entity value:

$$\hat{\nu} = \frac{0.008260}{1 + \frac{D-A}{E}} = \frac{0.008260}{1 + \frac{-5.214}{22.43 \times 40}} = 0.008308$$

and

$$\hat{\phi} = \frac{0.08722}{1 + \frac{D-A}{E}} = \frac{0.08722}{1 + \frac{-5.214}{22.43 \times 40}} = 0.08773.$$

We convert these two numbers into the normalized estimates that we need, using equations (12.3) and (12.4) with $\Delta t_d = 1/12$. The resulting drift and volatility estimates are $\hat{\mu} = 0.09970$ and $\hat{\sigma} = 0.3039$ respectively. We use monthly time steps in our binomial tree, so that the up and down moves can be found by evaluating equations (12.7) and (12.8) with $\Delta t_m = 1/12$. We find that $U = 1.0917$ and $D = 0.9160$.

---

9. Many royalty trusts report only the amount of gas equal in value to their total net profits interests, which is the measure required by the Financial Accounting Standards Board. That is, they divide the estimated net cash flows to be received by the trust by an estimate of the gas price. This expresses the *net* proceeds with gas as the numeraire, whereas we need a measure of the *gross* proceeds.

10. The implication of a predictable depletion rate is demonstrated in Problem 16.1.

The starting point for estimating the risk-neutral probability of an up move is equation (3.2), rewritten in the form

$$\pi_u = \frac{ZR_f - X_d}{X_u - X_d} = \frac{\left(\frac{Z}{X}\right)R_f - D}{U - D}. \tag{16.4}$$

We have already estimated U and D, and estimation of R_f is straightforward. All that remains is estimation of Z/X, the ratio of the price of the spanning asset to the current level of the state variable.

Shares in our comparison firm effectively give ownership of developed reserves that are in production, while the state variable is the price of developed reserves that are not yet in production. The former are generating cash flows, but being depleted in the process; the latter are currently producing no cash, but are not being depleted. Despite these differences, it is still possible (in principle) to replicate the spanning asset, as we explained in Section 14.2.1. The idea is that we purchase enough developed reserves in production, reinvesting the dividends we receive in additional shares, so that—after allowing for the depletion of this reserve due to production—we end up holding the required quantity of reserves. In order to implement such a transaction we need to know two things: the rate at which the reserves in production are being depleted and the dividend payout rate.

If a gas field's reserves are being depleted at rate δ and it contained Q_0 Bcf of gas at date 0, it will contain just

$$Q_t = e^{-\delta t} Q_0$$

Bcf after t years of production. Solving this equation for δ shows that the depletion rate implied by the two different levels of reserves equals

$$\delta = \frac{1}{t} \left(\log Q_0 - \log Q_t \right).$$

The underlying properties for Hugoton held developed reserves of 431.399 Bcf at the end of 1999 and 352.732 Bcf at the end of 2007. Thus, the reserves are being depleted at the rate

$$\delta = \frac{1}{8} \left(\log 431.399 - \log 352.732 \right) = 0.02517,$$

or approximately 2.5% per annum.

The dividend payout rate is the difference between the overall rate of return from investing in a firm's shares and the growth rate in the share price. $100 invested in Hugoton shares at the end of 1999 would have increased in value to $472.55 by the end of 2007 if all dividends were reinvested, and to $221.07 if none were reinvested.[11] Thus, the overall rate of return is

$$\frac{1}{8} \left(\log 472.55 - \log 100 \right) = 0.19412$$

---

11. Recall that all prices are expressed in December 2007 dollars.

per annum, while the capital gain is

$$\frac{1}{8}(\log 221.07 - \log 100) = 0.09916$$

per annum. The (continuously compounded) dividend payout rate is

$$y = 0.19412 - 0.09916 = 0.09496,$$

or approximately 9.5% per annum.

Now we are in a position to construct a replicating portfolio for our spanning asset. This portfolio must have a payoff equal to 100 Bcf of developed reserves exactly one period from now. Suppose we buy a shares in the royalty trust now and reinvest all dividends. If each share represents b Bcf of developed reserves now, then it will represent just $be^{-\delta \Delta t_m}$ Bcf of reserves after one period has elapsed. Because we are reinvesting all dividends, we will own $ae^{y\Delta t_m}$ shares after one period has elapsed, or the equivalent of $abe^{(y-\delta)\Delta t_m}$ Bcf of reserves, with no cash flows received in the meantime. This portfolio has exactly the same payoff as one unit of the spanning asset, provided that $abe^{(y-\delta)\Delta t_m} = 100$. Thus, the replicating portfolio contains exactly

$$a = \frac{100}{b}e^{-(y-\delta)\Delta t_m}$$

shares in the royalty trust. From the law of one price, the price of the spanning asset must equal the cost of this many shares in the royalty trust, which represents $100e^{-(y-\delta)\Delta t_m}$ Bcf of developed reserves. Since 100 Bcf of such reserves are currently worth X, this quantity of reserves must be worth $Xe^{-(y-\delta)\Delta t_m}$. Therefore the current price of the spanning asset is

$$Z = Xe^{-(y-\delta)\Delta t_m}. \tag{16.5}$$

Thus, we can use the dividend yield and depletion rate of a comparison firm to estimate the term, Z/X, that we need in order to calculate the risk-neutral probability of an up move. In the case of Hugoton, we have

$$\frac{Z}{X} = e^{-(y-\delta)\Delta t_m} = e^{-(0.09496-0.02517)\Delta t_m} = e^{-0.06979\Delta t_m}.$$

With monthly time steps (so that $\Delta t_m = 1/12$), we have $Z/X = 0.9942$.

Because the firm's development lease covers a ten-year period, we use the yield on ten-year Treasury inflation-protected securities (TIPS) at the end of 2007, which was 1.73%, to form our estimate of the risk-free real interest rate. Interest on TIPS is paid semi-annually, so that the implied return on a one-year risk-free bond is

$$\left(1 + \frac{0.0173}{2}\right)^2 = 1.01737.$$

It follows that the return on a one-period risk-free bond is $R_f = (1.01737)^{\Delta t_m}$. With monthly time steps we have $R_f = (1.01737)^{1/12} = 1.001436$. Given the up and down moves estimated above, equation (16.4) implies that the risk-neutral probability of an up move equals $\pi_u = 0.4532$ throughout the tree.

Now we turn to calibrating the development-cost component of our model. Recall that we split development of the field into M distinct stages, all of which must be successfully completed in order to develop the gas field. Each attempt to complete the latest stage lasts one period and is successful with probability q. As we show in Appendix 16.A, the length of time required to complete the project has mean $\bar{T} = M\,\Delta t_m/q$ and standard deviation

$$s = \frac{\Delta t_m}{q}\sqrt{M(1-q)}$$

(both in years). For the problem being considered here, we are given $\bar{T}$ and s. We therefore solve these equations for M and q to obtain

$$M = \frac{\bar{T}^2}{s^2 + \Delta t_m \bar{T}} \quad \text{and} \quad q = \frac{\Delta t_m \, \bar{T}}{s^2 + \Delta t_m \bar{T}}. \tag{16.6}$$

With an average development time of four years, a standard deviation of one year, and monthly time steps, we calculate $M = 12$ and $q = 0.25$.[12] The probability density function of the time required to develop the field is shown in Figure 16.3.[13]

Anticipated capital expenditure is $60 million per year which, for simplicity, we will assume is paid at the start of each year. Using equation (4.13), we can show that

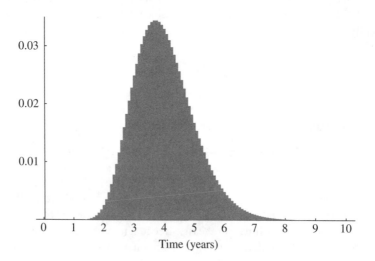

Figure 16.3. Probability density function for the time required to develop the field

---

12. Our model requires that M is an integer, so that some rounding may be required in practice. However, it is not necessary for the parameters used here.

13. The graph plots the function $\psi(n; M, q)$ given by equation (16.7) in Appendix 16.A.

the present value of capital expenditure of I per period, from dates 0 to $n-1$, equals

$$\left(1-\left(\frac{1}{R_f}\right)^n\right)\frac{R_f I}{R_f-1}=I\left(\frac{1-\left(\frac{1}{R_f}\right)^n}{1-\left(\frac{1}{R_f}\right)}\right)=I\left(\frac{1-\left(\frac{1}{1+r_f}\right)^{n\Delta t_m}}{1-\left(\frac{1}{1+r_f}\right)^{\Delta t_m}}\right).$$

If n periods span one year (so that $\Delta t_m = 1/n$), then we choose I such that this present value equals \$60 million. That is, we set the cost of each development attempt equal to

$$I=60\left(\frac{1-\left(\frac{1}{1+r_f}\right)^{\Delta t_m}}{1-\left(\frac{1}{1+r_f}\right)}\right),$$

where r_f is the risk-free interest rate for a term of one year. With monthly time steps, we obtain $I = 5.040$.

16.4 RESULTS

We start with a simple back-of-the-envelope analysis of the problem that would be appropriate if there were no development-cost risk and the firm had no timing flexibility. Development is expected to take four years and cost \$60 million per year (before tax), so suppose—for now—that the field is developed after exactly four years. From the discussion leading up to equation (16.5), the current market value of an asset with a payoff $\Delta t = 4$ years from now that is equal to the level of the state variable at that date must equal

$$X_0 e^{-(y-\delta)\Delta t} = 189.6 e^{-(0.09496-0.02517)\times 4} = 143.49$$

million dollars. The market value of the (post-tax) development expenditure would equal

$$(1-0.4)\left(60+\frac{60}{1.01737}+\frac{60}{(1.01737)^2}+\frac{60}{(1.01737)^3}\right)=140.35$$

million dollars if all development expenditure were tax-deductible as soon as it occurred. If decisions were made on the basis of these calculations, the firm would begin developing the field immediately and it would estimate the market value of the development rights to be \$3.14 million.

In contrast, a thorough analysis of the development problem that the firm actually faces needs to consider the development-cost risk together with the flexibility created by the firm's option to develop the field any time within the next ten years. We report the results of such an analysis in the remainder of this section.

Optimal Development of the Gas Field

When we implement the solution approach in Section 16.2 using the calibration described in Section 16.3, we find that the development rights are initially worth

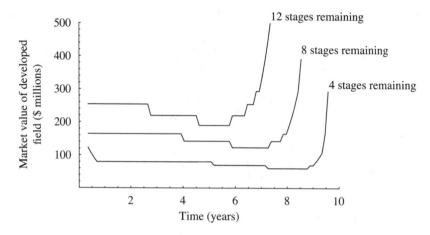

Figure 16.4. Development threshold for a natural gas field

$25.94 million. The earliest that development should begin is at date 4, and then only if the first four moves are all up. Thus, not only are the development rights much more valuable than the back-of-the-envelope calculation above, but that calculation would also lead to a suboptimal development policy.

We can calculate the development threshold for various stages of development. Three examples are drawn as functions of time in Figure 16.4. Initially, with 12 stages remaining, the firm should attempt development only when the market value of the developed field would lie above the top curve. When there are eight stages remaining, attempting development is optimal only when the market value lies above the middle curve; when there are just four stages remaining, the corresponding threshold is shown by the bottom curve.

The field is currently estimated to be worth $189.7 million if it were fully developed, placing it below the initial development threshold in Figure 16.4. Therefore the firm should not begin developing the field immediately; it should begin development within the first three years of the lease if the estimated market value reaches $269.4 million during that period. As Figure 16.4 shows, the optimal development threshold falls as each stage is completed, so that the next stage will begin immediately after the current one is completed. Development should be interrupted only if the estimated market value of the completed project falls sufficiently far during the course of finishing an individual stage that it moves below the optimal development threshold.

Figure 16.4 shows that the development thresholds have a U-shape, initially slowly decreasing as time passes, and then rapidly increasing as the firm runs out of time to complete development. As for the timing options we met in Part II, we can break the investment threshold into the sum of a break-even threshold and a premium reflecting the delay option that is destroyed whenever the firm invests. As time passes—and the date when the development rights must be relinquished approaches—the break-even threshold increases and the delay-option premium falls.

- The expected payoff from attempting to develop the field falls as time passes (holding all else equal) due to the reduced probability that development will be completed in time. Thus, the market value of the developed field must exceed a higher threshold as time passes in order to compensate the firm for the reduced probability that it will actually be able to exploit the developed field. In other words, the break-even threshold rises.
- The delay-option premium falls because the firm's timing flexibility is reduced as the time remaining to develop the field falls.

As Figure 16.3 shows, development is unlikely to take more than six years. Thus, in the early years of the lease, the break-even threshold is largely unchanged as time passes, while the option premium falls. Late in the lease's life, the delay option is almost worthless, so that the delay-option premium cannot fall much further. However, the break-even threshold rises rapidly. This explains the U-shape of the thresholds in Figure 16.4.

The owner of the development rights is exposed to two sources of risk: unexpected changes in the market value of developed reserves and unexpected capital expenditure. The magnitude of the first source is described by the volatility parameter σ, while the magnitude of the second source depends on the parameters M and q in a manner we describe shortly. We analyze the effect of these two sources of risk in the remainder of this section.

The Effect of Volatility in the Market Value of Developed Reserves

We begin by performing sensitivity analysis on the state variable's volatility σ. Our analysis will focus on the effect that changing σ has on the market value of the development rights at date 0 and on the optimal development policy. Table 16.1 shows what happens when we increase σ from 0.2 to 0.5. The first two entries in each row give the volatility of the state variable (σ) and the market value of the development rights at date 0 ($V_M(0, 0)$). The final three entries give the development threshold required for attempting completion of the next stage two years from now to be optimal, given that 12, 8, or 4 stages remain to be completed. For instance, when $\sigma = 0.2$, if the first stage has still not been completed two years from now, then the firm should only attempt development at that time if the market value of the developed field would exceed $212.9 million; when $\sigma = 0.4$, the firm should only attempt development if the market value would exceed $301.1 million.

Higher volatility means that the market value of the gas field when development is finally completed will be drawn from a much wider range of possibilities. Increases in the state variable that would have been large with volatility at its calibrated level will be even larger when volatility is greater; reductions that would have been large will also be larger. The firm will develop the field in the former case, so that it fully benefits from the increased upside risk. However, its ability to relinquish the development rights in the latter case allows it to mitigate the downside risk. This is consistent with the behavior in the second column of Table 16.1, which shows the development rights increasing in value as volatility increases.

The increased asymmetry in upside and downside risk due to greater volatility raises the value of the option to delay incurring development expenditure. As a result, the payoff from immediate development activity needs to be higher for immediate investment to be optimal. Consistent with this, the final three columns of Table 16.1 show that the optimal development threshold increases as volatility increases.

The Effect of Development-cost Risk

Now we turn to the role of development-cost risk. The distribution of capital expenditure is determined by the number of development stages, M, and the probability of success at each attempt, q. In order to focus on the role of risk, we vary M and q in such a way that the expected development time equals four years, as in our baseline analysis above. Thus, once we have specified M it follows that

$$q = \frac{M \Delta t_m}{\bar{T}} = \frac{M}{48}.$$

The standard deviation of the development time is then

$$s = \frac{\Delta t_m}{q}\sqrt{M(1-q)} = \frac{4}{M}\sqrt{M\left(1 - \frac{M}{48}\right)} = 4\sqrt{\frac{1}{M} - \frac{1}{48}}$$

years. As we increase M, each attempt to complete a stage becomes more likely, and the standard deviation of the required development time falls. By the time we have reached $M = 48$, the gas field will be developed after exactly 48 attempts, so that there is no development-cost risk.

Table 16.2 shows what happens to the market value of the development rights when we increase M from 1 to 48. The first three entries in each row report the number of stages (M), the probability of success required for the average development time to remain at four years (q), and the standard deviation of the

Table 16.1. Sensitivity Analysis of the Volatility of the Market Value of Developed Reserves

σ	$V_M(0,0)$	Development Threshold		
		$m = 12$	$m = 8$	$m = 4$
0.2	15.35	212.9	150.6	67.1
0.3	25.53	268.2	159.5	79.8
0.4	36.10	301.1	189.7	94.9
0.5	46.56	337.9	253.2	142.1

Table 16.2. Sensitivity Analysis of Development-cost Risk

M	q	s	8-year Lease		10-year Lease		12-year Lease	
			$V_M(0,0)$	X^*	$V_M(0,0)$	X^*	$V_M(0,0)$	X^*
1	0.021	3.96	35.34	189.7	37.71	189.7	39.29	189.7
2	0.042	2.77	26.67	189.7	30.16	226.1	32.27	226.1
4	0.083	1.91	23.19	226.1	27.12	226.1	29.33	269.4
6	0.125	1.53	22.62	226.1	26.42	226.1	28.48	269.4
8	0.167	1.29	22.55	226.1	26.15	269.4	28.08	269.4
12	0.250	1.00	22.73	226.1	25.94	269.4	27.77	269.4
16	0.333	0.82	22.91	226.1	25.90	269.4	27.64	269.4
20	0.417	0.68	23.06	226.1	25.91	269.4	27.57	269.4
24	0.500	0.58	23.20	226.1	25.93	269.4	27.55	269.4
36	0.750	0.33	23.60	269.4	26.08	269.4	27.57	269.4
48	1.000	0.00	24.39	269.4	26.50	269.4	27.81	269.4

development time (s). The next three pairs of entries show the market value of the development rights at date 0 ($V_M(0,0)$) and the development threshold required to attempt completion of the first stage two years from now (X^*). The pairs correspond to leases lasting eight, ten, and twelve years, respectively. We see from the table that increasing development-cost risk (that is, moving up the table) first lowers the market value of the development rights and then raises their market value; the shaded cells indicate the level of development-cost risk that minimizes the market value of the development rights for each lease.

Two things happen as development-cost risk rises. First, the firm can be less confident in its ability to delay development and still be able to develop the field before the rights expire. This reduces timing flexibility and therefore makes the development rights less valuable. Second, the possibility of completing development in a very short time (and therefore of beginning to produce gas relatively soon) is increased, which makes the rights more valuable. The table shows that the first effect dominates when both risk and timing flexibility are relatively low.

Increasing development-cost risk also affects the optimal development threshold in two distinct ways, but now the two effects reinforce each other. First, the firm's timing flexibility falls, lowering the market value of the delay option that is destroyed when the firm attempts to complete a development stage, and therefore lowering the payoff that is required for investment to be optimal. Second, the increased likelihood of very rapid development raises the investment payoff for any given level of the state variable. Thus, in order for the investment payoff to exceed the value of the delay option, the market value of a developed field does not need to be as high when development-cost risk rises, partly due to the lower value of waiting and partly because of the higher investment payoff. This intuition is consistent with what we see in Table 16.2, where greater development-cost risk leads to a lower development threshold.

16.5 PROBLEMS

16.1. **(Demonstration)** Denote the quantity of reserves in a gas field at date j by Q_j and the market value of each unit of reserves by P_j, so that the gas field itself is worth $X_j = P_j Q_j$. Suppose that the reserve quantity declines at rate δ, so that

$$Q_{j+1} = Q_j e^{-\delta \Delta t_d},$$

and that the price of reserves evolves according to

$$\log P_{j+1} - \log P_j = \nu + u_{j+1}, \quad u_{j+1} \sim N(0, \phi^2),$$

for some constants ν and ϕ. Derive an expression for $\log X_{j+1} - \log X_j$ and discuss the significance of this result.

16.2. **(Practice)** Implement the model described in Section 16.2 with $\Delta t_m = 0.25$. (Note that the values of M and q will have to change to reflect the new step size.)

16.3. **(Demonstration)** In this problem we estimate the RADR for our state variable.

    (a) Calculate the risk-adjusted growth factor implied by our calibration.

    (b) In Section 16.3 we estimated that the market value of developed gas reserves that are in production has an average annual growth rate of approximately 10.0%. Explain why this implies an estimate of the average annual growth rate for the state variable equal to 12.5%.

    (c) Use this information to estimate a RADR for the state variable, expressed in percent per annum.

16.4. **(Demonstration)** We calibrated the development-cost process using equations (16.6). We were fortunate that our choice of Δt_m led to an integer solution for M, but this will not always be the case. An alternative approach is to specify the number of development stages (M) and then calculate the values of Δt_m and q that match the mean and standard deviation of the development time.

    (a) Solve equations (16.6) for Δt_m and q.

    (b) Calculate the values of Δt_m and q for the following numbers of development stages: 1, 2, 4, 8, 12, 16, 20.

16.5. **(Practice)** Suppose that there are two phases to developing the gas field. Phase I will take one year on average with a standard deviation of six months; Phase II will take three years on average with a standard deviation of one year. The lengths of time to complete the two stages are statistically independent. Describe how to modify the model described in Section 16.1 so that it reflects the two development phases.

16.6. **(Discussion)** Discuss the extent to which the firm learns about the eventual total development cost over time, given the current model set-up. Discuss the strengths and weaknesses of our approach. Describe various ways to modify the model that would enhance the role that learning plays.

16.A APPENDIX: THE DISTRIBUTION OF THE DEVELOPMENT TIME

We begin by deriving the probability that exactly n attempts are required to develop the field, which we denote by $\psi(n; M, q)$. The only way that exactly n attempts will be required is if (i) $M - 1$ of the first $n - 1$ attempts were successful and (ii) the nth attempt is also successful. The first condition occurs with probability

$$\frac{(n - 1)!}{(M - 1)!(n - M)!} q^{M-1}(1 - q)^{n-M}.$$

Since the second condition occurs with probability q, and the outcomes of all attempts are independent, the probability of both conditions occurring is

$$\psi(n; M, q) = \frac{(n - 1)!}{(M - 1)!(n - M)!} q^{M}(1 - q)^{n-M}. \tag{16.7}$$

This is the function that is plotted in Figure 16.3.

The expected value of the number of attempts required to achieve M successes is

$$E[n] = \sum_{n=M}^{\infty} n\psi(n; M, q)$$

$$= \sum_{n=M}^{\infty} \frac{n!}{(M - 1)!(n - M)!} q^{M}(1 - q)^{n-M}$$

$$= \frac{M}{q} \sum_{n=M}^{\infty} \frac{n!}{M!(n - M)!} q^{M+1}(1 - q)^{n-M}$$

$$= \frac{M}{q} \sum_{n=M}^{\infty} \psi(n + 1; M + 1, q)$$

$$= \frac{M}{q}.$$

The last step is a consequence of the probabilities $\psi(n + 1; M + 1, q)$ having to sum to one.

We can use a similar procedure to show that

$$E[n(n + 1)] = \sum_{n=M}^{\infty} n(n + 1)\psi(n; M, q)$$

$$= \sum_{n=M}^{\infty} \frac{(n + 1)!}{(M - 1)!(n - M)!} q^{M}(1 - q)^{n-M}$$

$$= \frac{M(M + 1)}{q^2} \sum_{n=M}^{\infty} \frac{(n + 1)!}{(M + 1)!(n - M)!} q^{M+2}(1 - q)^{n-M}$$

$$= \frac{M(M+1)}{q^2} \sum_{n=M}^{\infty} \psi(n+2; M+2, q)$$

$$= \frac{M(M+1)}{q^2},$$

which implies that

$$E[n^2] = E[n(n+1)] - E[n] = \frac{M(M+1)}{q^2} - \frac{M}{q} = \frac{M(M+1-q)}{q^2}.$$

Therefore the variance of the number of attempts required to achieve M successes is

$$\text{Var}[n] = E[n^2] - (E[n])^2 = \frac{M(1-q)}{q^2}.$$

Since each step in the binomial tree represents Δt_m years, the length of time required to complete the project has mean $\bar{T} = M \Delta t_m / q$ and standard deviation

$$s = \frac{\Delta t_m}{q} \sqrt{M(1-q)}.$$

17

Mothballing an Ethanol Plant

Total US ethanol production rose from 1.6 billion gallons in 2000 to 6.5 billion gallons in 2007 (EIA, 2008, Table 4a). The increased output reflected rising capacity from a wave of investment in new production facilities. Despite the increasing supply of ethanol, the spread between the ethanol price and the cost of its main inputs (corn and natural gas) continued to widen, at least for a while. However, ethanol prices fell in the middle of 2006 and corn prices began to rise. By 2008 construction of many partly-completed ethanol plants had been halted. Some completed plants had suspended operations and some had defaulted on debt obligations.

It is the end of May 2008 and the owner of an operational ethanol plant is considering temporarily suspending production, mothballing the plant, or shutting it down permanently. Suspending production requires no immediate expenditure and allows full production to resume at very short notice. However, there will still be substantial ongoing cash outflows while production is suspended. Mothballing reduces these cash flows significantly, but at a cost—mothballing the plant takes time and money, and subsequently resuming production takes even more time and money. Thus it is worth mothballing the plant only if the owner is confident that he will not want to produce ethanol for a reasonable length of time but is not convinced that complete abandonment is warranted. One of our tasks in this chapter is to help the owner determine just how bad conditions in the ethanol market have to get before mothballing is optimal.

The plant is capable of producing 100 million gallons of ethanol each year from 36 million bushels of corn and 3.5 trillion British thermal units (Btu) of natural gas. The futures prices for corn, ethanol, and natural gas at the end of May 2008, reported in Table 17.1, show why the plant's owner is concerned.

Table 17.1. Futures Prices at the End of May 2008

	Exchange	Delivery Date			
		Jun.	Jul.	Sep.	Dec.
Ethanol ($/gal)	CBOT	2.391	2.398	2.420	2.436
Corn ($/bu)	CBOT	5.927	5.992	6.124	6.264
Gas ($/MMBtu)	NYMEX	11.399	11.556	11.672	12.374
Margin ($/gal)		−0.142	−0.164	−0.193	−0.252

Prices for delivery in June 2008 are \$2.391 per gallon of ethanol, \$5.927 per bushel of corn, and \$11.399 per MMBtu of natural gas. Since the plant requires 0.36 bushels of corn and 0.035 MMBtu of natural gas to produce each gallon of ethanol, the implied cost of production is

$$0.36 \times 5.927 + 0.035 \times 11.399 = 2.533$$

dollars per gallon, \$0.142 more than the ethanol futures price. As is shown in Table 17.1, the situation is even worse for more distant delivery dates, with the owner losing \$0.252 per gallon of ethanol sold in December 2008.

Wages and administration currently cost the owner \$5.5 million each year, transportation costs \$20 million, and plant maintenance costs \$1.5 million. Transportation costs are only incurred when the plant is producing ethanol. The owner estimates that maintenance costs will fall by 50% while the plant is idle and by 95% when it is mothballed. Wages and administration costs will fall by 95% while the facility is in mothballs. There will be time lags involved in putting the plant in and out of mothballs and these will play an important role in determining the optimal operating policy. The owner estimates that it takes one month and \$500,000 to mothball the plant and three months and \$2.5 million to bring it back to operational status. This expenditure includes wages and other costs paid during the mothballing and reactivation processes. The cost of preparing the plant for sale and cleaning up the site are such that the net proceeds from shutting the plant permanently are negligible. All costs are assumed to be constant in real terms. The plant has a useful life of ten years.

17.1 SETTING UP THE MODEL

The processing plant produces ethanol from corn and natural gas. Its profitability depends on the gross processing margin, which is the amount by which the price of ethanol exceeds the cost of these inputs. We take the gross processing margin as the state variable for our model. Assuming that the only significant contributor to the plant's revenue is ethanol, it equals

$$X = P - 0.36C - 0.035G,$$

where P is the price of ethanol in dollars per gallon, C is the price of corn in dollars per bushel, and G is the price of natural gas in dollars per MMBtu.

Each date that the plant is operational it can either produce Q gallons of ethanol or it can temporarily suspend production. If it produces ethanol then its cash flow equals $QX(i, n) - C_P$, where C_P denotes all costs other than those of purchasing corn and natural gas. The plant's cash flow equals $-C_S$ each date that production is suspended. Each date that the plant is mothballed the firm's cash flow equals $-C_M$, reflecting expenditure on low-intensity maintenance, security, property taxes, and so on.

We assume that no expenditure is required to switch between producing ethanol and temporarily suspending production. However, it will take N_M periods to undertake the mothballing process and lump-sum expenditure of I_M must be incurred as soon as the process begins. Reversing the mothballing procedure is also costly. We assume that it will take N_R periods to reactivate the plant and that lump-sum expenditure of I_R must be incurred as soon as the reactivation procedure begins. The mothballing and reactivation procedures cannot be interrupted. The plant can be abandoned whenever it is operational or in mothballs; if it has not been abandoned before date N then it must be abandoned at that date. Abandonment is irreversible. A net salvage value of S is received as soon as the plant is abandoned.

The tax rate T reflects federal, state, and local taxes. We assume that the plant has already been fully depreciated, so that the depreciation tax shield has zero value. The return on one-period risk-free bonds is R_f.

17.2 THE SOLUTION PROCEDURE

The decision tree for the owner's problem is shown in Figure 17.1 for the special case where it takes $N_M = 2$ periods to mothball the plant and $N_R = 3$ periods to reactivate it. The extension to different mothballing and reactivation lags is straightforward.

At date 0 the plant is operational and the owner must take one of four possible actions: produce ethanol (action P), temporarily suspend production (action S), abandon the plant (action A), or start to mothball the plant (action M). If he takes either of the first two actions then the plant will still be operational at date 1 and the choices available to the owner will be the same as at date 0. If he abandons the plant then the decision tree terminates at date 0. Therefore, the only new possibility at date 1 that we need to consider is that one stage of the mothballing procedure has been completed. Our assumption that mothballing cannot be interrupted means that all the owner can do in this situation is complete the second stage.

The plant will be in one of three states at date 2: operational, with one stage of the mothballing procedure completed, or with two stages completed. The choices available to the owner for the first two are as described in the preceding paragraph, so that we only need to consider the situation when two mothballing stages have been completed. If mothballing takes more than two periods then all the owner can do is complete the next stage. However, if (as in Figure 17.1) mothballing only takes two periods then the situation is more complicated: the owner must

$n = 0$ $n = 1$ $n = 2$ $n = 3$ $n = 4$ $n = 5$ $n = 6$

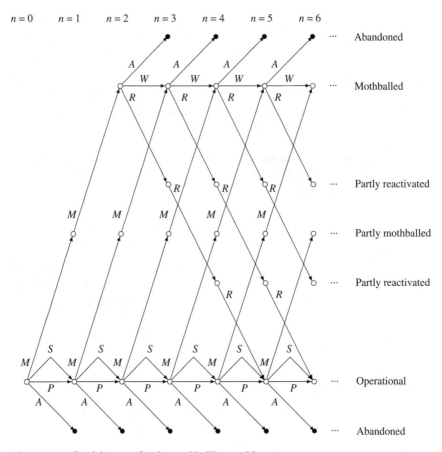

Figure 17.1. Decision tree for the mothballing problem

keep the plant in mothballs (action W), abandon the plant (action A), or begin to reactivate it (action R). If he takes the first action then the plant will still be in mothballs at date 3 and the choices available to the owner will be the same as at date 2. If he abandons the plant then the decision tree terminates at date 2. If he begins to reactivate the plant, then at date 3 one stage of the reactivation procedure will have been completed. Our assumption that reactivation cannot be interrupted means that all the owner can do in this situation is complete each successive stage until the plant is once more operational.

If we continue to work forward in time like this, we eventually complete construction of the decision tree in Figure 17.1. The decision tree reveals several distinct project states, each one requiring its own binomial tree. We need to construct $1 + N_M + N_R$ trees in total:

- One tree for the state variable, $X(i, n)$.
- One tree for the market value of the plant while it is operational, $V_O(i, n)$.

- N_M trees for the market value of the plant while it is being mothballed, $V_{M,m}(i, n)$, where $m = 1, 2, \ldots, N_M$ denotes the number of steps in the mothballing process that have been completed.
- $N_R - 1$ trees for the market value of the plant while it is being reactivated, $V_{R,m}(i, n)$, where $m = 1, 2, \ldots, N_R - 1$ denotes the number of steps in the reactivation process that have been completed.[1]

Because we assume that the plant is abandoned, and its net salvage value received immediately, at date N, all market-value trees have the same terminal condition:

$$V_O(i, N) = V_{M,m}(i, N) = V_{R,m}(i, N) = (1 - T)S. \qquad (17.1)$$

However, the recursive equations differ across the various project-states.

We begin by considering the case that the plant is operational when it enters node (i, n). The plant can produce ethanol, generating post-tax cash flow of $(1 - T)(QX(i, n) - C_P)$, or suspend production, generating post-tax cash flow of $-(1 - T)C_S$.[2] In either case, the plant will be worth $V_O(i, n + 1)$ or $V_O(i + 1, n + 1)$ at date $n + 1$, depending on whether an up or a down move occurs. However, the owner of the plant has two other alternatives. He can begin the mothballing process, in which case the post-tax cash flow is $-(1 - T)I_M$ immediately and the plant will be worth $V_{M,1}(i, n + 1)$ or $V_{M,1}(i + 1, n + 1)$ at date $n + 1$. Finally, he can abandon the plant altogether, generating a payoff worth $(1 - T)S$. Provided he follows a value-maximizing policy, the operational plant is worth

$$
\begin{aligned}
V_O&(i,n) \\
&= \max \Bigg\{ (1-T)(QX(i,n) - C_P) + \frac{\pi_u(i,n)V_O(i,n+1) + \pi_d(i,n)V_O(i+1,n+1)}{R_f}, \\
&\quad -(1-T)C_S + \frac{\pi_u(i,n)V_O(i,n+1) + \pi_d(i,n)V_O(i+1,n+1)}{R_f}, \\
&\quad -(1-T)I_M + \frac{\pi_u(i,n)V_{M,1}(i,n+1) + \pi_d(i,n)V_{M,1}(i+1,n+1)}{R_f}, \\
&\quad (1-T)S \Bigg\}.
\end{aligned}
\qquad (17.2)
$$

Suppose, instead, that the plant has completed m stages of the mothballing process when it enters node (i, n). If the process is not yet completed, so that

---

1. There is no need to consider a separate tree for $m = N_R$, since the relevant market value in this case is $V_O(i, n)$; that is, the plant is fully operational as soon as stage N_R of the reactivation procedure is completed.

2. We assume that the owner has sufficient income from other sources that the expenditure of C_S can be used to reduce his tax immediately.

$m < N_M$, then all the owner can do is continue the mothballing operation. Thus

$$V_{M,m}(i,n) = \frac{\pi_u(i,n)V_{M,m+1}(i,n+1) + \pi_d(i,n)V_{M,m+1}(i+1,n+1)}{R_f}. \quad (17.3)$$

However, once the process has been completed the owner has the option to reactivate the plant or to abandon it, as well as to keep it in mothballs. If he begins the reactivation process, the post-tax cash flow is $-(1-T)I_R$ immediately and the plant will be worth $V_{R,1}(i,n+1)$ or $V_{R,1}(i+1,n+1)$ at date $n+1$. If he decides to keep it mothballed for at least one more period then the cash flow is $-(1-T)C_M$ immediately and after one period elapses the plant will be worth $V_{M,N_M}(i,n+1)$ or $V_{M,N_M}(i+1,n+1)$ at date $n+1$. If he abandons the plant altogether, the payoff is $(1-T)S$. Thus, the mothballed plant is worth

$$V_{M,N_M}(i,n)$$

$$= \max \left\{ -(1-T)I_R + \frac{\pi_u(i,n)V_{R,1}(i,n+1) + \pi_d(i,n)V_{R,1}(i+1,n+1)}{R_f}, \right.$$

$$\left. -(1-T)C_M + \frac{\pi_u(i,n)V_{M,N_M}(i,n+1) + \pi_d(i,n)V_{M,N_M}(i+1,n+1)}{R_f}, \right.$$

$$\left. (1-T)S \right\}. \quad (17.4)$$

Finally, suppose that the plant has completed m stages of the reactivation process when it enters node (i,n). All the owner can do is continue the reactivating operation. If there is more than one period remaining in the reactivation process, the plant will still not be fully operational after one period elapses, so that it will be worth $V_{R,m+1}(i,n+1)$ or $V_{R,m+1}(i+1,n+1)$ at date $n+1$. Thus its value at date n equals

$$V_{R,m}(i,n) = \frac{\pi_u(i,n)V_{R,m+1}(i,n+1) + \pi_d(i,n)V_{R,m+1}(i+1,n+1)}{R_f}. \quad (17.5)$$

However, when there is just one period remaining in the reactivation process, the plant will be fully operational after one period elapses. That is, it will be worth $V_O(i,n+1)$ or $V_O(i+1,n+1)$ at date $n+1$. It follows that the plant is worth

$$V_{R,N_R-1}(i,n) = \frac{\pi_u(i,n)V_O(i,n+1) + \pi_d(i,n)V_O(i+1,n+1)}{R_f} \quad (17.6)$$

one period before reactivation is complete.

We now have all the recursive and terminal equations needed to derive an optimal policy for operating the ethanol plant, as well as to determine its market value. Because of the presence of switching options, it is simplest to follow a similar approach to that sketched in Table 10.1 and fill in all of the market-value trees simultaneously, starting with their terminal conditions and working from right to left. The procedure is summarized in Table 17.2.

Table 17.2. Summarizing the Solution Procedure

Variable	Recursive	Terminal
$V_O(i, n)$	(17.2)	(17.1)
$V_{M,1}(i, n)$ $\quad \vdots$ $V_{M,N_M-1}(i, n)$	(17.3)	(17.1)
$V_{M,N_M}(i, n)$	(17.4)	(17.1)
$V_{R,1}(i, n)$ $\quad \vdots$ $V_{R,N_R-2}(i, n)$	(17.5)	(17.1)
$V_{R,N_R-1}(i, n)$	(17.6)	(17.1)

17.3 DATA AND CALIBRATION

Our main focus is on calibrating a binomial tree for the state variable (the gross processing margin). Although the state variable is not the price of a traded asset, it is derived from such prices, which influences the calibration approach we adopt. The margin can take negative values and is likely to be mean reverting, with entry by new processors stopping the margin from ever getting too high and exit by existing processors stopping it from ever getting too low. Therefore we assume that the margin follows the mean-reverting process discussed in Section 14.1. Estimating the parameters for this process would be straightforward if historical data on the margin were available.

Recall that, via equation (3.2), the risk-neutral probability of an up move at node (i, n) depends on the price of the spanning asset at that node. For the situation considered in this chapter, the spanning asset has a payoff equal to the margin one period in the future. Because the state variable is built up from spot prices, we can replicate the spanning asset using a portfolio of one-period-ahead futures contracts. Specifically, the portfolio comprising one long position in an ethanol futures contract, 0.36 short corn futures positions and 0.035 short gas futures positions, and an appropriate holding of one-period risk-free bonds, has exactly the same payoff as the spanning asset. If historical data on the period-ahead futures prices were available, we could calculate the corresponding prices of the spanning asset, estimate the relationship between the state variable and this price, and use it to estimate the risk-neutral probabilities.

We would like to use historical data on spot prices and period-ahead futures prices for ethanol, corn, and natural gas. Unfortunately, spot price data for these commodities are affected by factors such as illiquidity, which can contaminate parameter estimates. Moreover, as we will see in Section 17.4, it is necessary to choose a small step size Δt_m, and we cannot observe such short-term futures prices. As a result, we cannot directly observe the data we would like to use.

However, futures contracts on all three commodities are traded with a selection of different delivery dates. We use data on the corn and ethanol futures contracts traded on the Chicago Board of Trade (CBOT) and the natural gas contracts traded on the New York Mercantile Exchange (NYMEX) to construct historical data for the state variable. The newest contracts are the ethanol futures, launched in March 2005 and still relatively thinly traded. This limits our sample period to just over three years. We use prices from these contracts to estimate the spot and month-ahead futures prices. Once we have estimated the relationship between the corresponding spot and month-ahead margins, we can infer the relationship between the state variable and the price of the spanning asset, which allows us to calibrate the risk-neutral probabilities.

We describe the details of this procedure shortly, but in the meantime we summarize our overall approach. We need to carry out the following steps to build the tree for the margin that is implied by our data.

1. For each commodity (corn, ethanol, and gas) we collect monthly data on the contracts with the nearest and the next-nearest delivery dates.
2. For each commodity and each month in our sample period we use a simple linear interpolation technique to estimate the spot price and month-ahead futures price consistent with the two observed futures prices.
3. We combine the three series of estimated spot prices to calculate a single time series of historical observations of the margin, which we convert into May 2008 dollars using the Consumer Price Index for all urban consumers. This procedure is repeated for the series of estimated month-ahead futures prices.
4. We estimate a mean-reverting process for the margin, using the technique described in Section 14.1.
5. We estimate the relationship between the month-ahead futures margin and the spot margin, infer the corresponding relationship between the period-ahead futures margin and the spot margin, and use this relationship to calculate the risk-neutral probabilities.

Constructing Spot and Futures Gross Processing Margins

Our data comprise end-of-month futures prices for contracts with the nearest and the next-nearest delivery dates. Each month, the time until delivery ranges from 0 to 5 months. We use the futures price for a contract with delivery in the next month as our estimate of the spot price, and that for a contract with delivery in the month after that as our estimate of the month-ahead futures price.[3] When one or both of these prices are not available (because the corresponding futures contracts

---

3. The contracts actually offer flexibility regarding exactly when delivery can occur. We assume that delivery occurs at the beginning of the delivery month. Since our data are measured at the end of the month, the futures price for delivery in the next month is effectively a day-ahead futures price. We use it as our spot price.

are not traded), we interpolate the observed term structure of futures prices to obtain an estimate of the missing prices.

If the nearest contract is for delivery n_1 months from now, while the second-nearest one is for delivery n_2 months from now, we use equation (12.23) to estimate the futures price for delivery t months from now:

$$\log \hat{F}_t = \left(\frac{n_2 - t}{n_2 - n_1} \right) \log \hat{F}_{n_1} + \left(\frac{t - n_1}{n_2 - n_1} \right) \log \hat{F}_{n_2}.$$

Whenever it is necessary, we use this equation with $t = 0$ to estimate the spot price or with $t = 1$ to estimate the month-ahead futures price.[4]

For example, at the end of May 2008 the futures price for delivery of corn in $n_1 = 1$ month was $F_{n_1} = 5.992$, while the futures price for delivery in $n_2 = 3$ months was $F_{n_2} = 6.124$. The implied spot price of corn has logarithm

$$\log \hat{F}_0 = \left(\frac{3 - 0}{3 - 1} \right) \log 5.992 + \left(\frac{0 - 1}{3 - 1} \right) \log 6.124 = 1.780,$$

which implies that the spot price is $\hat{F}_0 = \exp(1.780) = 5.927$ dollars per bushel. The spot prices of ethanol and natural gas at the end of May 2008 are \$2.391/gal and \$11.399/MMBtu, implying that the gross processing margin equals $X_0 = -0.142$ at the end of May 2008. We take this as our starting value for the state variable.

The three curves in the left-hand graph in Figure 17.2 show the estimated spot prices of corn, ethanol, and gas, while the right-hand graph plots the corresponding margin. The margin reached its highest level in the middle of 2006, when the price of ethanol rose and the price of natural gas fell. Shortly afterwards, the ethanol price fell steeply and the corn price rose, contributing to a rapid decline in the margin. The steady decline in the margin since then is the result of a stable ethanol price and climbing corn and gas prices.

One question we have to confront is whether the behavior evident in these graphs is representative of future behavior. If we believe it is, then it is appropriate to calibrate the model using data from the entire sample period. An alternative view is that the wave of new investment in ethanol production facilities means that the boom period in the first half of 2006 is unlikely to be repeated in the future. In that case, our analysis might be misleading if it relied on data from the full sample period. However, it is not feasible to restrict the sample to the post-boom period: there are too few observations for any parameter estimates to be reliable. We use the full sample period, from March 2005 to May 2008, thus making the implicit assumption that the behavior of the margin during that period is representative of what can happen over the remaining lifetime of the ethanol plant we are analyzing.[5]

---

4. When $t = 0$ we actually extrapolate from the two observed futures prices. However, the same formula for $\log \hat{F}_t$ applies in this case.

5. In practical applications we might carry out a sensitivity analysis on the parameters describing the behavior of the margin, as in Problem 17.3. In addition, Problem 17.4 shows what happens when we use only the post-boom period to calibrate the risk-neutral probabilities.

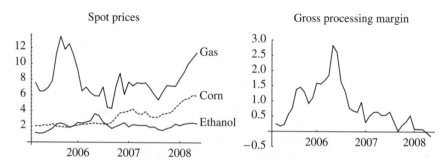

Figure 17.2. Price history of corn, ethanol, and natural gas

Note: Estimated spot prices for corn ($/bu), ethanol ($/gal), and natural gas ($/MMBtu), converted into May 2008 dollars using the Consumer Price Index for all urban consumers. The gross processing margin is measured in dollars per gallon. Estimates are calculated using futures prices from CBOT (corn and ethanol) and NYMEX (natural gas).

Calibrating the Binomial Tree for the State Variable

Estimating the AR(1) model for the gross processing margin using the ordinary least-squares method results in the estimated relationship

$$X_{j+1} - X_j = \underset{(0.08858)}{0.08191} - \underset{(0.0821)}{0.1105 X_j} + u_{j+1}, \quad \mathrm{Var}[u_{j+1}] = 0.1202, \qquad (17.7)$$

where the numbers in brackets indicate the standard errors of the associated parameter estimates. It follows that the parameters we need in order to evaluate the equations in (12.13) are

$$\hat{\alpha}_0 = 0.08191, \quad \hat{\alpha}_1 = -0.1105, \quad \hat{\phi} = \sqrt{0.1202} = 0.3467.$$

Since the data are monthly, we have $\Delta t_d = 1/12$. Substituting these parameters into the equations in (12.13) shows that the normalized estimates of the required parameters are

$$\hat{a} = 1.405, \quad \hat{b} = 0.7413, \quad \hat{\sigma} = 1.272.$$

From the discussion in Section 12.1.2, these parameters imply that in the long run the margin is normally distributed with mean $\hat{b} = 0.7413$ and standard deviation $\hat{\sigma}/\sqrt{2\hat{a}} = 0.7588$. The implied half-life of shocks to the margin is $(\log 2)/\hat{a} = 0.4933$ years, or almost six months. That is, half of each shock to the margin is expected to have died out after six months.

Recall from equation (14.1) that the state variable evolves according to

$$X(i, n) = X_0 + (n - 2i)\hat{\sigma}\sqrt{\Delta t_m}.$$

We saw in Section 14.1.1 that this is equivalent to adding $U = \hat{\sigma}\sqrt{\Delta t_m}$ to the state variable each time there is an up move, and adding $D = -U$ each time there is a down move. For example, if we break each month into 30 time steps (so that $\Delta t_m = 1/360$), then $U = 0.06704$. From equation (14.4), the actual probability of an up move at node (i, n) equals

$$\theta_u(i, n) = \frac{1}{2} + \frac{(1 - e^{-\hat{a}\Delta t_m})(\hat{b} - X(i, n))}{2\hat{\sigma}\sqrt{\Delta t_m}} = 0.5215 - 0.02905X(i, n)$$

whenever this number lies between 0 and 1; if it is negative we reset it to 0, while if it exceeds 1 we reset it to 1.

Calibrating the Risk-neutral Probabilities

Now we turn to the calculation of the risk-neutral probabilities. Recall from Section 3.3 that the risk-neutral probability of an up move at node (i, n) is

$$\pi_u(i, n) = \frac{F(i, n) - X(i + 1, n + 1)}{X(i, n + 1) - X(i + 1, n + 1)},$$

where $F(i, n)$ equals the futures price for a contract on the state variable for delivery one period in the future. Since $X(i, n + 1) = X(i, n) + \hat{\sigma}\sqrt{\Delta t_m}$ and $X(i + 1, n + 1) = X(i, n) - \hat{\sigma}\sqrt{\Delta t_m}$, this reduces to

$$\pi_u(i, n) = \frac{1}{2} + \frac{F(i, n) - X(i, n)}{2\hat{\sigma}\sqrt{\Delta t_m}}.$$

In this chapter we suppose that

$$F(i, n) = c_0 + c_1 X(i, n), \tag{17.8}$$

for some constants c_0 and c_1, in which case the risk-neutral probability of an up move at node (i, n) is[6]

$$\pi_u(i, n) = \frac{1}{2} + \frac{c_0 - (1 - c_1)X(i, n)}{2\hat{\sigma}\sqrt{\Delta t_m}}. \tag{17.9}$$

We therefore need to estimate the relationship between the period-ahead futures margin, F, and its spot counterpart, X. We do this indirectly, by first estimating the relationship between the month-ahead futures margin and the state variable and then inferring the relationship between the period-ahead futures margin and its spot counterpart. The reason for this approach (rather than using the period-ahead futures margin directly) is that at this stage we do not know how small the time step (and hence the length of each period) needs to be. It is preferable to estimate the relationship for a given futures margin and then use this information to calculate the risk-neutral probability for whatever time steps we wish to consider.

---

6. There are four exceptions. When $\theta_u(i, n)$ equals 0 or 1 we set $\pi_u(i, n)$ equal to 0 or 1 respectively. Otherwise, whenever $\pi_u(i, n)$ is negative we reset it to 0, while if it exceeds 1 we reset it to 1.

As we demonstrated in Problem 12.14, if the period-ahead futures margin and the state variable are everywhere related as in equation (17.8), then the m-period futures margin equals

$$F_{m+n}(i, n) = \frac{c_0(1 - (c_1)^m)}{1 - c_1} + (c_1)^m X(i, n)$$

at node (i, n). We regress the month-ahead futures margin on a constant and the spot margin, to obtain

$$F_{1 \text{ month}} = \hat{\gamma}_0 + \hat{\gamma}_1 X + v,$$

where $\hat{\gamma}_0$ and $\hat{\gamma}_1$ are the estimated coefficients and v is the error term. If we wish to represent each month by m time steps in our binomial tree, then the corresponding estimates of c_0 and c_1 are the numbers $\hat{c}_0$ and $\hat{c}_1$ that satisfy

$$\hat{\gamma}_0 = \frac{\hat{c}_0(1 - (\hat{c}_1)^m)}{1 - \hat{c}_1} \quad \text{and} \quad \hat{\gamma}_1 = (\hat{c}_1)^m.$$

It is straightforward to show that

$$\hat{c}_0 = \frac{\hat{\gamma}_0(1 - (\hat{\gamma}_1)^{1/m})}{1 - \hat{\gamma}_1} \quad \text{and} \quad \hat{c}_1 = (\hat{\gamma}_1)^{1/m}, \tag{17.10}$$

which are the parameters we use in (17.9).

Figure 17.3 shows the scatter plot of the month-ahead futures margin against the spot margin, using our full data set. When we regress the month-ahead futures margin on a constant and the spot margin we obtain

$$F_{1 \text{ month}} = \underset{(0.02122)}{-0.03202} + \underset{(0.0199)}{0.9055X} + \hat{v},$$

which corresponds to the dashed line in Figure 17.3. The slope coefficient is less than one, indicating that shocks to the state variable are not fully passed on to the price of the spanning asset. For instance, if the current margin increases by \$1 per gallon then the price of the month-ahead futures margin increases by approximately \$0.9055 per gallon. This is what we expect to see with mean reversion, since the increase in the margin is expected to be offset in the future as the force of mean reversion pulls it back towards its long-run level. This anticipated movement restricts the increase in the futures margin.

Based on this empirical relationship, we set $\hat{\gamma}_0 = -0.03202$ and $\hat{\gamma}_1 = 0.9055$, and then use (17.10) to estimate the coefficients required to evaluate the risk-neutral probabilities in (17.9). For example, when each month is represented by 30 (approximately daily) time steps, we find that $\hat{c}_0 = -0.001119$ and $\hat{c}_1 = 0.9967$. In this case the risk-neutral probability of an up move at node (i, n) equals

$$\pi_u(i, n) = 0.4917 - 0.02464X(i, n).$$

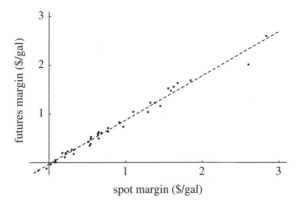

Figure 17.3. Relationship between spot and futures gross processing margin

Note: Estimated spot and one-month-ahead futures gross processing margin, measured in dollars per gallon, converted into May 2008 dollars using the Consumer Price Index for all urban consumers. Estimates are calculated using futures prices from CBOT (corn and ethanol) and NYMEX (natural gas).

Calibrating the Remaining Parameters

Calibrating the remaining parameters in the model is straightforward. The ethanol plant has a useful life of ten years, so we use the yield on ten-year Treasury inflation-protected securities (TIPS) as the basis of our risk-free interest rate. The ten-year rate was 1.58% at the end of May 2008. Since TIPS pay interest semi-annually, this implies a return on a one-year risk-free bond of

$$\left(1 + \frac{0.0158}{2}\right)^2 = 1.01586.$$

It follows that the return on a one-period risk-free bond is $R_f = (1.01586)^{\Delta t_m}$. We assume the tax rate is $T = 0.4$, reflecting federal, state, and local taxes.

The plant is capable of producing 100 million gallons of ethanol each year, or $Q = 100\Delta t_m$ million gallons per period. When the plant is producing ethanol, its operating expenditure amounts to $27 million each year or $C_P = 27\Delta t_m$ million dollars per period. Since transportation costs fall to zero while the firm is idle, and maintenance costs fall to $0.75 million, operating expenditure is just $6.25 million per year, or $C_S = 6.25\Delta t_m$ million dollars per period, while production is suspended. When the plant is mothballed, wages and administration cost $0.275 million and maintenance costs $0.075 million, for a total cash outflow of $0.35 million per year or $C_M = 0.35\Delta t_m$ million dollars per period. Mothballing the plant takes $N_M = 1/(12\Delta t_m)$ periods and $I_M = 0.5$ million dollars; reactivating it takes $N_R = 1/(4\Delta t_m)$ periods and $I_R = 2.5$ million dollars. The salvage value is $S = 0$ and all trees extend out as far as ten years or $N = 10/\Delta t_m$ periods.

17.4 RESULTS

Choosing the Step Size

The one parameter that we did not specify in Section 17.3 was the length of each time step in the binomial tree, Δt_m. Although it is a crucial input into our analysis, it is quite different from the other inputs. It does not relate to the facility being analyzed, nor to the market in which the facility operates. Rather, it is a parameter that determines how we go about conducting our analysis. We are trying to model a world that evolves continuously, so that ideally we would use a value of Δt_m that is extremely small. However, small time steps lead to very large binomial trees and time-consuming calculations. Therefore, we make Δt_m as large as possible, subject to the condition that our results would be approximately the same if we used a smaller Δt_m. Our first task is to find such a step size.

Figure 17.4 plots the market value of the facility at date 0 as a function of the number of steps per month. The graph shows that even using a tree with approximately weekly time steps (four steps per month, or 480 steps in the tree in total) can lead to a misleading estimate of the plant's market value. Convergence is rather slow and exhibits the oscillating pattern familiar from derivative pricing applications of the binomial option pricing model.[7] In the analysis below we break each month into 30 time steps, which should ensure reasonably accurate results.[8]

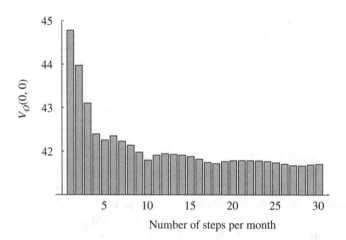

Figure 17.4. Market value of the plant for various step sizes

---

7. See, for example, Tian (1999).

8. This means that our ten-year trees have 3600 time steps, clearly too many for us to build the binomial trees in a spreadsheet. Fortunately, it is quite straightforward to implement our valuation model in many common programming languages.

Should the Plant be Mothballed?

Now that we have identified a suitable step size, we use our model to analyze the optimal operating policy for the plant. Table 17.3 shows the three most important binomial trees over the first 11 days. The top panel shows the gross processing margin, while the middle panel shows the market value of the plant while it is still operational. The top group of shaded cells in this panel indicates nodes where it is optimal to produce ethanol, while the bottom shaded cell indicates the region where immediately mothballing the plant is optimal. The bottom panel reports the market value of the plant when the mothballing procedure has been completed, with the shaded cells showing where reactivation of the plant should begin.

Inspection of the binomial trees reveals that the owner of the plant should suspend production immediately and only resume production once the gross processing margin takes values of 0.260 dollars per gallon or above. If, in the meantime, the margin reaches −0.879 dollars per gallon, the owner should begin the mothballing procedure. Reactivating the mothballed plant is only optimal once the margin reaches 0.193 dollars per gallon. We do not have space to show the remainder of the trees here, but they reveal that these three thresholds do not change until the plant approaches the end of its ten-year life.

These results show that, even though the plant is currently losing money, it is too early to place it in mothballs. Suspending production reduces the outflow of cash to some extent while retaining the ability to resume production immediately. In contrast, whereas mothballing allows the owner to reduce the plant's ongoing expenditure, it significantly reduces flexibility. In particular, taking the plant into and then out of mothballs requires four months and expenditure of at least $3 million. As a result, it is optimal to delay beginning the mothballing procedure until the owner can be confident that he will not want to reactivate the plant for a substantial period.

The owner also faces a difficult decision once the plant is mothballed: when to begin reactivation. Notice that it is optimal for reactivation to begin once the threshold has reached $0.193/gal, which is less than the point at which production would resume at an operational facility. That is, it would be optimal to reactivate a mothballed plant before it would be optimal to resume production at an operational one. The reason for the difference in behavior can be found in the reactivation lag. Production can be resumed at an operational plant immediately, while reactivating a mothballed plant takes three months. Thus, the plant's owner needs to begin reactivation relatively early, hoping that the margin will have moved far enough back towards its long-run level of $0.741/gal that operating the plant will be profitable by the time the reactivation is complete.

How Much is the Plant Worth?

If each month is split into 30 time steps and an optimal production policy is followed, the ethanol plant is worth $41.7 million at date 0. Figure 17.5 plots

Table 17.3. Optimal Operating Policy for an Ethanol Production Facility

$X(i,n)$	0	1	2	3	4	5	6	7	8	9	10	11
0	-0.142	-0.075	-0.008	0.059	0.126	0.193	0.260	0.327	0.394	0.461	0.528	0.595
1		-0.209	-0.142	-0.075	-0.008	0.059	0.126	0.193	0.260	0.327	0.394	0.461
2			-0.276	-0.209	-0.142	-0.075	-0.008	0.059	0.126	0.193	0.260	0.327
3				-0.343	-0.276	-0.209	-0.142	-0.075	-0.008	0.059	0.126	0.193
4					-0.410	-0.343	-0.276	-0.209	-0.142	-0.075	-0.008	0.059
5						-0.477	-0.410	-0.343	-0.276	-0.209	-0.142	-0.075
6							-0.544	-0.477	-0.410	-0.343	-0.276	-0.209
7								-0.611	-0.544	-0.477	-0.410	-0.343
8									-0.678	-0.611	-0.544	-0.477
9										-0.745	-0.678	-0.611
10											-0.812	-0.745
11												-0.879

$V_O(i,n)$	0	1	2	3	4	5	6	7	8	9	10	11
0	41.7	42.4	43.2	44.1	45.1	46.1	47.3	48.6	49.9	51.3	52.9	54.5
1		41.0	41.7	42.4	43.2	44.1	45.1	46.1	47.3	48.5	49.9	51.3
2			40.4	41.0	41.7	42.4	43.2	44.1	45.0	46.1	47.2	48.5
3				39.8	40.3	41.0	41.6	42.4	43.2	44.1	45.0	46.1
4					39.2	39.8	40.3	40.9	41.6	42.4	43.2	44.0
5						38.7	39.2	39.7	40.3	40.9	41.6	42.3
6							38.3	38.7	39.2	39.7	40.3	40.9
7								37.8	38.2	38.7	39.2	39.7
8									37.4	37.8	38.2	38.7
9										37.1	37.4	37.8
10											36.8	37.1
11												36.5

$V_{M,N_M}(i,n)$	0	1	2	3	4	5	6	7	8	9	10	11
0	40.8	41.3	41.9	42.5	43.1	43.8	44.6	45.4	46.2	47.1	48.9	48.9
1		40.3	40.8	41.3	41.9	42.4	43.1	43.8	44.6	45.4	46.2	47.1
2			39.9	40.3	40.8	41.3	41.8	42.4	43.1	43.8	44.5	45.3
3				39.4	39.8	40.3	40.7	41.2	41.8	42.4	43.1	43.8
4					39.0	39.4	39.8	40.3	40.7	41.2	41.8	42.4
5						38.6	39.0	39.4	39.8	40.2	40.7	41.2
6							38.3	38.6	39.0	39.4	39.8	40.2
7								38.0	38.3	38.6	39.0	39.3
8									37.6	37.9	38.2	38.6
9										37.3	37.6	37.9
10											37.0	37.3
11												36.8

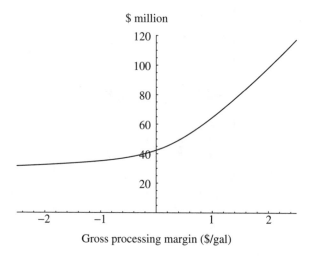

Figure 17.5. Market value of an ethanol production facility

the market value of the plant three months from now as a function of the gross processing margin.[9] The graph shows that even if the margin falls to very low levels the market value of the plant can only fall to approximately $27 million. However, there is considerably greater upside potential, with the plant being worth more than $100 million if the margin were to return to the levels of early 2006. The ability to respond to low levels of the margin by suspending production, or to go further and mothball the plant, until the margin moves back towards its long-run level, puts a floor under the plant's market value.

As well as estimating the market value of the plant, we can use real options analysis to help the plant's owner develop an intuitive understanding of how the various real options embedded in ethanol production contribute to its market value. One approach is to value the plant with various combinations of these options removed. The three options that we have identified are the ability to temporarily suspend production, to mothball the plant, and to abandon ethanol production altogether. The easiest way to eliminate the production-suspension option is to reset the expenditure while production is suspended, C_S, to such a large positive value that it is never optimal to suspend production.[10] Similarly, we can effectively eliminate the mothballing option by setting the expenditure required to mothball the plant, I_M, to such a large positive value that mothballing is never optimal. Finally, we can effectively eliminate the abandonment option by setting the salvage

---

9. The graph is constructed by drawing a scatter plot with $X(\cdot, 90)$ on the horizonal axis and $V_O(\cdot, 90)$ on the vertical axis.

10. An alternative is to rewrite the relevant recursive equation, (17.2), by excluding the payoffs corresponding to the disallowed options.

Table 17.3. Isolating the Contribution of
Various Real Options

Suspend	Mothball	Abandon	$V_O(0, 0)$
•	•	•	41.7
	•	•	33.4
•		•	35.1
•	•		41.5
•			33.6
	•		33.2
		•	1.6
			−328.2

value, S, to a very large negative value (except at the terminal nodes, where we keep the original salvage value).

Table 17.3 reports the market value of the plant with various combinations of real options removed. The market value ranges from −328.2 million dollars, when the owner must operate the facility at all times, to 41.7 million dollars when all options are available. We need to be careful when interpreting the values in the table, because the various options can interact. Thus, while the abandonment option contributes value of just $41.7 - 41.5 = 0.2$ million dollars when suspension and mothballing are possible, it contributes $35.1 - 33.6 = 1.5$ million dollars when only suspension is available. Nevertheless, inspection of the table indicates that the abandonment option is the least important of the three that we consider: removing it has less impact than removing either of the other two options. Although suspension and mothballing contribute similar amounts to the overall market value (for example, removing the suspension option reduces value by $8.3 million, while removing the mothballing option reduces it by $6.6 million), they are not simply substitutes for each other. Indeed, the plant is significantly more valuable when the owner can suspend and mothball relative to when he has only one of these options: $41.5 million versus (at most) $33.6 million. That is, much of the plant's value comes from the owner's ability to suspend production for short periods *and* to mothball the plant for long periods.

17.5 PROBLEMS

17.1. **(Practice)** At the end of April 2006 the ethanol futures prices for delivery in May and June were $2.725/gal and $2.610/gal respectively. The futures prices for delivery of corn in May and July were $2.380/bu and $2.492/bu respectively. The futures prices for delivery of natural gas in June and July were $6.555/MMBtu and $6.810/MMBtu respectively. Use this information to calculate the spot and month-ahead values of the gross processing margin at the end of April 2006.

17.2. **(Practice)** Implement the model described in Section 17.2 with each month represented by two periods.

17.3. **(Practice)** In this problem we use the implementation in Problem 17.2 to examine how some key parameters affect the market value of the ethanol plant.

    (a) Calculate the market value of the plant at date 0 for the following values of $\hat{a}$: 0.6, 1.4, 2.2, 3.0, 3.8. Keep all other parameters at their calibrated levels.

    (b) Calculate the market value of the plant at date 0 for the following values of $\hat{b}$: -1, 0, 1, 2, 3. Keep all other parameters at their calibrated levels.

    (c) Calculate the market value of the plant at date 0 for the following values of $\hat{\sigma}$: 0.4, 0.8, 1.2, 1.6, 2.0. Keep all other parameters at their calibrated levels.

    (d) Calculate the market value of the plant at date 0 for the following values of $\hat{\gamma}_0$: -0.05, -0.04, -0.03, -0.02, -0.01. Keep all other parameters at their calibrated levels.

    (e) Calculate the market value of the plant at date 0 for the following values of $\hat{\gamma}_1$: 0.86, 0.88, 0.90, 0.92, 0.94. Keep all other parameters at their calibrated levels.

    (f) Discuss the results.

17.4. **(Practice)** When we restrict the sample period so that it begins in September 2006 (that is, immediately after the large reduction in the gross processing margin), the estimated relationship between the month-ahead futures margin and the spot margin is

$$F_{1\ \text{month}} = \underset{(0.01940)}{-0.05706} + \underset{(0.0391)}{0.9219X} + v.$$

Use the implementation in Problem 17.2 to calculate the market value of the plant at date 0 using this relationship. (Keep all other aspects of the calibration unchanged.) Discuss the results.

18

Where to from Here?

Although this chapter marks the end of this book, it should really be just the "end of the beginning" of our development of real options analysis. The case studies in Chapters 15–17 have shown the potential of real options analysis and how to put the components of that analysis together. However, they have also suggested some areas where we might wish to develop or extend the tools we have available. In this chapter we make some very brief comments about how our real options toolkit might be expanded.

18.1 IMPROVED NUMERICAL ALGORITHMS

As we found in Chapters 15 and 17, it can be necessary to have a very large number of steps in our binomial trees in order for the results of our analysis to converge—that is, for our results not to depend on the precise size of each time step. Since this can make calculation of the trees quite time consuming, it is desirable to improve our approach so that it can deliver comparable accuracy from smaller trees. There is an existing literature that discusses many different methods for improving the efficiency of numerical techniques for implementing derivative pricing models. Although this literature mainly focuses on pricing financial derivatives, many of its insights have the potential to improve the efficiency of real options analysis.

The easiest techniques to implement use the estimates generated by our approach in various ways that speed up convergence. One possibility, motivated by Breen (1991), is to analyze the model for several different restricted exercise policies and combine the resulting market-value estimates using the so-called Richardson extrapolation technique. For example, in considering the simple investment timing option of Section 7.2, we might analyze the problem assuming that investment can only occur at the expiry date N, reconsider it assuming that investment can occur only at date $N/2$ or N, and then consider it one last time assuming investment is allowed at date $N/4$, $N/2$, $3N/4$, or N. A specific linear combination of the three corresponding market values then provides an approximation to the true market value that has been found to be quite accurate.[1] Other techniques improve performance by making minor modifications to the way in which our standard technique is implemented. For example, Tian (1999) uses slightly different values for U and D from our equations (12.7) and (12.8). At least for the case of European options, he is able to apply an extrapolation technique that improves the efficiency of the algorithm.

Much more substantial modifications to our binomial framework have been found to improve numerical efficiency. For example, Boyle (1988) replaces the binomial tree for the state variable with a trinomial tree. In this case, each period the state variable can move up, move down, or be unchanged. The derivation of the risk-neutral pricing formula in Section 3.1 will no longer be valid in this case, because it is impossible to replicate a future cash flow that can take three possible values when we can trade just two assets (a risk-free bond and the spanning asset). Nevertheless, it is possible to derive a valuation formula that, like our equation (3.1), uses numbers that we can interpret as probabilities to calculate expected payoffs that we then discount using the risk-free interest rate. As we saw in Section 12.1, we must choose three parameters when we calibrate a binomial tree: U, D, and the probability of an up move, θ_u; θ_d is determined by the requirement that $\theta_u + \theta_d = 1$. For a trinomial tree, θ_d can be chosen independently of θ_u, giving us one additional degree of freedom. It has been found that this extra parameter, if chosen carefully, can lead to more efficient numerical algorithms.

However, there is one important point to remember: most of these techniques have been developed with the pricing of financial derivatives in mind. Problems involving real options will often feature more complicated decision trees and the state variables will often be mean reverting (in contrast to financial derivative applications, which will often assume the logarithm of the state variable follows a random walk). What works for one type of derivative and a random walk will not necessarily work for a compound option problem with a mean-reverting state variable. Nevertheless, this literature offers the prospect of some useful insights for practitioners of real options analysis.

18.2 GREATER ECONOMETRIC SOPHISTICATION

A crucial part of any real options analysis is modeling the future behavior of the state variable. This involves choosing a process for the state variable, estimating a

---

1. However, while this method might tell us about the market value of the project rights, it does not give us an indication of the optimal investment policy. Moreover, it really only offers significant improvements in numerical efficiency if we can use the short cuts described in Section 4.2.1, which may not be the case if the state variable is mean reverting.

set of normalized parameters, and then building the binomial tree itself. We have seen how to estimate a random walk and one particular mean-reverting process, as well as how to build the corresponding binomial trees. However, we have not developed any objective method for choosing one approach ahead of the other, so that our choice must currently be based on the underlying economics of the state variable and an assessment of the economic significance of any mean reversion that we detect in the data.

There are many more possible processes for the state variable than the two that we have considered in Chapters 12 and 14. For example, we have considered one mean-reverting process, but there are many others—all with slightly different characteristics—that we could use instead. In addition, there are some realistic features missing from the processes that we have considered, such as seasonality. For example, seasonal patterns in corn and natural gas prices may well affect the gross processing margin we used in Chapter 17.

We need to be able to estimate the parameters that specify whichever process we adopt. Ideally, we would also be able to objectively select one particular process from the range of processes that are available to us. The tools of modern econometrics can help us achieve both of these goals. For example, unit root tests can be used to assess whether or not commodity prices are mean reverting. However, even with the use of very sophisticated econometrics, we still have to exercise our judgment regarding crucial modeling decisions. For instance, Pindyck (1999) argues that the results of unit root tests on energy prices can still be inconclusive with over 100 years of annual data.

Having chosen a process for the state variable and estimated the required parameters, our next task is to build a binomial tree to represent movements in the state variable over time. Different processes lead to different sizes and probabilities of up and down moves. Nelson and Ramaswamy (1990) give details of one approach that can be applied to a wide variety of different processes.

18.3 MULTIPLE STATE VARIABLES

Throughout this book we have restricted attention to models in which there is a single state variable. This made the derivation of the risk-neutral pricing formula a straightforward application of the law of one price, and also allowed us to keep the models and solution algorithms reasonably simple. Moreover, many practical situations can naturally be modeled in terms of a single state variable.

However, there may be situations in which we would like there to be more than one state variable. Consider, for example, our analysis of an ethanol production facility in Chapter 17. Factors affecting the price of corn may differ from those affecting the price of ethanol, which may differ from those affecting the price of natural gas. As a result, perhaps our analysis would have been improved had we modeled the behavior of the ethanol price and the input prices separately, rather than collapsing everything down into a single variable (the gross processing margin) as in Chapter 17.

Even when there is a single relevant commodity price, we may wish to allow for multiple state variables. There is now a quite extensive literature on the behavior of commodity prices in which the convenience yield is treated as a state variable in addition to the commodity spot price.[2] This is in contrast to our approach in Section 12.2.2, where (as we demonstrated in Problem 12.13) we effectively treated the convenience yield as an explicit function of the spot price. Treating the convenience yield as a state variable in its own right introduces a random component to the relationship between spot and futures prices that might better reflect reality.

If we wish to incorporate multiple state variables, we need to change the way in which we describe the state of nature at each date. It is no longer sufficient to describe the state of the world by the date (n) and the number of down moves (i) because different state variables might have moved in different directions. We need to allow each state variable to have its own sequence of up and down moves, so that the state of nature at date n is described by a vector, with one element for each state variable, each element giving the number of down moves for the corresponding state variable. For example, if there are two state variables, then state $(2, 3, n)$ arises at date n if there have been two down moves in the first state variable and three down moves in the second one. This is the approach adopted by Boyle et al. (1989).

The precise specification of the risk-neutral valuation formula changes when there is more than one state variable, but the intuitive interpretation is unchanged from that of equation (3.1). The market value of an asset at date n still equals the sum of the current cash flow and the present value of the cum-dividend market value one period in the future. Moreover, this present value is calculated by discounting the expected value (which is evaluated using numbers that we interpret as risk-neutral probabilities) at the risk-free interest rate.

Because the overall form of the valuation formula is unchanged, apart from altering the structure of the binomial tree, the approach to real options that we have developed in this book carries over largely unchanged. For example, we still need to build the decision tree for each problem we solve, we still need to build a market-value tree for each distinct project state, and we still fill in the nodes of these trees by working from right to left and using the dynamic programming technique introduced in Chapter 5. All that changes is that instead of there being two branches growing out of each node (as in a binomial tree), now there are four or more. This means that the number of nodes grows very rapidly—and the calculations can be time consuming—but in principle the situation is not much more complicated than our single-variable case.

The two extensions described in Sections 18.1 and 18.2 become even more important once two or more state variables are included in a model. For example, when calibrating the model we need to consider the correlation between changes

2. One of the most important papers in this literature is Schwartz (1997).

in the state variables, as well as their individual volatilities. In some cases, the univariate techniques we developed in Chapter 12 can be used with little change—for example, the logarithms of two state variables may each follow a random walk, with just the correlation between the noise terms needing to be estimated in addition to the usual parameters. Because the number of nodes in the trees grows extremely rapidly, implementing the numerical valuation technique efficiently becomes especially important. For example, Kamrad and Ritchken (1991) generalize the multinomial trees in Boyle et al. (1989) in ways that lead to greater numerical efficiency for the cases they examine.

Bibliography

Ana Aizcorbe. Price measures for semiconductor devices. Board of Governors of the Federal Reserve System, 2002.

Kaushik Amin, Victor Ng, and S. Craig Pirrong. Valuing energy derivatives. In Robert Jameson, editor, *Managing Energy Price Risk*, chapter 3, 57–70. Risk Publications, London, 1995.

Tom Arnold and Richard L. Shockley. Real options, corporate finance, and the foundations of value maximization. *Journal of Applied Corporate Finance*, 15(2): 82–88, 2002.

Tom Arnold, Timothy Falcon Crack, and Adam Schwartz. Implied binomial trees in Excel without VBA. *Journal of Financial Education*, 32: 37–54, 2006.

Jonathan B. Berk, Richard C. Green, and Vasant Naik. Valuation and return dynamics of new ventures. *Review of Financial Studies*, 17(1): 1–35, 2004.

Phelim P. Boyle. A lattice framework for option pricing with two state variables. *Journal of Financial and Quantitative Analysis*, 23(1): 1–12, 1988.

Phelim P. Boyle, Jeremy Evnine, and Stephen Gibbs. Numerical evaluation of multivariate contingent claims. *Review of Financial Studies*, 2(2): 241–250, 1989.

Richard Brazee and Robert Mendelsohn. Timber harvesting with fluctuating prices. *Forest Science*, 34(2): 359–372, 1988.

Richard Breen. The accelerated binomial option pricing model. *Journal of Financial and Quantitative Analysis*, 26(2): 153–164, 1991.

Mohammed M. Chaudhury and Jason Wei. Upper bounds for American futures options: A note. *Journal of Futures Markets*, 14(1): 111–116, 1994.

Congressional Budget Office. FASABs exposure draft "Accounting for Federal oil and gas resources": CBO's alternative view. Congressional Budget Office, 22 May 2007.

John C. Cox, Stephen A. Ross, and Mark Rubinstein. Option pricing: A simplified approach. *Journal of Financial Economics*, 7: 229–263, 1979.

Michael A. Cusumano, Yiorgos Mylonadis, and Richard S. Rosenbloom. Strategic maneuvering and mass-market dynamics: The triumph of VHS over Beta. *Business History Review*, 66(1): 51–94, 1992.

Graham A. Davis. Estimating volatility and dividend yield when valuing real options to invest or abandon. *Quarterly Review of Economics and Finance*, 38: 715–754, 1998.

Avinash K. Dixit. Investment and hysteresis. *Journal of Economic Perspectives*, 6(1): 107–132, 1992.

Avinash K. Dixit and Robert S. Pindyck. *Investment Under Uncertainty*. Princeton University Press, Princeton, 1994.

EIA. Short-term energy outlook. Energy Information Administration, June 2008.

Eugene F. Fama and Kenneth R. French. The CAPM: Theory and evidence. *Journal of Economic Perspectives*, 18(3): 25–46, 2004.

Martin Faustmann. On the determination of the value which forest land and immature stands possess for forestry. *Allgemeine Forst- und Jagd-Zeitung*, 25: 441–455, 1849. English translation by William Linnard in Michael Gane (ed.), *Martin Faustmann and the evolution of discounted cash flow*, Commonwealth Forestry Institute Paper 42, University of Oxford, 1968.

Federal Accounting Standards Advisory Board. Accounting for Federal oil and gas resources. Federal Accounting Standards Advisory Board, 21 May 2007.

John R. Graham and Campbell R. Harvey. The equity risk premium in January 2007: Evidence from the global CFO Outlook Survey. *ICFAI Journal of Financial Risk Management*, 4(2): 46–61, 2007.

Mark Grinblatt and Sheridan Titman. *Financial Markets and Corporate Strategy*. McGraw-Hill, New York, 2nd edition, 2002.

James E. Hodder, Antonio S. Mello, and Gordon Sick. Valuing real options: Can risk-adjusted discounting be made to work? *Journal of Applied Corporate Finance*, 14(2): 90–101, 2001.

James L. Howard. U.S. timber production, trade, consumption, and price statistics 1965 to 2005. Resource Paper FPL RP 637, U.S. Department of Agriculture, Forest Service, Forest Products Laboratory, 2007.

Michael Hsu. Spark spread options are hot! *Electricity Journal*, 28–39, March 1997.

Wen–yuan Huang. Impact of rising natural gas prices on U.S. ammonia supply. WRS–0702 U.S. Departmant of Agriculture, 2007.

John C. Hull. *Fundamentals of Futures and Options Markets*. Pearson Education, Upper Saddle River, New Jersey, 6th edition, 2008.

Margaret Insley and Kimberly Rollins. On solving the multirotational timber harvesting problem with stochastic price: A linear complementarity formulation. *American Journal of Agricultural Economics*, 87(3): 735–755, 2005.

Jens Carsten Jackwerth. Option-implied risk-neutral distributions and implied binomial trees: A literature review. *Journal of Derivatives*, 7(2): 66–82, 1999.

Jens Carsten Jackwerth and Mark Rubinstein. Recovering probability distributions from option prices. *Journal of Finance*, 51(5): 1611–1631, 1996.

Bardia Kamrad and Peter Ritchken. Multinomial approximating models for options with k state variables. *Management Science*, 37(12): 1640–1652, 1991.

David Kesmodel. Miller gives lime-and-salt beer a shot at boosting sales. *Wall Street Journal*, 12 June (B1), 2007.

David G. Luenberger. A correlation pricing formula. *Journal of Economic Dynamics and Control*, 26(7): 1113–1126, 2002.

John McCormack and Gordon Sick. Valuing PUD reserves: A practical application of real option techniques. *Journal of Applied Corporate Finance*, 13(4): 110–115, 2001.

Alan J. Marcus. Efficient asset portfolios and the theory of normal backwardation: A comment. *Journal of Political Economy*, 92(1): 162–164, 1984.

Stewart Mayhew. Implied volatility. *Financial Analysts Journal*, 51(4): 8–20, 1995.

William R. Melick and Charles P. Thomas. Recovering an asset's implied PDF from option prices: An application to crude oil during the Gulf crisis. *Journal of Financial and Quantitative Analysis*, 32(1): 91–115, 1997.

Antonio S. Mello and Unyong Pyo. Real options with market risks and private risks. *Journal of Applied Corporate Finance*, 15(2): 89–101, 2002.

Daniel B. Nelson and Krishna Ramaswamy. Simple binomial processes as diffusion approximations in financial models. *Review of Financial Studies*, 3(3): 393–430, 1990.

James L. Paddock, Daniel R. Siegel, and James L. Smith. Option valuation of claims on real assets: The case of offshore petroleum leases. *Quarterly Journal of Economics*, 103(3): 479–508, 1988.

Robert S. Pindyck. The long-run evolution of energy prices. *Energy Journal*, 20(2): 1–27, 1999.

Robert S. Pindyck. The dynamics of commodity spot and futures markets: A primer. *Energy Journal*, 22(3): 1–29, 2001.

PJM. PJM markets and operations. 2006.

Richard J. Rendleman. Option investing from a risk-return perspective. *Journal of Portfolio Management*, 109–121, May 1999.

Mark Rubinstein. Implied binomial trees. *Journal of Finance*, 49(3): 771–818, 1994.

Eduardo S. Schwartz. The stochastic behavior of commodity prices: Implications for valuation and hedging. *Journal of Finance*, 52(3): 923–973, 1997.

Nelson D. Schwartz. The un-Enron. *Fortune*, 145(8): 132–137, 15 April 2002.

Kenneth Skog and Christopher Risbrudt. Trends in economic scarcity of U.S. timber commodities. *Resource Bulletin FPL 11*, U.S. Department of Agriculture, Forest Service, Forest Products Laboratory, 1982.

Han T.J. Smit. Investment analysis of offshore concessions in the Netherlands. *Financial Management*, 26(2): 5–17, 1997.

Jeremy C. Stein. Rational capital budgeting in an irrational world. *Journal of Business*, 69(4): 429–455, 1996.

David Stires. The unmaking of the un-Enron. *Fortune*, 150(5): 123–125, 6 September 2004.

J. Alex Tarquinio. Not an oil baron? You can still get oil royalties. *New York Times*, 17 October 2004.

Thomas A. Thomson. Optimal forest rotation when stumpage prices follow a diffusion process. *Land Economics*, 68(3): 329–342, 1992.

Yisong Tian. A flexible binomial option pricing model. *Journal of Futures Markets*, 19(7): 817–843, 1999.

Sheridan Titman. Urban land prices under uncertainty. *American Economic Review*, 75(3): 505–514, 1985.

Courland L. Washburn and Clark S. Binkley. On the use of period-average stumpage prices to estimate forest asset pricing models. *Land Economics*, 66(4): 379–393, 1990.

Index